OXFORD MEDIEVAL TEXTS

General Editors

C. N. L. BROOKE   D. E. GREENWAY
M. WINTERBOTTOM

MAGNA VITA SANCTI HUGONIS

THE LIFE OF ST HUGH OF LINCOLN

MAGNA VITA SANCTI HUGONIS

THE LIFE OF ST HUGH OF LINCOLN

VOLUME TWO

EDITED BY

THE LATE DECIMA L. DOUIE

Formerly Reader in History, University of Hull

AND

DAVID HUGH FARMER

Reader in History, University of Reading

CLARENDON PRESS · OXFORD

1985

Oxford University Press, Walton Street, Oxford OX2 6DP
London New York Toronto
Delhi Bombay Calcutta Madras Karachi
Kuala Lumpur Singapore Hong Kong Tokyo
Nairobi Dar es Salaam Cape Town
Melbourne Auckland
and associated companies in
Beirut Berlin Ibadan Mexico City Nicosia

Oxford is a trade mark of Oxford University Press

Published in the United States
by Oxford University Press, New York

First published by Thomas Nelson and Sons Ltd 1961
Reprinted with corrections and published by Oxford University Press 1985

British Library Cataloguing in Publication Data
Adam, b.c. 1150, Chaplain of St. Hugh
[Magna vita Sancti Hugonis. English & Latin].
Magna vita Sancti Hugonis = The life of St. Hugh of Lincoln.
—(Oxford medieval texts) 1. Hugh of Lincoln Saint   2. Catholic church—Bishops—Biography
3. Christian saints—Biography
I. Title.   II. Douie, Decima L.   III. Farmer, David Hugh
270.4'092'4   BX4700.H8
ISBN 0-19-822207-6 v.1
ISBN 0-19-822208-4 v.2

Library of Congress Cataloging in Publication Data
Adam, of Eynsham, fl. 1196–1232.
Magna vita Sancti Hugonis = The life of St. Hugh of Lincoln.
(Oxford medieval texts)
Text in English and Latin; introd. in English
Reprint. Originally published: Edinburgh; New York:
Nelson, 1961. With new pref.
Bibliography: p.
Includes index.
1. Hugh, of Avalon, Saint, 1135?–1200.
2. Christian saints—England—Biography.
I. Douie, Decima L. (Decima Langworthy), 1901–1980.   II. Farmer, David Hugh.
III. Title.   IV. Title: Life of St. Hugh of Lincoln.   V. Series.
BX4700.H8A62 1985   282'.092'4 [B]   84–27385
ISBN 0–19–822207–6 (v. 1)
ISBN 0–19–822208–4 (v. 2)

Printed in Great Britain
at the University Press Oxford
by David Stanford
Printer to the University

282.924
Hug
Aba

CONTENTS

ABBREVIATIONS

AA.SS.	*Acta Sanctorum,* (1685-)
AA.SS.O.S.B.	*Acta Sanctorum, Ordinis S. Benedicti* (ed. J. Mabillon, 1668-)
C. and Y.	Canterbury and York Society
Canonization Report	H. Farmer, 'The Canonization of St Hugh of Lincoln', *Lincs. Architectural and Archaeological Society Papers,* 1956, 86-117
C.S.E.L.	*Corpus Scriptorum Ecclesiasticorum Latinorum,* Vienna 1866
E.H.D.	*English Historical Documents,* (ed. D. C. Douglas London 1953-)
Gir.	Giraldi Cambrensis Opera (R.S.), 7 volumes
Le Couteulx	C. le Couteulx, *Annales Ordinis Cartusiensis,* Montreuil 1888-91, 8 volumes
M.V.	*Magna Vita Sancti Hugonis* (references are to books and chapters)
O.H.S.	Oxford Historical Society
P.L.	Migne, *Patrologia Latina,* (Paris 1879)
R.S.	Rolls Series
Thurston	H. Thurston, *The Life of St Hugh of Lincoln,* (London 1898)
T.R.H.S.	*Transactions of the Royal Historical Society*
Witham Chronicle	A. Wilmart, 'Maître Adam, chanoine Prémontré devenu Chartreux à Witham,' *Analecta Praemonstratensia,* IX (1933), 207-37
+	adds
om	omits

Note : Scripture references are to the Vulgate and Douay Version ; liturgical references, unless otherwise stated, are to the *Missale Romanum* and the *Breviarium Monasticum O.S.B.*

LATIN TEXT
and
ENGLISH TRANSLATION

LIBER QVARTVS

Prologvs

Vt autem, temporis serie paululum intermissa, pro
etatum ordine adhuc sicut cepimus pauca referamus,
post exactam infantilis *a* necnon eui puerilis historiam,
adholescentium est mentio breuiter subnectenda, sicque
per succedentium gradus etatum usque ad mortuorum
exequias narratio *b* extendenda, in quorum diligentis-
sima executione post Tobiam nemo reperitur adequasse
Hugonem. Qui, ut superius innotuit, singula uite sue
momenta diuinis mancipando preceptis, id iure promeruit ut pluribus in quolibet etatis gradu existentibus
etiam ipse prodesse ualuisset. Factus uero etatis iam
integre et pontificali officio insignitus, sepeliendis mortuis
tantam uisus est sollicitudinem impendisse, ut misericordie huius premio reposito in futurum, sub presenti
quoque tempore singulari donaretur honore sepulture.
Quod tunc plenius, fauente *c* Domino, exponetur, cum
quarto huic ac penultimo gestorum illius libro imponetur
meta. In cuius exordio ista duximus prelibanda.

Capitvlvm I

De Martino scrinifero Hugonis, qui ab eo casu tonsus,
mox seculo renuntians effectus est monachus.

Deputauerat custodie pontificalium scriniorum

---

a infantibus B
b *om* B
c faciente B

I

BOOK FOUR

PROLOGUE

To resume after this short digression my original chronological scheme, after dealing with his relations with babies and children, I must add something about his relations with the young and continue with each successive stage of life to his burial of the dead. With the exception of Tobias no one equalled Hugh in the zealous discharge of the duty of burying the dead. The dedication already mentioned by me of every moment of his life to the divine will was what enabled him, as was only just, to be of assistance to many people of all ages. When he was already elderly and had been raised to the office of a bishop, his zeal for burying the dead was so manifest that in addition to the reward reserved for him in heaven, he was accorded in this world a funeral of exceptional magnificence. This, if God so will, we will describe later more fully, when we have completed this fourth and last book but one concerning his deeds, to which I have decided to prefix this, by way of a preface.

CHAPTER I

Concerning Martin, Hugh's wardrobe keeper, who happening to be tonsured by him, shortly afterwards abandoned the world and became a monk.

The venerable bishop Hugh had entrusted the

reuerendus antistes Hugo iuuenem quemdam, modestum quidem moribus et pudicum, set uanitatis mundane non plene uacuum nomine Martinum. In scriniis autem uasa et uestimenta aliaque huiusmodi sacra, quorum in altaris ministerio usus erat, continebantur. Moris erat horum custodem et baiulum, quamuis laicum, tamen quia inter ecclesiastica uersabatur cum clericis ministeria, tonderi ut clericum, et tunicam propriis uestibus super-indutum lineam creditis deseruire obsequiis. Martinus, huic de recenti subrogatus officio, tonsionem suscipere iubetur ab episcopo. Quam ille triduo iussionem, pudore obsistente non bono, distulit adimplere, uariis per dies singulos excusationibus uelare nitens, cum argueretur omissi precepti, uoluntariam inobedientiam.

Hoc episcopus aduertens, reportantem ab ecclesia die quadam post missas scrinia obseruat, eumque in ulteriorem secutus exedram, cincinno capitis illius digitos innectens, ' Ecce,' ait, 'quia tonsorem non repperisti qui ordinatam tibi faciat tonsuram, ego ipse tondebo te.' Hec dicens, sumptis forpicibus, cesariem illius in rotundum circumcidit. Quo facto, mox iuuenculus in lacrimas resolutus, genibus sancti pro-uoluitur, constringensque manibus fortiter pedes eius, ' Domine,' inquit, 'per misericordiam Dei adiuro uos, audiatis parumper me. Quia enim dextera uestre sanctitatis capiti meo signum abstulit mundane uanitatis, oro quatinus a mundi huius laqueis penitus me absoluere uelitis. Nam reuera amputata per manus uestras coma secularis [a] meas ulterius ceruices minime pregrauabit. Vtque mentis propositum per manus uestre obsequium celitus michi inspiratum, manifestius pandam ; uiluit michi prorsus hoc nequam seculum, appeto mona-

[a] + uanitatis X

custody of his episcopal wardrobe to a young man named Martin, whose manners and character were admirable and beyond reproach, although he was not absolutely immune from worldly vanity. The plate, vestments and other articles used at mass were kept in the wardrobe, and it was the custom that their guardian and keeper, although a layman, should be tonsured and wear a linen surplice over his garments when at work, since he was employed amongst clerks on work suitable for clerics. Shortly after his appointment Martin was ordered by the bishop to be tonsured, but out of vanity he put off obeying this command for three days. Each day when he was rebuked he gave a different excuse for his deliberate disobedience.

The bishop was aware of this. One day after mass, seeing him carrying back the cases, he followed him into the ante-room at the further end and running his fingers through his curly hair, said, ' As you have not found a tonsurer to give you the tonsure I ordered, I shall tonsure you myself.' As he spoke, he took the scissors and cut his hair into a circle. When he had finished the youth suddenly burst into tears, and fell down at the saint's knees. He clutched his feet convulsively and said, ' I beseech you, my lord, by God's mercy to hear me for a little while. Your reverend hand has removed the mark of worldly vanity from my head, and I beseech you to free me now completely from the snares of this world. My head will no longer be weighed down by the locks suitable for a secular profession which your hands have removed. I will make known to you my purpose, divinely inspired by your handiwork. I now count this wicked world as dross, and desire to become a monk. From henceforth I shall devote myself entirely to God, and completely abandon the vanities of this

chatum. Deo in posterum me totum deuoueo, seculi ex toto pompis renuntio. Prosequatur, obsecro, gratia uestra, qua per uos merui preueniri gratiam Dei, ut et ipsa subsequatur me, que iam preuenit, omnibus diebus uite mee. Per uos religionis merear suscipere uestem per quem modo suscepi caracterem.'

Quid multa ? Cum *a* episcopus hec quasi dicta puerilia duceret negligenterque acciperet, dissimulabat quippiam referre auditis, processitque iam commessurus ad triclinium. At ceteris uescentibus, edax desiderii flamma depascebatur *b* Martini precordia, adeo ut uix contingere sineret *c* corporea alimenta, pre interni ardoris quo medullitus estuabat uehementia. Finito conuiuio, accedit seorsum ad cunctos singillatim quos in tali censebat negotio magis exaudibiles fore episcopo. Quorum pedibus aduolutus, aures, animos affectusque eorum singultibus pulsat, mouet fletibus, precibus pietate plenis inclinat, ut estuanti *d* penes episcopum suffragia conferant, quo per eum salutaris desiderii consequatur effectum. In talibus uero diebus persistens indefessus et noctibus, tandem post triduum optinuit quod perseueranter postulauit. Expiata siquidem triduana eius inobedientia ex dilate, non minori tempore, exauditionis mora, sciens uir clementissimus temperamentum misericordie sue, fecit ad se accersiri uirum uenerabilem priorem sancti Neothi. Vtque absoluamus compendio quod gestum est, sancto cetui eiusdem ecclesie *e* suum fauorabiliter Martinum sociari petiit et impetrauit. Compertam namque a precedentibus annis Beccensium habuerat idem iuuenis laudabilem prorsus institutionem, nec non et ordinatam familie sancti Neothi conuer-

a om B   *b* depascebat QX
c sineretur QX   *d* + sibi X
e celle Q : cellule X

world. Through you I have been found worthy to be vanquished by the grace of God and therefore I beg you that by your prayers this grace which has now overcome me may remain with me all the days of my life. Deign to bestow on me the monastic habit, since you have already given me the mark of the cleric.'

What happened next? The bishop treated his request as a childish fancy and did not answer, but went to the hall where he was to dine. The rest ate, but Martin's heart was consumed with the ardent flame of his desire which would scarcely allow him to eat owing to the intensity of the fire which consumed him to the marrow. When the meal was over, he privately approached everyone in turn who he thought might have influence with the bishop in this matter. He flung himself at their feet, and assailed their ears, hearts and feelings by his sobs ; his tears moved them, he aroused their pity by his passionate prayers that they would intercede with the bishop for one who was in torment, that through him his pious intention might be achieved. He followed this course perseveringly for some days and nights, and at length after three days obtained what he had so persistently asked for. The kindly bishop, knowing how to temper mercy with justice, as a penance for his three days' disobedience delayed answering his prayer for no less a period. He then summoned the venerable prior of St Neots, and to sum up what happened, he asked him to receive Martin as one of the monks of that monastery. His request was gladly granted. The young man had heard a few years earlier of the high reputation of the discipline of the congregation of Bec, and also of the excellence of the religious life at St Neots, and so decided to be professed under Bec

sationem : unde professione illis astringi, isti uero
habitationi preelegerat coniungi.¹ Cui prouisor pius
et uestitum contulit regularem et diem susceptionis
illius ad habitum sacrum sollempni refectione uniuersis
fratribus exultabilem fecit. Martinus uero que Dei sunt
non minus facere quam scire infatigabiliter studens,
prosequente pia eius uota gratia Christi, in bonitate,
in ᵃ disciplina, in scientia quoque adeo in breui profecit
ut omnibus eius profectus et admirandus et imitandus
esse censeretur.

Quem postea ad subdiaconatus gradum nutritius
suus cum gaudio ingenti promouit, applaudentibus hiis
qui eum nouerant, et inuicem quiddam tale dicentibus :
'Quidnam accidit filio Cis ?' ² Audiebant eum apostolica
siue prophetica uoce altissona, celeritate inoffensa
scripta legentem ; uidebant eum inter Natinneos ³
tunica decoratum polimita, leuiticis iuxta pontificem
ministeriis subseruientem, ac dicebant : 'Num et Saul
inter prophetas ? ' ⁴ Erat namque in eo cunctis mirabile,
quod in semetipso unicuique uidebatur impossibile, ut
in etate scilicet iam prouectiore tam cito litteras sciret
quas in tenerioribus annis minime didicisset.

At Martinus admirantium laudibus non dico non ᵇ
extollebatur, immo nec quidem leuiter mouebatur,
quin potius coeuos et consodales quondam suos firmis-
simis rationibus arguebat uanitatis, ad studium eos
inuitans uite correctioris.ᶜ Rogauit etiam pontificem
quatinus a domino abbate Beccense suis dignaretur
precibus optinere, ut ad domum matricem de Becco

ᵃ et Q
ᵇ om B
ᶜ correctionis B
¹ St Neots, founded c. 972, was refounded as a cell of Bec c. 1079. It
generally had 12-18 monks, besides the conventual prior.
² 1 Kings 10 : 11

and join St Neots.[1] His holy patron gave him the monastic habit, and made the day on which he received it a festive one for all his brethren by providing a sumptuous repast. Martin indeed tried earnestly to know and do God's will, and by Christ's grace carried out his pious purpose. In a short time he had advanced so much in virtue, in knowledge and the monastic way of life, that his progress seemed to everyone a subject for admiration and imitation.

His patron had the immense joy of raising him to the sub-diaconate. Those who had known him highly approved, and said one to another. ' What has befallen the son of Cis ? ' [2] They heard him reading the epistles and prophecies in a clear voice rapidly but without stumbling, and saw him with Nathineans [3] clad in an embroidered tunicle serving the bishop amongst the deacons, and said, ' Is Saul also among the prophets ? ' [4] What seemed amazing to all of them, since each of them felt it would have been impossible in his own case, was that although already grown up he had learnt to read so quickly, without having received any instruction during his childhood.

Martin was not puffed up by their praise and admiration, which had no effect at all upon him. Instead he brought forward convincing arguments to convict his contemporaries and former companions of levity, and exhorted them to reform their lives. He also asked the bishop to approach the lord abbot of Bec, and obtain permission for him to go to the mother house at Bec and stay there for a long period, that he might be more fully instructed in the rites and customs of his holy

---

[3] In 1 Esdras 8 : 20, the Nathineans minister to the Levites. St Isidore comments that subdeacons are found in the book of Esdras, and are called Nathineans. (*De Ecclesiasticis Officiis* II, 10. P.L. 83, 790)

[4] 1 Kings 10 : 11

ueniendi et in ea diutius persistendi copia daretur sibi, quo sacri ordinis perfectius informaretur cerimoniis et probatissimorum quos ibi nouerat esse plenius instrueretur monachorum exemplis. Agebat hoc magno utique zelo religionis, illud secum reputans : ' Dulcius ex ipso fonte bibuntur aque,' [1] item illud melioris poete : 'Ibunt sancti de uirtute in uirtutem.' [2] Consecutus est autem post modicum tempus, interuentu presulis, pie huius petitionis effectum. De cuius nuper conuersatione et industria, tam ab ipsius abbate quam et ab aliis pleraque didicimus satis commendabilia.

Dicat unusquisque quod sentit : nobis miraculo superiori quo puer a periculo precipitis est ereptus torrentis, [3] hoc longe prestantius uidetur miraculum. Ibi quippe uim uirtutis sue oblitus est amnis, ut puerulus liberaretur illesus. Apparuit igitur, nature mutato ordine, humor solidus in fluuio, sicut olim ardor friguit in camino.[a] [4] At in Martino utriusque signi nouitas innouata est, set ordine quo excellentiore eo et utiliore. In illis ab ignibus et aquis caro, utrisque in posterum obnoxia tandemque peritura, uite mortali ad tempus modicum reseruata est ; in Martino, cum carne perpetim et anima uicturo, illud propheticum adimpletum est et cum psalmista eidem cantare permissum, ' Transiuimus per ignem et aquam, et induxisti nos in refrigerium.' [5] Verum de hiis philosophari largius aliis relinquamus. Nobis enim tramite cepto dum adhuc grandis restat uia, ad alia properandum est retexenda in seruo suo magnifice semper operantis Christi magnalia.

---

[a] + babilonico X

order, and model himself upon the excellent monks there, about whom he had heard. He did this out of religious fervour, because he thought that ' waters from the fountain-head the sweeter taste,' [1] or, to quote a better poet, ' the saints shall go from strength to strength.' [2] Within a short space of time, owing to the intervention of the bishop, his pious petition was granted. His abbot and others told us much about his exemplary later life, and all the information we received was highly satisfactory.

Everyone is at liberty to express his own opinion, but to me it seems a greater and much more amazing miracle than that of the boy snatched from the torrent.[3] In this last case, the river lost its natural quality to let the boy escape unharmed. The order of nature being changed the flowing stream became solid, just as of old the fiery furnace grew cold. [4] In Martin both miracles were repeated in a much finer and more profitable way. In the former miracles, the body which is the destined victim of fire and water and must perish in the end, was preserved from both to enjoy a short span of mortal life, whereas in Martin's case whose body and soul were destined to live eternally, the prophetic words of the psalmist were fulfilled and he could sing with him, ' We have passed through fire and water and Thou hast brought us to safety.' [5] I will, however, leave it to others to make any further reflections on these events. Much of the path I set out upon still remains to be covered, so I must hasten to relate other wondrous works which Christ was always performing through his servant.

[1] Ovid, *Epistulae ex Ponto*, iii, v, 18
[2] Ps. 83 : 8
[3] See above, I, p. 133
[4] cf. Dan. 3
[5] Ps. 65 : 12

Capitvlvm II

De alterius conuersione iuuenis, qui mentis simul et corporis per episcopum nostrum consecutus est medelam.

De conuersione alterius iuuenis relatio subinfertur que longe quidem posterius accidit, set pro similitudine historie precedentis ei congrue subnecti meretur. Quam ita Saluatoris clementia noscitur operata ut eam, mediante genitricis sue pietate melliflua, Hugonis quoque merita uideantur peregisse. Cuius euentum compendiose perstringimus ne prolixitate gestorum lectoris studium pregrauemus. Euenit autem postremis regni incliti regis Ricardi temporibus.[1]

Ea sane tempestate idem princeps in grauem aduersus episcopum iram exarserat ; adeo ut, machinante et per familiaria sibi perditionis uasa insistente totius bonitatis inimico, iusticiariis suis de Anglia districte precipiendo mandauerit quatinus omni [a] occasione postposita, in suas recepissent [b] manus episcopi Lincolniensiumque canonicorum bona, ipsosque possessionibus cunctis spoliassent.[c] Huius uero simultatis origo et finis suo plenius loco assignabitur, cuius ad hoc mentio hic agitur, quatinus per ea que sequuntur illud beati apostoli testimonium erga bonum uirum euidenter monstretur impletum, quo de electis Dei idem uas electionis quod interius fideliter tenet exterius fidenter asserendo profert :[2] 'Scimus,' inquiens, 'quoniam diligentibus Deum omnia cooperantur in bonum.' [d] Excitauerat sane liuor serpentis antiqui contra diligentem Deum, Deoque dilectum militem suum egregium

---

[a] om B
[b] reciperent X
[c] spoliarent X
[d] + hiis qui secundum propositum uocati sunt sancti X

Chapter II

Concerning the conversion of another young man, whom our bishop healed both in body and mind.

Although it took place a long time later, I shall give here an account of the conversion of another young man, which can best be recounted here because of its resemblance to the preceding. This too was manifestly wrought by our merciful Saviour, at the intercession of his compassionate mother, in such a way as to make it appear that it had been done through the merits of Hugh. We shall describe it as shortly as possible in order not to overburden our readers by a detailed account of what happened. The incident occurred in the last year of the reign of the illustrious king Richard.[1]

At that particular time, the son of perdition, the enemy of all good, wickedly devised by means of his favourite vessels of iniquity to kindle the wrath of the king so greatly against our bishop that he sent peremptory orders to his justiciars in England immediately to seize the goods of the bishop and canons of Lincoln and confiscate all their possessions. The cause of his anger and its outcome will be described more fully in the right place, but I mention it here because the sequel shows the absolute truth of the words of the apostle in the case of this holy man. The vessel of election expressing his most sincere convictions about the elect of God said, ' We know that all things work together for good for those who love God.'[2] The malice of the ancient serpent had stirred up strife and fierce persecution against the

---

[1] i.e. in 1198 ; see below, II, pp. 95-102
[2] Rom. 8: 28

factiose admodum persecutionis acerbitatem, set ad insipientiam sibi. Ex eo namque congressu uictus ipsemet multipliciter et confusus, in malignitatis sue felle contabuit ; Christi uero miles, quem uiribus impar temere impetiit, cum triumpho multiformi gloriam amplissimam reportauit.

Huius siquidem occasione certaminis, episcopus regem aditurus, qui tunc in partibus agebat transmarinis, Rouensem peruenit ad urbem. Accessit ad eum ibidem quidam iuuenis, quem perniciosius suis illaqueauerat dolis hostis humani generis. Qui mediante interprete, neque enim uel ipse pontificis uel pontifex ipsius sufficienter dinoscebat loquelam, miserabilem in hunc modum de seipso recensuit tragediam :—

' Cum,' inquit, ' dudum adholescentulus, discretionis adhuc minus capax, uagis ducerer affectuum motibus, contigit me infelicem ex insidiis aduersarii humane salutis detestabile enormis cuiusdam piaculi incurrisse crimen. Nec contentus lapsu simplici, lapsum adieci lapsui ; sicque, quod deterius est, crimini addendo crimen, longam in criminum lapsibus feci consuetudinem. Erat scelus meum sui qualitate nimis horrendum cuius horrorem quadruplicauerat loci, temporis et persone, cum sui ipsius immanitate consideratio. Nil ex peccatorum circumstanciis supremo defuit mali cumulo, nisi forte ignorantia iuris semiplena. Suasus preterea et illectus ab alio, primitus immo semper fere peccabam.

' Nuper uero sacerdote quodam uerbum Dei predicante in ecclesia me indignissimum turbis accidit confluentibus interesse. Qui cathalogum retexens capitalium criminum, in hoc, cuius eram michi *a* conscius, uerbi diuini fortius gladium uibrans, eius dampnabilem adeo exaggerauit feditatem ut me pene crederem terra

a om B

friend and beloved and gallant knight of God, but to his
own undoing. He came out of that conflict beaten and
greatly confused, and corrupted by his own rancour and
spite. Christ's soldier, however, whom he had rashly
attacked with unequal resources, gained great glory
from his considerable victory.

This conflict forced the bishop to go to the king who
was then abroad. When he reached the city of Rochester,
a young man came to him whom the wiles of the enemy
of the human race had ensnared to his destruction. He,
by means of an interpreter, since he had not sufficient
knowledge of the bishop's native tongue nor the bishop
of his, related his sad history as follows :—

' When I was still a stripling, and being incapable of
reasoning, was a prey to roving appetites, I happened,
wretch that I am, through the craft of the enemy of
man's salvation, to commit a horrible and dreadful
crime. Not content with one fall, I fell several times,
and worst of all by sinning repeatedly, sin became
habitual to me. My crime was of its nature a terrible
one, and its heinousness was quadrupled owing to con-
siderations of place, time and person in addition to its
utter monstrosity. Every circumstance increased my
sinfulness, except perhaps my partial ignorance of the
law. At first, however, and indeed almost every time I
sinned I was led astray by the persuasion of another
person.

' Recently, all unworthy, I happened to be in a
crowded church where a priest was preaching the word
of God. He went over the list of mortal sins, castigating
particularly the one of which I knew I was guilty. He
so dwelt on its shameful and damnable character that I
almost believed that the earth would open suddenly and
swallow me up, and that I would fall alive into hell. I

subito dehiscente absorbendum, ac uiuum in infernum collapsurum. Tantam denique mentis confusionem incurri ut extra meipsum me funditus putarem effectum.

' Diem uero illum, cum prima sequentis parte noctis,[a] in lacrimis expendi et singultibus ; cum [b] ecce, post noctis medium, lassatum pre tristitia corpusculum in soporem resoluitur, uisaque michi est astitisse femina inestimabili prefulgens decore, talia ferens [c] monita desolato. " Noli," ait, " miselle, desperare. Larga est clementia et magna potentia Filii mei qui neminem uult perire. Surgens uero diluculo sacerdotem inquire, quem tibi non ignotum designo ex nomine, eique fideliter, pure et integre peccata tua confitere." Hiis dictis, uisio michi cum sompno ablata est. Ego de nocte consurgens michi iniuncta peregi. Nec multo post, confusionis mee ruborem non sustinens, locum insuper perditionis mee exhorrescens, discessi clanculo a domo genitricis mee et a ciuitate in qua natus et conuersatus infeliciter eram.

' Pergenti uero, set quo tendendum uel ubi consistendum michi commodius esset nescienti, occurrit anxianti [d] et merenti uir ex improuiso horrendi aspectus, statura prolongus, capillo rufus, qui ore terrifico hec michi est locutus : " Pessime," inquit, " offendisti Deum et eius genitricem ; quos si uelis quouis pacto habere propitios, ipsum necesse est corpus extinguas, quo eis totiens iniuriosus extiteras. Erras enim si credas quod in eodem uasculo quod tot contaminationibus polluisti, quicquam diuine sinceritati acceptum operari queas." Vix dictum impleuerat et ecce peregrini adueniunt, beati martiris Thome busta petituri, ad quorum presentiam qui loquebatur repente disparuit. Ego in formidinem simul et desperationem licet uehementer

---

[a] nocte B   [b] tum Q
[c] referens Q   [d] anxiato X

felt so terribly distracted in mind that I seemed utterly beside myself.

'I spent that day and the early part of the night, sobbing and weeping. Just after the middle of the night when my body, exhausted by grief, sank into slumber, there seemed to be standing by me a lady of exceptional beauty, who gave me this counsel in my desolation : " Do not despair, unhappy man. Boundless is the mercy and great the power of my son, and His will is that no-one should perish. Arise at dawn, and seek the priest, whom I shall name and who is not unknown to you, and confess your sins to him truthfully, completely, and without any omissions." When she had spoken thus, the vision vanished and I woke. Rising whilst it was still night I carried out the instructions I had received. Shortly afterwards, being unable to endure my shame, and, moreover, hating the scene of my destruction, I secretly left my mother's house, and the city where I had been born, and had lived so wretchedly.

' Whilst I wandered, not knowing where it would be best for me to go or to stop, there suddenly appeared to me in my grief and anxiety a man frightful to behold. He was very tall with red hair and addressed me in a terrible voice, " Wretch, you have so greatly aroused the anger of God and His mother that if you desire to recover their favour, your only means is by the destruction of your body, which has made you utterly hateful to them. You are mistaken if you believe that with a vessel which you have contaminated with so much poison you can do anything acceptable to the divine goodness." He had hardly finished speaking when the pilgrims on their way to the tomb of the blessed martyr Thomas arrived, on whose appearance he who had been speaking to me disappeared. In spite of being very much

impulsus, signaui frontem tamen signo salutari ; pergensque itinere cepto merens, uixque pre cordis dolore gressus proprios regens, hac ipsa die qua *a* michi hec dicta sunt, in hanc circa horam tertiam deuenio urbem. Immissum quidem fuerat animo meo, et antequam hominis predicti suasionem uisibiliter percepissem ut memet ipsum interficerem. At postmodum hec in me fortius preualuit cogitatio, fecissemque quod ille suggesserat, nisi paululum animaret miserum *b* recordatio uisionis premisse qua *c* michi aliquantulum blandiebar de Saluatoris nostri sueque genitricis misericordia. Nam et hoc pro constanti olim acceperam quod quicumque sibi ipsi necem inferret, eternaliter procul dubio periret. Tam uero infesta michi fuit et adhuc existit, ista ut credo inimici suggestio, quod bis hodie perrexi ut meipsum de ponte huius uille precipitarem in fluuium. At primo quidem ob meantium *d* multitudinem reuocaui pedem ; secundo, aduentus uester insinuatus auribus meis per uestros precursores, a iam imminenti me suspendit precipitio. Mox enim ut comperi uestre sanctitatis presentiam affuturam, omni fluctuatione cordis explosa, in tante cepi discretionis alloquium respirare.'

Talibus ab eo peroratis, episcopus breuiter eum pro tempore adhortatus, data benedictione, monet quatinus ad usque Doroberniam sua uestigia subsequatur, ibidem plenius et liberius salutis consilium necnon et auxilium percepturus. Paret ille monitis salutaribus. Qui ueniens Cantuariam, sacra eius instructione firmatus et intercessione adiutus, a temptatione pestifera funditus in perpetuum liberatur. Perhendinante autem ibidem pontifice et tempus nauigationi congruum per dies fere quindecim prestolante, idem penitens, iam in fide et

<hr>

a quo B   *b* *om* B
c quam B   *d* commeantium QX

overcome by dread and despair, I made the sign of the cross on my forehead, and sadly set out once more on my journey, although my grief made it difficult for me to walk, and on the very day these words were spoken to me, at about the third hour I reached this city. Even before I had seen and listened to the persuasions of the man I have mentioned, I had entertained the idea of killing myself. After this my inclinations grew stronger, and I would have done as he had suggested, if the memory of the vision I have described had not given me, wretched sinner as I was, a faint hope and confidence in the mercy of Our Saviour and His mother. Also I had formerly taken it for granted that whoever killed himself was certainly eternally damned. Nevertheless this suggestion, coming as I believe from the enemy, had such an effect on me and still has, that twice today I have been on the point of throwing myself from the town bridge into the river. On the first occasion the crowd of passers-by caused me to draw back, and on the second just when I was about to hurl myself over, the news of your arrival reached me through the attendants whom you had sent ahead of you. As soon as I heard of your Lordship's coming, all the turmoil of my heart subsided, and I began to breathe more freely at the prospect of conversing with someone of your great wisdom.'

Having heard the youth's tale the bishop gave him a few short instructions, and his blessing, telling him immediately to follow him to Canterbury, where he would receive fuller and more ample spiritual direction and aid. He took this excellent advice and, coming to Canterbury and receiving strength and help from his admirable counsels and prayers, he was ever afterwards entirely free from his dreadful temptation. The bishop remained there for almost fifteen days awaiting favour-

deuotione preualidus, consistebat in eadem urbe per unam circiter septimanam. Disponebat uero summorum limina apostolorum orationis gratia quamtocius inuisere.

Ceterum rem inauditam illi nouimus interea accidisse. Subito namque secus utrumque femur et circa uerenda eius caro illius ita computruit ut duo altrinsecus foramina, seu potius fosse bine, horrende amplitudinis et profunditatis apparerent ; cum ipse tamen ex tam immenso uulnerum hiatu nichil penitus sentiret doloris. Ostendit autem, metu grauioris periculi, cuidam fidelissimo uiro, curandorum uulnerum notitiam habenti, nomine magistro Reginaldo Pistori, locum illum putridum ; a quo accepimus quia iam pene usque ad intima uiscerum [a] carnes eius putride defluxissent.

Insinuatur ista episcopo, qui ceram iubet uulneribus imponendam dari, quam tunc forte appositam [b] foco, ad conficienda in usus necessarios luminaria, ut est consuetudinis, ministri calefaciendo mollem tractabilemque reddebant. Res mira : ut enim hedera Ione, sub una nocte exhorta, sub una itidem nocte confugientibus ad penitentiam Niniuitis exaruit, ita repentina istius penitentis ulcera in cicatricem citius redacta sunt, quibus ne signum quidem obductionis repente superfuit. Qui totus iam euangelico more, anima scilicet sanatus et corpore, sumptis sollempniter pera et baculo, apostolica ut proposuerat menia petiit : optentaque benedictione summi pontificis in Angliam reuersus ac Cisterciensis ordinis habitum indutus, bone conuersationis merito non minus rem sibi quam nomen conuersi perseueranter uendicauit.

----

[a] uiscera X
[b] + in B[1]

able weather for sailing, and his penitent, now strong in faith and devotion, also remained in the city for about a week. He determined however, to go as soon as he could on pilgrimage to Rome.

Meanwhile a most remarkable thing befell him. Suddenly the flesh round both his thigh bones and privy parts gangrened and two holes, or rather caverns of a terrible size and depth appeared and yet he felt no pain at all from these immense and yawning wounds. For fear that they might become worse, he showed those putrid sores to a very devout man and a skilled healer of wounds, Master Reginald Baker, who told us that his rotting flesh had fallen away almost to the bowels.

Hearing this, the bishop ordered that some wax which his servants happened to have set by the fire at that very moment to warm and soften it for making candles as the custom is, should be applied to the wounds. Wondrous to relate, just as Jonah's gourd which grew up in one night and withered in the same space of time when the Ninevites did penance,[1] so the wounds of the penitent suddenly became mere scars, and very soon not even a trace of a scar remained. He being completely cured in mind and body, as in the gospel miracle stories, formally assumed his scrip and staff and set out for Rome, as had been his intention. After receiving the pope's blessing he returned to England where he assumed the Cistercian habit, and by his perseverance in holy living deserved the title of ' conversus ' in fact as well as in name.

[1] cf. Jonas 4 : 7-10

CAPITVLVM III

Qualem se erga lepre maculatos contagione exhibuerit ;
et de commendatione inaudite dulcedinis Saluatoris ab
ore Hugonis sepius iterata ; et de munificentia ipsius in
omnes passim necessitatem patientes.

Verum ista retexendo auctori totius nequitie Sathane
insultamus, qui uirtutis uiro dum *a* cunctis malitie sue
insidiatur uiribus, in sui ipsius perniciem liuoris proprii
refusum semper ingemuit uirus. Set quia ad hec,
historie pretermisso ordine, dum etatum processus
exsequimur quibus sancti merita claruerunt, quasi per
excessum quemdam stilum defleximus, ad gestorum
seriem hunc denuo retorqueamus ; quatinus eumdem
ipsum ubique, tam uidelicet in cunctis uite sue momentis
quam et in etatibus singulis, et uerum Deitatis extitisse
cultorem et hostis antiqui enituisse uictorem demons-
tremus.

Iam enim ex premissis satis innotuit quia innocentie
uerus amator, omnipotens Conditor, famulo suo
innocentissimo ad immensum *b* laudis preconium, per
ora innocentium necdum quidem loquentium set
arridentium perhiberi uoluit testimonium, eo nimirum
uerius quo et diuinius, eoque constantius quo et in-
corruptius, eo demum credibilius quo miraculosius. Ita
Dominus serenissimus sue singularis prerogatiue sueque
partem glorie contulit seruo deuotissimo ; ut sicut eum
etas innocens non loquendo set moriendo meruit confiteri,[1] ita per eandem *c* istius merita gestiendo et
alludendo faceret commendari ; et qui precursori suo
prius dedisse legitur spiritum gratie quam uite quo

a Dei B   *b* mansurum X
c + innocentiam X

Chapter III

How he treated those afflicted with leprosy, and how the praises of the unutterable sweetness of the Saviour were often upon Hugh's lips, and how generous he was to all who were in want.

To relate such things is to attack Satan, the author of all evil, who when he used all the resources of his guile against this holy man always groaned to find the poison of his malice turned to his own destruction. Because of this, in describing the heroic acts which brought fame to the saint at the different periods of his life, my enthusiasm has caused my pen to stray from the correct chronological order to which I shall now once more return. My purpose is to show how, wherever he was, at every moment of his life and in his dealing with people of all ages, this sincere lover of God won many outstanding victories over the ancient enemy.

Enough has been said already to show how the omnipotent Creator who holds innocence so dear chose through the mouths of innocent babes who could not speak as yet but only smile, to bear witness to His servant that he shared their innocence. The divine inspiration, their own innocence and finally the marvel itself made their testimony sincere, faithful and convincing. Thus the God of peace conferred on His devoted servant a share of his own especial privilege and glory for, as the Holy Innocents confessed him not by word but by their deaths,[1] so he caused the same to commend his servant's virtues by their playful gestures. Moreover, He who gave to his precursor the spirit of grace to greet him

---

[1] Collect for feast of Holy Innocents (Dec. 28)

salutaret se,[1] prius daret paruulis cultorem suum
agnoscere quam posse intelligere se. Quique benedictum
regnum suum a pueris Hebreorum uoluit collaudari,[2]
ipse militis sui de hoste uersuto triumphum, per etatem
similem ab illius tyrannide potenter sepius liberatam,[a]
sublimi preconio decreuit propalari. Qui etiam a
nuptiis, uini ex aqua facti consecratis pariter et letificatis
miraculo, ad celibatus gratiam per seipsum suum
inuitauit futurum euangelistam tunc adholescentem,[3]
ipse per infidelitatis torporem iam deficientem iuuenem,
carnalibus de cetero ualefacturum illecebris, ad fidei
calorem speique letitiam reuocauit per Hugonem.
Hugo bene uiuendo suumque auctorem benedicendo,
impleuit illud propheticum : ' Per singulos gradus meos
pronuntiabo eum.' [4] Vicissim quoque idem Dominus et
auctor suus in singulis etatum gradibus gratificauit et
glorificauit eum, ut senes cum iunioribus laudent nomen
eius, in omnibus laudabile atque magnificum per
largifluum gratie sue donum.

Quia uero ex prelibatis iam ista patuerunt, quid
restat modo nisi ut ea que per seruum suum ad com-
munem utriusque, sui uidelicet et ipsius gloriam, passim
Dominus in quibusdam personis, causis, temporibus et
locis magnifice gessit temptemus uel ex parte referre ;
ac demum qualiter eum in senectute bona et uenerabili,
quamquam minus diuturna, feliciter quiescentem in
gaudium suum admiserit, studeamus intimare ?

Cuius inter alia pietatis insignia, quantam egrotantibus curam, quantam lepre etiam tabe laborantibus

---

[a] liberatum X

even before he was born,[1] gave to these children the ability to recognise His servant before they possessed understanding of Himself. Also, He who willed that the Hebrew children should praise His kingdom as blessed,[2] decreed that the victory of his knight over the guile of the enemy, should be proclaimed by those of a similar age set free from his tyrannical yoke. He too who Himself invited the future evangelist, then a youth, from his marriage feast hallowed and gladdened by the miracle of the water changed into wine to a state of celibacy, through Hugh converted a youth already a prey to langour and despair to ardent faith and joyous hope, and the renunciation of the lusts of the flesh.[3] Hugh by his holy life and his gratitude to his Creator, fulfilled the words of the prophet, ' I will proclaim him with every step I take.' [4] His Lord and Creator in return gave men of every age reason for gratitude and thanksgiving for the superabundant grace conferred on him, so that old and young might praise, exalt and magnify his name in everything.

As all this is plain from what has gone before, it only remains for me to attempt to relate at least some of the great works wrought by God through His servant on various persons, and on various occasions, times and places to their mutual glory, but especially to his. Finally, I shall try to describe his beautiful and holy old age, brief though it was, and his happy death and admission into the joy of his Lord.

It is impossible adequately to record amongst the other marks of his devotion, his great compassion and

[1] cf. Luke 1 : 41
[2] cf. Mark 11 : 10
[3] Adam here refers to the legend that St John the Evangelist and St Mary Magdalene were the bridegroom and bride at the marriage feast of Cana, and that at the call of Christ St John at once left his bride to follow him.   [4] Job 31 : 37

benignitatem impenderit, quis digne commemoret?
Hiis nimirum, pedes propriis sepe manibus diluens et
extergens, osculisque demulcens, nummos insuper cibo
refectis et potu largiri consueuerat. Faciebat hec
secretius coram paucis arbitris in camera sua tredecim
sepius personis, cum tot inueniri potuissent in locis
quibus ipse interfuisset.[a] Erant preterea in quibusdam
fundis episcopii matricule, in quibus non pauci, huius
morbi incommodo detenti, tam uiri quam femine
sustentabantur. Hiis, preter assignatos a predecessoribus
suis redditus, uaria in multis rebus subsidia cum omni
diligentia conferebat ; frequenter quoque [b] ad eos in
propria accedens persona, ac cum paucissimis ex sibi
adherentibus uiris timoratis et deuotis, medius inter illos
in cella residens secretiori, uerbis optimis releuabat
animos [c] eorum, dolentibus quodammodo materna
lenitate blandiens, et ad spem retributionis eterne
desolatos temporaliter afflictosque sustollens, morum
quoque bonorum documenta suauitate mira interserens
uerbis consolatoriis. Ita, si quid de eis reprehensibile
percepisset, ne admitteretur, suadebat ut eos et admissi
uehementer [d] peniteret, et ulterius admittendi audacia
seu uoluntas nulla eis remaneret. Ante exhortationis
uero alloquia, semotis interim iussu eius feminis, mares
singillatim circumiens exosculabatur, singulis se inclinans
et quos cerneret atrocius iam tabe confectos diutius ac
suauius complexans.

Parce, Ihesu bone, infelici anime ista referentis.
Non enim latet scientiam, quod lateat utinam ultionem
tuam, quanto michi [e] fuerit horrori tumidas et luridas,
saniosas et deformatas, oculis euersis aut effossis,

---

[a] *Here* X *insert incident about William de Monte and the lepers almost verbatim*
from canonisation Report
[b] *om* B [c] animos. Sicut autem eorum doloribus X
[d] uehementius X [e] sibi B

tenderness towards the sick, and even to those afflicted
with leprosy. He used to wash and dry their feet and
kiss them affectionately, and having refreshed them with
food and drink give them alms on a lavish scale. He
often did this privately in his chamber with few people
present to thirteen patients, when that number could be
found in the place where he was. There were hospitals
on certain of the episcopal manors, where many men
and women afflicted by this disease were maintained.
He made a practice of giving gifts of many different
kinds to these in addition to the revenue already assigned
to them by his predecessors, and frequently visited them
himself with a few of his more God-fearing and devout
retainers. He would sit in their midst in a small inner
room and would comfort their souls by his kindly words,
relieving their sorrow by his motherly tenderness, and
encouraging those who were so desolate and afflicted in
this life to hope for an eternal reward, combining with
amazing gentleness words of consolation and exhortations
to good conduct. Also if he noticed any tendency to
wrong-doing, he would exhort them not to give way to
it, and if they had done so to repent, and from henceforth neither to dare nor desire to do wrong. Before
his address the women withdrew at his command and
he went to kiss the men one by one, bending over each
of them and giving a longer and more tender embrace
to those whom he saw worse marked by the disease.

Have pity, sweet Jesus, on the unhappy soul of the
narrator ! I cannot conceal, would that it were concealed from your vengeance, how much I shuddered not
merely to touch but even to behold those swollen and
livid, diseased and deformed faces with the eyes either
distorted or hollowed out and the lips eaten away ! To
an eye darkened by arrogance the pearl of God did not

labiisque absumptis, facies non modo cominus attingere
set uel eminus aspicere. Lippienti quippe pre superbia
oculo interiori, non fulgebat in sterquilinio margarita
Dei. Verum seruus tuus, cuius plenissime oculos auertisti
ne uiderent exteriorem uanitatem [1] internam capiebat
plenius claritatem ; unde sibi ornatiores uidebantur qui
infestiorem forinsecus preferebant [a] deformitatem.

Iccirco tales predicabat esse felices, tales paradisi
flores et preclaras corone regis eterni esse dicebat
margaritas. Hos fiducialiter et secure expectare Salua-
torem memorabat Dominum nostrum Ihesum Christum,
qui reformet corpus humilitatis eorum, configuratum
corpori claritatis sue ; [2] cum e diuerso formidolosi
expectent sublimem affuturum iudicem, qui modo de
corporis specie gloriantes, illius per mentis refugiunt
elationem humilitatis et munditie conformitatem.

Agens uero seorsum cum familiaribus suis de tanta
Saluatoris nostri clementia, qui miserrimos quosque in
uita presenti totiens ore diuino beatificat in euangelio suo,
nunc Lazarum inducendo ulcerosum in sinum Abrahe
ab angelis perductum, nunc seipsum in infirmis asserendo
infirmum,[3] mira cum dulcedine omnium auctorem
dulcedinum attollebat. ' O,' inquit, ' quam felices erant
qui uiro adeo dulci familiarius adherebant ! Quam [b]
michi dulce foret, quecumque is seu pedibus calcasset
seu qualibet corporis sui parte contigisset uel manibus
attrectasset, osculis lambere, oculis apponere, intimis
etiam, si fieri posset, uisceribus inserere ! Quid dicam
de humore superfluo, si quid tamen fas est superfluum
dicere quod fluxerit de ligno [c] uite ; quid, inquam, de
humore illo sentiam quem forte de uasculo tante bene-

---

[a] perferebant B
[b] Quantum X
[c] unguine X

gleam in the mire. But Your servant, whose eyes You had completely blinded to external superficiality,[1] saw clearly the internal splendour, and therefore those seemed to Him the more beautiful who outwardly were the most horribly diseased.

For this reason he declared such to be blessed, and called them the flowers of Paradise and the lucent pearls in the crown of the eternal king. These, he said, could confidently await the coming of Our Saviour Jesus Christ who would transform their vile bodies into the glory of His risen body.[2] Those on the other hand must dread the coming of the heavenly judge, who now gloried in the beauty of their bodies, but through pride refused to conform themselves to His meekness and purity.

Speaking when alone with his friends of the marvellous mercy of Our Saviour who had so often in the gospels testified with His own divine mouth to the blessedness of those who had been most wretched on earth, as, for example when He declared that Lazarus with his sores was borne by angels to Abraham's bosom, and that He Himself shared the afflictions of the afflicted.[3] Hugh used to extol in glowing terms the author of all goodness. ' O,' he exclaimed, ' how fortunate were the companions of this gracious man ! How sweet I should have found it to have beheld and kissed His footprints, or, if it had been possible, to have held close to my heart anything which His hands or any part of His body had touched ! What shall I say of His excretions, if it is not impious to call an excretion what flowed from the Tree of Life ? What, I say, should I feel about the sweat which perchance flowed from the Vessel

---

[1] cf. Ps. 118 : 37
[2] cf. Phil. 3 : 21
[3] cf. Luke 16 : 22 and Matt. 25 : 36

dictionis effundi ratione assumpte infirmitatis contingebat ? Certe non solum, si daretur facultas, illum diligentius colligerem, set omni nectare dulcius illum haurirem labiis, faucibus imbiberem, et abditis uiscerum precordiis ipsum reconderem. Quam uero miseri sunt qui aliud quicquam timent quam adeo dulcem offendere ! Quam gemendi sunt qui aliud quippiam dulce reputant aliudue expetunt quam sic dulci dulciter adherere, dulciter parere ! Nescio quid iam possit amarum sentire, qui dulcis huius dulcedinem iugi didicit meditatione in interno cordis palato dulciter ruminare.' [1]

Hec uir sanctus de celesti uulnerum nostrorum medico sentiens, hec dicens, hec etiam que premisimus de menbris illius infirmantibus proferens, hec illis impendens, euidenter satis exprimebat quanto interius ferueret igne diuine pariter et fraterne dilectionis. Qui etiam in commune quibusque indigentibus tantas largiebatur elemosinas, ut preter illa que multis sepe specialibus ex causis, nunc interpellatus, nunc ipse uoces preueniens necessitatem patientium, secretius erogabat, annuas omnium rerum suarum obuentiones usque ad tertie partis estimationem, sub certa constitutione in opera expendisse non dubitetur misericordie.

Capitvlvm IV

Quod inter micantes gladios et exertas [a] in capud suum dexteras tertio pro assertione iustitie seipsum inermem obiecerit. Et quod exercendo gladium ecclesiastice districtionis, plurimos dederit in reprobam mortem carnis.

[a] extentas X

of such great blessedness, owing to His assumption of our infirmity ? Certainly, if I were given the chance, I would not only carefully collect it, but would devour it with my lips and imbibe it as something sweeter than honey, and would treasure it in the depths of my heart. How wretched are they who dread anything except to offend so sweet a friend ! How much to be pitied are they who esteem anything else sweet, or desire anything except to cleave lovingly to such a lover, and lovingly obey Him ! To my mind nothing can seem hard to a man who has through meditation experienced His sweetness, and sweetly digested it in the depths of his heart.' [1]

The openly expressed feeling of this saintly man for the divine Healer of our wounds, and his words and acts concerning his sick members described by me show plainly how afire he was with love for God and his neighbour. He gave so lavishly to those who were in need that it is estimated that at least a third of his yearly income was devoted to almsgiving. This did not include any special cases which he privately relieved, either because he was asked to do so, or because he forestalled the requests of the needy for assistance.

CHAPTER IV

How on three occasions, in the interests of justice, he thrust himself unarmed amongst men brandishing naked swords over his head and clenching their fists, and how

---

[1] This surprising rhapsody is a ' period-piece ' in medieval devotion, inspired by St Bernard's fresh emphasis on the importance of affective devotion to the Humanity of Christ. The doctrinal principle that Christ's body was adorable because of its union in His Person with the Godhead can be traced back to the councils of Ephesus (435) and Constantinople (553).

Regis mitissimi atque fortissimi preconia sacra nobis insinuante Scriptura, dicitur de Dauid quod ipse erat tenerrimus ligni uermiculus.[1] Ligni quippe uermiculo sicut nichil lenius inuenitur cum premitur, ita cum premit nil se exerit eo mordacius. Vnde fit ut nulla prorsus res tam minute terebrare sufficiat lignum durissimum ut solet minutus ille mollisque uermiculus, qui et duritiem soluit [a] in puluerem et ostendit tabidum quod solidum putabatur.

Que plenius assignare [b] in uirtutibus uiri de quo specialiter a Domino perhibetur, quod inuenerit uirum secundum cor suum,[2] dum constet non esse temporis seu operis huius, inspicere libet an forte in Hugonis nostri moribus hec inueniantur siue operibus. Preconia namque uiri admirabilis mirifice exprimunt uocabula tria hec, quibus qualitas ipsius diffinitur cum dicitur : ' Ipse erat tenerrimus ligni uermiculus.' In tenerrimo docetur lenis et mansuetus, in ligno fortis et robustus, in uermiculo humilis ostenditur, inque suis oculis modicus et despectus. Quam uero is extiterit per lenitatem mentis tenerrimus, quamque fuerit ex humilitatis gratia quasi uermiculus, sibi scilicet uilis et apud se minimus, ex hiis perpendi euidentius poterit, que iam in medium utcumque protulimus sicut a primordio uite illius supra digeste lectionis insinuat textus. Nunc igitur de fortitudine illius inflexibili aliqua subicienda sunt, unde clareat manifestius quantum se exhibuerit in censura iustitie, qui tantus in humilitate, tantus quoque innotuit in spiritus suauitate.

Vbi uidetur imprimis breuiter recensendum quam egerit fortiter in superborum presumptionibus coher-

----

[a] *om* B
[b] assignari X

his excommunications consigned many persons to a horrible death.

Holy Scripture singing the praises of David, the gracious and mighty king, describes him as a most tender woodworm.[1] Nothing is easier to squash than a woodworm, and nothing is more deadly when it attacks. Thus nothing destroys the hardest wood as completely as this small soft worm, which turns its firmness to dust, and converts its solidity to rottenness.

There is obviously no time here, nor is it the purpose of this work to enlarge upon the virtues of the man of whom the Lord said that He had found a man after His own heart,[2] but it is permissible to examine whether our Hugh displayed the same qualities in his deeds and general behaviour. The three words of this prophecy ' He was a most tender woodworm,' are an amazing description of the character of this remarkable man. ' Tender ' denotes gentleness and compassion, ' wood ' courage and strength, and ' worm ' humility, for in his own eyes he was despicable and of no account. The description already given by me of his youth and of the middle period of his life must make it obvious how tender he was by reason of the sweetness of his disposition and how the gift of humility made him regard himself as a worm, and the vilest and least of men. I must now give some instances of his undaunted courage which will make it abundantly clear that his humility and gentleness were combined with an equally strong determination to maintain the cause of justice.

First, therefore, I must briefly recount how, in order

---

[1] 2 Kings 23 : 8, with the *Glossa Ordinaria* on this text
[2] Acts 13 : 22

cendis, quam incunctanter armatorum sepe se *a* inermem
ingesserit turmis, quam *b* steterit inter micantes gladios
et exertas dexteras : in Lincolniensi primum ecclesia,
deinde in Holandia ac demum in Norhamtona, nudo
capite constans et intrepidus. Minus uero dixi steterit
cum, huc illucque discurrendo, gladium Spiritus tota
cum libertate in furentes et frementes conspiratores seu
intrusores uibrauerit, tradens contumaces Sathane in
interitum carnis ut spiritus saluus fieret *c* in die Domini.[1]
Cuius eo constantia sublimius emicuit,*d* quo ibidem
uirorum fortium robur formidini euidentius cessit ;
eoque illius confidentia illustrius claruit quo suorum
diffidentia comitum et officialium in tanto se discrimine
apertius propalauit.*e* Hiis namque non modo ad aras
confugere parum fuit, immo et sub ipsis mensis dominicis
se abscondere uidebatur minus tutum. Quibus ita
fugientibus et latebras fouentibus Hugo persistebat solus,
cedebatque labiis intentantes gladios ceruicibus suis.
Cuius magnanimi audacia, necnon et protegentium se
angelorum custodia, ipsiusque diuine uirtutis armatura,
fracti et confusi, apud Lincolniam tam clerici quam
laici, apud Holandiam milites et armigeri, apud
Norhamtonam quoque burgenses infensi, cesserunt
plures uni, seuientes miti, tranquillo turbati.

Apud Holandiam tamen, quod pretereundum non
est, Willelmus de Aualun,[2] episcopi consobrinus milesque
acerrimus, generosi sanguinis uena incalescens, cum
stricto mucrone quidam armatorum pontificem funesta
pararet ferire audacia, iam percussuro se fortiter obiecit.

---

a ipse B
b quamque X
c fiat o
d enituit X
e probauit Q

to restrain the violence of angry men, he bravely and intrepidly often advanced unarmed into the midst of an armed band, and stood calm, undaunted and bare-headed amongst the naked brandished swords and clenched fists, first in the cathedral at Lincoln, then in Holland and finally at Northampton. To say he stood is inexact, for he rushed hither and thither, brandishing the sword of the Spirit at will against his enraged and furious adversaries and assailants, delivering the con-tumacious to Satan for the destruction of their bodies that their souls might be saved in the day of the Lord.[1] On that occasion his courage and fortitude were the more conspicuous and amazing, since even brave men were afraid and his companions and officials completely lost their nerve when exposed to such danger. To them it was insufficient to flee to the altars, and even to hide under them gave them no sense of security. Whilst they fled and took refuge in dark corners, Hugh remained alone and castigated with his tongue those who raised their swords to brain him. His magnificent courage and the protection of his guardian angels, which armed him with divine might, caused the enraged clerks and laymen at Lincoln, the knights and squires at Holland, and the burgesses at Northampton to give way out of shame. Thus a raging and riotous mob was quelled by one calm and undaunted man.

It should not however be omitted that at Holland the bishop's kinsman, William of Avalon,[2] a very valiant

---

[1] cf. 1 Cor. 5 : 5. The occasion was probably the anti-Jewish riots in 1190 at Stamford, Lincoln and Northampton. One of the Stamford rioters, killed by a fellow-thief for his plunder at Northampton, was believed by the townspeople to be the martyr of Jewish assassins. Thus was begun a lucrative cult suppressed by St Hugh (cf. *infra,* p. 201 and William of Newburgh, *Historia Rerum Anglicarum* (R.S.), lib. IV, cc. VIII-IX, pp. 310-7).

[2] Probably St Hugh's brother; see below pp. 164 and 171.

Cui etiam ui magna extorquens gladium ni prohiberetur
districtius a presule, eum absque uulnere abire non
siuisset. Horum si uellemus exprimere diffusius causas
tumultuum, pararet *ᵃ* forsitan lectori prolixitas inconsulta
fastidium. Vnde tantisper hoc loco hec uel tetigisse
sufficiat, bonique pastoris predicabilem fidelibus commendasse instantiam ; *ᵇ* qui sibi commissarum ouium
errorem, etiam cum periculo capitis sui, dissimulare
noluerit incorrectum.

Quamobrem non immerito animam suam pro suis
monstratur ouibus posuisse, quamuis eam tollere ab eo
nullus preualuerit ¹ ; illius nimirum hanc dextera con-
seruante illesam, de cuius manu eruere uel perimendos
ne pereant, uel saluandos nemo potest rapere ut
intereant. Hic tamen uelud semper in manibus suis,
cum fortissimo superius memorato rege Dauid, animam
suam portans,² seipsum periculis impauidus exponebat.
Timere siquidem nescius, aduersis uero cedere dedig-
natus, ut contempnebat mortem, sic uitam honesto *ᶜ*
postponebat. Karitatis namque apostolice sibi plene
conscius, securius dicebat in hiis omnibus, in quibus
ultra humanum modum presidere eum cuncti mira-
bantur : ' Karitas Dei urget nos ³ ; neque enim mors
neque uita, neque instantia neque futura, neque
periculum *ᵈ* nec gladius, neque sublimitas aut profundum, set nec creatura alia separabit nos a karitate
Dei que est in Christo Ihesu Domino nostro.' ⁴ Ita uero
paratus erat *ᵉ* iuxta formam apostolicam omnem in

ᵃ pareret X
ᵇ iustitiam X
ᶜ honestati X
ᵈ B *omits these two words*
ᵉ *om* B

¹ cf. John 10 : 15, 18
² cf. Ps. 118: 109
³ 2 Cor. 5: 14
⁴ Rom. 8: 38-39

knight whose noble blood boiled in his veins when one
of the armed men had drawn his sword and was reck-
lessly preparing to strike a deadly blow at the bishop,
bravely resisted the striker just as he was about to strike.
With great force he wrenched his sword away from him
and, if the bishop had not prevented him, would not
have suffered him to go away unwounded. If we were
to describe the causes of these riots in more detail the
reader might be bored by the unusual length of our
narrative. Therefore, let it suffice to have briefly
touched upon them now, and to have set before the
faithful the memorable example of the Good Shepherd,
who even at the risk of His own life, would not leave the
flock committed to his care uncorrected.

He is thus rightly described as having laid down His
life for his sheep though no one was strong enough to take
it from Him ;[1] for God's right hand preserved it unharmed, from whose grasp no-one can either snatch
away those doomed to perdition to save them from their
fate, nor take those destined for salvation and bring them
to destruction. Hugh, like the most valiant king David
whom I have just mentioned, always took his life in his
hands[2] and undauntedly exposed himself to danger.
Indeed, he did not know what fear was and scorned to
yield to his enemies ; disdaining death he preferred
honour to life. Having himself experience of the charity
of the apostle he could say with confidence on all these
occasions when to the amazement of all he seemed super-
human, ' The love of God constraineth us,[3] for neither
life nor death, nor things present nor to come, neither
danger nor the sword, neither height nor depth indeed,
nor any other creature shall separate us from the love of
God which is in Christ Jesus our Lord.'[4] For this
reason he was ready, following the example of the

gladio Spiritus ulcisci inobedientiam, ita eius quoque
ultioni celestis animaduersio celerem subinferebat
uindictam, ut in Deum contumaciter delinquentibus
sicut ipse nullatenus parceret, sic quemcumque zelo
iustitie spirituali idem mucrone percelleret, citius nisi
resipisceret, corporali pariter exitio interiret. Hinc
rebelles quosque et iuris ecclesiastici uiolatores, de sua
quandoque potentia presumentes insolenter ac pre
tumore *a* mentis ad minas interdum procaciter erum-
pentes, sic uoce terrifica obiurgabat, ' Quid de uestris,'
inquiens, ' uiribus uel armis contra manum Omnipotentis *b*
presumitis, quando nobis etiam indignis et infirmis hec
manus adeo potentia contulerit arma ut eis humana
nullatenus coequetur armatura ? Loricas nostras iacula
uestra non penetrant, galee nostre uestros enses non
formidant.*c* Nostris uero ensibus nec cassides uestre nec
thoraces resistunt. Vos si quando carnem ceditis, set
animam prorsus contingere non ualetis ; gladius noster
et corpus perimit et morti non transitorie set eterne
eorum quos percellit animas adicit.'

Iam uero si conemur uiritim exponere quam multos
in reprobam tradiderit mortem solo anathemate, quam
horrendo plerique legis diuine contemptores interierint
fine, qui secundum duritiam suam et cor impenitens
iram sibi thesaurizantes, benedictione spreta et eius
maledictione retenta, de suis renuerunt peruersitatibus
emendari, nec etiam si plurimi conficiantur libri,
poterunt omnia que scribenda sunt sufficienter explicare.
De quorum tamen numero pene innumerabili uel
paucos exempli gratia commemorasse non erit inutile,
cum ad fidelium consolationem atque eruditionem
infirmorum hanc placuerit superne maiestati erga

---

a timore Bo
b Omnipotentem Q
c uestros enses non formido X

apostle, to smite the disobedient with the sword of the Spirit, and the divine vengeance followed swiftly after his sentence. He never spared sinners hardened against God, and those whom he struck with the spiritual sword in his zeal for righteousness, unless they quickly repented all died suddenly. He used to rebuke those who arrogantly believed that they could defy and rebel against ecclesiastical law with impunity and in their wrath used at times insolent and threatening language, with these terrible words : 'How can you dare to trust your own power and arms against the hand of the Almighty whose power and might has given us, weak and un-worthy though we are, weapons infinitely superior to any human ones ? Your lances cannot pierce our corselets, our helmets are proof against your swords, but your steel tunics and headpieces cannot resist our blades. You can sometimes slay the body, but are unable to touch the soul. Our sword destroys the body, and condemns the souls of those whom it transfixes not to temporal but eternal destruction.'

If we were to attempt to describe how he delivered many over to a miserable death by his excommunication alone, and how very many more who defied the divine law and following the dictates of their stubborn and impenitent hearts laid up for themselves wrath by scorning his blessing and remaining under his malediction and, by refusing to repent of their sins, came to a horrible end, it would take many books and even then everything which should be written would not have been sufficiently covered. It will, however, not be amiss to select a few examples from these innumerable cases, since it pleased the divine majesty for the consolation of the faithful and the instruction of the weak to make manifest his just vengeance upon sinners, in order that

peruersos iuste animaduersionis districtionem euidentius
exercere ut impleretur illud psalmiste : ' Letabitur iustus
cum uiderit uindictam, manus suas lauabit in sanguine
peccatoris,'¹ itemque illud ᵃ dictum a sapiente : ' Flagel-
lato pestilente, sapientior efficitur paruulus.'²

CAPITVLVM V

De quodam milite cuius uxor, partum mentita proprium,
supposuit in fraudem germani uiri sui fetum alienum.
Et de quorumdam interitu post excommunicationem
uiri Dei tanto se facinori immiscentium.

Erat in territorio Lincolniensi miles quidam iam
prouectioris etatis, uxorem habens sterilem.³ Habebat
quoque fratrem eque militem, industrium et prudentem,
quem iuris hereditarii si absque liberis decederet,
habiturus uidebatur successorem. Inuidebat huic uxor
sua, uerens ne forte uiduata marito sub illius deueniret
dominatum, erga quem placitum numquam gessisset
affectum. Nequitie igitur uiperee dolis incitata, ut ei
consequende hereditatis precluderet aditum, quia partum
non habebat proprium, supposuit sibi alienum. Refertis
siquidem ac tumentibus interna fraude uisceribus,
ceruical precingit exterius, simulatque uterum intumes-
cere puerperio qui solummodo scelere fetabatur infando.
Miles in cuius preiudicium uersute malignitatis com-
ponitur stropha, dolum sibi strui deprehendens, set doli
artificem nec conuincere nec cohibere sufficiens, rem

ᵃ om B
¹ Ps. 57: 11
² Prov. 19 : 25, 21 : 11
³ This knight was called Thomas of Saleby, his wife Agnes, his brother
William of Hartshill and their supposititious child Grace. William made

the words of the Psalmist should be fulfilled, ' The just man shall rejoice when he perceives retribution, he shall wash his hands in the blood of the wicked,' [1] and also the saying of the wise man, ' The chastisement of the evil-doer makes the child wiser.' [2]

Chapter V

How the wife of a certain knight in order to defraud her brother-in-law pretended to be pregnant and passed off another woman's child as hers, and how some of the participators in such a crime died as a result of the bishop's excommunication.

There was in the county of Lincoln a knight already advanced in years, whose wife was barren.[3]   His brother, an honourable and worthy knight, was by hereditary right his lawful heir if he died without children. His wife disliked the brother and having never concealed her feelings, feared that if she were left a widow he would be her guardian. As she had no child of her own, with serpentine guile and wickedness she passed off another child as hers, in order to shut him out of the inheritance. With a belly swollen and big with deceit, she fastened a cushion over her womb, to pretend that she was pregnant, but in reality her crime was all that she had conceived. The knight to whose prejudice the malicious and cunning device had been planned, seeing that he was being tricked, but being unable either to

his claim against Thomas and Agnes at Michaelmas 1194 in the king's court at Westminster, but St Hugh claimed that the case belonged to ecclesiastical jurisdiction (cf. *Abbreviatio Placitorum*, p. 3 and *Rotuli Hundredorum*, 3rd Edward I, I, p. 294; also cf. *Rotuli Curiae Regis* (London, 1835), I, p. 78).

defert ad notitiam amicorum. Rimatur sollicitius consilii remedium set minime repperit oportunum.

Interea mulier decumbit lecto, ficte parturitionis indulget suspiriis. Quesitam uero a uico proximo muliercule cuiusdam recens *a* natam prolem femineam in publicum edit ; ac ueluti a se ueraciter enixam omni cum diligentia studiosius enutrit. Cuius etiam ueriorem ad se accersiuit genitricem, eique nutriendi pignoris proprii delegat *b* sollicitudinem. Dum talia geruntur non procul a Lincolnia, contigit instare iam resurrectionis Dominice festa Paschalia. Accedens igitur miles muliebri circumuentus astutia ad pontificem, astipulantibus sibi uiris discretis, quos fama certior tanti perflauerat maleficii, omnem rei cunctis audientibus adeo suspecte pandit rationem. Nec uero cuiusnam esset filia seu quemadmodum a falsa genitrice adquisita, per quam sibi exhereditatio parabatur, adhuc certius sibi innotuerat.

Motus autem uehementer uir iustus et pius ad audita, maligne maritum mulieris ad se iubet quamtocius accersiri. Quem secretius euocatum *c* discutit instantius, instruit et coarguit, tantique reatus confessionem ab eo elicere magnopere insistit. Verum ille, coniugis nimium procacis plus iurgia quam Dei iustitiam pertimescens, eius quoque sibilis preincantatus uipereis, criminis huius se primum inficiatur habere conscientiam. Vrgente demum episcopo et publice estimationis argumenta *d* acriter inferente, quibus patebat uerisimillimum esse nec ei sobolem nasci potuisse iam ualitudinario et seni, nec eum uideri ignarum uxorii *e* commenti, artatus euidenti ratione, hac tandem seipsum responsione

a recenter QX
b delegauit Q
c aduocatum Q
d argumentum . . . quo X
e uxoris X

prove or prevent it, brought the matter to the notice of his friends, and pressed them for their advice, but received no satisfactory answers.

Meanwhile the woman took to her bed, and groaned as if she were in travail. She produced a newborn female infant which she had procured from a woman in a village in the neighbourhood, and brought it up with as much care as if it had been really her own. She summoned the true mother, and made her foster-mother to her own child. These events occurred not far from Lincoln just when Easter was approaching. The knight who had been defrauded by a woman's guile came to the bishop accompanied by certain men of repute who had already heard rumours of the malicious fraud, and told the whole story which aroused the suspicions of all who heard it. Nobody yet knew for certain to whom the female infant belonged or how her reputed mother had obtained her with the intention of disinheriting him.

The righteous and holy man was greatly roused when he heard about it and immediately summoned the husband of the wicked woman to his presence. When he came he interrogated him privately, charged him with it, and rebuked him, trying hard to make him confess his guilt. He, however, fearing the scoldings of his shameless wife more than the wrath of God, and ensnared by her crafty tongue, at first denied his complicity in the crime. At last under pressure from the bishop, who bluntly told him that the general belief was that, since he was so old and sickly, the child could not possibly be his and that he was unlikely to be unaware of his wife's wiles. At length, being driven into a corner he gave himself away, saying ' For a long time, owing to my bad state of health, I have had very little intercourse with my wife. I should like, if you will allow me, to

deludit, ' Quia longo,' ait, ' tempore, corporis incommodo premente, coniugis secreta minus perfecte noui, uolo, si placet, arcius de hiis ab illa perdiscere ueritatem. Quicquid uero inde michi compertum fuerit, uobis mane nuntiabo, uestro indubitanter pariturus consilio, super omnibus que fuerint iuxta rei inquisite seriem utilius exequenda. Tum presul, satis admonitum in hiis eum uerbis abire[a] permittens, ' Scias, ' inquit, 'die crastina excommunicationis sententia omnes illos a nobis sollempniter ac terribiliter feriendos, qui huius mali auctores extiterint[b] aut fautores, si minus forte quod polliceris fueris executus.' Sic ille dimissus et ad suos reuersus, sterili puerpere queque audiuit a pontifice uel que pontifici retulerit ipse, seriatim exponit.

Ad hec illa infrendens et infelicem illum procaciter obiurgans, redire ad fidelem consiliarium eum penitus dissuasit. Qui male adquiescens dominatrici, cui ordine prepostero diu consueuerat ancillari, resedit domi, crimen adiciens mendacii precedenti errori. Facta est dies crastina que fuit sacrosancte resurrectionis Dominice Paschali sollempnitate gloriosa. Episcopus, habito sacre exhortationis uerbo ad populum, cunctis negotii huius pandit euentum, enormitatem exaggerat maleficii ; se non defuturum asseuerat quin tanto pro uiribus occurrat piaculo ex censura pastoralis officii. Cumque perdocuisset plenius quanti sit criminis non modo[c] in fratrem proprium set uel in quemuis proximum quippiam huiusmodi attemptasse, unde necessario contingat eum, cum omni posteritate sua, irremediabili dispendio subiacere, quod etiam peccati genus sub sue mole nequitie ad mortem sepe sui perpetratores dicebat irremissibiliter astringere ; omnes illos uinculo innodauit[d] anathematis

---

[a] adire B   [b] extiterunt B
[c] tantummodo Q   [d] + districti X

learn the truth about this from her. Tomorrow morning I will let you know whatever I find out, and will be ready to take your counsel on what can best be done about everything which transpires from my investigations.' The bishop then let him depart with a final warning. ' Know,' he said, ' that tomorrow we shall launch a solemn and terrible sentence of excommunication against the perpetrators of this evil deed and their abettors, if you do not do what you have promised.' After this dismissal he returned home and gave the barren mother a full report of his conversation with the bishop.

The brazen woman's reaction was to abuse him so vigorously that the unhappy man was dissuaded from returning to his faithful counsellor. Reluctantly yielding to his tyrant, whom contrary to the order of nature he had long been accustomed to obey, he stayed at home, and added the sin of deceit to his former error. The following day was the most holy and glorious feast of our Lord's Resurrection, and the bishop, having preached to the people, described the whole business to them, making plain the seriousness of the crime, and asserting that he must bring the full weight of his episcopal authority to bear upon such an offence. Having informed them of the enormity of committing such a sin not only against one's own brother but against any of one's neighbours, since it meant that he and his descendants would irrevocably lose their rights, he said that that kind of sin was of such immense seriousness as to cause the eternal death of its perpetrators. He then excommunicated all who had dared by means of the fictitious birth described to deprive the knight, who has already been frequently mentioned, of his inheritance.

qui de partus predicti suppositione exheredationem militis sepius memorati minime timuissent procurare.

Nec uero in longum distulit in traditos sibi ex sententia uiri iusti sue seuitie Sathanas tyrannidem exercere. Virum *ᵃ* namque sequenti nocte inuadens, qui peruersitatem coniugis dissimulando potius fouit quam increpando correxit, eius subito animam extorsit. Repente etenim in lectulo apparuit mortuus, in quem se locauerat, quiete ut credidit pausaturus. Audiant hec et pertimescant qui subditum sibi infirmiorem sexum ad facinus sequuntur siue flagitium, nec terrentur exemplo prothoplasti, quem a serpente uxor circumuenta extorrem paradisi et debitorem morti, tante cum suis posteris addixit calamitati. Enimuero, iuxta sententiam uiri sapientis : ' Non est capud super capud colubri, et non est nequitia super nequitiam mulieris.' Ve peccatori cuius ' sors super ipsam cadit ! ' [1]

Que utraque *ᵇ* sententia in hac muliere euidenter patuit : cuius ita furor pertinax et ira adeo dura fuit ut proprium tam exitialiter uirum perdidisse non ei sufficeret, nisi et ceptam contra eius germanum nequitiam hostiliter adimpleret. Perstitit enim confirmare sermonem nequam, debitam sibi retentans maledictionem, et indebitam alumpne sue uindicans hereditatem. Excluso igitur legitimo herede a fraterna successione, datur regio munere infantula cum ipsa hereditate cuidam iuueni qui frater erat Hugonis de Nouauilla, summi scilicet in regno forestarii. Quem, etatis uix quartum implentem annum, disponebat idem nuptiali more sollempniter sibi desponsare, precauens nimirum ne forte qualibet occasione priuaretur talis patrimonii adquisitione.

ᵃ Verum B
ᵇ utique X

Satan did not long delay to exercise his cruel sway over those delivered over to him by the sentence of this holy man. On the following night he suddenly claimed and seized the soul of the man who had connived at his wife's wickedness by concealing it, instead of rebuking and correcting it. He was found dead in the bed on which he had lain down to enjoy, as he thought, a quiet rest. Let this be a lesson to those who are led into crime and sin by the weaker sex which should be subject to them, and are not forewarned by the example of our first parent, whose wife, beguiled by the serpent, brought upon him and his descendants the awful fate of exile from Paradise, and death. Truly, as the wise man said, ' No head is more cunning than that of the serpent, and no iniquity more iniquitous than that of a woman.' Woe to the sinner whom fate unites with her ![1]

Both these sayings are obviously applicable to this woman, whose rage and fury were so strong and persistent that the tragic loss of her husband did not deter her from carrying out her wicked device against her hated brother-in-law. She continued to maintain her lie, in spite of the anathema which was so well deserved, and claimed the inheritance for her child. The lawful heir thus being excluded from his brother's estate, the child and her lands were given by the king to a certain youth, the brother of Hugh de Neville, the chief forester of the kingdom. Although she was not yet four years old, he decided that their marriage should be solemnly celebrated, fearing that something might prevent his acquisition of her inheritance.

[1] Ecclus. 25 : 22, 26

Quod ubi innotuit episcopo qui generali sepius constituto inhibuerat etatis indiscrete copulam nuptialem, mox etiam speciali prohibuit interdicto ne quis presbiterorum seu fidelium quilibet Christianorum hiis presertim nuptiis presumeret interesse. Prospiciebat in hoc perhenni simul et temporali multorum indempnitati, consulens etiam iuri communi ne uidelicet ante plenius cognitam et discussam rei huiuscemodi ueritatem in cuiusuis partis preiudicium tale iniretur connubium.

At episcopo citius post hec ob quedam negotia in Neustriam ad regem profecto, conueniunt in uico quodam remotiori iuuenis predicti fautores et consanguinei ; ibique simplicitate abutentes seu cupiditate sacerdotis illius loci, sollempni coniungunt more in facie ecclesie militi infantulam, illustri rusticanam, ingenuo ex seruili conditione procreatam. Tanta fuit auiditas alieni iuris occupandi ut nec ingenuitatis degenerata conditio nec salutis manifesta proditio infaustas nuptias prepediret. Regresso interea de *a* transmarinis episcopo que gesta sunt citius innotescunt. Hinc presbiter, talium minister nuptiarum, suspensione ab eodem pariter beneficii multatur et officii ; in reliquos uero uetiti sui transgressores, cum iuri coram eo parere contumaciter detrectarent, excommunicationis sententia promulgatur.

Interea ficte matris cubicularia, cuius ministerio proles aliene genitricis quesita est et inuenta, terrente conscientia, primum ad penitentialem *b* ecclesie Lincolniensis, sancte recordationis magistrum Willelmum de Branfed[1] subdecanum, et ipsius demum hortatu ad

---

a a Q ; a partibus X
b + seu penitentiarium X
[1] William of Bramfeld, subdean of Lincoln from 1198 until he was murdered in the cathedral on 25 September 1205, frequently occurs as witness to charters (cf. K. Major, *Registrum Antiquissimum*, V. pp. 97, 151, 156, 168 ; *Annales Monastici* (R.S.), Waverley Annals, p. 257).

When this was reported to the bishop, as he had frequently issued constitutions forbidding the marriage of those who had not yet reached the years of discretion, he now gave a special order forbidding any priest or devout Christian to be present at the wedding. In this matter he was considering alike the eternal and temporal security of many people and the claims of justice, for he thought that such a marriage before the truth had been fully sifted through investigations in the law courts would be to the prejudice of the parties concerned.

Immediately afterwards, the bishop having set out. for Normandy on account of certain business with the king, the relatives and friends of the young man assembled in a remote village, and there, taking advantage of either the simplicity or the greed of the parish priest, married him to the child publicly in church, thus uniting a peasant of unfree birth to a noble. Their lust to acquire what legally belonged to someone else was so great, that neither the servile condition of the bride, nor the obvious risk of damnation could deter them from the ill-omened marriage. As soon as the bishop returned from abroad, they informed him of what had taken place. He suspended the priest who had celebrated the marriage, and sequestered his benefice, and publicly excommunicated all those who had flouted his prohibition, and who had contumaciously refused to appear before him in defiance of the law.

In the meantime, the maid of the false mother who had sought for and procured the child of another mother, being conscience-stricken, came first to the penitentiary and sub-dean of the church of Lincoln, Master William de Bramfeld [1] of pious memory, and then by his advice to the bishop, to whom, shedding abundant tears, she made known exactly what had

ipsum accedens episcopum, omnem rei ordinem cum magna ⸢detegit profusione lacrimarum. Tunc episcopus de hiis omnibus certior effectus, secretum quidem apud se interim habet,[a] quod secretius audiuit, latam uero pridem sententiam singulis circumquaque per ecclesias diebus dominicis renouari publice demandauit.

Quod aliquamdiu ut fuit impletum, machinatrix et materia huius mali mulier infelix, reuersa demum in se, cepit horrere opus adeo perniciosum a se commissum. Tandemque animata consilio prudenti, accedit pariter secum assumpta delicti sui conscia et ministra, cubicularia prenotata, ad episcopum ; primoque illi soli, deinde pluribus uiris discretis, inter quos et ille qui hec scripsit presens fuit, reatum suum flebiliter confitetur : se proprium maritum prodidisse,[b] se fratrem eius circumuenisse, illum ad mortem, hunc ad proscriptionem et exheredationem uoce gemebunda protestatur. Que uniuersa Cantuariensi metropolitano, tunc temporis regni totius iustitiario,[1] sollicite per episcopum insinuantur, fratribus quoque et amicis alieni patrimonii ut predictum est insidiatoris, cunctis etiam primoribus fere et baronibus curie Anglicane.

Nichilominus uero sponsus puelle insonter noxie cum suis incumbit consiliariis possessioni nocenter adepte. Asserunt enim iuxta leges Anglie cuiusque sobolem legitimam discerni, quam uxoris maritus legitime quoad uiueret legitimam habuisset. Arcetur itaque huius pretextu sententie heres legitimus ab ingressu possessionis hereditarie. At interim, ob reuerentiam magis episcopi quam propter euidentiam uniuersis pene notificate rei,

---

[a] habuit QX
[b] perdidisse QX
[1] Hubert Walter, archbishop of Canterbury 1193-1205, was also Justiciar 1193-1198.

occurred. The bishop then, now having full information about everything, kept to himself for the time being what had been revealed to him secretly. On the next day, however, he ordered that the sentence he had already launched should be published every Sunday in the churches of the neighbourhood.

A little while after this had been done, the wretched woman whose machinations were responsible for this evil act came at last to her senses, and began to feel misgivings about the horrible sin she had committed. Finally, she had the excellent idea of coming to the bishop, bringing with her the maid who had been her confidant and partner in sin. She first with many tears confessed her guilt to him in private, and then again in the presence of many honest men including the writer, declaring amid her sobs that she had betrayed her husband, and cheated her brother-in-law, the former to his death and the latter out of his lawful inheritance. All these things were reported by the bishop to the archbishop of Canterbury, who was then justiciar of the whole kingdom,[1] as well as to the brothers and friends of the despoiler of the property of another person, and to almost all the nobles and barons of the Curia Regis.

In spite of this, the husband of the girl who was the innocent cause of the wrong, and his counsellors kept possession of what they had wrongfully acquired, declaring that according to the laws of England a child was regarded as legitimate whom the husband of a woman had recognized as legitimate during his lifetime. On this pretext the legitimate heir was prevented from entering into his inheritance. Meanwhile, however, more out of respect for the bishop than because the story was generally known, no definite judicial sentence was given against him.

non sinebatur contra eum iudiciaria diffinitio sententialiter proferri.

Iterato autem constantissimo iuris propugnatore in Normanniam transfretante, inque discessu suo sepius protestante quia si hanc miles sibi ut proponit in coniugem acceperit, rusticam profecto se habere nouerit, nec de illa plurimum gaudebit, homines rursus factiosi *a* conspiratione facta, diem partibus statuunt, quo diffinituum litigii huius calculum apud Londonias proferendum procrastinatione remota edicunt.

Igitur Adam de Nouauilla, hoc enim nomen erat uiro qui puellam duxerat, stipatus propinquorum turmis, Londonias festine petens, nocte diem precedente qua iudices sibi terram illam promiserant in solidum adiudicandam, cuius solummodo eatenus optinebat custodiam, non procul ab urbe hospitio suscipitur. Cuius dum fautores et consiliarii de forma dande sentential cum iudicibus in ciuitate sollicite deliberant, ille in diuersorio letus et temulentus lecto excipitur ; set sopori mortem socians subito extinguitur, solusque ad tribunal iustioris iudicis, factorum recepturus uicem, tam imparatus quam nil tale arbitratus extemplo pertrahitur. Timendum autem ne forte cum improperio ibidem audierit ex sententia districti iudicis quod sepius uertebatur in ore ueridici ipsius sui preconis. Cum enim incognitum sibi et peregrinum quondam nomen forestariorum crebrius audiret uir sanctus, querelis etiam oppressorum ab eis hinc inde crebrescentibus, barbare nuncupationi alludens dicere consueuit, 'Recte,' inquiens, 'homines isti et satis proprie nuncupantur forestarii ; foris namque stabunt a regno Dei.' [1]

---

a facinorosi X

This indefatigable champion of justice again crossed the sea to Normandy. At the time of his departure he openly declared on more than one occasion that if the knight took her to wife as he intended, he should realise that he had united himself to a serf, and would not enjoy her for very long. These crafty men devised a scheme by which a day was fixed for the parties on which the case was to be settled at London without the possibility of further postponements.

Therefore Adam de Neville, the girl's husband went hastily to London with a great company of relatives, and on the night before the day on which the judges had promised that the land would be irrevocably adjudged to him, for up till then he had only had the custody of it, lodged at no great distance from the city. Whilst his counsellors and supporters were in the city discussing earnestly with the justices the wording of the verdict, he went joyously to bed somewhat intoxicated, and died unexpectedly in his sleep, and alone and unprepared, for he had expected nothing of the kind, appeared before the tribunal of a more impartial judge to receive retribution for his crimes. It is to be feared that there to his shame he heard from the lips of the most just Judge the sentence so often given by his loyal spokesman. Whenever the holy man heard the name forester formerly strange and unknown to him, and from every side the growing number of complaints from their victims, he used to say, making a pun on their barbarous name, ' These men are aptly and very properly called foresters, for they will remain outside the kingdom of God.' [1]

---

[1] This punning ' etymology ', attributed to St Hugh by Walter Map (*De Nugis Curialium*, i, 9) was in accordance with contemporary humour. Other examples given by K. Strecker, *Introduction à l'étude du latin mediéval*, p. 31 include ' Presbiter qui prebit iter ' and ' Bononia quasi plena bonis '.

Isto itaque taliter sublato ac de tabernaculo suo celitus euulso, datur eius uidua, nuptiis adhuc minus apta, cuidam cum alterius patrimonio regis cubiculario. Quo iam, post sancti ex hoc mundo excessum, in fata progresso, tradita est puella miserabilis in manus uiri tertii, prioribus illis longe peioris, quem ob innumeras iniurias ecclesiis pluribus illatas, multiplicis tenet implicitum nexus anathematis. Quis huius futurus sit finis, iam opera eius precedentia ad iudicium, non incertis, ni caueat sibi, preloquuntur indiciis. Mulier quoque que hec est machinata, uitam aliquamdiu in dolore protractam et erumpna morte dudum clausit amara.[1]

Capitvlvm VI

De quodam forestario, de quodam etiam diacono et de quadam adholescentula, et de quibusdam aliis, uiri iusti maledictione in carnis interitum datis.

Alius quidam forestarius, episcopi maledictione retenta, infra dies paucos ex quo tradi meruit Sathane in interitum carnis,[2] crudelis interiit sententia mortis. Nam a quibusdam, quos in foresta sua quam seruabat inuentos insolentius more suo tractare disposuit, ita peremptus est ut, brachiis amputatis et capite auulso, fustes quidam satis exigui, pro quibus ab eodem [a]

---

[a] + satis Q ; + nimis X

[1] In July and Michaelmas 1199 William of Hartshill brought a case against Adam de Neville, the first husband of his brother's supposititious child, who is described as being in his custody, offering the king 500 marks for a favourable judgment. *Rotuli Curiae Regis* I, p. 452 and *Rotuli de Oblatis et Finibus* (ed. T. D. Hardy), I John, pp. 20-21. Adam was apparently still alive in 1201 (*Rotuli Cancellarii*, Record Commission 1833, p. 175), so that Adam's story of his sudden death immediately after winning his case is untrue. His widow was given by John to Norman de Camera, and after

This man being thus removed and snatched away from the world by God, his widow, although still too young for wedlock, was given with another's patrimony to one of the king's chamberlains. He also died, but after the saint's departure from this world, and then the wretched girl was surrendered to a third husband, much more wicked than her former ones, who on account of the innumerable outrages committed by him against various churches, had many times been excommunicated. His past deeds proclaim in no uncertain manner what his future fate will be unless he takes warning. The woman who was responsible for the whole business, ended a life passed for some time in misery and distress by a tragic death.[1]

Chapter VI

Concerning a forester, a deacon and a girl, and certain other persons who died as a result of the excommunication of the holy man.

Another forester who was under the bishop's sentence of excommunication, a few days after he had been delivered over to Satan to the destruction of the flesh,[2] perished in a very horrible way. He was murdered by certain men whom he had found in the forest where he held office and had intended to treat in his usual barbarous way. Having cut off his arms and head, his

---

his death before January 22, 1205 to Brian de Insula. *Rotuli de Oblatis et Finibus*, pp. 40, 240 ; *Rotuli Clausi* (6 John), pp. 17-17b. All three marriages were childless and the inheritance reverted to William of Hartshill's son. *Rotuli Hundredorum* (Record Commission 1812), I, p. 294.

[2] I Cor. 5 : 5

iniuriati fuerant qui eum peremerunt, inter cadauer
truncatum et capud exsectum necnon et alia menbra
feraliter excisa hinc inde posita per loca tria relinque-
rentur,*a* in signum uidelicet et testimonium illius nequitie
qua in finitimos quosque tyrannicam rabiem consueuerat exercere.

Diaconus nomine Ricardus de Waura militem quemdam uocabulo Reginaldum de Argentun super crimine
impetebat regie proditionis.[1] Erat uterque de episcopatu
Lincolniensi. Erat uero pluribus non incertum falso
militem impeti a clerico. Hiis episcopus cognitis
diaconum per censuram ecclesiasticam nititur a temeri-
tate sua cohibere. Inhibet sub interminatione anathematis ne in foro seculari hominem, presertim ad iudicium
sanguinis, audeat pertrahere diaconus. At ille, de regio *b*
qui eum tuebatur elatus fauore, monita pariter et minas
pontificis contempnebat. Nam et Cantuariensis archiepiscopus, qui et publicus tunc regni iustitiarius
habebatur, cuius eum protectioni rex Ricardus impensius
commendauerat, episcopo dicitur iniunxisse ne contra
honorem regium clericum compelleret a prosecutione
inite accusationis desistere.

Verum Petri imitator uerus, in hoc sicut et in
similibus sepe mandatis illius, sui potius officii iura quam
hominis attendebat uerba. Nam quia magnus ille uir,
ut ipse ueraciter perhibere solebat, utrumque sibi
gladium commissum habebat—erat namque, sicut
potestate ordinaria metropolitanus et auctoritate apost-

---

a relinquuntur B²
b regis X

murderers left his truncated body, and severed head and limbs in three different places along with the medium sized cudgels which they were carrying in the forest on account of which he had proceeded to maltreat them, as a witness to his cruel and oppressive treatment of the people of the district.

A deacon, named Richard de Waure, had charged a knight named Reginald de Argentan with treason.[1] They both belonged to the Lincoln diocese, and very many persons were convinced that the accusation made by the clerk was false. When the bishop heard this he did his best to deter the deacon from his wicked act by ecclesiastical censures. He forbade him on pain of anathema to be so bold as to implead a man in a secular court, especially in a case involving the death penalty or mutilation. He, however, relying on royal favour and protection, despised the admonition and threats of the bishop, for the archbishop of Canterbury, who was then justiciar of England, and to whose protection the king had commended him, was alleged to have forbidden the bishop to compel the clerk to give up the prosecution once he had begun it, since this would be a slur on the king.

But Hugh, like a true imitator of Peter, when he received this and similar mandates, put the duties of his office before the orders of any man. This powerful man, as he used to say himself with perfect truth, had both swords committed to his custody, for he was metropolitan

---

[1] Richard of Waure's case against Reginald de Argentan at Michaelmas 1194 was not for treason but felony and breach of the king's peace. He alleged that Reginald and his accomplices had broken into his house by night, and had committed robbery, besides wounding him and killing two of his servants. The defendants pleaded his excommunication as an exception, so it is possible that Hubert Walter absolved him in order that the case could be tried. *Rotuli Curiae Regis* (6 Richard I, 1194), I, pp. 6, 60.

olica totius Anglie legatus, ita uice quoque regia super forenses iudices arbiter summus—episcopus quid a quo idem loqueretur gladio *a* prudenter et caute discernere studebat. Vnde quotienscumque aliquid monebat aut iubebat quod materiali potius quam gladio congrueret spirituali, non uerebatur uir Dei dicere ei quod in Actibus suis summis pontificibus dixisse leguntur Apostoli, 'Obedire oportet Deo magis quam hominibus.' [1] Quamobrem clericum rebellem et discipline contumaciter resistentem ecclesiastice, pontificali non distulit uigore percellere. Suspendit itaque ab officio et beneficio nolentem iugo subdi canonico.

Qui ad legatum perueniens, per eum de facto a suspensione optinuit relaxari. Hinc tumore plenus accedens ad episcopum, sub presentia multorum optimatum regni, tam uidelicet procerum quam et episcoporum, minari cepit grandia. Iactabat uero se a iurisdictione Lincolniensis episcopi taliter iam legati auctoritate exemptum, quod de cetero nullatenus omitteret propter illum, quin et domino regi omnem fidelitatem exhiberet, eique iustitiam de suis optinere proditoribus decertaret. Insultans *b* quoque episcopo, asserebat se relaxatum a suspensione qua ipsum, ut dicebat, minus licite punire decreuisset.

Ad hec ille, non eneruis nauicule Petri gubernator, suo ut semper more illato terrore constantior, qui, ut de quodam sancto legitur, ' In diebus suis non extimuit principem,' [2] ita cunctis audientibus infit, ' Incassum sane super huiuscemodi,' inquit, ' relaxatione tibi blandiris ; nam excommunicandum te incontinenti noueris, si iuri parere super excessibus tuis ulterius

---

a episcopus quidem Hugo uenerabilis a quo Archipresul loqueretur gladio X
b Insultabat asserens X

in his own right, and by papal authority legate throughout England, and also the king's representative above
the other secular justices.   The bishop therefore en-
deavoured to decide after careful investigation by virtue
of which sword he had issued his instructions.   Wherever
he ordered or advised anything which pertained rather
to the material than to the spiritual sword, the man of
God had no scruples about saying to him as we read in
Acts that the apostles did to the high priests, ' It behoves
us to obey God rather than men.' [1]   For this reason he
did not desist from using his episcopal authority against
this clerk, who had rebelled against and was obstinately
refusing to submit to ecclesiastical discipline.   He
suspended him from his office and benefice because of
his defiance of canon law.

The clerk went to the legate and obtained from him
the revocation of the suspension, and being highly elated
by this he accosted the bishop and used very threatening
language towards him in the presence of many of the
magnates, nobles and bishops of the kingdom.   He
boasted that the legate had by his authority exempted
him from the jurisdiction of the bishop of Lincoln, so that
from henceforth he need have no scruples on account of
him in manifesting upon every occasion his loyalty to the
king, and in striving to bring traitors to justice.   He also
jeeringly told the bishop that the suspension which he
had, as he asserted, illegally imposed on him, had been
removed.

He, however, being a bold helmsman of the boat of
Peter, was habitually made the more determined by
threats, and like a certain saint who is described as
' never in his life fearing those in authority ',[2] answered

---

[1] Acts 5 : 29
[2] Ecclus. 48 : 13

detrectaueris.' Quid multa? Illo contumaciter obstre-
pente, et tamquam ore regio minas furiosas intonante,
episcopus eum innodare nec timuit nec distulit sollempni
anathemate. Qui legatum adiens, queritur de episcopo
qui *a* in eius preiudicium regisque dispendium adeo, ut
allegabat, proterue excommunicasset eum. A quo
tandem et litteras impetrauit ad episcopum quatinus pro
absoluto haberet eum, utpote a se absolutum. Cui
episcopus, tali perlecto mandato, ita dixit, ' Si centies te
dominus archiepiscopus duxerit absoluendum, centies
aut etiam sepius *b* te scias a nobis reexcommunicandum *c*
quamdiu te uidebimus in presumptionis tue amentia
irreuocabiliter induratum. Tu uideris quanti habeas
sententiam nostram. Nos enim hanc omnimodis ratam
habemus et firmam.'

Sic ille abscedens, iamque metu tante illius constantie
aliquantulum corde fractior, pollicetur deliberaturum se
utrum iuxta quod exigebatur super parendo iuri coram
episcopo uellet cauere necne. Qui cito post hec a
quodam suo puero securi letaliter percussus in capite,
proh dolor, prius exhalauit animam quam erroris sui
insinuaret penitentiam. Vno enim ictu excerebratus et
repente extinctus, formidabilem illam *d* in se uiri
sapientis sententiam est expertus : ' Semper,' ait,
' iurgia querit malus, angelus autem crudelis mittetur
contra eum.' [1]

De hoc item clerico nequaquam ducimus pretereundum silentio quia in monachum se recipi, modico ante
ista tempore, in quodam petierat religioso cenobio.

---

a quod X
b + ultra X
c excommunicandum Q
d *om* B
[1] Prov. 17 : 11

so that everyone heard, ' You flatter yourself quite groundlessly about this alleged relaxation, for you must realise that you are *ipso facto* excommunicate if you refuse any longer to submit to the jurisdiction of the Church on your transgressions.' He denied this defiantly and angrily threatened him with the king's displeasure, but the bishop boldly and immediately again solemnly excommunicated him. He went to the legate and complained of the bishop, who to his prejudice and, as he alleged, in contempt of the king had dared to excommunicate him. He received letters from Hubert to the bishop to hold him as absolved, since he himself had absolved him. The bishop having read the mandate, addressed him thus : ' If the lord archbishop declares a hundred times that you are to be absolved, be assured that just so often we shall again excommunicate you as long as we see you truculently maintaining your mad defiance. Make up your mind what importance you should attach to our sentence, for we are absolutely convinced of its legality and validity.'

He then left and being at the time somewhat shaken and cowed by so much determination, promised himself that he would consider whether or not he would give the necessary securities to appear before the bishop and obey the law. Soon afterwards, however, one of his pages struck him a fatal blow on the head with an axe, and he unfortunately drew his last breath before he had shown his sorrow for his sin. A single blow brained him and he died suddenly; the terrible words of the sage were indeed fulfilled : ' The evil man always seeks strife, but a tormenting angel will be sent against him.' [1]

I do not think I should omit to mention that this clerk had a little while previously sought admission into a certain monastery as a monk. His petition was granted,

Quod dum ei fuisset concessum, suum interea cognoscit
decessisse germanum cui iuxta primogenita paternum in
hereditatem cesserat patrimonium. Qui hereditatem
cupiens optinere fratris absque liberis defuncti, fratris
pro se mortui sortem repudiauit, qui fratribus suis per
seipsum dixit : 'Qui non renuntiauerit omnibus que
possidet *a* non potest meus esse discipulus.'[1] Merito igitur,
qui eius pro terra reliquit discipulatum, qui suis promittit
discipulis in hoc seculo centuplum et in futuro uitam
eternam,[2] et terram quam optauit cito perdidit, et de
uita etiam temporali exemplo terribili citius emigrauit.
Misit enim manum ad aratrum set respiciens retro
amisit, ni misereatur Omnipotens, regnum celorum.[3]

Adholescentula quedam Oxoniensis, cuiusdam
burgensis filia, conuicaneo cuidam iuueni legitime nupta,
alterius amore iuuenis amplius succensa, priore con-
tempto sponso, illi est de facto coniugata. Que super
hoc impetita a sponso priore atque conuicta, monebatur
diligentissime ab episcopo quatinus primo se redderet
marito. Ipsa uero, dissuasa a matre, que in consilio
nequam alteram se filie sue exhibebat Herodiadem, ante
se morituram quam ei nupturam procaciter clamitabat.
Tunc uir Domini, apprehensa eiusdem sponsi illius
dextera, miscensque terroribus blandimenta,[4] 'Si uis,'
inquit, ' esse filia mea, obaudi iussioni mee et suscipe in
pacis osculo cum Dei benedictione maritum tuum.
Alioquin reuera de cetero non parcam tibi nec perniciosis
consiliariis tuis.' Iussit quoque uirum eius in osculo
sancto pacis sucipere eam. Quod dum ille implere
uellet, infelix illa impudentissime expuit in faciem eius
cum prope esset altare, presensque *b* cum pluribus uiris

---

a B *omits these two words*
b presens B

but meanwhile he learnt that his brother, to whom the family inheritance had come according to the law of primogeniture, had died without children. He, desiring to obtain the inheritance of his earthly brother renounced that of the Brother who had died for him, and had Himself said to His brethren ' He who does not renounce all that he possesses cannot be my disciple.' [1] Deservedly, therefore, one who had for earthly riches given up being a disciple of the One who promised to His disciples a hundredfold in this world, and eternal life in the world to come,[2] soon lost the land he had coveted, and was removed from this earthly life in this terrible way. He had indeed put his hand to the plough and, by looking back, lost the kingdom of Heaven, unless God be merciful to him.[3]

A young girl at Oxford, the daughter of one of the burgesses, and already wedded to a certain youth of the same town, was inflamed by a stronger love for another youth, and deserting her husband, actually lived with him as his wife. Her husband accused her and proved the charge, and the bishop earnestly admonished her to return without delay to him. She, however, was dissuaded by her mother, who showed herself another Herodias in her wicked advice to her daughter, and declared defiantly that she would rather die than live with him. The man of God then took her husband by his right hand, and combining persuasion with threats [4] said, ' If you desire to be my daughter, obey me and give your husband the kiss of peace with God's blessing. If you do not, I shall not spare you and your evil counsellors.' He also ordered her husband to give her the kiss of peace, which he would willingly have done,

---

[1] Luke 14: 33   [2] cf. Mark 10 : 30
[3] cf. Mt. 19: 29   [4] *Rule of St Benedict*, c. 2

reuerentissimis adesset tantus sacerdos et turba fidelium
multa in ipsa ecclesia pariter constituta. Tunc uniuersis
ob tantam contumeliam uiro illatam uehementer erube-
scentibus, episcopus uoce terribili ait, 'Quia noluisti,'
inquit, 'benedictionem set maledictionem dilexisti, ecce
apprehendet te maledictio', moxque excommunicauit
eam. Que in propria contumaciter abscedens,[a] post
dies paucos sibi ad inducias utilius secum deliberandi
celesti pietate concessos, cum magis induraretur cor eius
et nullatenus resipisceret, prefocata ab hoste maligno,
delicias repente illicitas et caducas tam perpetuis quam
iustis commutauit suppliciis.

Itidem clerico cuidam Eboracensis diocesis nomine
Willelmo, suam qua iniuste eum spoliauerat quorumdam
uiolentia, restituendam ecclesiam auctoritate decreuerat
apostolica, quem pars aduersa diutius ab ingressu
possessionis sibi adiudicate manu repellebat armata.
Miles namque, illius uille dominus in qua sita erat
ecclesia litigiosa, suum fratrem in eandem ingressum per
intrusionem armis tuebatur, uiribus nitens illicite occu-
patam uendicare illi possessionem. Fouebant quoque
partem intrusoris tam ecclesiastici quam et mundani
iudices et optimates illius regionis. Tandem Willelmus
nimiis iam laboribus confectus, sumptibus quoque dum
sepius curie Romane suffragium in propria implorat
presentia, plurimorum etiam hinc inde auxilia peruigili
set parum utili [b] requirit instantia, penitus exhaustus,
totus conuertitur ad unicum oppressorum refugium, ad
inuictum iuris patronum, eiusque flebilibus uocibus
interpellat subsidium.

---

[a] quam . . . abscedentem B
[b] peruigili . . . utili pugili B . . . inutili X

but the wretched girl impudently spat in his face, although he was near the altar and the bishop himself was present in the church with many important ecclesiastics and a great multitude of the faithful. Everyone was deeply shocked at such outrageous behaviour towards her husband. The bishop said very sternly, 'As you have spurned my blessing and have desired my curse, my curse shall fall upon you,' and immediately excommunicated her. She went home still stubborn and during the few days vouchsafed to her by the divine mercy to come to a better frame of mind, her heart became more hardened and not in the least repentant. Then being suddenly strangled by the devil, her illicit and temporary delights were exchanged for perpetual torments as she richly deserved.

Once as a judge delegate Hugh decreed that a clerk of the diocese of York named William should be restored to the church, from which his enemies had ejected him by violence and had for a long time forcibly prevented him from taking possession of it. The knight who was lord of the manor to which the church under dispute belonged, had intruded his own brother and kept him there by force, trying hard to maintain his claim to what he had illegally seized. The ecclesiastical and secular judges as well as the chief men of the district supported the intruder. At last William, when practically broken and ruined by all the trouble and expense he had been put to, in having to journey several times to the Curia to secure help, and in trying hard but vainly to procure assistance from many people everywhere, had recourse to the only refuge of the oppressed and undaunted champion of justice, and with tears implored his aid.

Indignatus itaque bonus Helie, Helisei quoque in zelo Dei emulator, auctoritate fultus apostolica, intrusorem prenominatum et ipsius complices dure maledictionis ferit sententia. Nec paulo tardius in sacrilegos deseuire cepit ultio diuina. Nam ut uiris plerisque religiosis referentibus nobis innotuit, alii ex hiis in amentiam uersi sunt, alii repentina morte miserabiliter preuenti inter-ierunt, aliis *a* e cauis orbibus oculi cum immensis cruciatibus exciderunt. Sic itaque uirtus absentis presentem ad nocendum innoxio perdomuit audaciam superborum : sic legitimo possessori suorum restituta est et defensa possessio bonorum : sic denique athleta fortis nostrique temporis ambidexter probatissimus, utraque manu pugnare utraque pro dextera [1] uti doctus, hos percutiebat et interficiebat, illos feriebat et uiuere faciebat : cadebantque ab eo a dextris et a sinistris. Citius enim quisque in mortem cecidit qui dextere ipsius ictum excepit. Aut enim corrigebatur, et Deo uicturus peccato moriebatur, aut corde induratus et incorrectus exitio tradebatur.

Capitvlvm VII

De pallii exactione quod sibi rex Ricardus ab ecclesia Lincolniensi asserebat deberi. Et quod mulctas pecu-niarias per officiales et archidiaconos a delinquentibus extorqueri prohibuerit.

Sentiens uero cruentus generis humani inimicus in sui graue dispendium uiri ubique uictoriosissimi uires preualere, a castris eorum quos eius tuebatur presentia

---

a alii B ; aliis et auis Q

The worthy rival of Elijah and Elisha in his zeal for God, being invested with papal authority, excommunicated the intruder I have already mentioned and his accomplices. Shortly afterwards divine vengeance overtook these profane wretches. I have heard from several devout men, that some of them went mad, others died miserably and unexpectedly, and the rest had their eyes put out and suffered immense torment. Thus even when absent he quelled the violence of arrogant men ever ready to injure the innocent, and thus lawful owners obtained restitution of their property and were protected in their possession of the same and, to conclude, thus the best champion of our age used both hands to equal advantage. He had been trained to fight with both hands,[1] to strike down and to kill, and to wound and to restore to life, and on all sides they fell before him. Those who received a blow from his right hand speedily died, for either they reformed and died to sin to live for God, or unrepentant and with hardened hearts, they were delivered over to hell.

CHAPTER VII

Concerning the tribute of a mantle, which king Richard declared was owed by the church of Lincoln, and how Hugh forbade his officials and archdeacons to impose fines on sinners.

The implacable enemy of mankind realising that this valiant man was always able to defeat him to his

---

[1] cf. St Ambrose, *Liber Officiorum*, lib. I, c. 40 (P.L. 16, 88)

eum arte callida nititur amouere, quatinus saltem elongato a certaminis loco insuperabili totius aciei protectore, in reliquo licentius *a* grassaretur agmine. Sciens namque serpens uirulentus uirum Dei libertatem ecclesie impensius zelare, qui nec subiectis sibi ecclesiis pecuniarias ullatenus exactiones imponeret, nec quibuscumque potestatibus, tale quid a sua exigentibus ecclesia, ulla ratione adquiesceret ; in talem eum perplexitatem conatur inducere ex qua, preter aliquod saltem inconueniens, haut facile quiuisset erumpere.

Armatus igitur astu *b* inueterate malitie, peruersas quorumdam mentes familiariter subditorum sibi instigat, per quos regis animos *c* contra episcopum ad nouas et inopinatas querelas excitaret. Suggeritur per eos regi ingentis cuiusdam debiti, quod ei annuatim soluere tenebatur, Lincolniensem episcopum esse detentorem ; unde et reus in eius, ut uulgo dicitur, misericordiam incidisset, et ad summam eris plurimi fisco ex diutina retentione refundendam addici potuisset. Nam Lincolniensis quidam olim antistes dictus Alexander,[1] qui tertius Hugonem precesserat, pallium centum argenti marcis appretiatum regi suo tempore imperanti aliquot impretermisse annis dedisse ferebatur. Cuius successor uocabulo Robertus idem aliquotiens egisse dicebatur. Hinc calumpnia in Hugonem deuoluta : non solum hoc quod eum pontificatus sui tempore quotannis debuisse prestare memorabant, anxie ab eodem repetunt, set etiam pro iniuriosa regii muneris subtractione ipsum ad regis nutum satisfactioni esse obnoxium, satis inuidiose decernunt. Nec tantum personam episcopi,

---

a libentius X
b astucia uiperee malitie X
c animum o

[1] In reality not Alexander but Robert Bloet began this payment. cf. Giraldus VII, pp. 33, 196

great detriment, used all his crafty devices to dislodge
him from the fortresses of those to whom his presence
was a protection, for if the leader of the always victorious
army were removed from the field, the remaining forces
would be entirely at his mercy.   The venomous serpent
knew that the man of God had such great zeal for the
liberty of the Church that he would never in any
circumstances impose monetary exactions on his subjects,
nor allow any other authority to make similar demands
upon his church on any pretext whatever.   He therefore
strove to entangle him in a net from which he could not
easily extricate himself without doing something which
he found particularly repugnant.

By means of his habitual craft and malice he worked
upon the depraved minds of certain of his chief servants
so that they caused the king to make new and unprecedented demands upon the bishop.   They told him
about a certain immense payment due annually, which
the bishop of Lincoln had held back, for which offence,
to speak colloquially, he was ' in mercy ', and could be
made to pay into the treasury a very large sum of
money as arrears over a long period.   One of the former
bishops of Lincoln, Alexander,[1] the third one before
Hugh, was alleged to have given at the command of the
king then reigning a cloak valued at 100 silver marks,
for several years in succession, and his successor Robert
was supposed sometimes to have done the same.   This
claim now devolved on Hugh, and they not only demanded
that he should pay at once the sum they said he should
have paid each year of his episcopate, but also very
maliciously decreed that having defrauded and offended
the king by withholding the tribute, he should pay in
addition whatever the king pleased.   They even alleged
that the church as well as the bishop who had taken over

immo et ecclesiam cuius ille et onera subisset et emolumenta perciperet, pro tempore Walteri sui decessoris qui nec ipse pallium regi debitum aliquando dedisset, et detentionis ream et redditionis debitricem esse perhibebant.

Conuentus super talibus ab ipso tunc rege Ricardo, episcopus uix tandem, nimirum *a* aduersante sibi ut ferebatur quam maxime archiepiscopo sepius memorato, pro tribus milibus marcarum, tam a repetitione *b* subtracti muneris quam et ab eiusdem in posterum collatione et se et suos eripuit successores, suamque perpetuis temporibus a prestationis illius onere absoluit ecclesiam. Nichil enim indignius, nichil sibi intolerabilius fore estimabat quam sponsam Regis eterni aut seipsum, illius pro tempore custodem, homini mortali censualem constituere et quodammodo uectigalem exhibere. Inuenit igitur artum licet et angustum foramen in maxilla leuiathan,[1] per quod illud effugeret morte illa molestius inconueniens, quo ecclesiam regine celi quam regebat terreno regi tributariam nitebatur fieri. Exemit igitur ecclesiam a seruitute degeneri, proprii nil metuens exilitati peculii. Paratior erat seipsum perpetue addicere egestati quam periclitanti minus adesse ecclesie *c* libertati.

Ceterum unde uiro liberalissimo hec tanta proueniet pecunia ? Qui omnes semper annuos redditus uel quoscumque prouentus ad impendia misericordie et in sumptus iuste necessitatis effundere erat solitus, cui numquam ultra presentis anni spatium quicquam pecunie erat residuum, quippe cum et mutuum es frequenter sumeret alienum ; unde perciperet *d* que regi persolueret tot milia talentorum ? Erat quidem paratum

---

a nimium o   *b* repetione B   *c* ecclesiastice X
d ubi inueniret Q : ubi, inquam, inueniret uel unde perciperet X

its obligations and was receiving its revenues was
responsible for the arrears due during the episcopate of
his predecessor Walter, who had never given the king
the cloak he was entitled to, and ought to pay up.

After some time and as the result of hard bargaining,
for the archbishop who has already been so often
mentioned was, as the story goes, his bitter enemy, the
bishop came to terms with king Richard. For three
thousand marks he freed himself and his successors and
his church from the burden for ever, for the tribute was
never to be again exacted nor again paid. Nothing
seemed to him more shameful and intolerable than that
the bride of the King of Heaven, or he himself, her
temporary steward, should pay taxes or tribute to any
human being. He therefore found a hole, albeit a tiny
one,[1] in the jaw of Behemoth, through which he could
escape from what he hated more than death, namely
that the church of the Queen of Heaven over which he
ruled should be compelled to pay tribute to any earthly
ruler. Thus, he freed his church from an ignoble
bondage, without taking into consideration the smallness
of his resources, for he was ready to doom himself to
permanent poverty rather than allow the least threat
to the liberty of the Church.

But how could such a generous man raise such a
sum ? He was accustomed always to devote the whole
of his annual income and any unexpected windfall to
works of charity, and to his necessary expenses. As he
never had anything over at the end of the year and
indeed often had to obtain a loan, how could he find
the wherewithal to pay the king so many thousands of
talents ? The obvious expedient was, if his own
resources failed, to exact the money from the pockets of

[1] cf. Job 40 : 21

ad manus consilium, si quod propriis deerat crumenis, a subiectorum uellet extorquere locellis.^a Set qui non modo pecuniam, immo et propriam pro sibi commissorum indempnitate in uotis semper habuerat ponere animam, qualiter eis suam extorqueret substantiam? Vel qui suam a prebitione ignobili eximere satagebat ecclesiam, quomodo aliorum ecclesias oneraret ut seipsum releuaret, et pro sua libertate iugum aliis imponeret seruitutis?

Iam itaque uiro Dei uidebatur unicum superesse remedium, quod et sibi erat satis uotiuum : ut ipse scilicet ad suam interim secedens Withamiam ibique solitarie degens, prouentus uniuersos totius episcopatus ad summam huius debiti persoluendam conuerti ordinaret. Gaudebat toto animo et exultabat quia non modo iustam et honestam, immo et necessariam se putabat inuenisse occasionem ut a mundanis tumultibus aliquamdiu secederet ac secretis celestibus eo suauius quo et liberius inhereret. Iam sibi blanditur et applaudit de assertione Pauli, scire se perhibentis, ' Quoniam diligentibus Deum omnia cooperantur in bonum.' [1]

Sperabat enim iuxta deliberationem suam ex inflicto rerum dispendio temporalium eternum mercari compendium fructumque ex breui capere ^b iactura copiosum. Verum ut hoc suum propositum notitie suorum intimauit clericorum, obniti uehementius uniuersi ceperunt, intolerabilem sibi prorsus illius tantam remotionem protestantes. Set et religiose persone innumere ne id fieret quod disponebat magnopere dissuadebant.

Denique uniuersis diocesis sue ecclesiasticis personis in commune placuit, ad exemptionem matricis sue ecclesie, pecuniam de suis copiis animo libenti conferre ;

^a loculis X
^b carpere X

his subjects. But how could he, whose aim it was to devote not only his money but even his life to the welfare of his flock, now take their property from them ? Could he who had worked to release his own church from an ignominious obligation, burden other churches to free his own, and lay the yoke of servitude on others to secure her freedom ?

To the man of God there seemed to be only one possibility, which indeed accorded well with his own desires, that he should return for a time to Witham and live there as a hermit, and set aside all the revenue of his bishopric to pay the sum due. It made him glad to be so completely convinced that he had not merely a good and legitimate excuse, but that it was absolutely essential for him to withdraw for a time from the disturbances of the world and surrender himself entirely to the delights of heavenly contemplation. He was already congratulating himself that he had proved for himself the truth of St Paul's well-known aphorism ' All things work together for good to them that love God ',[1] hoping and believing that his temporal losses would be to his eternal profit, and that abundant fruit would be gained from a short period of penury. When, however, he informed his clergy of his intention, they were strongly opposed to it, and declared that they could not bear the idea of his going so far away. Very many devout persons also tried hard to dissuade him from doing so.

Finally all the clergy of the diocese came to a common decision, which was that they would willingly provide the money for the redemption of their mother church out of their own revenues. They unanimously petitioned the bishop most earnestly that since he was their dear

[1] Rom. 8 : 28

unanimiter quoque, ut patrem et defensorem pium atque fortissimum, ipsum obnixius flagitabant episcopum ne huius rei gratia suam ab eis aliquatenus presentiam absentaret. Ita, multum licet inuitus et coactus, filiorum suorum petitionibus et consiliis adquieuit amicorum, sue preponens desiderio uoluntatis pium generalitatis decretum. Suis uero districtius inhibuit officialibus ne a quouis hominum quicquam exigere amplius presumerent quam quod uoluntate spontanea quilibet obtulisset.[1] De proprio autem peculio, quantum facultas admisit, dari precepit. Sicque prouinciales potius ecclesias quam earum matrem ecclesiam Lincolniensem a turpi simul et graui diu inolite iugo seruitutis semel eripiendo, perpetue restituit libertati. Nam quod citra cuiusque grauamen a clericis semel modo perceperit [a] eorum, ut sic dicatur, redemptor et manumissor, hoc immo multo amplius non sine plurimorum grauamine extorquere solitus erat uterque prememoratus huius tributi inuentor ac redditor, palliata scilicet sub pretextu regalis pallii ambitione pontificali. Quod tamen ex nobis dicere non audemus set hoc dicimus ex sententia plurimorum qui sepius ex tali diuitum colludio egestati sue gemebant illudi. Nam et ipse rex edoctus ut credebatur a quibusdam, lac suarum ouium usque ad expressionem butiri libenter ac frequenter emulgentibus,[2] hoc episcopo potius quam sibi profuturum dixerat, qui more decessorum suorum multa sumeret a suis clericis, unde uix pauca daret pro pallio appendendo ipsius [b] humeris. At uerus et bonus pastor, quantum oues sibi creditas diligebat, tantum immunitatem illarum zelabat ; quantum uero ad se pertinebat, sicut omnem auaritiam sedulo fugiebat, ita

---

[a] percepit QX
[b] suis Xp

father and valiant champion, he would not leave them even for a moment on this pretext. He therefore, although reluctantly and much against his will, yielded to the prayers of his friends and spiritual sons, and sacrificed his personal inclinations to the general consensus of opinion. He issued strict orders to his officials, however, that they were not to demand more from anyone than he had offered to give,[1] and also commanded that, as far as his resources permitted, his own revenues should be used.

Thus, by one act he freed the churches of the diocese as well as the Mother Church for ever from a shameful and heavy burden which they had borne for a long time. He can aptly be described as the liberator and manumitter of his clergy since he took from them on this one occasion only, less than the amount of the obligation, whereas the two bishops already mentioned, the offerer and the payer of the tribute caused considerable financial hardship to very many, by exacting this sum and a good deal more, thus making the king's cloak a cloak for their own covetousness. I am not asserting this on my own authority, but am repeating the views of a large number of persons who often complained that their poverty was due to the rich combining to deceive them in this particular way. Even the king, when informed by certain pastors who frequently and gladly milked their flocks until they obtained butter,[2] is believed to have asserted that the bishop would gain more than he did himself since like his predecessors he would extort large sums from his clergy and give little for the cloak which he hung on the royal shoulders. The

---

[1] This was in accordance with Hugh's synodal decree : ' Precepit ne pro iustitia exhibenda vel acceleranda datur vel accipiatur aliquid.' Benedictus Abbas, I, p. 357.
[2] cf. Prov. 30 : 33

et occasionem auaritie summis, ubi posset, nisibus iugiter euellebat.

Vnde et mulctam pecuniariam a quibuscumque delinquentibus tam archidiaconos suos quam eorum officiales ac decanos exigere prohibebat, nimirum uerens ne pro muneribus aliquem aut opprimerent insontem, aut in suis excessibus sontem fouerent, iuxta illud antiqui legislatoris, ' Munera excecant oculos sapientum et subuertunt uerba iustorum.'[1] Itemque illud Scripture alterius suis crebro officialibus ingerebat, ' Ignis deuorabit tabernacula eorum qui munera libenter accipiunt.'[2]

E contrario illis frequenter asserentibus plus terrere improbos pecunie dampnum quam excommunicationis probrum aut etiam corporalium afflictionem penarum illis indicendarum, ille e diuerso asserebat id sue negligentie ascribendum qui remissius se haberent in corripiendis et districtius cohercendis illis qui peccassent, nec eos tam studiose obseruare ut illi iniunctam explerent satisfactionem quam obseruarent ut sibi pollicitam enumerarent pecunie taxationem. Illis interdum pro se allegare studentibus ac dicentibus beatissimum archiepiscopum et martirem Thomam huiusmodi a delinquentibus sumpsisse mulctas, ille confestim respondebat, ' Credite michi,' inquit, ' non iccirco sanctus fuit; alia enim uirtutum merita sanctum exhibuerunt, alio meruit titulo palmam reportare martirii.'

faithful and good pastor, on the other hand, loved the sheep committed to his care as much as he desired to secure their freedom, and his horror of avarice made him do his best to prevent whenever he could any temptation to covetousness. This was why he forbade his archdeacons, their officials and the rural deans to impose fines on offenders, for he was very much afraid that bribes might cause them to punish the guiltless and encourage the guilty in their offences, in accordance with the opinion of the old lawgiver, ' Gifts blind the wise, and annul the sentences of the righteous.' [1] He also used to quote often to his officials that other passage from the Scriptures : ' Fire shall devour the tabernacles of those who willingly accept bribes.' [2]

They, for their part, used often to argue that offenders disliked the loss of money more than the shame of excommunication or even corporal penances. To this he replied that this must be due to their own negligence and apathy in correcting and dealing sternly with sinners, for they took much less trouble to see that they performed the penances imposed upon them, than they did to secure payment of the amount of money they had been promised. When they tried to defend themselves by declaring that the most holy archbishop and martyr Thomas had taken fines in this way from offenders he immediately replied, ' Believe me, this did not make him a saint, his other conspicuous virtues showed him to be one, and he deserved the martyr's palm for another cause.'

[1] Exodus 23 : 8 ; Deut. 16 : 19
[2] Job 15 : 34

Capitvlvm VIII

Quod ius patronatus in monasterio Hegneshamensi contra ipsum regem Anglorum in curia ipsius multo sudore optinuerit.

Viro itaque sancto hoc ordine liberato ac laqueo uenantium nutu Dei contrito, inuidia peruersorum que utcumque superari potuit, quiescere a consuetis malitie sue artibus nesciuit. Iterum namque uiri simpliciter gradientis pedibus nouas struit pedicas, iterum recentes molitur insidias. Nouis siquidem fraudium cuniculis [a] ad antiqui iuris ecclesie sue haut leue preiuditium conatur surripere.

Cum enim ab aduentu Normanorum in Angliam, bellico sibi iure subactam, per annos centum et eo amplius ecclesia Lincolniensis continue et inconcusse usque ad id temporis patronatum gesserit Egneshamensis cenobii, hanc ei dignitatem surripere maligni quidam pertinaciter sunt aggressi. Beatus sane pontifex Remigius, quem in breui post triumphatam insulam, gloriosum habuit cathedralis ecclesia Lincolniensium fundatorem, uastatam, fugatis hostili metu fratribus, abbatiam reformauerat prenotatam.[b] Quam sibi auctoritate regia inclitus triumphator Willelmus ita confirmauit [c] in propriam, ut preter ipsum episcopum eiusque successores, nulla in eam uendicare presumeret ecclesiastica seu laicalis persona quamcumque dominationem.[1]

Accidit autem ut anno presulatus beati Hugonis decimo uenerandus cenobii huius rector et abbas migrauit ad Dominum nomine Godefridus, qui a diebus regis Stephani usque ad tempora regni penultima Ricardi

---

[a] fraudum cumulis X   [b] reformauit QX prenominatam X
[c] confirmasse dicitur X

Chapter VIII

How after much labour Hugh recovered in the king's court his patronage over the monastery of Eynsham against the Crown.

Although the holy man had been set free in this way and the snare of the hunters had been broken by God's hand, he was not able to overcome the envy of the evil-doers, or to make them abandon their malicious devices. Once more it laid traps for the feet of the man who walked uprightly, and again lay in wait for him. Once more it attempted to cheat him, by hatching new plots to the serious prejudice of the ancient rights of his church.

Certain evil persons made a determined attack on the right of patronage over Eynsham exercised continually and without challenge by the church of Lincoln for a hundred years or more, since the arrival of the Normans and their conquest of England. Blessed bishop Remigius, who had founded the magnificent cathedral church of Lincoln shortly after the conquest, had refounded the ruined abbey, from which the monks had fled out of fear of the enemy. The mighty Conqueror William had in virtue of his royal authority confirmed his possession of it, on terms which excluded the lordship of any clerk or layman except the bishop and his successors.[1]

It befell, however, in the tenth year of the episcopate of blessed Hugh, that the venerable abbot Geoffrey who had ruled and governed the abbey for about forty-four years from the days of King Stephen to the later years of the reign of Richard, the son of King Henry,

---

[1] For these documents cf. H. E. Salter, *Eynsham Cartulary* I, pp. 32, 36-77.

filii regis Henrici annis circiter quadraginta quatuor
loco eidem noscitur prefuisse. Quo episcopus audito,
misit iuxta morem antiquum ex suis clericum unum, qui
abbatie custodiam in manus suas reciperet ac rerum
monasterii una cum fratrum diligentia sollicitudinem
gereret, quousque abbatis instituendi canonica electio
celebrari potuisset. Ceterum tam uacantis custodiam
abbatie quam substituendi abbatis debitam facultatem,
qui regiis in Anglia preerant negotiis, episcopo nitebantur
auferre. Nam rex ea tempestate in transmarinis con-
fligebat cum Francorum rege.

Complures itaque uiri prudentes et episcopum
sincere diligentes persuadere ei conati sunt, ne ut dici
solet, contra ictum fluminis brachia,[1] ob aduersantium
multitudinem atque potentiam interim minus ualida,
inaniter fatigando exereret.[a] Asserebant namque regis [b]
genitorem Henricum generali constitutione decreuisse
ut uniuerse regni sui abbatie in sua manerent donatione.
Nec fore estimabant de facili ut contra patris decretum
filius, eo ut uidebatur in multis pertinacior, gaudere eum
sineret priuilegio, auitis licet temporibus optento.
Denique negotium hoc laboris plenum, modice fructuosum, multimodis dampnosum nullatenus monebant
attemptandum. Metiendum cum labore etiam fructuoso
laboris fructum suggerebant, nec maxima subeunda [c]
rerum innumerabilium dispendia, que iam certius
preuiderent ex hac controuersia sibi suisque emersura,
ubi quod intendebat [d] assequendi spes esset fere nulla,
forte etiam assecuti utilitas parua.

Talia suggerentibus uir singularis confidentie mireque

---

[a] contra ictum obaduersantium atque potentiam, interim brachia
minus ualida inaniter fatigando exerceret X
[b] *om* B   [c] *om* B   [d] attendebat X

migrated to the Lord. On learning the news, the bishop in accordance with the ancient custom sent one of his clerks to take over the custody of the abbey and administer its temporalities with the assistance of the monks until a canonical election of the new abbot could be held. The king was at that time abroad fighting against the French king, and those who governed England for him, did their best to deprive the bishop of his custody of the vacant abbey and of his right to appoint the abbot.

Many shrewd men out of sincere affection for the bishop tried to persuade him that on account of his numerous powerful enemies, he should not, to use the common phrase, wear himself out in vain by struggling feebly against the stream.[1] They told him that Henry, the king's father, had made a general ordinance by which all the abbeys of the kingdom were to be in his gift. They thought it very unlikely that the son who seemed in many matters more determined than the father would allow him to exercise his privilege although it had been obtained in the days of his ancestors, in spite of his father's decree. Finally they counselled him on no account to undertake a business which would cause him infinite trouble, and bring him no profit but involve him in considerable risks. They pointed out that for labour to be fruitful its fruits must be reaped, and the heavy losses of every kind which they foresaw would certainly ensue both to himself and his friends from this conflict should not be risked. There was almost no hope that the course he intended to pursue would be successful and even if it were, it was hardly worth while.

To such suggestions this man of amazing faith and

---

[1] cf. Ecclus. 4: 32.

discretionis confestim respondit, ' Absit,' inquiens, ' ut
mortalium quispiam tale decretum statuere presumat,
unde Deo nostro et beatissime celi regine quod suum est
auferre preualeat. Huiusmodi leges, et si iuste essent,
futuris duntaxat negotiis formam darent ; non etiam
conuellerent statuta priorum. Quis uero predecessorum
meorum tali subscripsit decreto, quo solo posset iuri non
immerito prescribi eatenus ab eisdem possesso ? Absit
enim ut persone cuiuscumque laicalis *a* statutum ecclesiastice libertatis infringat priuilegium. Michi uero non
contingat ut qualiscumque timore potestatis seu quante-
cumque formidine difficultatis ius ecclesie domine mee,
quantum in me est, sinam deperire. Cum enim sit satis
pudendum a maioribus adquisitas, ab antiquis defensas,
non etiam augere dignitates sancte ecclesie atque
libertates, quam est probrosum si ex inertia *b* inutilis
atque ignaui rectoris a sue integritatis statu decidant, que
per strenuum dispensatorem augmentari ac in melius
prouehi debebant.'

Talia prosequens continuis duobus semis annis nec
sumptibus *c* nec proprio sudori parcens, tum pro
expedienda libertate canonici status prefati monasterii,
tum pro tuenda dignitate sua, inuictissime tam contra
regem ipsum quam et contra plerosque subdolos clam
sibi aduersantes, cis citraque mare decertans, tandem
fauente Domino celebri potitur triumpho. Recognito
namque per sacramentum uiginti quatuor fidedignorum
clericorum pariter et laicorum quid iuris predecessores
sui in illo habuissent cenobio, adiudicatur ei eiusdem
patronatus in regis curia. Hinc ei restituitur abbatie
uacantis custodia, preficiendi quoque abbatis iurisdictio
plena et absoluta.

a + preeminentie X
b materia B
c B *omits these two words*

wisdom answered immediately : ' God forbid that any mortal should dare to make a decree by which they can deprive our God and the blessed Queen of Heaven of what is theirs ! Such laws, even if they were just, would create dangerous precedents for the future. Let them not destroy the ordinances of our ancestors. Which of my predecessors agreed to such an ordinance, on the sole strength of which the rights they had possessed up till then could not unjustly be taken away from them ? God forbid that ecclesiastical liberties and privileges should be infringed by the decree of any layman ! It is impossible for me out of fear of any powerful person, or the dread of any difficulty whatsoever to allow the rights of my church to be sacrificed, if I can help it. Indeed since it is a matter for shame not to increase the privileges and liberties of Holy Church acquired and defended of old by our predecessors, how disgraceful it would be if through the indifference of a weak and cowardly ruler its condition should decline, when it is the duty of a vigorous steward to improve and ameliorate it ! '

He pursued this policy steadily for two and a half years, sparing neither labour nor money, fighting undauntedly to preserve the freedom and canonical status of the aforesaid monastery and also the Church's own rights both against the king and against many others who were his secret enemies, both here and overseas, and at length with God's assistance he won a notable victory. Twenty-four trustworthy recognitors, half of whom were clerks and half laymen, testified on oath to the rights of his predecessors over the monastery, and its patronage was adjudged to him in the king's court. Hence the right of custody during vacancies was restored to him and his right of appointing the abbot was completely established.

Post que in propria ad eam accedens persona, per dies octo mansit in ea cum fratribus loci tamquam benignissimus pater cum filiis karissimis ingrediens et egrediens, cum eis in communi refectorio pariter conuescens, eosque uino iocunditatis et dapibus sue largitatis copiose reficiens. Tractabatur interea iussu eius in conuentu super electione futuri abbatis. Expleta uero ebdomada una, accitis abbatibus uicinis aliisque religiosis uiris, presentatur episcopo monachorum electio ac sollempniter confirmatur ab episcopo.[a]

Quibus rite gestis, pastor egregius Lincolniam proficiscitur, ibique in cathedrali ecclesia electus Egneshamensis cum fauore cunctorum atque letitia eius benedictione sacra in abbatem honorifice promouetur. Instructoque sollempni conuiuio tam clericis quam abbati et monachis suis, discumbebat utriusque cohortis dux inclitus in medio eorum, mirum in modum gaudens et exultans in Domino, eo quod instar pastoris summi [b] boni alias oues adduxisset que essent ex ouili alio,[1] ut efficerentur de cetero unus grex iste et ille oues, et esset utriusque unus pastor, qui sic mutuo sibi ecclesiam confederasset et abbatiam, uti foret perpetim utraque unum. Dedit quoque abbati nouo uirgam pastoralem argento et ebore pulchre uermiculatam, cum cifo ingenti atque insigni. Locum etiam ipsius commissum regimini pluribus ampliauit beneficiis et donariis decorauit, ac paterno semper affectu tam ipsum quam gregem ei subditum fouit et dilexit.[2]

---

[a] ipso X ; eodem p
[b] summe QX

After this he paid a personal visit and remained there for eight days with the monks, going in and out among them like a devoted father with his dear sons, and eating with them in the refectory, and refreshing them greatly by the wine of his good humour, and the excellent fare of his kindliness. In the meantime discussions about the election of the future abbot took place among the community by his command. After a week had passed the neighbouring abbots and other monks were summoned, and the monks presented the abbot elect to the bishop who formally confirmed the election.

When all this had duly taken place, the excellent pastor set out for Lincoln and in the cathedral church there, amid general approbation and rejoicing, the elect of Eynsham received his solemn benediction as abbot. There was a great banquet for the clergy as well as for the abbot and his monks, at which the great bishop sat presiding over both groups. He was exceedingly glad and gave thanks to God that like the good Shepherd he had brought other sheep who had belonged to another sheepfold into his own,[1] and that henceforward these and his other sheep should be one flock and he himself shepherd of both, and that he should unite the cathedral and the abbey under himself, so that both should be one for ever. He gave the new abbot a pastoral staff, beautifully inlaid with silver and ivory, and a large and magnificent cup. He showered favours on the house under his rule, and enriched it by his gifts, watching over the abbot and the flock he governed with fatherly affection and care.[2]

---

[1] cf. John 10 : 16

[2] Abbot Geoffrey died in 1196 ; his successor, Robert of Dover was blessed at Lincoln on 11 Nov. 1197 (Gervase of Canterbury, I, 543-4). Adam now joined Hugh's household.

CAPITVLVM IX

Quod specialis ei gloria, sicut et patrono suo beato quondam Martino, in ordine fuerit monastico. Quod Withamiam frequenter adire consueuerit. Qualiter uiros seculares instruere, qualiter quoque sexum femineum monere solitus sit. Et de prerogatiua ueritatis, castitatis et caritatis ipsius. Necnon et de custodia sigilli sui.

Erat namque ei, sicut et patrono suo beato Martino, semper gloria in ordine monastico.[1] Inter cuius multiplicem ac misticam uarietatem post Cartusienses carius et familiarius amplexabatur Cluniacenses[2] ceterosque illius habitus, quos silentia claustri sub negotioso otio spiritualiter nouerat excolentes. Hoc autem artioris erga istos dilectionis studium emulatio sancti Hugonis Gratianopolitani indiderat ei. Hic enim beatus episcopus, precipuus olim adiutor et informator eorum qui prouide atque sanctissime ordinem Cartusiensem primitus instituerunt, huius ab adholescentia sua conuersationis [a] professor extitit et deuotissimus obseruator.[3]

De quo uerbum quoddam eleganter ab eo sepius prolatum, ut a beato nostro accepimus Hugone, illius scilicet et nominis et sanctitatis herede, dignum ducimus huic commendare historie. Cum enim habitu nigro idem presul inclitus et monachus eximius nitidissimam mentis et corporis obtegeret sanctitatem, et e diuerso Cartusienses sui amictu nitescerent albo, a quibusdam

---

[a] + scilicet Cluniacensis ordinis X

[1] cf. Sulpicius Severus, *Epistola* III : ' monachorum qui eo die fere ad duo milia convenisse dicuntur, specialis Martini gloria' (C.S.E.L. I, p. 150)

[2] Like Giraldus, Adam seems to designate Black Benedictines in general by the term *Cluniacenses*. cf. Dom D. Knowles, *Monastic Order in England*, App. XXII, p. 719.

CHAPTER IX

How, like his patron the blessed Martin, his chief glory
was the monastic life, and how it was his custom
frequently to visit Witham. His instructions to men and
women living in the world, concerning the real meaning
of truth, chastity and charity. Also, about the custody
of his seal.

For him as for his patron blessed Martin the monastic
life was always the ideal one.[1] Of the many types of
religious vocation the one which after the Carthusian
appealed most to him was the Cluniac [2] or Benedictine,
since these orders knew how to value and make busy use
of the silence and leisure of the cloister. The example of
St Hugh of Grenoble had given him a greater enthusiasm
and a closer affection for them. This blessed bishop had
formerly been the special friend and patron of the venerable and wise founders of the Carthusian order, and had
from his youth onwards devoutly followed and imitated
its way of life.[3]

I think it right to set down in this book one of his
most frequent sayings both because of its appropriateness
and because Hugh his namesake and the inheritor of his
sanctity quoted it to me. This excellent bishop and
model monk concealed his remarkable purity of mind
and body under his black habit, in contrast to the
Carthusians whose white cowls were symbolic of theirs.

---

[3] Hugh of Grenoble, born in 1052, became bishop of that town in 1080 ;
he was a zealous reformer. He once retired to the Benedictine abbey of
Chaise-Dieu and took the habit there, but the pope refused his resignation,
and he resumed the government of his diocese. He had welcomed St Bruno
and the first Carthusians to his diocese in 1084 and remained on the
friendliest terms with them till his death in 1132. He was canonised in 1134.

illorum interdum dicebatur ei, ' Cur, domine episcope,
qui ordinem nostrum tantopere iugiter fouere et eum
tot precipuis illustrare documentis studuisti, qui et apud
nos ac inter nos quasi unus ex nobis crebrius manere
dulcissimum semper habuisti, nobis etiam, deposita
amictus nigredine, in uestitus assimilari candore hactenus
neglexisti ? ' Ad hec nobilis ille et carne et in Domino,
uoce non ignobili interioris sui status nobilitatem
declarans, aiebat, ' Numquam profecto cuculla ista,
quamlibet pulla uideatur, uerecundie iniuriam fecit
michi ; et ego qua ratione repudii contumeliam facerem
illi ? '

Et hec quidem sanctus de sancto, de Hugone Hugo,
ad edificationem nostram qui ei candidis induto
adherebamus in scemate nigro, referre solitus erat.
Adiciebat quoque ordinis sui tenore antiquitus sancitum
haberi ut liberum sit professis suis,[a] si obseruationes illas
suis probauerint uiribus aut moribus non satis congruere,
ad istorum instituta conuolare.

Ad suam uero Withamiam singulis propemodum
annis semel aut bis secedere uir sanctus consueuerat.
Qui, licet ubicumque locorum constitutus, perfecte rem
nominis exprimeret Iacob et Israel, hic tamen liberius
dilecte sue [b] fouebatur amplexibus, et uberius pascebatur
decore formose Rachel, perfectius hic tediose declinabat
Lye lippitudinem. Hic, quasi Helye et Enoch con-
tubernio iungeretur, mundi turbines tranquillitate
paradisi se mutasse gaudebat.[1] Cetus namque gemini
consistentium ibi monachorum atque conuersorum, quasi
duos illos pretendere uidebantur iustitie atque innocentie
precones, quos hactenus de communi morte mundi
omnipotentia Conditoris noscitur sequestrasse. Hii

---

[a] ut licitum sit professoribus suis X
[b] *om* B

Some of them used to ask him, ' Why, lord bishop, since you are so devoted to our order, which devotion you have shown by your many favours, and have also always found exceptional satisfaction in staying often with us as if you were one of us, have you still not troubled to change your black habit for our white one ? ' This man, noble by birth and also in the sight of God, showed the nobility of his mind by his fine answer, ' I have never been ashamed of this cowl, however drab it seems, so why, by abandoning it, should I bring it into disrepute ? '

These words of one St Hugh, another St Hugh used to repeat for the edification of us black monks who were his disciples in spite of his white habit, adding that originally the statutes of his order had decreed that if any of its members found its way of life did not suit either their health or their temperaments they should be free to join other orders.

The saint used to withdraw to Witham once or twice almost every year, although wherever he was the names of Jacob and Israel could rightly be applied to him. Here, however, he could freely enjoy the embraces, and feast fully on the beauty of his lovely Rachel, and get away completely from the dreariness of blear-eyed Leah. Here, as if in the company of Elijah and Enoch he could boast that he had exchanged the storms of the world for the peace of Heaven.[1] The twin bands of monks and lay brethren who dwelt there seemed symbolic of those two protagonists of justice and innocence, the only persons whom up till now the almighty Creator has snatched away from this mortal life. These indeed like

---

[1] Elias, Enoch and Rachel were all considered as types of the Contemplative Life. The name Jacob was thought to signify *luctator vel supplantator*, and Israel *videns Deum*.

nempe sicut et illi, pre ceteris pene mortalibus serene, secure et tranquille perfruuntur uite quodammodo celestis suauitate.

Inter medios istarum sortium Domini cleros dormiens eiusdem uinee Domini Sabaoth in partibus illis plantator primus, inebriabatur ab ubertate domus Domini ; set minime derisus a Cham, uenerabatur a Sem et Iaphet.[1] Et quidem uerecundiora sua detegebat eis a quibus abluta et detersa uelabantur uestigia eius pallio gemine confessionis, si quo fedabantur puluere mundane conuersationis. Sic quoque tenacius custodiebat uestimenta sua, ne uel ad modicum in qualibet sui parte nudus ambularet,[2] quo eius quantulacumque turpitudo diuinis siue angelicis aut etiam humanis conspectibus appareret. Sciebat namque iuxta apostolum se factum spectaculum huic mundo et angelis et hominibus,[3] et Dominum scrutari Ierusalem in lucernis.[4] Erant uero ibi plurimi probabiles trapazete qui librarent, examinarent atque diiudicarent secum figuram et pondus et metallum eorum que tractabat dominicorum talentorum, ne quid forte in eis leue, ne quid minus uel purum uel legitimum inueniri potuisset.[5] Manebat more aliorum in cella solitaria que semper ei absque inhabitatore uacua seruabatur, in qua meditabatur et orabat, reficiebatur cibo et sompnum capiebat.

Inde ad publicum quandoque, ut salutaret aduentantes sibique loqui cupientes progrediens, celestibus quodammodo radiis, ex consortio sermonis Domini cornutam gerere diligenter intuentibus uidebatur faciem,[6] quam miri cuiusdam leporis comitate totiusque

---

[1] cf. Ps. 35 : 9 ; Gen. 9 : 20-3   [2] cf. Apoc. 16 : 15
[3] cf. 1 Cor. 4 : 9   [4] cf. Soph. 1 : 12
[5] Cassian taught that a monk should discern the origin and value of his own thoughts like a clever money-changer (probabilis trapezita) discerns true and false coin. *Collatio I*, 20-21 (C.S.E.L. XIII, pp. 29-33).
[6] cf. Exodus 34 : 29

them enjoyed more than the rest of the human race a life of peace and tranquillity which was a foretaste of the bliss of Heaven.

This first planter of the vine of the Lord of Hosts in our land, whilst he dwelt in the midst of these chosen priests of God, was inebriated by the abundance of the house of the Lord, but was not mocked at by Ham, although honoured by Shem and Japhet.[1] He revealed to them the things of which he was ashamed and if any of the dust of life in the world had dirtied his feet these were washed, dried and covered by them with the cloak of a sincere confession. He used to wear his garments with great care, lest any part of him however small should be uncovered as he walked,[2] that is, lest the smallest failing of any kind should be apparent to God or his angels or to men. To quote the apostle, he knew ' that he was made a spectacle to this world, to angels and to men '[3] and that ' God would search out Jerusalem with lanterns '.[4] There, there were very many expert money-changers who could weigh, examine, and judge with him the shape, weight and metal of the talents of the Lord, lest any light, alloyed, or false ones should be discovered among them.[5] He, like the others, remained alone in the cell, which was always reserved exclusively for his use. Here he meditated and prayed, and ate and slept.

He sometimes emerged from his privacy to greet visitors, who had come to speak with him, and on these occasions those who looked at him carefully observed that he was horned by the celestial rays caused by his familiar converse with God.[6] His wonderful courtesy, graciousness and gentleness made his face even more attractive to those who spoke with him. Moreover, ' from out of the abundance of the heart, the mouth

suauitate dulcedinis palliabat, ac colloquentibus sibi frontem contemperabat.[a] Interea ex habundantia cordis loquebatur os eius,[1] eratque sermo eius in corde audientis musto comparabilis, ignitus uidelicet et dulcis, quippe quem introduxerat rex in cellam uinariam.[2] Qui iuxta ordinatam in eo diuinitus caritatem, omnibus propinabat pro status sui et ordinis exigentia, doctrine salutaris poculum, melle quidem celestis sapientie conditum set discretionis libramine temperatum.

Nam laicis atque secularibus, angelice illius uite statum collaudantibus et de sue mundane uite impedimentis conquerentibus, quos tamen nec uelle nec posse sciret ad perfectiora instituta uiuendi transire, huiusmodi proferebat instructionem, 'Haut solum,' inquit, 'monachi set nec heremite tantummodo atque solitarii consequentur regnum Dei. Denique cum unumquemque iudicabit Dominus, nequaquam id expostulabit quod heremita quisque non fuerat aut monachus, set hoc potius reprobo cuique exprobrabitur quod minime extiterit ueraciter Christianus. Nam tria quedam a quolibet sunt exigenda Christiano, ex quibus si uel unum illi cum iudicabitur defuerit, nomen illi Christianum prodesse non ualebit. Nocebit potius nomen sine re, quia dampnabilior est falsitas in ueritatis professore. Exigitur autem ut uirtus et ueritas habeatur beati nominis huius, quatinus indesinenter teneatur caritas in corde, ueritas in ore, castitas quoque in corpore non fallaciter Christiani.'

Disserebat de hiis sepe uir Dei diffusius, harum ostendens atque distinguens uirtutum proprietates et differentias ; docens etiam coniugatos, mensure sue

---

[a] ac . . . contemperabat. *om* B

speaketh ',[1] and his words were to the hearts of those who heard them, like wine sweet and fiery, and coming from one whom the King had taken into His wine cellar.[2] He, being inspired by the love of God, gave to each the draught of sound doctrine according to his state and profession, spicing the cup with the honey of heavenly prudence and discrimination.

To lay persons who praised this angelic way of life and lamented the hindrances of life in the world, and whom he knew had neither the intention nor the capacity to follow a better way of life, he gave the following advice, ' The kingdom of God is not confined only to monks, hermits and anchorites. When at the last, the Lord shall judge every individual, he will not hold it against him that he has not been a hermit or a monk, but will reject each of the damned because he had not been a real Christian. A Christian is expected to possess three virtues, and if, on the day of judgment he lacks any of them, the name of Christian will be useless to him. The name without the reality is in itself a condemnation, for falsehood is the more horrible in a professor of truth. That blessed name must really represent the virtues it implies, and all sincere Christians must have loving hearts, truthful tongues and chaste bodies.'

The man of God often developed this further, by describing and defining the properties and differences of these virtues. He taught that even married people, who never rose above the natural obligations of their state, should not be considered to be devoid of the virtue of chastity but equally with virgins and celibates would be

---

[1] cf. Matt. 12 : 34
[2] cf. Cant. 2 : 4

limites minime transcendentes, castitatis decore nequaquam priuandos, set cum uirginibus pariter et con-
tinentibus superne beatitudinis gloria donandos. Sic
sanctus simplicium animos informabat, quatinus sub
compendio quodam totius Christianitatis *a* sue sibi
estimarent summam depingi, atque de cetero seque
suosque uerbo quodam abbreuiato et perspicuo com-
monere atque instruere forent ydonei. Eius namque ad
homines indoctos, ut Scriptura de prudentibus dicit, erat
doctrina facilis [1] ; nam inter perfectos loquebatur
sapientiam [2] quibusque exercitatissimis in studio
sapientie admirandam.

Illa uero eius ad simpliciores predicatio, quemadmodum erudiebat auditores, ita interdum nos prouocabat
qui uite illius eramus inspectores, doctrine illius formulam
adeo efficacem ad subtiliorem morum eius considera-
tionem referre. Monebat sane nos hec totiens repetita
ac cum tanto semper mentis ardore prolata eius
exhortatio, scrupulosius hec uirtutum insignia in moribus
eius perscrutari et uita. A quibus demum animaduersum
est et,*b* quantum nostra tulit estimatio, certius deprehen-
sum, omnes quos nouimus mortales culmine excellen-
tioris prerogatiue ipsum in predictis uirtutibus esse
supergressum.

De cuius interim caritate, ut de singulis uirtutibus
hiis aliqua breuiter tangamus, de caritate, inquam, que
illi ad Deum et proximum semper in corde fuit, quamuis
dignum aliquid uix quisquam effari queat, iam superius
tamen, prout imperitie nostre sub tanto compendio
possibile fuit, nonnulla digessimus.

De priuilegio etiam eximie castitatis celitus èi
collato, illud in superioribus habetur expressum [3] quod

---

a + uocationis X
b in X

admitted to the glory of the heavenly kingdom. Thus the holy man impressed on the minds of ordinary people, that they must consider that their vocation was summarised by the name Christian, and that they must be able to understand and explain the meaning of this short and simple word to their friends. His instructions to the unlearned were, as the scriptures say of the wise, easy to comprehend,[1] but his words to the perfect were of such depth [2] that they amazed even those who had great experience of spiritual things.

The things he said to simple folk not merely taught his audience, but also inspired us who had an intimate knowledge of his way of life to examine his character more carefully in the light of his admirable teaching. It was in fact these repeated instructions and the exhortations given always with such fervour which made us observe the fruits of the same virtues in his own life and behaviour. My own observations enable me to assert and testify that as far as I can judge he excelled everyone I have ever known and had attained to a higher degree of perfection in the virtues I have mentioned than they had.

I will now deal very briefly with his charity and with each of his other virtues. Concerning the love of God and of his neighbour, I can say that his heart was always full of it, and although no words can describe it adequately, I have nevertheless already said something about it as far as lack of space and my own limitations permitted.

I have also described above [3] what I often heard from his own truthful lips about the amazing gift of chastity granted to him by God, that is how he was cured of his painful temptation by means of a vision, and how both

[1] cf. Prov. 14 : 6
[2] cf. 1 Cor. 2 : 6
[3] See above, I, pp. 49-52

a ueracissimis ipsius labiis nostris sepe fuit auribus infusum, qualiter scilicet per uisionem curata temptationis sue plaga, cordi simul et carni eius perpetua sanitas fuerit restituta.

De cuius priuilegii munere securus, religiosas interdum matronas similiter quoque et uiduas more aliorum episcoporum suo in mensa lateri assidere faciebat. Palmis etiam mundissimis capita illarum constringens atque consignans, aliquotiens etiam pectori suo castissimo leniter imprimens, eas de sectandis uestigiis sanctarum feminarum ubertim instructas, Deoque data benedictione commendatas, in pace dimittebat. Mulieribus quoque uerbum dulcedinis *a* plenum et memoria dignum usu familiari dicere consueuerat. Vt enim ad diligendum feruentius Conditorem ipsas prouocaret, ' Satis,' aiebat, ' a sexu femineo Deus omnipotens diligi promeruit, qui nasci de femina non refugit. Magnificum quoque ac uere dignum ex hoc omnibus feminis priuilegium contulit. Nam cum uiro concessum non sit quod sit uel dicatur pater Dei, hoc tamen prestitum est mulieri ut sit parens Dei.'

Iam uero tantam in ore ueritatem habebat ut nullus sermo ab eius exiret labiis cui sentiret aliquid inesse falsitatis. Nam pro cautela uitandi cuiuscumque falsi, cum referebat quippiam seu que egisset uel audisset recensebat, aliquo semper temperamento utebatur in hiis etiam que indubitanter uerissima esse nouerat, ut diceret, ' Sic nobis occurrit modo,' aut aliquid in hunc modum quo temeritatem assertionis false funditus declinaret.

Nec minori quoque obseruantia ueritatis sigilli sui reuerentiam tuebatur, nichil umquam non uerum in litteris eo signandis *b* contineri permittens. Vbi adeo scrupulosus fuit quod, iuxta tritam scribendi formulam cum citatorias *c* alicui ederet, in eis nullatenus poni sineret, ' Meminimus nos te alias citasse ', ne forte quod in sua non erat memoria, in ea esse mentiretur sua cartula.

---

dulcedine X   *b* sigillandis X   *c* + litteras X

his heart and flesh were from that time onwards completely freed from it.

The confidence given him by this exceptional favour caused him to imitate the other bishops and occasionally invite devout matrons and widows to eat at his table. He used to lay his holy hands on their heads and make the sign of the cross and even sometimes reverently embrace them. After giving them copious exhortations to follow in the footsteps of the women saints, and commending them to God, he sent them away with his blessing and in peace. A favourite saying of his concerning women should be remembered because of its beauty. To encourage them to love their Creator more ardently he used to say, ' Almighty God certainly deserves to be loved by women, for he did not disdain to be born of a woman, and thus conferred a special honour on the whole sex. To no man was it granted to be called the father of God, but to a woman alone was it accorded to be God's mother.'

He laid such store on truthfulness, that he would never utter a word which he felt was not absolutely true. To avoid any possibility of falsehood, when he was describing anything which he thought he had done or heard, he always, even if he was convinced that it was completely true, made some qualification, such as, ' So it seems to me now ', or something like that. This was a precaution against any accidental untruthfulness.

His use of his seal was marked by the same scrupulous truthfulness, for he never permitted the letters issued under it to contain anything not strictly true. An example of his extreme conscientiousness was his refusal ever to allow the usual formula, ' We remember that we have cited you before,' to be used in letters of citation, in case he did not really remember it, and so the document would lie.

Capitvlvm X

De modo sue conuersationis apud Witham.

Ne cui uero minus credibile uideatur hoc quod de spiritali quadam uultus ipsius claritate in eo relucente cum egrederetur a cella sua supra tetigimus, aliud quiddam satis de eo suis familiaribus notum, a multis sepe non absque stupore et admiratione notatum, ueracissime huic narrationi duximus breuiter inserendum. Quotiescumque enim a longinquis partibus ad illam sibi dilectam tendebat solitudinem, mox ut a remotis finitimam eius ingrediebatur regionem, nitor quidam insolitus, colore decenter *a* rubicundo superfusus, genas ei cum facie simul tota uestire consueuit. Ipse quoque intima cordis sui ad primum illius loci conspectum ineffabili quadam iocunditate spiritualis gaudii sentiebat perfundi, quod suis quoque familiaribus sepissime fatebatur.

Quo iam consistente apud Witham, tantam in eo omnium sensuum innouationem superna efficiebat gratia ut subito intus simul et extra renouari uideretur sicut aquile iuuentus sua.[1] Deposito quidem exterius pallio quo utebatur in publico, quod ex nigro erat uel subrufo panno candidis agnorum pellibus foratum, pelles induebat arietinas nullo panni tegmine coopertas. Cilicio, ut semper, tegebatur ad nudum, hinc tunicam in medio superinducto *b* uelabat pelliceo. Lectisternia eius hec tantum erant : sagum, ceruical et pelles. Mane cum manus de more ablueret, ut ministerio *c* nullo, ita nullo utebatur manutergio.

Missam deuotissime, duobus contentus ministris, sacrista scilicet loci et suo capellano, cotidie celebrabat.

---

a recenter o   *b* superinduto X ; superindutam m   *c* ministro QX

CHAPTER X

Concerning his way of life at Witham.

In case what I have mentioned above about the spiritual radiance of his face when he emerged from his cell should seem incredible to anyone, I think that another fact about him often noticed by his attendants, many of whom observed it with wonder and amazement, should be briefly and truthfully described in this work. Whenever he returned from distant parts to his beloved place of retirement, as soon as he approached the neighbourhood a delicate rosy flush used to mantle his cheeks and even his whole countenance. He often told his attendants that he felt that the first sight of the spot filled his heart with indescribable joy and spiritual delight.

Whilst he was at Witham, divine grace effected such a restoration in every one of his faculties that it seemed that like the eagle both physically and mentally he had renewed his youth.[1] He laid aside the outer cloak of black or russet cloth lined with white lambswool which he wore in public, and wore sheepskin without a cloth covering. The hair-shirt which he wore, as always, next to his skin was concealed by a tunic worn under his leather cloak. His bedding consisted of only a blanket, a bolster and skins. When he washed his hands at dawn as was his custom, he had no attendant to serve him, and he did not use a towel.

He daily celebrated mass very devoutly, with only two assistants, the sacristan of the monastery and his chaplain. He spent the week in the convent like any

[1] cf. Ps. 102 : 5

Suam quoque, tamquam simplex monachus, agebat in conuentu septimanam, aquam die dominica benedicens, missam et horas diebus singulis more solito percantans. Anulo pontificali excepto, in reliquis sacerdotalibus indumentis a consuetudine Cartusiensium in nullo penitus differebat. Vtuntur enim alba et amictu, stola, fanone atque planeta planis et candidis, nec ornatis serico nec aurifrisio seu gemmis.¹

Diebus dominicis post cenam cum ceteris monachis ad hostium refectorii cum silentio et grauitate procedebat, ubi panis unus singulis ad totius ebdomade uictum a fratre interius existente ᵃ prebebatur. Sepe tamen de licentia prioris ex cophino siue ex archa qua mice condebantur, a fratrum cellis seu a refectorio collecte, crustulas duriores et minutias fragmentorum pre ariditate iam torridas, propriis manibus colligebat ; non quod suus ei panis non sufficeret et superhabundaret, set hec dicebat sapidiora sibi quam solidum panem uideri. Reuera quidem benedictionibus condita iustorum gratius sano palato eius sapiebant. Scutellas, non modo quibus ei pulmenta fuissent ministrata set quas fortuitu illotas alicubi reperisset, delectabiliter gaudebat eluere,ᵇ tanta eas diligentia manibus digitisque nitidissimis intus exteriusque defricans et poliens ac si calicem Dominicum se contrectare putaret.²

At uerendum nobis est ne, minima hec de uiro tanto diutius referentes, grauioris censuram lectoris offendamus. Que tamen eo minus prudens lector pro minimis reputabit quo maioris fuisse humilitatis sagaciter aduertit

---

ᵃ consistente Q
ᵇ abluere X
¹ Three Carthusian chasubles of the 12th century, made of white dimity cloth, on which plain woollen orphreys of different colours were sewn according to the season's liturgical colour, were kept at the Grande

other monk, blessing the holy water on Sundays, and celebrating mass and chanting the hours daily just as he always did. Except for his episcopal ring, his priestly vestments, a plain white alb, amice, stole, maniple, and chasuble, were completely Carthusian, since they were not of silk, nor embroidered with gold thread or jewels.[1]

On Sundays after supper he went with the other monks slowly and silently to the door of the refectory where one loaf, his food for the whole week, was given to each of them by the brother inside. Often, however, with the prior's permission, he would take with his own hands from the hamper or chest where the pieces of bread from the cells of the brethren or from the refectory had been put, hard crusts and tiny morsels already exceedingly dry and stale. He did not do this because his own loaf was not more than enough for him, but because he said that he found these more tasty than a new loaf. In fact, what had been spiced by the blessings of holy men seemed more delicious to his healthy digestion. He loved washing, not only the bowls in which his own vegetables were given to him, but any which he found by chance anywhere dirty, rubbing them as carefully and polishing both the exterior and the interior with his own spotless hands and fingers, as if he believed that he was handling the Lord's chalice.[2]

I fear that my readers will criticise me for describing at length these trivial acts of this distinguished man. To the discriminating reader, however, the conscientious performance of such insignificant duties by a priest of

---

Chartreuse until the French Revolution. See *La Grande Chartreuse par un Chartreux*, pp. 39-40. Hubert Walter, according to the Witham chronicler, was so astonished at the simplicity of a chasuble used there that he at once ordered one of his own, worth sixty shillings, to be given to the monastery.

[2] cf. *Rule of St Benedict*, c. 31 : ' Omnia vasa monasterii cunctamque substantiam ac si altaris vasa sancta conspiciat.'

quod tantus sacerdos hec minima et extrema tam sollerter impleuit. Ne tamen nimis protrahatur in longum hec nostra qualiscumque narratio, innumera preterire decreuimus sub silentio que ab eo gesta ibidem et dicta nobisque experta, multorum si scriberentur edificationi erant profutura. Ceterum historias texenti sic de rerum multiplici copia feriati lectoris est satisfactio procuranda, ne occupati negotiosa intentio estimetur pregrauanda ; set nec erit unde nobis studiosus auditor de iure succenseat, quod et fastidioso nos aliquatenus morem gerere deprehendat. Nam et auidis interdum conuiuis alimenta que minus sufficiunt, dum edendi appetitum suggerunt, menbrorum nutrimento utilius inseruiunt. In simili uero causa a uiro doctissimo longe ante nos dictum recolimus, quia ' multa non proderunt cui pauca non sufficiunt.' [1]

Hoc tamen, ut tandem de sua, quodam quasi uiolento narrandi compendio, extrahamus solitudine uerum nostri temporis Christi preconem, hoc inquam uel breuiter dixisse liceat, quia sicut magni precursoris Domini et baptiste uenerator eximius et strenuus extitit imitator, ita in hac presertim heremo constitutus, dirigebat indesinenter uias Domini.[2] Qui etsi praua ibidem non inueniebat que dirigeret uel aspera que complanaret, set plana tamen et directa que inuenisset ad perfectiora dirigebat, ut impleretur illud Scripture dicentis : ' Iustus iustificetur adhuc et sanctus sanctificetur adhuc.' [3] Quod in se per uirum iustum et sanctum accitari unusquisque sentiebat, qui eius exemplo in Iordane baptizari, in spiritu uidelicet humilitatis peramplius et perfectius mundari consentiebat.

[1] Sulpicius Severus, *Dialogus* I, 18 (C.S.E.L. I, p. 170)
[2] cf. John 1 : 23 ; Luke 3 : 5
[3] Apoc. 22 : 11

such eminence will be a striking example of his great humility. I have, however, decided to omit very many of the things which he did and said whilst there, of which I have first-hand knowledge, although to write them down would instruct and edify a large number of people, in order not to make my biography too long. It is the task of a biographer to satisfy a leisured reader with a variety of fare, and yet avoid overburdening a busy one. The serious reader will have no just cause to be annoyed with me if he sometimes finds me considering the interests of the critical one, since food which seems insufficient for hungry guests and merely whets their appetite is the best nourishment for the body. I remember a very wise man saying long ago in connection with a similar matter that ' a man who is not content with a little, will not be satisfied with a lot.' [1]

After all this, let my brief narrative intrude, as it were, by violence and bring Christ's truest herald of our own day from his retreat. We do not apologise for this very compressed description of his life there, since like the great forerunner of our Lord, the Baptist, for whom he had a great veneration, and whose example he did his utmost to follow, he indefatigably made straight the way of the Lord especially when in the wilderness. [2] Although he did not find there anything crooked to be made straight or any rough places to be made smooth, yet he raised to greater perfection the straightness and smoothness he found there in order that the words of the scriptures might be fulfilled, ' The righteous man shall be yet more righteous and the saint more holy '. [3] Each man felt this brought to pass by the agency of this just and holy man, who wished like Christ to be baptised in Jordan, that is to have the humility to be more fully and perfectly cleansed.

Et ipse quidem omni tempore semel in ebdomada, id
est die sabbati, purissime confessionis lauacrum frequen-
tabat. Quod de traditione inuiolabili ordinis sui exequens,
nullatenus omittebat. Quin etiam crebrius hoc ageret,
mox ut aliquis ex quocumque facto, dicto, cogitatu,
scrupulus preter solitum eius animo subortus fuisset.
Frequenter quoque, iterata innumeris uicibus confessione,
quicquid ab infantia se meminisset *a* delicti commisisse,
Domino reuelari eiusque uicarii cui confitebatur oratione
ueniam optinere satagebat. Quasi uero minus esset
quicquid totius anni tempore alias fecisset, tunc in
auribus discretissimis uenerabilium seruorum Dei cum
ingenti cordis contritione id agere impensius curabat,
indesinenter conquerens quod bona, si qua ex dono Dei
in se essent, ex suo reatu fieret quod pura satis non
prodirent, mala uero sua *b* non aliud quam pura mala
fuissent.

CAPITVLVM XI

De uiro opinatissimo, magistro scilicet Adam, qui ex
abbate Driburgensi Cartusiensis apud Witham effectus
est monachus.

Erat uero apud Witham uir summe, ac in rebus
diuinis pene dixerim incomparande eruditionis et
doctrine, qui dimissa abbatia ordinis Premonstrensis
quam regebat, ad huius se conuersationis stadium *c*
mirabiliter sublimando deposuerat. Dicebatur magister
Adam de Driburch.*d* Qui amore preuentus uite
contemplatiue, cuius a primeuo iuuentutis flore felici
desiderio estuauerat, cuius et primitias diu iam felicius

---

a inuenisset X   *b* *om* B
c studium X   *d* *om* t ; de Brabantia X

He always, once a week, on Saturdays, made a full confession and received absolution. This practice he never omitted because it was a fixed tradition in his order. Indeed, he did so more often if his mind was more than usually troubled about any of his deeds, words or thoughts. Often, also and on many occasions, he would confess to God whatever sins he remembered having committed since his early childhood and would strive to obtain pardon through the prayers of His earthly representative, to whom he made his confession. If he did not go as far as this he took pains to confess when there to the wisest of the venerable servants of God whatever he had done elsewhere during the year, with immense contrition of heart, always maintaining that if there were any good in him it was a gift from God, and was qualified by his sinfulness, whereas his wickedness was nothing but wickedness unrelieved.

Chapter XI

Concerning the very distinguished man, Master Adam, who from being abbot of Dryburgh, became a monk at Witham.

There was at Witham, a man of very great, I might almost say, incomparable knowledge and experience in the things of God, called Master Adam of Dryburgh, who resigned the rule of the Premonstratensian house of which he was abbot, to embark upon a more perfect and exacting way of life.

He had been seized with a love for the contemplative life, which he had thirsted for and blessedly aspired after from the first bloom of his youth, and after tasting its

prelibauerat, datis sibi celitus pennis columbe, ad hanc
solitudinem conuolauerat, ubi per quina circiter
annorum lustra sub felicissimo contemplationis sompno
requiescebat.[a][1]

Cum isto frequentissimum erat sancto pontifici
colloquium. Hii quasi gemine tube argentee ductiles,[2]
celestis eloquii nitore splendentes ac regularis discipline
exercitiis subtilius elimate,[b] mutuis se sublimium exhor-
tationum clangoribus ad fortia militie spiritualis studia
incitare non desistebant.

Ingerebat heremita pontifici ex Scripturarum eloquiis[c] exempla perfectorum et dicta prelatorum, incusans
modernorum inertiam pastorum quorum adeo mores
et studia ab eximiorum uestigiis exorbitarent suorum
decessorum, adeo degenerarent a uirtutibus eorum.
Interea et ad ipsum cui loquebatur reflectens sermonem,
' Te,' inquit, ' homines plurimi tamquam bonum ac
magnum ecclesie Dei rectorem mirantur ; set queso te,
ubi saltem umbra digni pastoris in gestis tuis relucet ?
Nec de mediocritate uite ac conuersationis tue nunc
michi sermo est. Sit modo cum imminentis iam illius
aduersarii faciem generalis uirtutum precedit egestas ;
sit, inquam, modo cum ad ianuam iam assistit filius
hominis nec inuenit fidem super terram ;[3] sit modo
preconio dignus qui pessimus non fuerit, uocetur beneficus qui mala quecumque potuerit proximo suo non
intulerit. Et hec quidem perfectio potentibus magna
uidetur, si aliquem iuuent et non uniuersos premant.
Tales nunc sancti habentur et laude digni.

---

[a] sub felicissimo superne contemplationis monte quiescebat X
[b] elimate . . . se . . . ad *om* B
[c] eloquiis *om* B (Scripturis B²)
[1] A Carthusian from c. 1188 until his death in 1212, Adam, according
to the Witham chronicler, was notable for his exact observance of the rule
and for the authorship of several works which he lists ; he was ' of medium

first delights for a long period, God gave him the wings of a dove and he had flown to this wilderness, where he had now reposed for twenty-five years or thereabouts, in the pleasant slumber of contemplation.[1]

He and the holy bishop often conversed together. They like two twin trumpets,[2] highly polished by their training in the monastic life, echoed and reflected the splendour of divine eloquence, and with alternate blasts of heavenly exhortation, never stopped rousing each other to greater valour in the spiritual warfare.

The hermit used to quote to the bishop from holy writ the examples and sayings of the holy apostles, upbraiding the lethargy of modern bishops, whose aims and practices showed such a departure from the virtues of their predecessors, that they had forsaken the path of even the worst of them. Then he attacked the bishop. ' Very many men extol you as a good and worthy ruler of the church of God, but, I ask you, are you even the pale reflection of a true bishop ? I am not now going to discuss the mediocrity of your life and behaviour. Now the general falling away heralds the coming of Antichrist, now the Son of Man is already at the door, nor will He find faith on earth.[3] In these times he is worthy of honour, who is not utterly depraved, and a man is called good who does not injure his neighbour to the utmost of his ability. Also, it is reckoned an act of the highest virtue on the part of the mighty, if they ever assist anyone, and do not tyrannise over everybody. These are now highly praised and spoken of as saints.

---

height, rather corpulent, with a bald head and a cheerful face, and very venerable with age.' See Introduction, vol.I, xxvi-xxvii and J. Bulloch, *Adam of Dryburgh*, London 1958.

[2] cf. Num. 10 : 2
[3] cf. Luke 18 : 8

'Quid uero de commissorum tibi negotiatione talentorum sentiemus?[1] Que lucra, quas usuras reportaturum te confidis inter illos egregios institores qui, omnia terre marisque pericula experti, non modo plantauerunt set etiam ornauerunt et munierunt ecclesiam sanguine suo? Hii ut fame pereuntes refocillarent, de longe portantes panem suum,[2] in hiis ultimis oceani sinibus [a] delitescentes nugas [b] qui perierant requisierunt, quos ab ipsis portis mortis ad ciuitatem Domini uirtutum reduxerunt. Illi quidem laborauerunt, et uos in labores eorum, non ad laborandum set pene dixerim ad lasciuiendum, ut autem temperantius loquar, ad ludendum et feriandum introistis.[3] Vnde uinea Domini Sabaoth inculta iacet, sentibus operta squalet. Conculcant eam omnes qui pretergrediuntur uiam, maceria [c] enim lapidum eius diruta est, et nemo est qui resarciat sepem eius.'[4]

Huiuscemodi satis innumera is prosequens,[d] ut erat fons exuberatissimus celestis doctrine, reciprocam ab episcopo petebat et recipiebat sermonis uicem.

CAPITVLVM XII

De quatuor uiris illustrissimis compendiosa Hugonis et edificationis plena narratio.

Sepissime ergo de sue regionis, quos modernis pene temporibus perfectam duxisse uitam nouerat, et monachis et heremitis et episcopis admiranda retexebat uirtutum monimenta. Ex hiis uero, exempli gratia, quatuor

[a] finibus X
[b] uagos X
[c] materia B
[d] eo prosequente B

'But what must I think of the talents given to
you to trade with?[1] What profits and interest do you
pride yourself on having acquired in comparison with
those holy merchant venturers who had knowledge of all
the perils of land and sea, and not only planted but
enriched and defended the church with their blood?
These carried their bread from afar,[2] to revive those who
were dying of hunger, and penetrated to those furthest
limits of the ocean and found their lost sheep who were
perishing, and brought them back from the gates of
death to the city of the Lord of Hosts. These indeed
laboured, and you, I would say, have entered into the
fruits of their labours to wax wanton, or to put it more
mildly, to play and make holiday.[3] Thus, the vineyard
of the Lord of Hosts remains uncultivated and neglected,
and the briars have grown up. All who pass by tread it
underfoot. Its stone wall has been destroyed, and no-one
is ready to repair its hedge.'[4]

He went on for a long time in this strain, for he was a
fountain overflowing with heavenly wisdom. At his
request the bishop answered him in the same way in his
turn.

CHAPTER XII

Hugh's short and edifying account of four illustrious
men.

He would often cite the exemplary virtues of the
monks, hermits and bishops of his own region, who in
comparatively recent times had lived an almost perfect

[1] cf. Luke 19: 13   [2] Prov. 31 : 14
[3] cf. John 4 : 38   [4] Isa. 5 : 5 ; Prov. 24 : 31

dumtaxat illustrissimorum uirorum mentionem nunc compendiose inducimus, de quorum gestis seu uerbis ^a maximam lectori edificationem sub exiguo uerborum impendio comparare studemus.

Et primo quidem duorum admodum uenerande sanctitatis uirorum de una eademque causa geminam set diuersam sententiam explicabimus, scilicet Hugonis Gratianopolitani antistitis, de quo paulo superius tetigimus, et sancti Ancelini Belensis reuerendi presulis ; quorum posterior Cartusiensis, prior uero Liridensis ^b monachus fuit.[1] Ille autem, cum mire esset uerecundie et summe pudicitie, nullam penitus feminarum dinoscibiliter intueri solebat preter unam solummodo, que eius, ob anime sue causam, nimium consilio indigebat.[2] Quam iccirco uir sanctus facietenus nosse uoluit, quatinus eam eminus consistentem et sibi loqui cupientem, ad se, cum esset oportunum, accersire potuisset. Cum super huiuscemodi cautela oculi in mulierem non figendi sermo haberetur coram memorato Belensi episcopo, dicere idem consueuerat, ' Ego sane,' inquit, ' feminas indifferenter quaslibet aspicio, set mox uniuersas excorio.' Quod ea ratione proferebat quod nimirum suo aspectui illecebrose cutis prestigium lenocinari non sineret, cuius animus affectu uoluptatis extrinsecum non intueretur nitorem, set potius motu doloris, ueluti pelle subducta, intrinsecus latentem conspicaretur corruptionis feditatem.

Itidem de Gerardo Niuernensium ^c quondam spectabili consule referebat, quia inter ceteras uirtutum dotes humilitate singulari preradiari consueuerit ac glorie

---

^a meritis X
^b Nerobridensis X : *read* Casa Dei.
^c Niuersiensium B (i.e. *of Nivernais*)

life. I will now briefly give as examples only four of these, whose deeds and words I shall try to relate in as few words as possible for the greater edification of my readers.

First, I shall describe two men of outstanding sanctity, alike and yet different : Hugh, bishop of Grenoble, whom I have already said something about, and St Ancelin, the venerable bishop of Bellay, the latter of whom was a Carthusian monk and the former a monk of ' Lirida '.[1] He was a man of amazing shame-facedness and great modesty, who never deliberately gazed on any woman, with only one exception, and she was in urgent need of spiritual counsel.[2] For this reason alone the holy man desired to know her by sight so that, when she was standing a long way off and wanted to speak with him, he could summon her to him when necessary. When this same bishop of Bellay was present and the need for caution in looking at women was under discussion, he used generally to say, ' I, indeed, see all women as one and the same, for I refuse to observe what they look like.' He explained this by saying that no-one could allow himself to be ensnared by a beauty that was merely skin-deep, for his heart would be moved to grief rather than to lust when he beheld their loveliness, if penetrating below the skin he should see the filth and corruption within.

He used also to describe Gerard, a former distinguished count of Nevers, who in addition to the other

---

[1] Anthelm, canon of Bellay and provost of Geneva, became a Carthusian monk at Portes, helped to rebuild the Grande Chartreuse after the avalanche of 1132, and became prior there in 1139. He held the first Carthusian General Chapter in 1141, but resigned his office in 1151. Soon after, however, he was appointed prior of Portes, and later bishop of Bellay. He died in 1178.

[2] cf. Guigo, *Vita S. Hugonis episcopi Gratianopolitani*, c. 4 (P.L. 153, 772-3)

inanis precipuus contemptor extiterit.[1] Qui cum
grauitatis et sapientie prerogatiua omnes excederet
finitimos proceres, tam a [a] Christianissimo Francorum
rege Lodowico quam et a cunctis regni optimatibus,
quasi onus omnium parens unico colebatur affectu.
Nichil in eius presentia uel etiam ipse rex ludicrum uerbo
aut facto proferre audebat. Vnde contigit ut tempore
quodam rex ludentibus forte assidens, consulis aduentu
comperto, scaccarium quod in medio erat summa cum
festinatione tolli iuberet. Timebat enim durius obiurgari
a uiro, si deprehenderetur huiuscemodi leuitati animum
intendisse. Quod non aliter quam rex timoratus
futurum dixerat, mox euenit. Nam superueniens
repente Girardus, regem dissimulare cupientem nec
ualentem quod ludentibus se miscuisset, ita increpitat,
' O te,' inquit, ' principem insignem et populi Dei
strenuum prouisorem, qui mentem regiam huiusmodi
ineptiis eneruiter subigis ! Cui omne uite tue momentum
uix sufficeret ut ea excogitares que in regimine ne
derelinqueres uel regni utilitatibus deesses, instruere
ac munire potuissent, quomodo in hiis uanis implica-
mentis et tempus expendis et uigorem mentis indecenter
resoluis ? '

Hic etiam inter consules ac nobiles uiros sepe in regia
quoque positus concione, horis sollempnibus ad orationem in partem secedere consueuit, flexis genibus aut toto
in terram prostrato corpore, cum lacrimis et singultibus
diuinam implorare clementiam. Quod dum sepe in
campis uel pratis aut quibusque locis publicis sub
aspectu cunctorum faceret, a suis interdum familiariter

[a] om B

virtues which he possessed was an outstanding and shining example of humility and displayed an especial contempt for worldly glory.[1] The wisdom and sagacity which made him pre-eminent amongst the nobles of the neighbourhood caused him to be loved as a father, not only by Louis, the most Christian king of the French, but by all the magnates of his kingdom. When he was present even the king did not dare to jest or indulge in idle amusements. Once when he happened to be taking part in a game, on hearing of the count's arrival, he hastily ordered the removal of the chess board around which the players were, for he feared that he would be sharply rebuked, if he was caught by him amusing himself. It happened soon, exactly as the frightened king had said it would, for Gerard, coming in unexpectedly, when the king tried unsuccessfully to conceal that he had been playing, thus rebuked him : ' Do you, a king, to whom has been committed the welfare of God's people, weakly allow your royal mind to be absorbed by such follies ? The whole of your life is hardly long enough to give you time to consider your shortcomings as a ruler and your failure to provide for the needs of your kingdom, and to rule and defend it adequately. How, therefore, can you so shamelessly waste your time and dissipate your energies on these idle allurements ? '

During his frequent attendance at the royal councils with the other counts and nobles, he used at the times of divine office to withdraw for prayer, and either on his knees or with his body prostrated on the ground, implore the mercy of God with tears. His friends sometimes took

---

[1] ' Gerard' count of Nevers must be an error here and at I, p. 32, for Count William II, who retired to La Grande Chartreuse c.1147 (see Walter Map, *De Nugis Curialium*, ed. M. R. James, rev. R. A. B. Mynors and C. N. L. Brooke, Oxford Medieval Texts, 1983, pp. 80-1 n.2)

corripiebatur, asserentibus quod ypocrisim aut cenodoxie
uitium hec redolere que agebat a plurimis dicerentur.
Ad que uir constantissimus in nullo penitus mouebatur,
stillantibus uero per genas ubertim lacrimis, uerbum
memoria dignum proferebat, ' Absit,' inquiens, ' absit
ut proditoris crimine ullatenus polluar, michi usurpando
gloriam Domini mei. Si adoro et exoro Deum meum,
non michi peccatori, set do gloriam sancto eius et
glorioso nomini.'

Cui tandem Lodowicus rex, cum Ierosolimam
petiturus de consilio magnatum suorum custodiam
delegare totius regni sui disponeret, ille onus oblati
honoris callide refugiens, asserebat se in uotis iamdudum
habuisse ut crucem sumeret et Ierosolimam uisitaret.
Quo rex audito hylaris efficitur, nec modicum exultans
quod tantum uirum sue peregrinationis comitem se
inuenisse speraret. Precepit uero quatinus, suis omnibus
concite dispositis, uotum suum adimplere maturaret.
Qui a rege dimissus, amicis suis ualefaciens, Cartusiam
profectus est ; ibique baltheo in funiculum, et serico
mutato in sagum, inter conuersos uere meruit computari ;
ubi crucem Domini cotidie tollens et ipsum indesinenter
sequens, uerus mundi peregrinus non ante destitit de
uirtute in uirtutem ire, quam mereretur in Syon Deum
deorum uidere.[1]

Ad quem uisendum post multum temporis spatium
filius eius egregie indolis adholescens profectus est, quem
ille paruulum, sibique hereditario iure successurum, in
patria sua olim dimiserat. Qui ueniens Cartusiam
patremque uidere [a] deposcens, didicit eum tunc in
superiores montes ad tondendas oues perrexisse. Quem
diutius expectatum tandem conspicit in habitu pau-

[a] + desiderans et X
[1] Ps. 83 : 8

him to task for doing this often in fields and meadows and public places where everyone could see him, saying that many people attributed what he did to hypocrisy or a desire to draw attention to himself. This strong-minded man was completely unmoved, and, tears rolling down his cheeks, made a memorable reply : ' God forbid, that I should ever be guilty of treason, by usurping the glory of my Lord. I worship and pray to my God thus, to glorify his holy and glorious name, and not myself, a sinner.'

When King Louis was about to set out for Jerusalem, on the advice of his magnates, he wanted to make him guardian of his kingdom, but he cleverly avoided accepting this burdensome office, by declaring that he had for some time been under a vow to take the cross and go to Jerusalem. This news delighted the king who was greatly pleased at the prospect of having such a man as his companion on his pilgrimage. He ordered him to make immediate preparations to fulfil his vow. Having taken leave of the king and bidden farewell to his friends, he set out for Chartreuse, and there, exchanging his baldric for the cord, and his silken robes for serge ones he was enrolled among the lay brothers. There, like a true pilgrim in this world, he took up the cross of the Lord daily, and following him without turning back, he went from strength to strength before he was rewarded with the sight of the Lord in Sion.[1]

After a long time his son, a youth of great promise, whom he had left in his own land when he was still a child so that he might inherit his estates, came to visit him. When he arrived at Chartreuse, he asked to see his father, and was told that he had gone into the mountains above to shear sheep. After waiting for some time, he at last saw him coming down in a very old habit,

perrimo deorsum uenientem, ac uellera recens *a* tonsa
ceruice onusta deferentem. Quem ille quidem minime
agnoscebat, set accepto a fratribus qui astabant hunc
suum esse genitorem, ualde animo compunctus occurrit
ei, tenensque uestigia eius et exosculans, pre gaudio cepit
lacrimari. Qui ad patris amplexus et oscula ab ipso
erectus, intuetur sinum ipsius et collum berbitionum
examine scatere. Quo iuuenis uiso nimium exhorruit,
ac uermes edacissimos tollere cupiens, talia *b* a milite
Christi fortissimo audiuit, 'Sine,' inquit, 'fili karissime,
istos uermiculos uermi qui non moritur preripere predam.
Votiuus omnimodis et delectabilis michi est morsus
istorum, per quos inexplebilem gehennalium edacitatem
uermium me, Domino miserante, spero euasurum.'[1]

Multa de huius uiri uirtutibus ac gestis et *c* alia
referebat, que gratia compendii sub silentio compellimur
preterire. Nunc uero, quia promisimus saltem de bis
binis uiris illustribus patroni nostri retexere narrationes,
cuiusdam uiri admirabilis a Morienne finibus oriundi
breuis est historia perstringenda, cuius nec granum
sinapis fidei, nec deuotioni rogus flammiuomus comparari
ualet.[2] Hic domo, liberis et uxore relictis, terram in
cuius medio Deus humanam est operatus salutem, contra
hostes salutifere crucis militaturus adierat. Vbi strage
innumera de perfidis sepe Agarenis *d* fortiter, ut erat
miles strenuissimus, exacta, tandem occulto Dei iudicio
qui Filio proprio non pepercit,[3] a gente furcifera *e* inter-
ceptus, captus et uinctus, in terram maumeticolarum
abductus est. Quod ad solatium prouenisse Christianorum, qui inter perfidos tenebantur seruili conditione
aut etiam carcerali squalore afflicti, plurimis claruit

---

and carrying the fleeces he had just shorn in a bundle on his head. He did not recognise him, but learning from the brothers who were present that it was his father, being much moved, he hastened to him, and seized and kissed his feet, weeping for joy. His father raising him, embraced him with a kiss. When the young man saw that his breast and neck were covered with lice, he was greatly horrified by the sight and wanted to remove the stinging worms, but the soldier of Christ prevented him, saying, ' My dearest Son, allow these little worms to rob the worm that dieth not of its prey, welcome their bites and find them sweet, because thanks to them, I hope by God's mercy to escape the insatiable appetite of the worms of Hell.' [1]

He said much more about the deeds and virtues of this man, which for the sake of brevity I am compelled to omit. Now, as I have promised to repeat the accounts given by my master of four illustrious men at least, I must give a short description of an excellent man who came from Maurienne, whose faith and devotion were even stronger than the grain of mustard seed and the burning fiery furnace.[2] He left his wife and children for the land where God redeemed mankind, in order to fight against the enemies of the cross of salvation, where, being a knight of great valour, he often slaughtered large numbers of pagan Saracens. At last, however, by the mysterious providence of God, who did not spare His own Son,[3] he was waylaid by this savage people, and after being captured and bound was taken off into Moslem territory. There he made it abundantly clear that he had been sent as a consolation to the Christians, living as slaves amongst the infidels, or enduring the horrors of imprisonment. Finally, he also was placed in

[1] cf. Mark 9: 43   [2] cf. Matt. 17: 20: Luke 17: 16: Dan. 3   [3] cf. Rom. 8: 32

indiciis. Qui tandem et ipse horrendo carceri addictus, cum multitudine captiuorum quos in libertatem glorie filiorum Dei captiua adhuc parturiebat filia Syon, diutino squalore exercetur, quo in superni regis ornamentum quandoque niue candidior assumi mereretur.

Contigit post hec, ut uir ille potens in iniquitate, qui hos tenebat in ferali conclusione, omnes pariter iuberet capitalem sententiam subire. Cuius sceleris executionem filio suo demandauit, qui adholescentie metam supergressus, rudimentis iam ceperat exerceri militaribus. Hec uero testium Christi passio eo erat die celebranda, quo egregius triumphator Laurentius palatium *a* summi regis meruit introire, corona celebri laureatus.

Tum uir memoratus, tali audita sententia, letissimus effectus, socios cepit uerbis potentibus animare ad agonem. ' O nos,' inquit, ' uiri fratres, o nos felices, quos licet indignos et peccatores, hodierna lux tanti dabit martiris esse consortes ! O quam beata lux, quam iocunda hodie nobis exoritur, qua, tenebris et angustiis procul pulsis, mundus paradiso, carcer captiuis mutabitur celo ! Nectar celicum, cuius suauitatem in hiis quoque reclusi angustiis cotidie meruimus prelibare, hodie se nobis toto infundet gurgite. Torrens uoluptatis intime, cuius hactenus quasdam stillas pregustauimus, rorem quo sumus delibuti in fontem nobis conuertet, quo erimus ad ebrietatem perpetuo satiandi. Iam *b* cum multitudine celestis exercitus, rosea quibus coronemur gestans serta, assistit Laurentius gloriosus huius diei patronus ; assistit, inquam, ut nos ad locum certaminis de ergastulo, ad triclinium eterni Regis de presenti exilio cum gaudio deducat infinito.'

---

a *om* B
b + pre foribus X

a horrible dungeon with a multitude of prisoners, whom the captive daughter of Sion was soon to bring forth into the glorious liberty of the children of God. There, by his long endurance of the filth, he earned the right to don eventually the snowy livery of the heavenly king.

Soon after this, the wicked tyrant, who kept them caged like beasts, ordered that they should all be put to death. He entrusted the execution of this foul deed to his son, who was still a youth and had hardly begun his knightly training. The day chosen for the martyrdom of these soldiers of Christ, was that on which the mighty victor Lawrence, crowned with his laurel wreath, entered the palace of the King of Kings.

The man I have mentioned rejoiced greatly when he heard his sentence, and roused his comrades to face the ordeal with these stirring words, ' We are indeed fortunate, my brethren, that in spite of our sinfulness and unworthiness, today's light will make us the companions of so famous a martyr. What a glad and blessed light has dawned for us this day, on which our captivity and darkness shall be ended for ever, and we shall exchange this world for Paradise and our prison for Heaven. The heavenly nectar, whose sweetness we have already daily tasted in this narrow prison, will today be ours to drain to the full. This overflowing torrent of inward delights of which until now we have merely sipped a few drops, will change the dew which has hardly wetted us, into a fountain from which we shall drink our fill eternally. Already, blessed Lawrence, today's patron saint is here with a multitude of the heavenly host, bearing the garlands of roses with which we shall be crowned. He is here, I say, to lead us from our dungeon to the place of conflict, and from our present exile to the infinite joy of the banquet of the Eternal King.'

Talibus peroratis, assunt carnifices, producuntur e carcere Christi uictime, exerunt funestas dexteras satellites Sathane, metuntur fruges Dominice, ethereis confestim apotecis inserende. Verum lictoribus hinc inde ceteros laniantibus, athletam fortissimum nullus impetebat. Ingerere se in percussorem nitebatur, set non reperiebat qui tangeret eum. Intuitus enim et miseratus filius principis qui huic palestre presidebat, canos uiri formamque corporis cunctis spectabilem, ab illius effusione sanguinis decreuerat supersedendum. Hunc igitur, ceteris omnibus ad sidera transmissis, a uinculis iubet relaxari atque ad suos abire illesum. Qui optata se ingemiscens fraudari corona, mestissimus reuertebatur ad propria.

Cunctis uero solebat palam referre quia iugiter, dum teneretur in predicto carcere, certa quadam diei *a* hora, una cum suis concaptiuis inestimabili perfrueretur odoris nectarei suauitate, cuius, ut asserebat, suauitatis modum aut magnitudinem nulla mortalium aut mens concipere aut lingua poterat explicare. Vnde nimio affectus tedio, super diuine illius uisitationis qua cotidie refici consueuerat priuatione, nec iam sustinens secularis consuetudinem uite, cum armaretur die quadam ut de more procederet cum suis ad condictum certamen exercitii militaris, digito locum quemdam designans non procul a suo stomacho, ingemuit et ait, ‘ Ve,’ inquiens, ‘michi misero, quia tantis bonis ad ista *b* mala, peccatis meis exigentibus, deuolutus sum. Verum tuam, o Fili Dei omnipotentis, exoro clementiam, quatinus hodie iubeas hic transfodi corpus istius peccatoris, ut hac saltem occasione mundi huius uinculis absolui, et de cetero tuis seruitiis ex integro ualeam mancipari.’

<hr/>

a die B   *b* tot X

When he had finished speaking, the butchers approached, and when Christ's victims had been taken from the prison the followers of Satan raised their murderous hands, and the corn of the lord was reaped to be gathered at once into the heavenly barns. Although the executioners massacred the others indiscriminately, no-one struck down this warrior. He tried hard to find an executioner but no-one laid his hands on him. The king's son who was in charge of the execution saw him, and out of compassion for his grey hairs and his impressive appearance stopped any further bloodshed. The rest having been dispatched to heaven, he ordered that his chains should be removed, and that he should be permitted to return to his friends unhurt, and he, lamenting that he had been deprived of the crown he had longed for, went back sorrowfully to his own country.

He told everyone that when he was in prison at one particular hour of the day he and his fellow captives were aware of an indescribably sweet odour, the deliciousness of which, he said, no mortal man could imagine or describe. He was much cast down by the loss of the divine favour which he had daily enjoyed, and found life in the world unbearable, and one day when he had armed himself to go as was his custom with his men to a tournament, he pointed a finger at a spot near his stomach and said with a groan, ' Alas, that I, wretch that I am, should because of my sins be brought from such bliss to this evil plight. I pray, O Son of Almighty God, that by your mercy, you will permit the body of this sinner to be pierced here today, that by this means at least I may be freed from the chains of this world, and may from now onwards dedicate myself entirely to your service.'

Quod et factum est. Nam perueniens ad campum supradicti certaminis, obuium habuit militem, qui lancea transuerberauit corpus eius. Quem, non sine luctu uniuerso omnium qui conuenerant, clipeo suo impositum et ad uicinum ordinis delatum Cisterciensis monasterium, Deo ibidem reliquerunt, ut optauerat, famulaturum. Qui mox ueste *a* donatus monachili, facilitate incredibili redonatur etiam integerrime sanitati.*b*

Cui postea moris fuit ut semper estiuo tempore Cartusiam uisitaret. Qui etiam diebus ibidem plurimis degens ac solitarie agens, singulorum uitam sancta curiositate explorabat ; morum instituta, uirtutum studia, ab uniuersis inquirebat ; ac demum, uelud apes prudentissima, a floribus redolentissimis mellis suscepto munere, ad suos redibat. Quicquid uero de perfectioris uite institutis ibidem didicisset, sic suis communicabat sodalibus, ut hoc propriis exprimere niteretur uirtutibus. Hic uero constitutus, Cisterciensium instituta uitamque extollebat ; inde ad Cistercienses regressus, Cartusiensium religionem preferebat. Sic itaque tam hos quam illos ad uirtutum incrementa ueluti quibusdam stimulis ex alterius laudibus incitabat. Non solum autem, set et in suis eos humiliabat laboribus et studiis ex prelatione mutua aliene sanctitatis. Tantus autem feruor in sancta religione tantusque rigor in conuersatione pia fuit ei ut esset omnibus sanctitatis speculum et exemplar probitatis.

Talibus uero Hugo noster suos alebat Withamenses ferculis uerborum, taliter eos fouebat spiritualibus quibusdam tegumentis, ne in arrepto tepescerent *c* sanctitatis proposito per exempla iustorum.

---

a iuste B
b sospitati X ; B² *adds* uel sospitati
c *om* B ; torpescerent m

It happened as he hoped. For in the lists he was attacked by a knight who pierced his body with his lance. Amid the lamentations of the whole company, he was laid on his shield and taken to a neighbouring Cistercian monastery, and there left, to enter the service of God, as he had wished. As soon as he had been given the monastic habit he made an amazingly quick and complete recovery.

He afterwards made a practice of visiting Chartreuse each summer, and spent a long time there living as a hermit. A holy curiosity caused him to investigate the manner of life of each of the monks. He asked everyone about the rule, customs and religious exercises, and having like a diligent bee taken a full toll of honey from the flowers, he finally returned home, and imparted to his fellow monks whatever he had learned there about a more perfect way of life, by striving to the best of his ability to imitate it himself.

When at Chartreuse he praised the customs and life of the Cistercians and when he returned to the Cistercians he gave the palm to the Carthusian order. Thus by alternately praising the one to the other he goaded them both on to greater virtue. He humbled them, not only by praising the sanctity of the other but by his own zeal and austerity. He was such a fervent monk, and lived such a holy and ascetic life, that all regarded him as the mirror and exemplar of sanctity and righteousness.

Such was the fare with which Hugh fed and regaled the Witham monks and by these examples of holy men he fostered their fervour for spiritual advancement, lest they should lose their original zeal.

CAPITVLVM XIII

Cuius maxime rei gratia Witham inuisere consueuerit.
Et de fratre Einardo iocunda narratio.

Eius quoque rei gratia ad eos uenire et quantum
licuit inter eos manere summopere cupiebat, quatinus
non tantum sumeret ab eis, set etiam impertiretur eis
quicquid posset gratie spiritualis. Quod nichilominus,
Domino cooperante, efficaciter adimplebat. Nam et
fortes exhylarabat et infirmos roborabat, uacillantes
stabiliebat, stabiliores *a* ad sublimiora prouehebat.

De quo genere illud eius opus iocundum fuit, quod
circa longe superius memoratum[1] fratrem Einardum
comiter et industrie gessit. Qui iam senex admodum,
utpote qui ab annis pene centum in diuersas mundi
partes pro instituendis illius ordinis domibus, a suis
Cartusiensibus longe lateque directus, demum iam
decrepitus huius negotii causa peruenerat Withamiam,
Cartusiam redire cupiebat. Videbat enim, opitulante
Dei omnipotentis misericordia, iam locum ipsum tam
interius quam exterius ad perfectionis culmen feliciter
enituisse. Disponebat igitur ad suos redire et cariosa
iam menbra bustis *b* sanctorum qui eum adholescentem
olim educauerant sociare. Verum cum cerneret suam
de die in diem uariis rationibus eludi intentionem, nec
iam ferret quo mens sua estuabat desiderii uehementiam,
ualedicens fratribus, tremulos baculo sustentans artus,[2]
abire cepit.

At episcopus solitis tunc in cella sua uacabat exercitiis
contemplatiue dulcedinis. Cauerat enim senex ille

---

a stabiles Xm   *b* bestiis B

[1] cf. MVI, p. 66

[2] cf. St Jerome, *Vita S. Pauli primi Eremitae*, c. 7 : ' Venerabilis senex
infirmos artus baculo regente sustentans.' P.L. 23, 22.

CHAPTER XIII

Why he was wont to derive so much spiritual benefit from his visits to Witham and the diverting story of brother Einard.

He greatly longed to go and stay with them as often as his duties permitted, not only to gain from them, but also to impart whatever spiritual benefits to them he could. This last indeed, with God's assistance he certainly did, for he inspired the strong to greater efforts, encouraged the faint-hearted, confirmed the wavering and raised the assured to higher achievements.

His wise and tactful treatment of brother Einard, who has been mentioned a long way back,[1] is an excellent example of his method. He was a very old man of nearly a hundred, and had been sent to different remote parts of the world by the Carthusians to establish houses of their order, and finally when he was already very feeble had come for the same reason to Witham, and longed to return to Chartreuse. He realized that by the grace of Almighty God, that place had by now reached both internally and externally the highest stage of perfection. He made up his mind therefore to return to his own people, so that his worn out body might be buried with those of the saints, who had formerly trained him in his youth. When he saw that he was being put off from day to day on various pretexts, he was carried away by the vehemence of the longing which absorbed his mind, and bidding his brethren farewell, he set out, supporting his feeble limbs by means of a stick.[2]

The bishop was then in his cell absorbed in contemplative prayer. The saintly old man had taken care not to inform him of his intention, knowing well that he

deuotus ne quod moliebatur ei citius innotesceret, a quo se maxime prepediendum multis iam argumentis certissime prenoscebat. Set non in longum res latere eum poterat. Mox ergo ita pedibus usque ad interiora uicini nemoris eum insecutus, hiis illum affatur, ' Parcat tibi,' inquit, ' omnipotens Deus, frater Einarde ! Quid enim est quod agere decreuisti ? Quid absque alumpno tuo recedere, meque solum et destitutum dulci nutritoris solatio in terra aliena relinquere cogitasti ? Et quidem non ignoro quam pio duceris desiderio, ut supreme iam uite tue reliquias inter sanctos Burgundie heremitas expendere ualeas. Verum me potius et ratio urget et uoluntas ut idipsum agam.' Extracto igitur anulo pontificali a digito et accersitis ad se clericis suis, ait eis : ' Ite quamtocius et hunc uobiscum anulum deferentes ac salutantes uerbis nostris dominos nostros Lincolnienses, denuntiate illis quatinus sibi alium prouideant et eligant pontificem, ut nobis de cetero [a] amicam liceat fouere solitudinem. Nimis diu est ex quo inter mundanos uersor turbines, sancte conuersationis dulcedini, in qua a puero coalui, uanas et amaras occupationes huius seculi non recte anteponens.'

Talia eo prosequente, timere cepit ac tremere uir ille desideriorum,[1] quem ducebat non dulcedo natalis soli set flagrans amor poli, stetitque stupefactus. Tunc clericis super tali infortunio conquerentibus, quo per eum suo forent pastore destituendi, et exaggerantibus uehementer incommodum huius mali, ille, suffusus lacrimis et ingemiscens grauiter, pedibus aduoluitur presulis sancti. Cumque ore facundo atque doctissimo laicus episcopo niteretur tum precibus tum rationibus persuadere, quia non ita liceret sibi diuinitus commissas relinquere oues, nec illum flecti conspiceret hoc modo,

---

[a] B omits these two words   [1] cf. Dan. 9 : 23

would certainly use the strongest arguments to dissuade him. But he could not conceal it from him for long, and he soon followed on his tracks into the heart of a neighbouring wood. He hailed him, ' Lord have mercy on us, brother Einard, what have you decided to do ? Do you really intend to go away without me, your nursling, and leave me alone in a strange land deprived of the consolation of my dear foster-father ? I fully realize how laudable your desire is to spend the last remaining years of your life among the holy hermits in Burgundy, so much indeed is this the case that my reason and inclination both force me to do the same.' He then removed his episcopal ring from his finger, and having called his clerks to him said, ' Go as quickly as you can, taking with you this ring, and greet on our behalf our lords, the canons of Lincoln. Tell them from us to make immediate arrangements for the election of another bishop, so that we may be permitted to enjoy our beloved retirement. Too long have we dwelt amongst the storms of the world, and foolishly preferred its empty and harassing business to the sweet and holy life in which we were reared from our youth.'

As he spoke, the man of desires,[1] who was inspired not by the attraction of his native land, but by his burning love of the heavenly country, stood amazed, and began to shake out of fear. Then the clerks took him to task for doing them the evil turn of depriving them of their bishop, and bitterly complained of this unfortunate mischance. He finally groaned heavily, and bursting into tears, cast himself at the bishop's feet. After this layman had tried by prayers and arguments to persuade the learned and ready-tongued bishop that it would be sinful thus to desert the sheep whom God had entrusted to him, and saw that he was unmoved, he

complectitur genua eius, dicens, ' Vere, ait, quamdiu
spiritus uitalis hos reget artus, non te permittam gregem
tuum relinquere, et plurimorum salute contempta, tui
ipsius tantummodo curam gerere. Melius michi est in
terra peregrina usque in finem morari et tandem morte
finiri, quam auctorem fieri tanti discidii. Redeamus
igitur ad solita, ne dum querimus que sunt nostra,
negligere culpemur que sunt Ihesu Christi.' Ita, quem
ab intentione recedendi a loco prius flectere tempore
multo nullus preualuit, prudentia uiri sancti in momento
non modo flectit, set etiam ut eo minime discedente et
ipse quoque non discederet cum uehementi instantia
ipsum exorare coegit. Inito itaque uicissim federe, quod
ille Withamiam non desereret nec iste Lincolniam,
redeunt alacres pariter, gaudente utroque se de alterutro
triumphasse.

De isto quoque uiro cum possemus innumera notitia
cunctorum digna referre, ne tamen uideamur a proposito
longius recedere, pauca saltem de insignibus eius gestis
summa curabimus breuitate perstringere. Dignissime
uero triumphalibus ducis illustrissimi titulis egregii
commilitonis sui memoriale credimus inserendum ; ut
cum quo in terris laboris et patientie, cum quo in celis
mercedis et corone particeps meruit ueraciter existere,
cum eodem quoque perhennis memorie celebritatem
apud homines ualeat optinere. Set nec adeo barbaram
sub celo gentem includit oceanus, que posset Einardi
apud se commorantis preconia non mirari, aut eius ad
celestia iam peruenientis merita laude celebri minime
uenerari.

Hic quondam a Cartusia in partes Hispaniarum
missus gratia informande cuiusdam noue domus ordinis
sui,[1] duos bone religionis uiros, in heremo degentes sibi
uicina, in magne familiaritatis gratiam susceperat.

finally caught hold of his knees and said, ' As long as I live, I will not allow you to leave your flock, and indifferent to the salvation of so very many persons, seek only your own. It will be better for me to remain in this foreign land till the end and die in it, rather than be the cause of such a betrayal. Let us both go back to our usual occupations, lest following our own inclinations, we are convicted of disobeying the will of Christ.' Thus by his skilful handling he was able to dissuade at once the man whom for a long time no-one had been able to persuade to change his purpose of leaving the place, and even made him urgently implore him not to depart provided he himself remained. They therefore struck a bargain that the one would not desert Witham nor the other Lincoln, and then returned triumphant, each congratulating himself on his victory over the other.

I could relate innumerable stories worth everyone's while to know about this man, but for fear of seeming to digress I shall confine myself to a brief account of the more remarkable events of his life, as I think it fitting that the memory of a valiant companion in arms should be preserved in this tribute to his illustrious leader. He certainly deserves always to be remembered by men along with the man whose trials and afflictions he shared on earth and whose crown and reward he shares in Heaven. No people in the world, however remote and uncivilized, have not wondered at and commended the works wrought by brother Einard amongst them, and have not praised and honoured him after his departure to Heaven.

Once when sent by the Carthusians to found a new house in Spain,[1] he made great friends there with two very

---

[1] The Charterhouse of Scala Dei in Catalonia was founded by Ildefonsus of Aragon in 1163. (cf. Le Couteulx, *Annales Ordinis Carthusiensis*, II, p. 251).

Contigit autem ea tempestate Saracenos, a finibus
Affrice in illas regiones irruptione facta multaque
hominum cede subito patrata, spolia inde cum preda
copiosa ad suos asportasse. Qui inter uiros quoque ac
mulieres quos predantes ceperant, heremitas Einardo
karissimos pariter abduxerunt. Quo ille cognito,
extorta *a* potius precibus importunis et lacrimis, a priore
et fratribus, quam ultro impetrata licentia, nauigauit ad
Affricam. Quo dum perueniret ac predictos Dei famulos
sollicite inquisitos demum inueniret, non ante destitit
uirum potentem qui eos captiuos tenebat, rogando,
monendo, penasque diuinitus inferendas minando, uelut
quibusdam precantationibus delinire, quousque eosdem,
quod uix sperare poterat ab homine gentili, absque
redemptionis pretio liberos impetraret dimitti. Cum
quibus reuersus ad propria, letabatur in Domino quasi
qui inuenisset spolia multa.¹ Tam libere uero et adeo
constanter cecitatem infidelium Agarenorum obiurga-
uerat, tanteque auctoritatis fiducia lucem eis Christiane
ueritatis annuntiauerat, ut nemo esset qui contempnere
illum auderet ; set uniuersi, ad primos eius affatus et
aspectus nutu Dei in stuporem uersi, non minimam
ei reuerentiam exhibebant. Erat quidem niuea canitie
reuerendus, uoce grauis, oculis diuinum quiddam
scintillantibus, ad indigna terribilis, ad congrua iocun-
dissimus et lenis.

Hic etiam cum uice quadam per fines apostatarum
Albigensium transiret, conferto cum eis sermone, audiuit
eos proteruis uocibus omnia ecclesie sacramenta blasphe-
mantes. Qui nimio contra impios zelo excandescens,*b*
accessit ad proximos illarum partium catholicos proceres

---

a exorta B
b exardescens X

holy hermits who lived in the vicinity. Just at that time the district was raided by Saracens from Africa, who massacred a large number of people and took back home with them an immense amount of booty. Amongst the men and women whom they had captured on their raid were the hermits to whom brother Einard was so devoted. On learning the news he extorted rather than obtained by his earnest prayers and tears permission from the prior and brethren, and sailed for Africa. Arriving there, he sought diligently for the aforesaid servants of God and having eventually found them, he never stopped entreating and exhorting and even threatening with the divine vengeance the chieftain who held them captive, until, as if under a spell he set them free without a ransom, an action scarcely to be expected from an infidel. He and they returned to their own country, the former giving thanks to God like one who had found much spoil.[1] He had attacked the blindness of the Saracens with so much freedom and vigour, and had made known to them with so much faith and conviction the light of Christian truth, that none of them dared to mock him. Instead, all of them, by God's providence were very much impressed by his personality and teaching and showed him every respect. He was a dignified old man with snowy hair, and a sonorous voice, and eyes shining with a divine light, terrible to evil-doers, but mild and gracious to the good.

He was on one occasion passing through the territory of the Albigensian heretics, and when he was speaking with them heard their shameless blasphemies against all the Christian sacraments. Blazing with righteous indignation at such profanity, he went to the nearest

[1] cf. Ps. 118 : 162

uirosque potentes ; induxitque eos ut sumptis armis in perfidos irruerent, et ex eis innumeros trucidarent. Vnde contigit ut illis in locis nullus erroris infandi assertor ulterius compareret. Iam uero huius facti exemplo longius propagato, brutum illud homunculorum pestiferumque genus magno fidelium sudore abrasum est, ac Deo miserante deletum.

Iam uero de Christi pugile fortissimo id quoque referendum est, quod ei infirmius surrepisse agnouimus, cum sit audire opere pretium. Nam et rigor pariter et moderatio sancti ordinis illius ex eo uehementer elucet, et uir strenuus, qui humanitus surreptione quadam impelli ad lapsum uidebatur, quam se ipso fortiter surrexerit subinde demonstratur. Cum enim Christi miles emeritus ac preualidus uinee Dominice operarius, quaquauersum dilatatam sacri huius ordinis religionem, ac si uitis electissime propaginem, annis iam innumeris rigare non destitisset, et iam centenarius Cartusiam, ubi sacre religionis olim puer susceperat habitum, reuersus, de cetero quieti operam dare disponeret ; repente iubetur in Daciam pergere ibique nouelle itidem plantationi, fundande scilicet de recenti cuidam domui, consuete solatium rigationis exhibere.[1] Tum ille non modice turbatus, nec tam itineris quamuis longioris satisque laboriosi fatigatione quam sibi ab olim suspectam gentis illius exhorrescens barbariem, signum sue fronti salutis imprimens confestim ait, ' A Danemarchia libera nos *a* domine.' Consueuerat enim, quamquam laicus et illiteratus, ad singula pene uerba scripturarum sermonibus quos usu didicisset uti.

Post hec aduoluens se pedibus prioris sui, supplicat

---

a me X

[1] This Danish Charterhouse was in existence c. 1174, but it was soon closed (cf. Le Couteulx, *op. cit.*, II, pp. 399-404.)

Catholic magnates and knights in those parts and persuaded them to take up arms and attack the heretics and slaughter large numbers of them. The result was that no preacher of that horrible heresy appeared again in that district. This act being widely known and imitated˙that perverted and pestilential people were by the vigorous efforts of the faithful and the mercy of God crushed and destroyed.

We must now relate something we heard to the discredit of this valiant champion of Christ, since the incident is very instructive, as it is an excellent illustration of the severe and yet temperate discipline of his holy order, and shows how this holy man, whom a certain human frailty caused to backslide, bravely overcame himself. When this veteran of Christ and indefatigable labourer in His vineyard had already watered the shoots of his chosen vine for an immense number of years, in every part of the world to which his holy order had spread, he returned when he was already a hundred to Chartreuse where formerly as a youth he had received the monastic habit. He intended from henceforth to live quietly there, but was suddenly ordered to go to Denmark to give the benefit of his customary watering to a new plantation there, that is to a recently founded house.[1] Being very much annoyed, not so much because of the journey which was long and fatiguing enough, but because he had for a long time hated and despised that barbarous nation, he made the sign of the cross on his forehead and exclaimed at once, ' Lord, deliver me from Denmark,' for although a layman and illiterate his language was generally that of the Bible which he had learnt by heart through constant repetition.

He then fell at his prior's feet, and begged hard that

instantius ne iam decrepitum cogat animos indocibiles
addiscendis hominum barbarorum ritibus ignotis subicere et ferendis eorum moribus, quos semper exhorruerit,
studium mentis uiolenter inflectere.   Memorabat iam
satis esse quod eatenus ad opera *a* huiusmodi decertasset,*b*
cui et etas et debilitas feriandum de cetero a tantis
laboribus iusta ratione prescriberent.   ' Qui enim a
remotis,' inquit, ' partibus huc tandem, respirandi
gratia et spiritum ad extrema preparandi, artus
fatiscentes referre tantopere curaui, quonam *c* pacto
nunc extra orbem ultra ipsum quoque oceanum mitti
habeo, presertim ad gentem cuius ne quidem linguam
noui ? '

Talia eo prosequente frustra, perstat prior in sententia, dicens probatam multo tempore industrie sue
experientiam   minoribus   illuc   dirigendis   fratribus
omnimodis fore pernecessariam.   Tamen ille grauiter
suspirans, ' O,' inquit, ' duram, o et amaram huius diei
conditionem ! proh dolor !   Qui tot annis obedientie
meritum tantopere colui, nunc compellor aut inobediens
inueniri, aut negotium milies supra mortis supplicium
michi semper exosum propter obedientiam experiri.
Ceterum istam, ut Deus adiuuerit, expiaturus inobedientiam, semel dico, Danemarchiam in hoc corpore
mortali degens numquam certe uidebo.'   Sic audaci uoce
locutus, singulorum pedibus in capitulo ubi hec gerebantur sese prosternit, ut pro se intercedant quatinus a
legatione   adeo   molesta   mereatur   dimitti,   fratrum
uniuersitati preces lacrimabiles fundit.   Set hec agendo
cum nichil proficeret nec quo iubebatur ire ullatenus
adquiesceret, ad terrorem aliorum extra habitationis sue
ianuam pulsus siue proiectus est.   In tantum quippe

a *om* B
b decreuisset B
c quondam B

he would not compel him when he was already so feeble to put up with savages and learn their strange and primitive ways, and constrain himself to endure their habits to which he had always had a marked aversion. He pointed out that he had already laboured long enough at work of this kind, and that his age and feebleness made it only right and reasonable that he should now be exempt from such tasks. ' Why should I, who have taken so much pains to drag my weary limbs home at last, from distant lands to rest and prepare my soul for the end, now have to be sent to the furthest limits of the world beyond the ocean, and to a people whose tongue I do not even know ? '

He pleaded in vain in this strain, for the prior would not change his mind, saying that his zeal and experience which had been tested over a considerable period would be absolutely essential there for the guidance of the younger brethren. He then said with a heavy sigh, ' Alas, how hard and bitter is my lot today ! After I have tried so hard to cultivate obedience for so many years, I am now compelled either to be disobedient or for the sake of obedience undertake a duty a thousand times worse and more hateful to me than death itself. I am ready, God help me, to do penance for this disobedience, but I declare once and for all that I will never see Denmark as long as I live.' He spoke boldly in this way, and prostrating himself at the feet of each of the brethren who attended the chapter, where these matters were arranged, implored them with tears to intervene on his behalf, that he might be excused from a mission he hated so much. His efforts were, however, in vain, and as he absolutely refused to go where he was ordered, as an example to the others he was expelled and put outside the door of the monastery. This holy order in its

prouida illius sacri ordinis censura inobedientie persequitur uitium, ut quemlibet etiam in re leuissima obedientie limites excedentem, a sua cum uoluerit societate eliminet.

Verum, ne multis immoremur, Einardus ille antiquus atque eximius ordinis Cartusiensis institutor et propagator, de ordine eiectus, extra fores Cartusie nudo sub aere iacens, fame torquebatur et frigore, ueniam quidem petens set petendo nil proficiens. Qui cum propriam supplicationem, ad optinendam quam querebat indulgentiam, prorsus cerneret inefficacem, ad emendicanda plurimorum suffragia, corpore seminudus et discalceatus, uniuersas pene ordinis illius domus adiuit. Erat uero tempus iam mediantis brume, cum omnis illa regio glaciali rigore et niuium congerie, flatibus quoque hibernis exasperata, etiam bene uestito ad gradiendum uidebatur incommoda. Nichilominus hic penitens nouus et innocens ueteranus, a castris in quibus tot lustra splendide militando transegerat, extorris non transfuga, per aspera montium per deuexa uallium ita ut erat nudulus digreditur. Nec enim qui, prothoplasti exemplo, paradisi habitationem per inobedientiam demeruerat, per expellentis *a* quoque misericordiam uestem pelliceam ut ille acceperat;[1] quia sepe in ira misericordie homo obliuiscitur, cuius semper Deus memoratur. Sic igitur interdiu incedens et noctu sub diuo recubans, compluta et congelata menbra nunc saxo cuilibet, nunc omnino *b* congesto niuium cumulo, rarius *c* uero nude credebat telluris gremio, cuius uidelicet et ubique superficiem nix densissima operuerat. Qui uersus demum, cunctorum pene totius ordinis priorum deprecatoriis onustus litteris, uenit, iam nocturnis incumbentibus *d* umbris, ad portam

---

a excellentis B   *b* om B
c raro X   *d* + tenebris et X

wisdom condemned the sin of disobedience so rigorously that anyone, whoever he might be, was expelled for the most trifling act of disobedience.

I must not, however, dwell too long on this. Einard, that old and tried founder and propagator of the Carthusian order, being expelled from his order, lay outside the precincts of Chartreuse with no roof over his head, and a prey to hunger and cold, seeking forgiveness, but obtaining no answer to his petition. When he found his own prayers were useless to obtain the pardon he sought, he went barefoot and half-naked to almost all the houses of his order to beg for their intercession. It was then mid-winter, when walking was unpleasant in that district even for the warmly clad, owing to the hard frost and heavy snow aggravated by the wintry winds. Nevertheless this new penitent, a blameless old man, an exile but not a fugitive from the fortresses where he had dwelt and fought so gallantly for so many years, wandered among the precipitous mountains and craggy valleys, almost naked. He had not even, like our first parent when he was expelled from Paradise for the sin of disobedience, a garment of skins provided for him [1] by the mercy of him who cast Him out, for man, unlike God who always remembers, often forgets in his anger to be merciful. Thus he passed his time walking by day and at night reposing under the stars, with his wet and frozen limbs stretched out either on a boulder or a heap of snow, or more rarely on the bare ground which was covered everywhere with a thick coat of snow. At last, he returned laden with supplicatory letters from almost all the priors of his order, and arrived, when the shades of night were drawing in, at the gate of Chartreuse.

---

[1] cf. Gen. 3 : 21

Cartusie. Quem frater portarius nec sub patulum tectum ianue ingredi permittens, cum esset nimia quoque celi intemperies, exterius in mediis niuibus pernoctare coegit. De cuius amaritudine noctis nimis immoderata uexatus,ᵃ mane tandem portario loquens Einardus, ita facete dixit, ' Revera,' inquit, ' frater karissime, si nocte hac inter collidentes pre frigoris tormento dentes meos faba extitisses, etiam nolens te funditus comminuissem.'

Qui tandem sub regulari satisfactione susceptus et a ᵇ Danemarchia ut petierat liberatus, ad Angliam non longe post in opus consuetum destinatur. Ita uero in Burgundia, quibus diu extiterat forma perfecte uiuendi,ᶜ exemplar demum effectus est perfectissime penitendi : et cuius uita stantes informauit ad iustitiam, eius penitentia quandoque lapsuros instituit ad indulgentiam. De cuius hodie perhenni memoria, dignis et gestis et dictis, tanta per totam fere Angliam uulgata sunt celebri sermone, quod hec ab ore narrantium etiam sine scribentis suffragio, nulla in euum, ut creditur, auferre preualebit obliuio. Qui biennio ferme antequam hec scriberentur, uicesimum sextum ut dicitur annorum transgressus lustrum, deficiens in senectute bona ¹ feliciter migrauit ad Dominum.

ᵃ *om* B
ᵇ *om* B
ᶜ + in Anglia X

The brother who was porter would not permit him to take cover under the penthouse roof of the door, in spite of the excessively inclement weather, but made him pass the night outside in the snow. When dawn at length came, brother Einard who had endured the extreme cold of the night, said jestingly to the porter, ' My teeth chattered so terribly last night, dear brother, because of the bitter cold, that if you had been a bean between them, I should have had to chew you up '.

At last, having done penance as prescribed in the rule he was received back, and excused from going to Denmark as he had begged, but was sent a little later to England on his usual task. Thus, in Burgundy where he had long been an example of perfect living he became finally an even better one of a penitent, and whilst his whole life had been an inspiration to the righteous, his repentance encouraged mercy in those who might one day find themselves backsliders. His memorable actions and sayings are so well known today in almost every part of England that I do not think that he needs the assistance of a writer to be always remembered on men's lips. Just two years before this was written he died, and departed peacefully to God at a ripe old age [1] being, it is alleged, about 130 years old.

---

[1] cf. Gen. 25 : 8

CAPITVLVM XIV

De incendio coquine, sub extremo recessu illius de
Witham innoxie peracto.

Verum iam forte plusquam satis hic noster apud
Withamenses perhendinauit stilus. Cui sollicite cauendum erat ne quando, sicut Hugoni nostro plerique
succensebant,ᵃ eo quod menstruas ibidem, immo plusquam bimenstres interdum moras internecteret, ita et
nobis pari iure nonnulli succenseant qui, intermissa
serie pontificalis historie, ad gesta rusticorum texenda
digressi uidemur. Quemadmodum namque illi secum
potius ad regis scaccarium pontificem maluissent residere
quam ad heremum secedere, ita forsitan et isti nos
mallent penitus reticere quam talia de ydiotis referre,
que sese sciunt, cum eximia litteratura sua, imitari non
uelle. Quibus nos eo in huiusmodi iustius morem
gerimus, quo ad ferendas detrahentium linguas Hugone
multo minus fortes sumus.

Hunc enim pene solum hec nostra infelicia tempora
uiderunt qui, ut ait ad regem David mulier prudentissima, ' Profecto tamquam angelus Domini, nec benedictione nec maledictione moueretur,' quominus ea liber-
rime foris ᵇ exequeretur que in intimo rationis sacrario
interius percepisset exequenda. Vnde, sicut ibidem
quoque subnectitur, ' Dominus Deus suus secum erat in
omnibus.' ¹

Verumptamen hoc interim nostro pro nobis lectori
satisfactionis studio ad mentem reducimus, quia semel
tantummodo, postquam uir sanctus ad pontificatum
accessit, calamus noster Withamiam scribendo attigerit ;

ᵃ succendebant B   ᵇ om B

CHAPTER XIV

Concerning the burning of the kitchen without further damage, an event which happened just before he left Witham for the last time.

Perhaps our pen has already paused too long at Witham. I must take great care lest, just as very many persons criticised my Hugh for spending a month and often over two months there, for the same reason I myself shall be criticised by some for interrupting my account of his episcopate to describe the affairs of country folk. Just as the former thought it less derogatory for a bishop to sit at the king's Exchequer with them than to withdraw to a hermitage, so the latter would perhaps prefer us to write nothing rather than give these anecdotes about illiterate men, whom, being fully aware of their own scholarship, they have no desire to imitate. I had better comply with their wishes, since I lack Hugh's indifference to un-justified criticism.

He seems to be almost the only person in our unhappy age to whom the words spoken by the wise woman to King David are applicable, 'Verily, like an angel of God, neither blessing nor curse diverted him from carry-ing out to the full whatever his conscience told him ought to be done'. Therefore, as is added there, 'the Lord his God was with him in all his works.' [1]

Meantime, I would remind my readers that owing to my wish to satisfy them this is the only place where, since the holy man became a bishop, I have let my pen describe Witham, although almost every year of his episcopate he used to go there, sometimes once and

[1] 2 Kings (2 Samuel) 14 : 17

ad quam ipse, toto pene quo episcopatum gessit tempore, nunc semel nunc sepius, prout oportunum ei fuit, singulis annis uenire consueuit. Hoc autem tempore potissimum autumpnali faciebat, quatinus dum sui ad fruges colligendas temporales studiosius uacarent, ille, dimissa suorum frequentia domesticorum in propria, eo fertilius quo et liberius carpende et in intimis anime sue apothecis recondende, inuigilaret annone spiritus. Ex eo autem quod premisimus constare recte considerantibus luce clarius potest, quanto breuitatis studio lectoris declinare fastidium, in aliis quoque eiusdem gestis satagimus ; qui uix pauca ex hiis que in loco ubi sepissime morabatur, ubi tot salutaria loquebatur, ubi tam spiritualia operabatur, summatim perstringendo replicamus.

Nunc igitur quid in ultimo eius ab inde recessu ibidem acciderit, solita compendiositate referemus ; ac sic ad eius abscessum ex hoc mundo ad domum non manufactam eternam in celis exponendum quanta ualebimus celeritate pertendemus. Nocte igitur que diem illum clausit, qua ultimum fratribus ualefecit, eos ulterius corporaliter non uisurus, id accidit quod referimus. Cum enim iam singulorum se orationibus, premissa confessione et absolutione uicissim petita et percepta, seorsum prius in eorum cellis commendasset ex more, demum in commune, licentia postulata et sollempni omnibus benedictione data, libato etiam pacis osculo, sub hiis uerbis que frequenti usu a caris suis discessurus proferebat, ab eis recessit, ' Nunc,' inquiens, ' commendo uos Deo et uerbo gratie eius.'[1] Hinc ad diuersoria fratrum laicorum, ubi clerici et seruientes sui commanebant, ibi mane crastinum expectaturus accessit.

---

[1] Acts. 20 : 32

sometimes more often, whenever he had an opportunity. He went most frequently in the autumn, since whilst his flock were engaged upon the gathering in of the earthly harvest, he, having sent most of his attendants to their homes, could concentrate more easily on getting in a richer harvest of spiritual fruit and garnering this in the depths of his soul. From my preceding descriptions of his other acts, it must be abundantly clear to all fair-minded persons, how hard I have tried to be concise in order to avoid boring my readers. I have continued to do this by dealing very briefly with just a few incidents out of those connected with the place where he so often stayed, and where he said so many profitable things, and did so many mighty spiritual works.

Now therefore I shall relate with my usual brevity an event which took place on his last visit, after which I shall go on as quickly as I can to describe his departure from the world to the eternal mansions in Heaven not made with hands. What I am going to describe took place on the night after the day on which he had said his last farewell to the brethren he was never to see again in the body. When he had made his confession and asked and received absolution, he commended himself to the prayers of each one of them, first privately in their cells and then collectively as was his custom, and having asked permission to depart he gave his solemn benediction to all of them and the kiss of peace, using the same words he always did when about to leave his friends, ' I commend you to God and to the word of His grace,' [1] and then departed from them to the lodging of the lay brothers, where his clerks and attendants were awaiting him, to wait there himself for the following morning. After resting there, he had entered the church for the night office, when suddenly an exceedingly brilliant light

Quo post quietem ad soluendas nocturnas Deo laudes ecclesiam ingresso, per uitreas ab occidua oratorii parte fenestras fulgor subito nimius illuxit, ita ut solis iubar eadem uideretur claritas excessisse. Vnde attoniti quidam qui ualuis ecclesie propius astiterant, festine erumpunt, cernuntque culinam *a* que proximis undique domibus pene fuerat contigua, porrectis longe in aera flammis, exuri. Quod episcopus agnoscens uehementer expauit, metuens scilicet ne in proxima forte edificia edax incendium deseuiret. Nec enim secus futurum situs et status edium circumquaque imminentium *b* cuiquam dictabat presumendum. Ipsa uero edicula, occasione seruientium episcopi necnon et hospitum episcopi, ut eorum usibus pulmenta coquerentur in ea, fuerat constructa ; eratque ex uirgulis ac uirgultis uicem parietum supplentibus contexta, stipula leui culmen ipsius tegente. Que ab aula hospitali sex aut septem uix pedum spatio disparata, tecto ipsius quod ex aridis erat scindulis confectum, e proximo imminebat. Cellule preterea lignee conuersorum usibus deputate haut procul in girum erant disposite. Ipsi nichilominus ecclesie uicinius astanti cum circumpositis undique officinis iustissime timebatur.

Cernens itaque uir prouidus hiis omnibus sui causa ineuitabile, ni diuina arceatur uirtute, imminere periculum, animo parumper *c* consternatus set plurimum de Saluatoris bonitate confisus, salutifere crucis signum contra ignem aliquotiens edidit. Intermittens uero cursum nocturnalis officii, quod ex parte iam inchoauerat, ante aram Dominicam sese protinus in orationem dedit. Nec prius destitit a prece quam, domuncula funditus absumpta, succubuisse flammas, incendia

a + seu coquinam X
b eminentium B
c pariter B

brighter even than the rays of the sun lit up the western windows of the oratory. The people nearest to the doors of the church were surprised and hastily rushed out to find that the kitchen which almost touched the nearest dwellings was on fire, and that the flames were rising upwards to a great height. When the bishop saw this he was much alarmed, for he feared that the devouring flames would probably attack the adjacent buildings. The position and nature of the surrounding ones indeed made it very likely that this would be their fate. It was a small erection with wattle walls and a thatched roof, constructed to serve as a kitchen for the bishop's retainers and other guests, scarcely six or seven feet away from the hall of the guest house, and almost abutting on to its roof, which was made of dry shingle. The wooden cells of the lay brothers were built in a circle not far off. Moreover, there was considerable reason for alarm about the church itself and the buildings around it which were near-by.

The prudent man saw that without a miracle all these buildings were irrevocably doomed and all because of him ; he was therefore for the moment perturbed, but having great confidence in the goodness of Christ, made the sign of the cross repeatedly in the direction of the fire. He also broke off the night office which he had already begun, and himself knelt in prayer in front of the altar of the Lord. He continued to pray until informed that the little building had been entirely consumed and that the fire was dying down ; no harm was done except for the loss of that building, which, even if it had been uninjured, would anyway have been pulled down deliberately. He had, in fact, often ordered that it should be replaced by a small stone building suitable for a kitchen, because he feared the very danger which

tepuisse nuntiantur, et quidem citra cuiuscumque rei
detrimentum preterquam illius solummodo edificii,
quod etiam si stetisset illesum, manibus hominum de
industria fuerat diruendum.   Iam enim sepius iusserat
ad usus necessarios lapideum, eo demolito, ibidem
construi domicilium ; hoc scilicet quod modo accidit
ueritus inde prouenire periculum.   Cuius mane incendium cum uniuersi mirarentur adeo extitisse in-
noxium, ille in Domino exultans aiebat : ' Benedictus
Deus, qui non solum presentem in tali casu timorem
nostrum consolari uoluit, set et futuri metus sollicitudinem sub nostra tandem presentia funditus amputauit.'

finally ensued. The next morning when everyone was amazed at the small extent of the damage, he gave thanks to God, exclaiming, ' Blessed be God, not only for His readiness to relieve our fears on this occasion, but also for His final and complete removal in our presence of any future fears and anxieties.'

LIBER QVINTVS

QVATVOR iam libellis de uita sancti patris nostri Hugonis antistitis, iuuante Christi gratia, utcumque explicitis, de eiusdem opitulatione confisi, quintum, quem et ultimum huius opusculi fore disponimus, subnexo inferius exordio, temptabimus adoriri. In cuius serie nulla penitus retexere decreuimus, nisi ea solummodo quibus presentialiter interfuimus, aut ea quoque que mox gesta per eum nobis intimata fuisse euidenter recolimus.

Hic uero narrationis sumetur initium de singulari deuotione qua preditus fuit erga studium sepulture mortuorum. Cui demum conclusionis causa *a* succedet postremum, de incomparabili sepulture simul et exequiarum honore et decore, quibus celitus donari meruit, uite iam peracto presentis agone. Media inter hec illa presertim continebunt, quibus docetur pro Anglicane ecclesie immunitate, tam contra regem Ricardum quam et contra eius iustitiarium, propriumque suum ipsius metropolitanum uiriliter decertando feliciterque Deo protegente superando, plurimum desudasse, atque ad postremum, ipsi regi suoque persecutori sepulture humanitatem exhibendo, insigniter triumphasse. Hiis quoque alia scitu digna de exordio regni Ioannis nunc iam anno ipsius quarto decimo mense tertio plurimum fatiscentis,[1] sensimque ut futurum ille predixerat deficientis, uidentur subicienda. Consequenter uero uti ipse Cartusiam et alia loca religione celeberrima adierit, reuersusque in Angliam, apud Londonias ad gaudia superne Ierusalem felici beatus excessu migrauit, temptabimus explicare.

a *om* Bo

BOOK FIVE

PROLOGUE

WITH Christ's help I have now finished four books of
the life of our holy father and bishop Hugh, so, trusting
in the same assistance, I shall now embark upon the
fifth, which begins below, and which it is my intention
to make the last. I have decided to include in it nothing
but what I myself witnessed, or what he himself related
to me shortly after the event.

I shall begin with a description of his amazing zeal
for the burial of the dead, for which he was conspicuous.
This makes the splendour of his own entombment, and
the pomp and magnificence of the funeral with which
Heaven so justly rewarded his virtues when the toils of
this present life ended, a fitting conclusion. The
principal matter of the middle of the book will be an
account of his great struggles for the liberty of the
English Church with King Richard and his justiciar, who
was also his own metropolitan. His gallant fight, thanks
to God's protection, ended successfully. His greatest
victory, however, was the magnanimity he showed at the
burial of the king, who had been his persecutor. To
this I thought it right to add certain details which
seemed worth recording about the beginnings of the
reign of John, whom we have now endured for fourteen
years and three months [1] and whose folly he foresaw and
prophesied. Then I shall attempt to describe Hugh's
visits to Chartreuse and other famous monasteries, and
his holy death at London after his return to England, and
his happy departure to the delights of the heavenly
Jerusalem.

---

[1] That is, July 1213 : Richard was killed 6 April 1199.

Capitvlvm I

Verba Hugonis de immensitate diuine ad hominem dilectionis. De ipsius immensa sedulitate circa officium sepulture, pro cuius executione bis distulit ad conuiuia regia uenire.

Memoriam habundantie suauitatis diuine erga humanum genus suauiter eructans[1] intimus [a] a secretis Deique amicus Hugo, hec et hiis similia que subinferimus suis sepissime in odorem suauitatis ingerebat auditoribus.

'Cum sint,' aiebat, 'innumera, que diuine ad hominem dilectionis declarant immensitatem, ea quam maxime inter cetera prerogatiuam singularis excellentie noscuntur preferre, que uel ante hominis ortum uel post ipsius occasum, homini non desinit conferre. Vt enim de hominibus qui modo oriuntur et occidunt pauca attingamus, ante cuiusque ortum, sue pro eo mortis pretium Deus [b] Dei Filius dedit ; Deus Pater eumdem Filium suum in mundum ut pro homine moreretur misit, Deus Spiritus Sanctus seipsum ei in pignus effudit.[c] Tota etiam simul Trinitas, unus Deus, sacramenta quibus mox natus et mundetur et muniatur et roboretur instituit, legis sue adminicula quibus regatur et erudiatur concessit, aliaque satis inexplicabilia utilitati ipsius multipliciter profutura indulsit. Quem post uite instabilis cursum occasu preuentum, cum a suis olim karissimis non sine tedio quodam respicitur, cum propriis quondam edibus anxia quadam parentum et filiorum festinatione propellitur, gratissima Dei sui benignitas sola a ceteris despectum non aspernatur. Extemplo namque, non solum spiritus angelicos in presidium anime ad factorem

---

[a] intimis Xp   [b] om X   [c] in pignus infudit o
[1] cf. Psalm 144: 7

CHAPTER I

Hugh's words about the greatness of God's love for man-kind. His immense concern for the burial of the dead, and how his discharge of this duty twice made him late for a royal banquet.

Ruminating lovingly in the depths of his soul upon the remembrance of the immensity of the divine love towards mankind [1] Hugh, the intimate friend of God, was wont frequently to urge this and similar considera-tions with great fervour upon his hearers.

' Although,' he would say, ' there are manifold proofs of the greatness of the love of God to man, obviously the most striking of these are the gifts His unfailing bounty confers on him either before his birth or after his death. To mention a few points concerning men who are now being born and dying, each one of them before he was born was ransomed by the death of God the Son. God the Father sent His Son into the world to die for man-kind, and in confirmation of this he received the out-pouring of the Holy Spirit. Thus, the whole Trinity, one God, instituted the sacraments by which shortly after his birth he is cleansed, strengthened and fortified and granted him the aid of the law to instruct and guide him, and conferred on him many other indescribable benefits. When the course of this transitory life is cut short by death, and his former friends regard him with distaste, and his children and relatives with anxious haste remove him from his former home, only the super-abundant loving-kindness of God does not spurn one whom everyone else rejects. Not only does He immedi-ately send His holy angels to guard the soul on its way back to its Creator, but He even dispatches His chief and

suum remeantis dirigit, uerum etiam primos et precipuos
quos in terris habet ministros, sacerdotes uidelicet et
alios *a* in sacris ordinibus positos, in obsequium funeris
mittit. Eis etiam quodammodo dicit :

' Cernitis,' inquiens, ' o sacerdotes mei, et meorum
que in mundo sunt palatiorum editui, cernitis facturam
meam quam semper amaui, pro qua Filio meo unigenito
non peperci,[1] set eum mortalitatis illius et mortis
participem feci ; cernitis, inquam, suis hanc amicis
quondam et necessariis effectam oneri, hanc quoque ab
eis quasi turbulenter eici et expelli. Eya, festinanter
occurrite ad me confugienti ; ymaginem Filii mei, pro
ea crucifixi, cum thimiateriis et cereis assumite ; ecclesie
mee signa in solempne classicum concutite ; uocibus
ymnidicis clarius concrepate ; basilice mee fores et
abdita *b* interiora pandite ; nec longius ab ara, Filii mei
corpus continente, fratris illius aut sororis lipsana *c*
deponite ; palliis denique pretiosis lecticam illius nunc
demum triumphantis *d* redimite, stipate lampadibus et
lucernis, assistentibus obsequentium cateruis quamuis
iacentem ambite. Iterata preterea Filii mei uotiua
immolatione, conuiuium pinguissimum instruite,*e* quo
et spiritus anhelus ac de concertatione mortalitatis
inolite set iam deposite adhuc irrequietus et fessus,*f* in
robur respiret ; et caro, habitatore pristino interim
uacuata matrisque terre gremio subinde confouenda,
sanctificatione irrigetur gratissima, quatinus sub die
ultima, contubernali olim precognito delectabiliter
socianda, alacriter refloreat, uiriditate eterna feliciter
induenda.'

Huiusmodi sententiam per singula pene uerba de
benigni Conditoris circa defunctos clementia proferens,

| *a* aliis B | *b* adita o | *c* bapsana X |
| *d* triumphalibus X | *e* construite B | *f* confusus X |

pre-eminent servants on earth, I mean, His priests, and those in the other holy orders, to bury him, giving them these instructions :

'You see, My priests and courtiers in My earthly palaces, this My creature whom I have always loved, and for whose sake I did not spare even My own only begotten Son,[1] but made Him the participator in its mortality and death. You see how it has become a burden to its former friends and kinsmen, who cast it out and drive it away with violence. Now, go in haste to meet it on its flight to Me, take up the image of My Son crucified for it with incense and candles, and toll the bells of My church with a solemn peal, and with the chanting of hymns open wide the doors of My church and its inmost sanctuary, and near the altar on which the body of My Son reposes, lay the remains of your brother or sister. Cover the bier of one victorious at the last with a rich pall, and with lights and torches go round the corpse accompanied by a throng of assistants. Renew the acceptable sacrifice of My son and prepare a magnificent feast, that the panting soul still restless and weary from the struggles of its ingrained but now cast off mortality may recover its breath and vigour. Let the body, now abandoned by its former inmate, be cherished for a time in the lap of mother earth, be watered by these holy rites, that on the last day, once more happily united with its former companion, it may blossom gaily anew, clad in the brilliant verdure of eternity.'

Such was the opinion of the most faithful and loyal interpreter of the will of God given in almost his very words, concerning the loving care of the Creator for the

---

[1] cf. Rom. 8: 32

hic eius dispensationis in multis conscius et fideles interpres euidenter satis prudentibus innuebat, quonam affectu, quoue respectu, ut tantam sepeliendis curam exhiberet, duceretur.

Generali siquidem inhibitione statuerat ne in uillis ubi ipse presens fuisset, sacerdos parochianus *a* quemlibet defunctum presertim etatis iam adulte traderet sepulture, nisi forte aliquando obstante incommodo, illo id exequi non ualente, de sua hoc ipsum permissione adimpleret. De adultis uero id precipue uolebat obseruari, quia hiis, si laudabiliter uixissent, propensiorem sciebat deferri honorificentiam, sin autem uitam duxissent culpabilem, nouerat eos uberiorem desiderare interuentionis instantiam. Ibat igitur passim ad uniuersos, eis que *b* mos exigit ecclesiasticus, summa cum alacritate exhibens, pauperibus luminaria uel cetera in funeribus desiderata per elemosinarium suum habundanter subministrari procurans.

Si quando, dum iter ageret, funus in quodlibet cimiterium prolatum *c* conspiceret, confestim equo descendebat. Ad feretrum uero accedens et aliquantisper orans, si librum non haberet competentem in quo inoffense legeret, cum iam circa dierum eius extrema aliquid soliti acuminis oculis ipsius deperisset, iunctus presbytero exequias celebranti, psalmos cum eo decantabat, et collectas inchoanti uel complenti Amen uel alia respondendo, uicem clerici, ne dixerimus ydiote adimplebat.[1] Si non defuisset codex ydoneus, ipse quod sacerdotis esset *d* prosequebatur ; orationes pronuntians, aquam benedictam aspergens, thurribulum circumferens, terram superiaciens ac reliqua illius officii sollicite complens. Post que, absolutionem cum benedictione adiungens, iter ceptum peracturus abibat.

dead and these completely convinced his more attentive listeners how great were the love and reverence which led him to devote such care to burials.

He issued a general decree forbidding any parish priest on one of his manors to bury a deceased person, particularly an adult, if he himself were there. If perchance he was prevented from doing so, the priest, with his permission, could perform the ceremony. He wished this to be done especially in the case of adults, for he felt that if they had lived good lives they deserved the highest consideration, and if they were sinners they stood in need of more intense and fervent intercession. He went therefore to everyone without respect of persons, doing for them whatever the rites of the church required, and making his almoner provide generously for the poor the lights and the other objects necessary in funerals.

Whenever he was on his travels and saw a corpse being borne to a cemetery he would immediately dismount and approaching the bier, would pray for a little while. If he had no book from which he could read easily—for at the end of his life his sight was failing—he would join the priest who was conducting the funeral and chant the psalms with him, and when he began or ended the collects, said the Amens and the other responses, thus fulfilling the function of a clerk, or it would be equally true to say of a mere layman.[1] If he had a book he could use he took the priest's part. He said the prayers, sprinkled the holy water, went round the bier with the censer, scattered the earth and devoutly performed all the other ritual acts, and after giving the absolution and blessing, went away to resume his journey.

[1] cf. 1 Cor. 14: 16

Plerumque autem in magnis consistens urbibus, dum ad unumquemque sepeliendum processisset, nuntiabantur ei alii atque alii passim per diuersas ecclesias sepeliendi. Qui magna cum alacritate uniuersos adibat, uniuersis singillatim debitum sepeliendi officium deuote impendens. Nec prius, quotlibet isti fuissent, a tante humanitatis munere destitit,[a] quam nullum superesse qui sepeliretur agnouit.[b] Querebantur nonnumquam et murmurabant petentes quilibet uiri, cum eo pariter commessuri, quia dum hoc diutius ageret, hora prandii iam dudum [c] preteriret. Verum ille numquam, seu ipse hos inuitasset, seu ab eis ille esset ad prandium inuitatus, siue huius rei siue alterius cuiuscumque obtentu negotii, huius omittebat pietatis opus exercere, dum ubi exerceret reperire potuisset.

Set parum est quod hec de minoribus referrimus personis, constat enim quia et a regibus inuitatus ad mensam idem effecerit. Nam et posterius apud Rothomagum a rege Ricardo, et prius olim ab eius genitore Henrico rogatus ad conuescendum,[1] tamdiu distulit ad palatium uenire, quamdiu in urbe repperit quos potuisset sepelire. Vnde regem utrumque cum optimatibus uel tota simul regali familia, in longum compulit ieiunia protelare, dum religiosum officium, nec per aulicos accersitus, contemplatione dignitatis seu uoluntatis humane ullatenus adquieuit omittere.[d] Vrgentibus uero ministris curie ut acceleraret ad regem expectantem et moras egre ferentem quamtocius uenire, ille, nichil festinantius agens, aiebat : ' Non est opus,' inquit, ' ut nos expectet ; uescatur in nomine Domini.' Suis itaque familiaribus dicebat, ' Expedit ut rex terrenus absque nobis prandeat, quam mandatum eterni Regis nostra

---

[a] desistebat X   [b] agnouisset X
[c] diu X   [d] nullatenus . . . amittere o

Often in big towns, when he was burying one person, he was told that there were many others awaiting burial in different churches. He went to them all with the greatest readiness and reverently buried each of them with full rites. However many there were, he never desisted from this work of charity until he had ascertained that there was no one left to bury. Persons of rank who were bidden to his table sometimes murmured because he continued this task long after the hour of dinner. He, however, would never neglect this pious duty because he had guests or was himself a guest, or because of any other business, as long as there was an occasion to perform it.

It is quite unnecessary to mention less important people, for it is well known that he did exactly the same when invited to royal feasts. At Rouen when asked by King Richard to dine with him, and on an earlier occasion when invited by his father King Henry, he delayed going to the palace as long as he found people in the city needing burial,[1] and thus compelled both kings and their magnates and attendants to continue fasting, for in spite of the representations of the courtiers, no consideration for the wishes of any person, however lofty his rank, could induce him not to discharge his priestly office. The royal attendants begged him to hasten as the king was waiting and angry at the delay, but he refused to hurry and replied, ' There is no need to wait for me, let them eat with God's blessing.' He said to his own companions, ' It is better that an earthly king should dine without me than that the command of the King of Heaven should be left undone by his unworthy servant.' It is perhaps a just conclusion that one who

---

[1] cf. Giraldus, *Vita S. Hugonis*, pp. 98-99

humilitas inexpletum pretereat.' Hinc fortassis animad-
uerti licet, diuinitus ei non immerito fuisse retributum,
ut qui duos reges ob pauperum sepulturam neglexerat,
ipse demum in funeris sui obsequium, cum uiris sublimibus multis reges duos adunatos haberet. Verum
hec suo inferius[1] loco plenius dicturi, interim cepta
prosequamur.

CAPITVLVM II

De paupere quodam secus uiam tumulato in Normannia.
De plurimorum sepultura in urbe Lincolnia. Et de
quodam prelato quem sepeliuit in Bermundeseia.

Quoniam hec apud Rothomagum, Normannorum
scilcet metropolim gesta, nec tamen a nobis uisa, set
ueraciter audita retulimus, libet ut in re simili quid in
eadem prouincia ipsi ab eodem actum uiderimus [a]
breuiter absoluamus. Die igitur quadam, iter agente
seruo Dei, contigit eum, non longe a castro quod
Argentum appellatur, tumulum recens sepulti humani,
ut uidebatur, cadaueris circa publicum aggerem cominus
perspexisse. Quo diligentius notato, confestim subsistit ;
mittensque protinus ad ruricolas, eminus aratro humum
proscindentes, didicit cuiusdam homunculi, ostiatim
pridem mendicantis alimoniam, ibidem busta [b] contineri. Defunctus namque idem egenus in pauperis
cuiusdam rus proximum incolentis domo, et a presbytero
illius parochie ob inediam neglectus, eo loco sepulturam
accepit, dum a quo portaretur ad cimiterium non
habuerit.[c] Quo uir piissimus audito altius ingemuit ;
moxque in pedes ab equo descendens, accepto quem fere
semper secum haberet codice, orationes cum psalmis,

[a] acta uidimus o   [b] bustum X
[c] habuit X   [1] c. 19

had neglected two kings to bury the poor was justly rewarded by God, when two kings together and many persons of high rank assisted at his funeral. I shall describe this more fully later when I come to it,[1] and in the meantime shall resume my narrative.

CHAPTER II

Concerning a poor man buried by the wayside in Normandy and many burials in the city of Lincoln. And also a certain prelate whom he buried at Bermondsey.

As I did not see these burials at Rouen the capital of Normandy but have merely set down accurately what I heard about them, it is only right that I should briefly relate a similar act of his in the same duchy which I actually saw. One day when the servant of God was journeying, he happened to see on the public highway not far from the castle of Argentan, a mound which looked like a grave. When he noticed it, he immediately stopped and sending to the rustics who were ploughing a little way off, he heard that it contained the body of a poor man who had formerly begged alms from door to door. The poor wretch had died in the hovel of a peasant who lived in the neighbourhood, and being ignored by the parish priest because of his destitution, had been buried in that spot, for no-one was ready to take him to the cemetery. Hearing this the most charitable of men groaned aloud, and quickly dismounted. He asked for the book which he always had with him, and slowly and devoutly recited the prayers and psalms used in the burial service. Afterwards he urged the bishop of the diocese to administer a sharp

quos recitari usus instituit sepulture, diligenter pro eo ac deuote percurrit. Postea uero episcopo loci attentius orando ^a suggessit quatinus in sacerdotem illum durius animaduerteret, qui homini Christiano propter illius inopiam sepulturam negauerat christianam.

Vidimus alio tempore, cum apud Lincolniam in crastino natalis Domini de glorioso Christi prothomartire Stephano missam deuotissime celebrasset, ut rogaretur a quodam cimentario, qui in fabrica ecclesie desudabat, quatinus fratris sui animam, nocte precedenti rebus humanis exemptam, auctoritate pontificali a peccatis absolueret Dominoque deuotione peculiari commendaret. Quod statim adimplens, inquirere cepit utrum eius adhuc corpusculum humatum fuisset. Quod in remotiori ecclesia necdum sepultum audiens seruari, iussit mox unum sibi, alium suo capellano, tertium famulo qui ante eum equitare consueuerat caballum adduci. Decreuerat enim cum hiis tantum tribus ad funus procedere. Set cum defuisset equus capellano, caballum seruientis eum precepit conscendere, et illum preeundo ad destinatum locum quamtocius properare. Sicque duobus tantum contentus equis, uno solummodo monacho et duobus pueris comitatus,^b peruenit ad corpus defuncti. Quo terre matris gremio paterna sollicitudine commendato, quinque deinceps ipsa die, si nos memoria non fallit, in diuersis successiue cimiteriis sepeliuit funera, per ipsorum sibi amicos designata.

Cum uero iam se hora tardior protraheret, ipseque cum cleri parte non modica ab archidiacono Bedefordensi inuitatus ad epulas solempnes, uenire differret, rogatur a multis et ab ipsis tandem qui ei suum mortuum

---

^a *om* B
^b contentus X

rebuke to the priest who had refused Christian burial to a Christian man, because of his poverty.

I was present on another occasion at Lincoln, on the morrow of Christmas, when after he had most reverently said the mass of the glorious proto-martyr of Christ, Stephen, he was asked by a mason who was working on the fabric of the cathedral to absolve by his episcopal authority the soul of his brother who had died the previous night, and to recommend him to God in his prayers. He immediately did this and then asked whether the body had yet been buried. On learning that it had been taken to one of the more distant churches but was not yet buried, he ordered that one horse should be brought for himself, another for his chaplain and a third for the servant who always rode in front of him, and decided to go with only these three to the body. When no horse was forthcoming for the chaplain he told him to mount the servant's, and to go as quickly as he could in advance of him to the place described. He himself, with only two horses and accompanied by a monk and two pages only, came to the dead body. With fatherly care he commended it to the lap of mother earth and afterwards, if my memory is correct, he buried that day five bodies at the prayer of their friends in different cemeteries one after the other.

It grew late, and he still delayed going to the banquet, to which he and a considerable number of the clergy had been invited by the archdeacon of Bedford. Many persons therefore, including finally even those who had informed him about their dead friend, begged him just to pray for the soul of the deceased and, having given it absolution, commend it to its Creator and not put off any longer going to the guests who had waited for him

annuntiauerant, quatinus pro defuncti anima tantisper orando et absolutionis suffragium porrigendo, eam Creatori commendaret et ad fatigatos pre diutina [a] expectatione conuiuas saltem post moras longissimas uenire ulterius non tardaret. Qui sibi ista suggerentibus non sine cuiusdam reprehensionis asperitate respondit : ' Et quare,' inquiens, ' uocem Domini nostri non attenditis,[b] ore sacro loquentis, " Meus cibus est ut faciam uoluntatem Patris mei qui in celis est ? " ' [1] Nec plura locutus, intermisso sancti Tobie instar prandio, maluit, ut monet Salomon, ad domum luctus quam ad domum ire conuiuii.[2] Iuit igitur, plurimumque ex sanctitatis sue presentia lugentes consolatus, eum sepeliens qui lugebatur, a luctu, ut pie creditur, Christo miserante, orando absoluit.

Quodam iterum tempore, Londonias ad generale colloquium [c] accersitis prelatis et proceribus Anglie, Lincolniensis episcopus eo pariter aduenit. Angebant quoque illum urgentissima ecclesie sue negotia, super quibus necessario erat cum amicis suis qui ad locum confluxerant tractaturus. Contigit uero die proxima, que statutum conuentus illius precessit diem, quemdam ex prelatis qui conuenerant subita preueniri egritudine, quam mox citato uite terminauit fine. De quo a multis ferebatur quia fuisset gule illecebris plusquam satis obnoxius et in potatione superflua nimis assiduus. Cuius decessu audito, licet ei parum notus extitisset, intime nichilominus pietatis uisceribus eidem condoluit et pro eo ad Dominum suppliciter intercessit. Protinus etiam explorari iussit quonam loci uel a quibus personis idem deberet tumulari. Renuntiatur ei quia in ecclesia Domini et Saluatoris nostri apud Beremundeseiam foret

for a long time and were wearied by his long delay. He replied to their representations with some tartness. ' Why', he said, ' will you not heed the words actually spoken by our Lord ? " My meat is to do the will of my Father who is in Heaven ".' [1] He said no more, and like holy Tobias missed his dinner, preferring, as Solomon counsels, to go into the house of mourning and not into the house of feasting.[2] He went therefore, and consoled the mourners greatly by his holy presence, and by burying him whom they mourned, he absolved him by his prayers, as we may trust, from torment through the mercy of Christ.

On another occasion, the bishops and magnates of England had been summoned to a council at London and the bishop of Lincoln attended as well as the others. He was troubled by some very urgent business in connection with his church, which made it necessary for him to consult his friends who had assembled there. It happened that on the next day, the one preceding the meeting of the council, one of the prelates who had come suddenly fell ill, and his illness soon ended fatally. Many ascribed it to his being much addicted to over-eating and excessive drinking. Although Hugh hardly knew him, the news of his death filled his compassionate heart with grief and he prayed earnestly to God for him. He at once ordered inquiries to be made as to who was to bury him and where. He was informed that the burial would take place at the church of our Lord and Saviour at Bermondsey, and that it was believed no bishop or abbot intended to conduct the funeral. None of the prelates who had been his neighbours, associates

---

[1] John 4: 34 ; Mt. 7: 21
[2] cf. Eccles. 7: 3 ; Tob. 2: 1-4

humandus, set nullus episcoporum siue abbatum eius
crederetur exequias celebraturus. Nemo enim uicinorum
aut familiarium seu carorum illi quondam prelatorum
deesse uolebat siue audebat sollempni conuentui qui
die sepulture illius apud Westmonasterium debuit
adunari.[1] Quod episcopus audiens, ' Nolit Deus,' inquit,
' quod talis persona, tot modo in hac pariter urbe con-
sistentibus prelatis, in hac suprema necessitate deseratur
ab omnibus nobis. Non ita faciemus proximo nostro :
nec enim sibi hoc quis fieri uellet ab alio.'[2] Disposito
igitur ut quosdam ex suis mitteret ad curiam, qui et
suam interim ibi excusarent absentiam, mane facto
perrexit ad exhibendam defuncto sepulturam.

Vbi die ipsa si ea que uisu, si que olfactu hausimus,
in medium proferamus, horrorem sane et stuporem
audientibus inferemus. In nos etiam aliquorum forte
indignatio concitabitur, asserentium scilicet quod inhumane cladis humane sortisque moribunde com-
munem erumpnam quam ibi conspeximus, publicis
auribus ingeramus. Ceterum, quia ex hiis suscepte
relationis portio magna dependet, nostramque in hiis
potius deflemus miseriam, quam aliene calamitati, quod
Deus auertat, aliquatenus insultamus, audiatur ad
omnium utilitatem quod dicimus. Sit notum uiuentibus
ad humilitatis prouectum, quod innotuit in defuncto ad
horroris cumulum ; sit quandoque [a] ad uirtutis emulationem, id etiam quod uiuus [b] circa defunctum, cui
propitietur Deus, ad intuentium exhibebat stuporem.

Visum est igitur iacens in feretro cadauer extinctum,
more quidem quorumdam prelatorum uultu nudatum,
set super carbonem denigratum. Erat sane reliquum
corpus alba sacerdotali set et casula indutum, set pre

[a] + extinguendis QX
[b] uiuis Q ; nimis X

and friends either wished or dared to be absent from the great council which was meeting at Westminster on the day of his burial.[1] The bishop hearing this said ' God forbid that a person of such importance, when there are so many bishops in this city, should be deserted in his last extremity by all of us ! We cannot act in this way towards our neighbour, nor would anyone wish this to be done to himself.'[2] He therefore decided to send certain members of his household to court to excuse his absence meanwhile, and set out at dawn to bury the dead man.

If I were to give details about what I saw and smelt on that day, my hearers would be utterly horrified and amazed. Some indeed might even rebuke me for making generally known what I saw, since it was merely the usual condition of the recently dead, and the common fate of the human race. As, however, much of the significance of what I shall relate depends on this, and my purpose in describing it is rather to deplore my own weakness than in any way to exult over the misfortune of another person, which God forbid I should do, my account should be to the general profit of all my audience. The knowledge of the ghastly state of the deceased should be an inducement to humility to those still living, and what the living man to the amazement of all who behold it did for the dead one, on whom God have mercy, should be an incitement to virtue.

We saw the corpse lying in its coffin, with the face uncovered as is usual in the case of bishops, but blacker than coal. The body was clad in the priestly alb and

---

[1] This was Simon, abbot of Pershore, who died at Bermondsey 11 May 1198 ; cf. *Annales Monastici* (R.S.) II, *Winchester Annals*, p. 67
[2] cf. Matt. 7: 12

tumore nimio eisdem uix inclusum. Nam cum adhuc dudum uegetabatur spiritu, ita grossitie uehementiori tumebat ut uix spirare potuisset. Iam uero postquam expirauerat, adeo interna sanies et torride estatis ignea intemperies distendebat exanimem, ut cernentibus prodigiosum uideretur. Verum quod ibi luminibus patebat tolerabile fuisset, si suo nares supplicio carere potuissent. Ceteri, quos feretro interdum approximare ordo poscebat, nares thure immisso aliisue aromatibus sibi precludebant; manibus quoque suaue fragrantia quedam ori sepius apponenda tenebant.ᵃ Solus episcopus, quo tamen nullus inueniretur nare sagacior, nullus tetri nidoris aspernatior, ita, horum tamen nichil admittens que leuare seu arcere solent aeris corruptelam, ita, inquam, iacenti astabat, ita et obambulabat ac si non in feretro set in cunis agentem mater paruulum suum fouendo circuiret. Post hec cum ad suum se contulisset hospitium, quidam ex suis, formidantes ne forte ex inspirato aeris contagio noxium quid precordiis eius insedisset, super hoc illum interrogare ceperunt. Quos ipse reputabat errare, nec quicquam eos insuaue ibidem hausisse, cum ipsemet, quo nullus eorum subtiliori uigebat odoratu, nil triste spirans in loco sensisset. Nimirum Christi ᵇ bonus odor, qui sibi reuera fuit odor uite in uitam, ipsum faciebat mortis putorem penitus non sentire.[1]

Die sequenti cum uenisset ad curiam, graui cepit pulsari calumpnia per comitem Leircestrie qui pagum optimum, eidem urbi contiguum, ipsi nitebatur auferre. Suggerebant etiam episcopo amici et consiliarii eius quatinus cum aduersario sub pacis forma transigeret, proponentes multa cause sue, quamuis satis iuste,

ᵃ apponebant X
ᵇ Proximi nimirum X

chasuble, but these had not been properly put on because it was so much swollen. Even during his lifetime he had been so fat and apoplectic that he could scarcely breathe, and now that he was dead, internal corruption and the fiery heat of an unusually hot summer had caused his corpse to swell so much that it seemed a monstrosity to all who saw it. The sight itself was just tolerable, but the smell was torture. The rest of them when the rites made it necessary to approach the bier from time to time, protected their nostrils by means of incense or other pungent spices, and frequently raised the sweet perfumes they held in their hands to their mouths. Only the bishop, although he had an unusually sensitive nose and a marked objection to unpleasant smells, did nothing either to lessen or remove the stink of corruption, and indeed stood and moved about, not as if by a bier, but like a mother watching over the cradle of a beloved child. Afterwards, when he had returned to his lodging, certain of his attendants, dreading lest he might have taken a serious internal infection from the contagion of the bad air, questioned him about it. He thought they must be mistaken about the horrible smell, as he, whose nose was more acute than theirs had noticed no unpleasant odour in that particular spot. Thus the exceedingly sweet perfume of Christ which was the very fragrance of his life, caused him to be completely unaware of the stink of death.[1]

The next day he went to the law courts for the beginning of a serious plea brought against him by the earl of Leicester, who was trying to get from him a valuable estate near the same city. The bishop's friends and counsellors suggested that he should come to terms

---

[1] cf. 2 Cor. 2: 15-16

admodum formidanda. Qui pertinaciam comitis atque insolentiam nimium aspernatus, omnibus consiliariis suis cum magne assertionis fiducia dixit : ' Sciatis pro certo quia, me in hac luce superstite, iste nullatenus sue intentionis praue sortietur effectum. Habeat sibi ad sue suorumque dampnationis cumulum, guerre quondam tempore extorta uiolenter instrumenta cartarum. Nos enim patrimonium domine nostre tuitioni nostre creditum, ipsa adiuuante, dum aduixerimus integrum retinebimus et in nullo penitus diminutum.' Cuiusmodi assertio plerisque tunc uiris prudentibus minus considerate uidebatur emissa, cum et colorem equitatis preferret actio impotentis, et tam regis quam pene totius curie fauor in comitis crederetur uota concurrere. Preualuit tamen uiri *a* sermo cogitatum suum plenissime iactantis in Domino.[1] De quo etiam illud pluribus mirum uidebatur quia numquam, more celeberrimo fori laicalis ubi lites ille agitabantur, se per internuncium de impossibilitate in iudicio comparendi uoluit excusare, quantocumque urgeretur discrimine ex litigantium improbitate, ne uel speciem mendacii uideretur incurrisse.

Post eius uero decessum comes quidem pagum quem petebat optinuit, set incontinenti lepre contagione percussus, mox corporis ualetudine et in breui post etiam uita carens, absque liberis decessit. Ante cuius obitum cum fratrem ipsius, episcopum uidelicet sancti Andree de Scotia, plurimi conarentur in cathedram uiri Dei, qui iampridem ad Dominum migrarat, subrogare ; uisum est nocte quadam per soporem nobili cuidam religioseque matrone quod cerneret predictum Dei famulum pontificem memoratum ambitionis estu succensum, dum

---

a + Dei X

with his adversary, giving many reasons why his case, although it was a good one, was a dangerous one to fight. He, however, was completely unmoved by the determination and unscrupulousness of the earl, and said with great firmness to his advisers: 'You can rest assured, that, as long as I live, he shall not get away with his wicked schemes, let him keep to his own undoing charters extorted by violence during a former war. Whilst we live we shall retain intact and without any losses, with her assistance the property of our Lady committed to our care.' This assertion seemed then exceedingly rash to very many prudent men, since justice was apparently on the side of the plaintiff and it was generally rumoured that the earl had the support of the king and almost all the justices. The words, however, of the man who put all his trust in God proved true.[1] During the course of the case, to the great amazement of almost everyone he would not, as is the custom in the secular courts, send a proctor with his formal excuses for non-attendance, however great the risk because of the unscrupulousness of his opponents, lest he should incur the least suspicion of not telling the truth.

After Hugh's death the earl did in fact obtain the estate which he had been seeking, but immediately contracted leprosy. His health declined rapidly and he died childless shortly afterwards. Before his death very many persons had tried to obtain for his brother, the bishop of St Andrews in Scotland, the see of the man of God who had some time ago departed to the Lord. One night a certain noble and devout lady had a vision as she slept. She saw God's aforementioned servant strike

---

[1] For the further history of this case cf. K. Major, *Acta Stephani Langton* (C. and Y. Society), pp. xxxviii and 56-58.

suum niteretur conscendere thronum, uirga pastorali durius percussisse sub pectore, ita ut uideretur qui ictum exceperat resupinus in terram coruisse.[1] Facto mane cum illa sompnium suis enarrasset, ecce assunt quidam mortem hominis illius, non sine stupore audientium, palam nuntiantes.[a]

Horum igitur adeo illustrium, adeo floribus huius mundi uernantium, tam abiectus, tam repentinus interitus, quid aliud hec scientibus innuit quam iura ecclesiarum euertere, seruosque Domini iniuste lacessere, supra modum excitiosum esse? Verum hiis pro utilitate legentium breuiter quasi per excessum intersertis, ea que sequuntur serie inconuulsa stilus absoluet.

CAPITVLVM III

De reuelatione cuidam clerico insinuata, qui in forma pueri misterii salutaris hostiam in manibus episcopi uidit.

Die quadam consistente episcopo in manerio iuris sui quod Bugdena [b] nuncupatur,[2] uenerunt ad illum quidam monachi, presentantes ei ad benedicendum uestes sacerdotales et calicem unum ualde speciosum.[c] Episcopus tunc a sepultura cuiusdam seruientis Laurentii Bedefordensis archidiaconi in ecclesiam uenerat, sacra missarum sollempnia celebraturus. Erat uero sabbatum; quo semper die si uacaret [d] de beata Dei genetrice Maria tam diurnum quam nocturnum officium solebat celebrare. Ad eum quoque sub die illo plures undique

---

[a] nuntiauit X   [b] Bukkedena Q   [c] pretiosum X   [d] uacabat X
[1] A dream about a bishop using his crozier as an offensive weapon is related in *Vita S. Eatae, Miscellanea Biographica* (Surtees Society), p. 125 ; cf. also W. Stubbs, *Memorials of St Dunstan* (R.S.) pp. 30, 57 and Matthew Paris, *Chronica Majora* (R.S.), V, pp. 429 and 470-471.

the above-mentioned bishop, who, kindled by over-whelming ambition was trying to ascend his throne, on the breast with his pastoral staff, so violently that as a result of the blow he fell flat on the ground.[1] Next morning she had just related her dream when, much to the astonishment of her audience, the news was brought of this bishop's death.

Should not the knowledge of the sudden and humiliating deaths of such illustrious men in the very spring-time of their worldly prosperity, bring home to people the grave peril of violating the rights of the Church, and doing grievous wrong to the Lord's servants? Having made this brief digression for the reader's benefit, my pen will now continue to the end without further deviations.

CHAPTER III

Concerning a revelation made to a certain clerk, and how he saw the host, which is the symbol of our salvation, in the shape of a child when the bishop consecrated it.

Once when the bishop was at his manor at Buckden [2] some monks came to him, bringing priestly vestments and a magnificent chalice for him to consecrate. He had just come from the burial of a servant of Laurence, arch-deacon of Bedford and was about to celebrate a solemn high mass. It was a Saturday, the day on which when-ever he could he always recited the day and night offices

---

[2] Part of St Hugh's manor at Buckden still survives. The following episode took place in 1194, the clerk concerned was Adam's own brother Edmund, who as a monk of Eynsham saw in 1196 a very famous vision of the next world, for which see Introduction, vol. I, p. ix.

confluxerant clerici, ecclesiasticis redditibus admodum ditati. Illis ergo in ecclesia iam presentibus, episcopus calicem superius memoratum in manibus, ut eum consecraret, tenebat nudatum. Quem cernens metallo, amplitudine et artificio satis conspicuum, ipsum ab altari in chorum detulit, omnibusque clericis prefatis eum exhibens considerandum, deuotam uirorum religiosorum circa diuini misterii et cultum *a* et uasa collaudabat sollertiam ; illis e contrario improperans *b* quod, multis ecclesiarum redditibus opulenti, ipsas nec libris nec uasis set nec aliis rebus necessariis conuenienter excolerent, set hiis omnibus egenas Christi basilicas spoliare potius quam ornare satagerent. Post hec, ingressus ad altare, missam deuotissime orsus est celebrare. Cumque ceteris iam rite peractis, ad eum peruenisset locum ubi eleuatam in altum hostiam benedicere moris est, mox in uerum *c* Christi corpus mistica sanctificatione conuertendam, cuiusdam clerici oculos superna clementia dignata est aperire ; eique sub specie infantis paruuli Christum suum demonstrauit mundissimis digitis sacri presulis reuerentissime contrectari. Erat uero idem puer forma quidem permodicus set diuino quodam nitore atque candore super estimationem hominis nimium decorus. Clericus qui hec uiderat mira deuotione, nec mirum, succensus plurimumque compunctus, tempus omne continuabat in lacrimis quod intercessit ab illa eleuatione usquequo interim *d* eam leuari cerneret, frangendam iam et sumendam sub trina sui partitione. In qua rursum eleuatione sub eadem qua *e* prius ymagine natum intuetur de uirgine Filium Altissimi, seipsum offerentem pro humana salute.

a ministerii cultum Xp   *b* improperabat X
c om B
d iterum uel interim ov ; iterum p
e om B

of Mary, the blessed mother of God. On that particular day, many clerks well endowed with ecclesiastical preferment, had come to him from different regions, and when they were in the church, the bishop was holding the chalice which I have already mentioned uncovered, as he was about to consecrate it. Perceiving its unusual size and the costliness of the material and workmanship, he brought it from the altar into the choir and displayed it to them for their examination, praising the zeal of the monks for the liturgy and the sacred vessels used in the blessed sacrament; rebuking at the same time those who, although enriched by the Church's revenues, did not endow their churches with books, vessels and other necessities, but tried rather to despoil than to adorn the poor churches of Christ with all these things. After this, he went to the altar and began with great devotion to celebrate mass. When in the course of the service he had reached the place where it is customary to consecrate the host, which has already been raised to be turned by the words of consecration into the body of Christ, God in His mercy deigned to open the eyes of a certain clerk and showed him Christ in the likeness of a small child in the chaste hands of the venerable and holy bishop. Although very tiny, the child was very lovely and of a supernatural brilliance and whiteness beyond man's imagination. The clerk who saw this not unnaturally felt great devotion and compassion, and wept continuously from the time of the elevation until he saw it elevated once more to be broken into three portions and partaken of. In the second elevation he saw the Son of the Most High, born of a virgin, in the same form as before, offer himself for the redemption of mankind.

Post hec, iam expletis omnibus que in ecclesia fuerant peragenda, clericus qui [a] ista conspexerat, accedens ad uerum Domini sacerdotem, taliter ei secretius est locutus, 'Domine pater, uobis,' inquit, 'habeo aliqua referre, que uestram, si placet, sanctitatem diligentius oporteat audire.' Cumque flexis genibus ista coram eo esset prosecutus, uir Domini cum eo secedens a turba seorsum [b] secus altare resedit, eique proferre que uoluisset leniter imperauit. Tum ille, 'In crastino,' inquit, 'festiuitatis Omnium Sanctorum, que hac ipsa septimana celebrata est, cum psalterium in quadam ecclesia decantarem pro animabus fidelium defunctorum, sicut ipsa die sollempnis exhiberi earum memoria solet, uox quedam subito auribus meis illapsa est que uerbis absolutissimis diceret, " surge," inquiens, " fili, et perge cito ad Lincolniensem episcopum, dicesque ei ex parte Dei quatinus moneat diligentius Cantuariensem Archiepiscopum, ut pariter secum solito uigilantius intendat ad corrigendum statum cleri et ecclesiarum. Nimis enim offenditur diuina maiestas per ea que indesinenter fiunt a rectoribus ecclesiarum et earum ministris. Sacerdotes enim et aliorum graduum persone omnimodo uitiorum genere, maxime autem luxurie sordibus fedati sacramentis diuinis ex indigno accessu iniuriosi existentes, ea irreuerenter sumendo atque tractando, quantum in se est polluere non uerentur. Ipse ecclesie indignis et Deo ob perditos mores inuisis passim ad regendum traduntur personis, a quibus sepe, more secularium prediorum, aliis atque aliis relinquuntur ad firmam, quod emphitosim alii nuncupant, utque uiles taberne sic ecclesie turpis lucri gratia sub annuo censu locantur ad questum. Hiis [c] de cura animarum, de indigentibus sustentandis

[a] + iam X   [b] deorsum B
[c] + personis X

After this, when the service had finished in the church, the clerk who had seen this thing approached the faithful priest of God and spoke with him apart. ' My lord and father,' he said, ' I have something to relate to you, to which, by your favour, your reverence should listen carefully.' When kneeling before him he had got thus far, the man of God took him away from the people and, seating himself near the altar, gently asked him what he wished to say. He answered, ' On the morrow of the feast of All Saints which was celebrated this week, I was in a church repeating the psalter for the souls of the faithful departed, since it is the custom on that day to make a solemn commemoration of them. Suddenly I heard a voice saying very distinctly the words, " Arise my son, and go quickly to the bishop of Lincoln, and tell him from God to admonish earnestly the archbishop of Canterbury that with his assistance he should devote himself more zealously than hitherto to the reform of the Church and the clergy. The daily acts of the rectors of churches and their assistants have deeply offended the divine Majesty. Priests and those in minor orders, although polluted by every sort of sin but particularly lechery, approach the holy sacraments unworthily and do not hesitate to profane them by handling and partaking of them irreverently. Everywhere churches are given to persons unfitted to rule them, whose depravity makes them hateful to God. These, moreover, often farm their churches to others and they in their turn to others, whilst others lease them just as if they were secular possessions. Thus the churches are let to make money for an annual rent to the highest bidder in the same way as taverns or shops. They never think of the cure of souls or of using the revenues of the church to assist the needy, but all the time greedily strive to stuff

ex fructibus ecclesie nullus est sermo ; set farciendis
crumenis quas uel luxus euacuet uel auaritia solummodo
erugini contingendas includat, tota indesinenter
auiditate inhiare non cessant. Hec et similia rectorum
uitia, in regendos contagiosa emulatione transfusa,
omnium fere tam minorum quam maiorum precordiis
dominantur. Hinc grandis furor et ira Dei imminet tam
populo quam uniuersis pariter inhabitatoribus terre
huius. Hiis [a] festinum inferetur exitium genti huic
misere, si non anticipet accelerata correctio iamiam
impendens [b] flagellum celestis uindicte."

' Hiis dictis, que uox audiebatur siluit. Ego siquidem
priusquam hec audirem, psalterio iam excurso usque
ad centesimum primum psalmum, flexis genibus coram
altari sancte Dei genitricis in orationem animum
uehementer intenderam. Oborta namque in mente mea
repente fuit memoria patris mei, ante non multos annos
in terra Ierosolimitana, quo religionis studio perrexerat,
defuncti ; indeque tantus subito compunctionis feruor
spiritum meum absorbuit, ut omissa penitus psalmodia
omnique strepitu labiorum suppresso, undatim ruentibus
ex oculis riuis lacrimarum, precordialibus tantum uotis
Domino [c] preces effunderem. Audita igitur hac uoce
que a proximo altari uidebatur emissa, uim compunctionis que me sibi totum uendicauerat, horror quidam
stupore mixtus confestim intercidit ; cepique mecum
attonitus mirari quis cui talia esset prosequendo locutus.
Sciebam enim neminem preter me cominus circa locum
ipsum constitisse. Igitur cum post longa pauide
cogitationis uolumina uocis auctorem nequiuissem ullatenus [d] deprehendere, consignans meipsum signo salutari,
intermisse orationis studium uehementiori quam prius

---

[a] Hinc X   [b] correptio . . . imminens X
[c] + uocis B   [d] nullatenus X

their money-bags, either to be dissipated by luxury or to be kept locked by avarice till rust eats them away. The bad example of these rectors has contaminated and corrupted their flocks. Almost all hearts from the least to the greatest are a prey to the same sins. God's fury and indignation will speedily fall on all the inhabitants of this land, and immediate disaster threaten this unhappy people, if correction does not at once anticipate the scourge of the divine vengeance now about to smite."

' After these words, the voice which I had heard was silent. Before I heard it, I had reached the hundred and first psalm, and had been kneeling before the altar of the holy mother of God praying heartily and with complete absorption. I suddenly remembered my father who had died a few years ago when on pilgrimage to Jerusalem and the greatness of the sorrow which filled my heart, made me stop my recitation of the psalter, and a flood of tears pouring from my eyes, I prayed to the Lord in silence, with prayers that came only from the heart. After I had heard the voice which seemed to come from the nearest altar, the grief which had mastered me gave place to horror and wonder, and in amazement I asked myself who had spoken these words and to whom, for I knew that I was alone in the church. Therefore, when after long and frightened deliberations I could find no explanation for the voice, I made the sign of the cross and resumed my interrupted prayers more earnestly than before. Almost immediately I heard the same voice saying exactly the same as before, word for word. Then I, since I could not find who was speaking, or the person he was addressing, decided that I had better go away, for I believed only that some sacred mystery was being enacted there by certain invisible

desiderio repetere cepi. Nec mora, et ecce iterum audio
uocem eodem sono eisdemque sillabis, eamdem quam
prius exprimere sententiam. Tunc ego, cum nec
loquentis personam nec illius cui sermo fiebat potuissem
aduertere, cedendum loco existimaui ; id tantum mecum
reputans quia aliquid sacratioris *a* misterii ibidem
agitaretur ab aliquibus quorum ego indignus existerem
archanis interesse. Adorato itaque Domino, signans
michi frontem a loco discessi.

   ' Cumque peruenissem ad ualuas ecclesie, occurrit
michi uirgo quedam religiosa ualde, que Domino in
ieiuniis et orationibus, in frigore et nuditate, die noctuque
deseruiens, ab ecclesia eadem rarissime, ab eius uero
atriis numquam pene recedebat. Hec cum predicta
audirentur, in remoto ecclesie angulo solitis uacauerat
orationibus. Que genibus meis aduoluta, rogabat
instantius quatinus, si fieri posset, aliqua sibi ex hiis que
interius ut asserebat michi dicta cognouerat, communi-
care studuissem.*b* Set qui nescius eram adhuc cui iam
dicta essent ea que audieram, illam uice uersa potius
duxi exorandam, ut ipsa que dignior me esset audire et
nosse interna misteria, reuelare dignaretur michi quod
de uocis celitus, ut ipsa fatebatur, emisse sententia ego
minime aduertissem. Ad hec illa : " Scio equidem bis
factum sermonem a Domino tibi, aliqua precipientem
que ego quidem minus aduerti, set quia tibi pre-
ciperetur certo certius intellexi." Tum *c* ego : " Ora,
inquam, soror in Christo dilecta, quatinus circa nos
beneplacitum suum Dominus adimplere dignetur. Super
talibus uero que modo prosequeris, ego certitudinem
nullam percepi." *d* Hiis a me dictis, ecclesiam ipse
egredior ; illa ad consueta orationum suarum latibula

---

a secretioris X   *b* studerem X
c cui X   *d* accepi X

beings, and that I was unworthy to be present at such mysteries. I genuflected out of reverence for the Lord, and making the sign of the cross on my forehead, left the place.

' At the door of the church I met a certain pious virgin, who served God day and night by prayer and fasting, and in cold and nakedness, and rarely left the church, being almost always in its precincts. When I heard the voice she had been praying as was her custom in a remote corner of the church. She fell at my feet and besought me earnestly to tell her if I could some of the things, which she declared she knew in her heart had been imparted to me. As I did not yet know for whom the things I had heard had been intended, I in my turn begged her, as one more worthy than myself to hear and understand divine revelations, that she would deign to interpret for me the meaning of the heavenly message, as she called it, since it completely baffled me.

' She replied " I know that God has twice spoken to you, commanding you to do something, but what I do not know, although absolutely certain that a command was given to you." I answered : " Dear sister in Christ, pray that God will deign to fulfil his will concerning me, for I am completely in the dark about the things you have mentioned." After I had said this, I left the church and she returned to her usual corner to pray. I then entered the bedroom of my lodging and spent the rest of the day until evening in prayer and fasting.

introrsum regreditur. Post hec, cubiculum ospitii mei ingressus, ibidem usque ad uesperam diem in orationibus ieiunus *a* exegi.

'Qui tandem lectulo exceptus, dum uariis estuaret animus horum *b* que premisi cogitationum fluctibus, uocem repente audiui, idipsum iam tertio quod primo et secundo intulerat replicantem ; hac tamen premissa insinuatione unde michi constaret quod ad me sermonem haberet. Ait namque, " Tibi dico, fili qui presens quiescis ; perge quam celerrime ad uirum uenerabilem episcopum Lincolniensem, eique ex parte Dei omnipotentis hec omnia que tibi in ecclesia iam secundo precepi nuntiare non differas." Cui statim ita respondi, " Et quomodo uir tante auctoritatis fidem habebit uerbis meis, cum ego et etate et ratione infirmior uix quicquam ei loqui sciam ? " Tunc is qui loquebatur ad hec respondens, ista *c* subiecit, " Fidem uerbis *d* tuis indubitatam idem uir habebit, cum ei pro intersignis ea insinuaueris que super altare coram eo uidebis, qua primum die ad illum perueniens ipsum sollempnia missarum celebrantem intueberis. Ne igitur differas parere eloquiis meis, set que tibi precipio deuotus exequere." Hiis dictis uox loquentis ablata est.

'Ego ad exequendum imperata plurimum animatus, modico prelibato sompno, de *e* nocte surrexi, clamque sociis meis iter ad uos inquirendum ita pedibus meis assumpsi. Huc autem ante introitum misse paulo ante ueni ; celebrantem diuina sanctitatem uestram deuotus obseruaui, intendens quoque sollicitius ad mensam dominicam coram uobis ; et in manibus uestris corpus Domini nostri Ihesu Christi, sub specie infantis paruuli bis supra calicem a uobis eleuatum, indignis licet oculis

---

a et ieiuniis B²   *b* + gratia QX   *c* ita X
d dictis X   *e* die B

'Finally, I went to bed, my mind being greatly troubled with the conflicting thoughts which I have described. Suddenly I heard the voice repeating for a third time what it had said on the first and second occasions, but now with an opening which convinced me that I was the person it was addressing. It said, " I command you my son, to get up and go as quickly as you can to the venerable bishop of Lincoln. Do not delay to inform him from almighty God of everything that I have twice commanded you in the church to tell him." I immediately replied : " How can a man of such importance believe me, who am so young and simple that I scarcely know what to say to him ? " My interlocutor then answered me in these words. " He will have complete faith in what you say, if you tell him as a proof what you will see on the altar when he is there on the first day of your visit, as you watch him celebrating a solemn mass. Therefore do not hesitate any longer to obey my instructions, but do exactly what I have commanded." After these words the voice ceased to speak.

' Being now very eager to obey my instructions, after a short sleep, I got up although it was still night, and without the knowledge of my companions I set out to seek you on foot. I arrived here a little before the introit of the mass and watched you intently whilst you celebrated. My attention was fixed on the table of the Lord in front of you, and my sinful eyes saw clearly twice in your hands the body of our lord Jesus Christ in the likeness of a tiny child on the chalice as you elevated it. Doubtless you yourself saw this much more clearly and for a longer space of time since you were nearer and much more worthy.'

euidenter conspexi. Quia uero idipsum et uos multo perspicacius, quia et diutius et uicinius et satis dignius perspexistis, non est ambigendum.'

Hec clericus ille fluentibus per genas lacrimis est prosecutus. Vir quoque Domini ubertim inter hec flebat. Cumque pariter aliquamdiu flentes, super hiis uerba plurima conseruissent, episcopus utriusque oculos et genas, suos uidelicet et clerici illius, sacris extergens digitis, osculatus est eum. Erat *a* idem clericus annorum circiter uiginti quinque. Precepit itaque ei quatinus hec reuerenter celare meminisset.*b* Preterea diligentius eum hortari studuit ut religionis habitum suscipere et religiosis moribus Domino seruire ex integro maturaret. Asserebat enim non esse conueniens ut qui talia uidisset et audisset in seculi uanitate ulterius spatiari uellet. Qui statim hiis se libentissime monitis pariturum respondit.

Post hec aulam iam pransurus ingreditur episcopus. Plurima igitur constipatus conuiuantium turba, hylaris et letus discubuit, clericum totiens memoratum in area non longe a loco sessionis sue precipiens simul recumbere. Qui die postera ab eodem cum benedictione dimissus et ad quemdam sibi familiarem monachum transmissus, monachus et ipse cito postea effectus religiose admodum conuersatus est.

Cui plurima quoque spiritualium uisionum misteria postmodum fuisse reuelata certissime experti sumus. Ex quibus non pauca, litteris dudum de mandato sancti presulis tradita, longe lateque uulgata noscuntur. A cuius ore hec ipsa que modo retulimus frequenter audiuimus. Cui inter alia id quoque reuelatum fuisse ab ipso accepimus, quia sanctam ciuitatem Hierusalem

---

a + autem QX
b celare meminisset celaret X

During the course of the clerk's narrative the tears were pouring down his cheeks, and as he spoke the holy bishop also wept abundantly. When they had wept together for a little while, and had conversed for a much longer space of time about the matter, the bishop with his own holy fingers wiped his and the clerk's eyes and face and then kissed him. The clerk was about twenty-five years old. The bishop charged him to take care out of reverence to conceal his vision, and moreover counselled him to take the monastic habit and to dedicate himself as a monk entirely to the service of God. He told him that it was not right for one who had heard and seen what he had to remain any longer in the world. He replied that he was very ready to take his advice.

After this the bishop entered the hall for dinner. Having an immense crowd of guests, he sat down with a cheerful and happy face, and ordered the clerk I have already mentioned so often to take a seat not far from his own. The next day he sent him away with his blessing to a certain monk with whom he was on friendly terms. Shortly afterwards this clerk became a monk and lived an exemplary religious life.

I know for certain that many other spiritual mysteries were subsequently revealed to him in visions. A few of these were written down by the order of our holy bishop, and were very widely known. What I have just related I have very often heard from his own mouth. One particular revelation among the rest which he imparted to me was that the holy city, which was captured recently

que pridem nostris temporibus a Saracenis occupata est, nostris quoque diebus miraculose ab eorum instantia omnipotentissima Redemptoris nostri eripiet clementia. Quod eo magis, fauente eiusdem Domini nostri pietate, confidimus adimplendum, quo iam plurima uidemus impleta que implenda adhuc ei didicimus *a* similiter preostensa. Set de hiis hoc interim dixisse sufficiat.

Capitvlvm IV

De eodem sacramento aliud stupendum satis mira- culum quod in Francia contigit. Et sententia memorabilis quam Hugo noster inde protulerit.

De uiuifico autem sacrosancte eukaristie sacramento adhuc referre quiddam non uidetur incongruum, quod in Galliis accidisse multis est manifestum. Quod licet cunctorum notitia fidelium estimemus *b* dignissimum, presenti tamen historie id a nobis minime fuisset insertum si non ad hoc *c* inserendum illius nos urgeret sententia, de re ipsa mirabiliter prolata, qui horum omnium que pagine huic inseruntur materia est et causa.

Hic igitur quodam tempore a Parisiensium digressus ciuitate, dum Trecas peteret, metatione prima hospitatus est in uilla quadam Ioi nuncupata.[1] Moris uero illi *d* fuit ubicumque hospitio sese excepisset, presbiterum cum ecclesie illius ministris *e* ad suam inuitare mensam ; uerbo frequenter utens cum liberali quodam iocunditate ad suum dapiferum, quo sepe olim usus est Dominus ad Hebreorum populum, ' Non deseras,' inquiens,

---

a + fuisse X
b existimemus X
c adhuc X
d illius X
e +suis X

in our own day by the Saracens, would be miraculously recovered from them also in our lifetime, through the mercy of our Saviour.   I am completely convinced that this will take place in God's good time, for I have seen many things come to pass which he told me it had been revealed to him would happen.   I have, however, said enough about these matters.

CHAPTER IV

Concerning another wonderful miracle which happened in France in connection with the same sacrament, and our Hugh's memorable words on this occasion.

It seems to me not amiss to describe here a miracle well known to many people, which happened in France in connection with the most holy and life-giving sacrament of the Eucharist.   Although I consider this wonder eminently suitable to be brought to the notice of all the faithful, I should not in any circumstances have inserted it here, if it had not been for the words spoken by the hero and subject of this biography on that occasion. Once when he had left Paris and was on his way to Troyes, he stopped for the night half-way, at the village of Joi.[1]   Wherever he stayed he made a practice of inviting the parish priest and his assistants to dinner, frequently saying jestingly to his steward, the words often formerly spoken by the Lord to the Hebrew people, ' Do not neglect the Levites within the gates of thy

---

[1] This episode probably belongs to Hugh's journey from Paris to Troyes in June 1200 ; cf. *infra*, pp. 156-7.

'Leuitas qui intra portas ciuitatis tue sunt.'[1] Illius itaque loci presbiter, a ministris more solito uocatus ad mensam episcopi, uenire obstinatius recusauit. Venit autem post prandium inuisere eum : uenit quoque non solum ut episcopo celeberrime opinionis salutationis obsequium exhiberet, set potius ut eius orationibus sese Domino commendari optineret. Venit etiam ut ei rem ualde stupendam que sibi dudum contigerat, de adorando corporis Dominici sacramento, et uerbis exponeret et ad uidendum ipsam rem, sub oculis adhuc in ecclesia sua positam, eum inuitaret. Erat enim idem sacerdos iam grandeuus et aspectu reuuerendus, corpore etiam toto, non tam pre etate quam pre abstinentie ut dicebatur rigore premarcidus, et cute ossibus insidente peraridus. Qui postquam salutauit episcopum, non potuit pre uerecundia quod optauit illi declarare per seipsum, set quibusdam ex suis hec seriatim exposuit in hunc modum.

'Cum essem iuuenis,' inquit, 'et gradum sacerdotii, nec annis adhuc nec moribus meis tanto apici digne respondentibus, conscendissem, contigit, insidiante hoste antiquo, ut crimen quoddam mortiferum incurrissem. A cuius necdum contagio aut remedio penitentie aut confessionis lauacro mundatus, ita ut eram et corde pollutus et corpore, mente insuper cecus et fide infirmus, quod dictu horrendum est, ad sacri altaris ministerium impudens et temerarius accedere consueui. Cumque die quadam sacris misse assisterem secretis, et criminis mei enormitatem in ipsa hostie salutaris consecratione, mente reuoluerem tacita, inter alias tenebrosi pectoris cogitationes hec mecum uersabantur in corde ; putasne illius corpus et sanguis hic a me sordidissimo peccatore ueraciter conficitur, tractatur et sumitur, qui candor esse describitur lucis eterne et speculum sine macula ?[2] Dum hec et alia hiis non minus stolida uersarem in

city.'[1] The parish priest, however, when asked in the usual manner by his attendants to the bishop's table, firmly refused the invitation. He came to visit him after supper, not so much to pay his homage to a celebrated bishop, as to obtain his prayers to God on his own behalf. His purpose was also to tell him of a miracle in connection with the most venerable sacrament of the Lord's body, which had happened to himself some time ago, and to invite him to see with his own eyes this wonder now exposed in his church. This priest was a very old and venerable-looking man, whose whole body was terribly thin, not from age but from fasting. In fact, the skin was tightly stretched over the protruding bones. After he had greeted the bishop, shame prevented him from making known to him what he wished, so he related it to certain of his retinue in these words.

' When I was a young man, I was raised to the priesthood, having neither the years nor the morals for so high an office, and it chanced that, tempted by the enemy of mankind, I committed a mortal sin. Although I had not yet cleansed or washed away the stain by penance and confession, and was polluted physically and spiritually as well as darkened in mind and weak in faith, horrible to relate, I used shamelessly and irreverently to celebrate mass. One day when I was assisting at this holy sacrament at the moment of consecration I was pondering over my terrible sin, and amongst the other thoughts which passed through my darkened mind and heart was : " Do you think that his body and blood is really consecrated, touched and partaken of by a wretched sinner like yourself, since it has the brilliance of eternal light or a spotless mirror ? "[2] Whilst these

---

[1] Deut. 14: 27
[2] cf. Wis. 7: 26

animo, peruentum est ad hoc ut frangenda esset
trifaria *a* more debito hostia sacrosancta. Quam ut per
medium fregi, mox cruor liquidissimus per fracturam
effluere cepit, qui mediam hostie partem quam manu
tenebam in carnis speciem subito conuersam rubore
sanguineo infecit. Quibus ego uisis pre timore totus
dirigui ; et pene exsensis effectus, perdito rationis
consilio, quicquid de ipsis sacramentis in manibus
tenebam in sacrum calicem decidere permisi. Erat tunc
ibi uidere quod usque in presens cernitur, seculis
omnibus stupendum miraculum ; uinum scilicet in
sanguinem et panem in carnem media sui partem
conuersam, rem pariter sacramenti et formam, significans
scilicet et significatum, sub gemina specie manifestissime
preferre. Que ut uidi has species inconuersibiliter
retinere, ea penitus non presumens, calicem patena,
patenam sacra palla cooperui,*b* misse officium per-
cantaui. Hinc populo dimisso, calicem cum sacrisque
in eo adhuc hodie continentur, loco congruo secus altare
reposui, debita reuerentia custodiendum. Post hec,
summi pontificis adiui presentiam ; rei huius seriem,
premissa confessione reatus mei, exposui ; absolutionis
beneficium, iniuncta michi satisfactione competenti, ab
ipso reportaui. Ad hec uero magnalia Dei presentialiter
contuenda, a multis huc per circuitum locis passim a
fidelibus concurritur, a quibus cum summa reuerentia
magnificatur Dominus qui facit mirabilia solus.[1]

' Hec sancto episcopo isti uobis cupio mediantibus
intimari, quo et illius merear ego orationibus apud
Dominum adiuuari, et ipse cum suis sociis in Domino
ualeat cum ista perspexerit amplius iocundari.'

---

a tripharie X
b + et Xp

and other equally evil thoughts were passing through my mind, the point was reached when according to the rite the most holy host must be broken into three. As I broke it, immediately blood began to flow copiously through the break, and the middle part of the host which I held in my hand suddenly took on the appearance of flesh and became blood-red. Seeing this I went rigid with fear, and almost fainted and, losing the use of my reason, I allowed the part of the sacrament which I was holding in my hands to drop into the chalice. Then could be seen there what can still be seen, an amazing miracle for all time, for the wine changed into blood and the half host into flesh ; the substance and form of the sacrament, the symbol and the reality, were clearly visible under both species. When I saw that these species remained unchanged, I did not dare partake of them but covered the chalice with the paten, and the paten with the corporal and went on chanting the mass. Then, having dismissed the people, I placed the chalice with the sacred elements which are still there today, in a suitable place behind the altar where they could be reverently preserved. After this I went to the pope, and having confessed my sin I told him everything, and when he had imposed on me a fitting penance, he gave me absolution. Large numbers of the faithful from the districts round come eagerly to see with their own eyes this wonderful work of God, and to praise and honour the Lord who alone worketh marvels.[1]

' I beg you on my behalf to relate these things to the holy bishop, so that he will deign to intercede with the Lord for me, and that he and his company may rejoice the more abundantly in the Lord, having witnessed these wonders.'

[1] cf. Ps. 71: 18

Hec igitur referentes episcopo quibus innotuerant a [a] presbitero, sperabant illum, non sine auida cordis deuotione, ad ea mox uidenda processurum. Verum ille ad audita confestim ita respondit, ' Bene,' inquit ' in nomine Domini habeant sibi signa infidelitatis sue. Quid ad nos de hiis ? Num miramur particulares ymagines huius diuini muneris, qui totum et integrum hoc celeste sacrificium cotidie intuemur fidelissimo aspectu mentis ? Intueatur illius exiguas portiunculas uisu corporeo, qui totum non intuetur fidei conspectu interno.' Hec dicens, commendantem se orationibus eius presbiterum, data benedictione abire permisit. Suorum uero curiositatem redarguens, in fidei soliditate ipsos non solum roborauit ; immo certius ea que fides prescribit quam ea que lux ista uisibilis ostendit, teneri debere a fidelibus et intelligi loculentissime declarauit. Sic itaque a proposito curiose uisionis illos cohercuit, et ad excitandum deuotionis aspectum pariter et amplexum, ad hec uera et uiuifica cordium alimenta mentes audientium erudiuit.

Ex premissis uero, necnon et ex aliis eius uerbis certius nobis persuasum tenemus, quia non semel tantum, ut supra ostensum est, immo etiam frequenter illi concessum sit, reuelata hominis interioris facie, illa singulariter de hoc sacramento uisu quodam intimo perspicere, que nobis inuisibilia docemur omnes pariter fide purissima credendo retinere.

CAPITVLVM V

De simultate Archiepiscopi contra episcopum propter frequentes quas ei faciebat exhortationes. De sollici-tudine episcopi in corrigendis moribus clericorum

[a] auctore X

Those who related the priest's tale to the bishop, expected that he would with eager devotion immediately set out to see the miracle. He, however, after he had heard them at once answered : ' It is well in God's name for him to keep for himself the proofs of his lack of faith. It is not our concern. Why should we gape at a sensory image of this divine gift, when every day we behold by faith this heavenly sacrifice, whole and entire ? Let that man look with his bodily eyes on the minute fragment, who cannot by faith internally behold the whole.' Having said this he gave the priest who had commended himself to his prayers his blessing and permitted him to depart. By rebuking the curiosity of his attendants, he did not merely strengthen their faith but showed them in a very impressive way that the truths of the faith should be accepted and believed by the faithful with greater assurance than what they saw by the light of common day. Thus he restrained their idle curiosity and by directing their devotion to inner sight and touch, he instructed his listeners about the true and living food of their souls.

From this and other sayings of his I am convinced that not once only as I have already shown, but several times he was permitted to see with the eye of the mind the inner mystery of the holy sacrament, which we are all taught to hold by believing it on faith although it is invisible.

CHAPTER V

Concerning the anger of the archbishop against the bishop because of his frequent rebukes, and concerning the bishop's earnestness in reforming the morals of the

diocesis sue. De cautela eiusdem in prebendarum collatione. Et de contradictione sua in concilio Oxonefordensi aduersus indebitam regis exactionem. Et de furore Ricardi regis contra eum et contra Saresberiensem episcopum subinde excitato. Et qualiter osculum ei rex, primo inuitus, post etiam sponte optulerit.

Set cum solito crebrius metropolitanum suum, solitoque instantius uir Dei, post factam sibi diuinitus ammonitionem, hortatur *a* quatinus omissis parumper quibus indefessus adherebat curis secularibus, studio potius indulgeret pontificalis officii quam reipublice administrationi, animum eius ad grauem contra se excitauit simultatem.

Sue uero iurisdictioni subditos tam clericos quam presbiteros ipse totis uiribus, per seipsum et per officiales suos, ad uite rectioris tramitem et discipline clericalis honestatem reuocauit. Nichil enim de paterna sollicitudine omittens, languidis sibi commissorum moribus infundebat uinum et oleum ; [1] ut seueritas coherceret districtionis quos curare non potuit lenitas pietatis. Quantum uero sudauerit quantumue profecerit ad correctionem subditorum in hac gemina ecclesiastice dispensationis exhibitione, non est facultatis nostre prout dignum esset exponere, cum hec etiam peritissimorum *b* ingenia uix multis sufficerent uoluminum prolixitatibus enodare.

Ecclesias quoque diocesis sue in omnibus pro posse suo ad statum curauit debitum erigere. Admittebat sedulo ad earum regimen uiros scientia et uita commendabiles ; hiis uero destitutos ab earum ingressu pro uiribus repellebat. In qua nimirum intentione quanto

---

a hortabatur o, hortaretur X
b perfectissimorum B

clergy of his diocese. His conscientiousness when collating to prebends and his opposition at the Council of Oxford to an unjust royal demand, through which he and the bishop of Salisbury incurred the anger of King Richard. How the king kissed him at first unwillingly, but later of his own accord.

After the divine message he had been given, the man of God urged his metropolitan more frequently and more earnestly than had been his custom to abandon for a season the business of state in which he was immersed, and devote himself more to his archiepiscopal duties than to the administration of the kingdom. This, however, merely made him the archbishop's bitter enemy.

His unflagging efforts and those of his officials were however successful in reforming the lives of the priests and clerks of his own diocese and in making them keep within the bounds of ecclesiastical discipline. He neglected nothing which his fatherly care suggested, and poured both oil and wine [1] into the wounds of his flock, restraining by sternness and severity those whom he could not cure by mildness and kindness. It is beyond my capacity to describe adequately his immense efforts, or the measure of his success in the reform of his people through the use of this double ecclesiastical authority. This would require many large books and would tax the ability even of writers of reputation.

One of his preoccupations was to restore as far as he could all the churches in his diocese to their right condition. He was very careful to put in charge of them only men of high character and learning, and to do his best to keep out men who lacked these qualities. The

[1] cf. Luke 10: 34

duceretur zelo ex ipsius uerbis melius perpenditur,
quibus de seipso ita sepissime fatebatur : ' Miror,'
inquiens, ' quosdam ut dicitur gaudere cum uacant
prebende aut ecclesie quas pro libitu possint nouis
possessoribus conferre. Vera enim de meipso loquor
quia nichil umquam in hac uita animum meum ita
adduxit ut anxia sollicitudo personas ydoneas eligendi
aut discernendi, quibus congrue posset regimen uacan-
tium prebendarum aut dignitatum ecclesie nostre
committi. Nec quicquam mundanum adeo me umquam contristauit ut error ille quo, ad multorum sepe
commendationem, talibus ecclesiastica concessi *a* beneficia, quos frustra credidi in canonicis disciplinis esse
strenuos, dum eos postmodum ecclesie ditatos bonis,
morum peruersitas ostendit fuisse ignauos.'

Et in hunc quidem modum sibi a quibusdam fuisse
surreptum non sine gemitu querebatur. Nouimus uero
eum pro huiusmodi errore diligentius cauendo, alicui
suorum collateralium de cuius sinceritate non parum
confidebat specialiter iniunxisse, ut si quid uel tenuiter
sensisset uel audisset sinistri de aliquo quem in ecclesia
sua beneficiare disponeret, hoc ei nullatenus celare
presumeret. Non quod ipse incertis de aliquo rumusculis
fidem esset habiturus, set ut a dubiis etiam certa quandoque eliceret, et conceptum ex incertis quoque laudibus
fauorem interim temperaret quousque, discussa super
auditis ueritate, inoffenso mentis iudicio quod ratio *b*
dictaret liberius exequeretur.

Plurimis uero Deum, ut sperabat, timentibus uiris
atque discretis iniunxit ut personas moribus et doctrina
probatas quas in gremium ecclesie sue oportunitate

a *om* B
b non B

words which he often used about himself best express how much he had this aim at heart. ' It amazes me that anyone can rejoice when prebends or churches are vacant, and they can give them at will to new incumbents. Speaking for myself, nothing in this life gives me more disquietude of mind than the careful selection of suitable people to whom I can confidently commit the prebends and dignities vacant in my church. Nothing in the world has ever grieved me so much as when by mistake I have given ecclesiastical preferment to people whom by general report I wrongly believed to be exemplary clergy, but who, after I had bestowed ecclesiastical endowments on them, proved to be unworthy and immoral.'

He used to complain bitterly that certain persons had misled him in this manner. I know that in order to do his best to avoid such mistakes, he gave special instructions to a member of his household in whose integrity he had great confidence, that if ever he had the smallest doubt, or had heard anything the least derogatory about anyone to whom he intended to give a benefice in his church, he should in no circumstances conceal it from him. It was not that he wished to believe idle gossip about people, but such rumours enabled him sometimes to find out the truth and caused him not to act upon a favourable opinion due to an over-partial report until the truth of what he had heard had been sifted, and he was able to feel that he was acting as an enlightened and well-informed judgment dictated.

He begged many persons whom he believed to be both God-fearing and discerning that they would seek out and bring to his notice men of established learning and character, whom when opportunity offered he could make members of his chapter. But alas, owing to the

concessa colligeret, sue notitie diligenter exploratas
intimarent. Set ue infelicitati humane infirmitatis et
ignorantie ! Nam et ex illis plerique, pro affinitatis aut
cuiuslibet necessitudinis seu familiaritatis optentu, cul-
pandos potius ei satagebant commendare ; quibus
interdum et ille non distulit, quamuis infideliter contra
se, immo contra Deum agentibus, fidem accomodare.
Ita se aliquotiens circumuentum a quibusdam sciebat
et gemebat ; tantamque hominum infidelium peruersitatem qui *a* Dei patientia suaque simplicitate purissima
abusi fuissent, magna de cetero cum detestatione
abhorrebat, et a suis quantum licuit consiliis eos
sequestrabat. Verum hec eo agente, et de lucris
Dominicis ex adquisitione fidelium animarum studiosius
satagente, non quieuerunt uirulenta contra eum serpentis
antiqui molimina. Set ne tedium generet lectori pagine
res singulas prout geste sunt prosequentis effluentia,
plurimis omissis, ea summatim ex hiis que acciderunt
exprimimus, que presenti opusculo credidimus *b* magis
oportuna.

Vno igitur anno et mensibus fere quatuor ante mortem
suam, rex Anglorum Ricardus in grauem contra ipsum
exarsit iram tali de causa. Ipso siquidem rege in
transmarinis agente ac contra Francorum regem Philippum acriter preliante, coacta est, uocante Archiepiscopo Cantuariense Huberto, ad generale colloquium
uniuersitas magnatum totius Anglie apud Oxenefordiam.[1]
Quibus Archiepiscopus, qui uice regis publicis presidebat
negotiis, regias proposuit *c* necessitates, qui sumptibus
et militantium copiis inferior, contra regem dimicaret
potentissimum, ad suam exheredationem et perniciem
totis nisibus aspirantem. Postulat demum quatinus
decernant in commune quo genere auxilii domino suo

---

a que B   *b* credimus X   *c* exposuit X

mischance of human partiality and blindness, many of
these, under the cloak of kinship or friendship or under
some other compulsion, did their best to recommend to
him unworthy men, and he sometimes was too ready to
believe them, although they were abusing his confidence,
and worse still, sinning against God.   He sometimes
realized and lamented that he had been deceived by
such people.   From henceforth he conceived a strong
prejudice against these utterly perverse and unscrupulous
men, who had tried God's patience and taken advantage
of his trustfulness, and, whenever he could legitimately
do so, he dismissed them from his council.   His actions
in this respect and his determination to do his utmost to
provide for the souls of the faithful by means of the
treasures of the Church caused him to be a prey to the
unceasing and venomous attacks of the ancient serpent.
However, lest the reader of these pages should be bored
by a full description of everything as it happened, I shall
omit most of it and relate very briefly those incidents
which I think most relevant to this present work.

Almost a year and four months before his death,
Richard, king of the English, became exceedingly angry
with him for this reason.   The king was across the sea,
engaged in a bitter struggle with Philip, king of the
French, and a general council of all the magnates of
England was summoned at Oxford by Hubert, archbishop of Canterbury.[1]   The archbishop, who presided
in the king's stead, explained the king's serious position.
With smaller resources and forces he was struggling
against a very powerful king, who was straining every
nerve to disinherit and ruin him.   Finally, he asked them
to decide as a body by what means they could best help
their lord in his desperate situation.   It was then

---

[1] For this episode see Introduction, vol. I, pp. xlii-xliv.

in tam *a* artis posito ualeant subuenire. Iam uero prefinitum erat ab hiis qui secum regiis ex toto nutibus ducebant parendum, ut barrones Anglie inter quos et episcopi censebantur, trescentos milites regi exhiberent qui suis sumptibus ei per annum integrum contra hostes transmarinos indesinenter militarent.

Requisito *b* super hoc in cetu illo assensu Lincolniensis episcopi ipse tacitus secum deliberans paulisper, cum prius tam primas Cantuariensis quam *c* Londoniensis episcopus Ricardus,[1] qui et decanatus priuilegio fungebatur inter episcopos, se suos et sua regie per omnia necessitati exposituros pronuntiassent, ita citius respondit, ' Nostis,' ait, ' o uiri prudentes et nobiles, qui in presentiarum adestis, me in partibus istis aduenam esse et de simplicitate conuersationis heremitice ad officium episcopale assumptum. Cum igitur ecclesia domine mee sancte Dei genitricis Marie mee dudum imperitie ad regendum fuisset commissa, consuetudines illius et dignitates, debita etiam et honera, solerter addidici ; in quibus conseruandis siue exhibendis, hactenus fere per tredecim annos[2] a rectis predecessorum meorum uestigiis non recessi. Scio equidem ad militare officium *d* domino regi, set in hac terra solummodo exhibendum, Lincolniensem ecclesiam teneri ; extra metas uero Anglie nil tale ab *e* ea deberi. Vnde michi consultius arbitror ad natale solum repedare et heremum more solito incolere, quam hic pontificatum gerere et ecclesiam michi commissam, antiquas immunitates perdendo, insolitis angariis subiugare.'

a om B   *b* + igitur Q   *c* + alter quidem X   *d* seruitium QX   *e* ad B

[1] Richard Fitz-Neal, bishop of London 1189-98, had been Dean of Lincoln at the time of St Hugh's election ; he later became royal treasurer and was author of the *Dialogus de Scaccario*.

[2] Adam here repeats his faulty chronology : the Council of Oxford was held in December 1197 when Hugh had been bishop for eleven years and seven months.

suggested by those who like him believed that every wish of the king should be unhesitatingly obeyed, that the barons of England amongst whom the bishops were included should provide him with three hundred knights to fight for a whole year across the sea at their expense against his enemies.

When the bishop of Lincoln was publicly asked to consent to this, he remained silent and thoughtful for a short time until first the primate, the archbishop of Canterbury and then Richard, bishop of London,[1] who held the office of dean amongst the bishops, had declared their readiness to devote themselves and their men and property to the king in his need. He then immediately answered to this effect : ' This noble and distinguished assembly will remember that I am a stranger in this land, and was raised to the episcopate from the seclusion of the eremetical life. Therefore when the church of our Lady Mary, God's blessed mother, was committed to my inexperienced hands, I took pains to find out its customs and privileges, and also its obligations and services, and in the performance and preservation of these for thirteen years [2] or thereabouts I have faithfully followed in the footsteps of my predecessors. I am well aware that the church of Lincoln is bound to serve the king in war, but only in this country, and it is a fact that no service is due beyond the frontiers of England. I should therefore prefer to return to my native land and resume my normal eremetical way of life rather than remain here as bishop and cause unprecedented burdens to be laid on the church under my charge by surrendering her ancient rights.'

Hoc eius responsum Archiepiscopus satis egre accipiens, suppressa paululum uoce, trementibus pre [a] indignatione labiis, a Saresbyriense episcopo nomine Hereberto [1] inquirere cepit [b] quidnam et ipse animi haberet super auxilio regi prospiciendo. Qui ad inquisita sic paucis respondit : ' Videtur michi quia citra ecclesie mee enorme preiudicium, aliud a me dici nequit uel fieri quam quod faciendum esse ex responsione domini Lincolniensis [c] modo audiui.' Ad hec nimium indignatus Archiepiscopus, primum in Lincolniensem uerbis amarissimis stomachatus, soluto concilio [d] nuntiauit regi per ipsum caruisse effectu negotium illius. Quo rex iam secundo et tertio per nuntios Archiepiscopi accepto, in ira et furore magno uniuersa que erant episcopi precepit quamtocius confiscari. Id ipsum mandauit et de Saresbyriensi episcopo fieri, qui Lincolniensis diffinitionem suo assensu comprobasset. Quid multa ? Saresbyriensis episcopus confestim proscribitur ; ueniensque ad regem, post iniurias, dampna atque uexationes et plurimas contumelias, uix tandem maxima pecunie summa pacem et possessiones suas redemit. In res uero et possessiones Lincolniensis episcopi nemo presumpsit manus extendere, dum et offensam eius metuunt incurrere, anathema uero illius subire [e] non aliter quam capitale supplicium formidabant. Protrahitur inter hec [f] tempus, a festo pene sancti Nicholai [g] usque ad kalendas Septembris, rege crebro mandante ut proscriberetur episcopus et regiis executoribus id exequi nulla ratione presumentibus.

Tandem uero, motus eorum maxime precibus, quos edicta urgebant regalia ut res illius iure fisci occuparent,[h]

[a] pro B   [b] adiecit QX
[c] + episcopi Q   [d] solito consilio B
[e] om B   [f] interim X
[g] + estiualis X   [h] occuparentur X

The archbishop took this answer badly, and in a low voice and with lips trembling from anger he asked Herbert, the bishop of Salisbury [1] what his opinion was about the provision of aid to the king. He replied to this question shortly and as follows : ' It seems to me that without great damage to my church, I cannot say or do anything else than what the bishop of Lincoln has just suggested ought to be done.' The archbishop now completely lost control of himself, and stormed at the bishop of Lincoln. Having dismissed the council, he informed the king that the latter was responsible for the rejection of his proposal. When the king had received two or three messengers from the archbishop, in great wrath and indignation he ordered that all the bishop's possessions should be confiscated. The same instructions were sent about the bishop of Salisbury who had supported the bishop of Lincoln. What next? The bishop of Salisbury suffered confiscation immediately ; only by going to the king, and enduring many insults and much rudeness and being put to great expense, was he able with great difficulty to buy back the king's favour and his own possessions by the payment of a large sum of money. No one, however, dared to lay hands on the lands and goods of the bishop of Lincoln, because they feared to offend him, and dreaded his excommunication as much as a death sentence. Nothing therefore was done almost from the feast of St Nicholas to the beginning of September, for the royal escheators dared not sequester the bishop's property in spite of the king's frequent peremptory orders.

At last, at the urgent request of the Exchequer officials, who were pressed by royal commands to

---

[1] Herbert le Poore, bishop of Salisbury 1194-1217

transfretauit ad regem. Ad quem, mediatore nullo
utens, per seipsum confidenter accessit. Reperiensque
illum in capella noui castelli Rupis de Andeli audientem
missarum sollempnia, in die doctoris eximii sancti
Augustini,[1] continuo salutauit eum. Stabat uero rex ipse
secus introitum hostii in solio regali, et duo episcopi,
Dunelmensis scilicet et Heliensis,[2] stabant secus pedes
eius. Cum ergo salutasset regem episcopus, ipse non
respondit ei uerbum, set cum illum parumper toruis
fuisset oculis intuitus faciem ab eo auertit. Cui episcopus
ait, ' Da michi osculum, domine rex.' Qui magis
auertit aspectum ab eo, uultumque et capud in partem
aliam declinauit. Tunc episcopus, circa pectus uestem
illius fortiter constringens, hanc uehementius [a] concussit,
iterum dicens, ' Osculum michi debes,' inquit, ' quia de
longinco ad te uenio.' Rex ad hec, ' Non,' ait, ' meruisti
ut osculer te.' Qui fortius concutiens eum per capam
quam stricta tenebat manu, confidenter ait, ' Immo,'
inquiens,[b] ' merui,' et adiecit ' Osculare me.' Tunc ille,
admiratus [c] fiduciam constantie eius, paululumque
subridens, osculatus est eum. Aderant ibi duo archiepiscopi et episcopi quinque, qui inter solium regis et
gradus altaris constiterant. Qui non procul a rege,
presulem hoc modo de rege iam triumphantem inter se
accisci cupientes, locum ei sessionis fecere. Quos ipse
directe pertransiuit ; ac secus cornu altaris gressum
figens, demissis obstinatius in terram luminibus, diuinorum tantummodo celebrationi animo intendebat.
Quem interea rex non parum curioso et pene continuo
aspectu considerabat.

----

[a] uehementer X
[b] om X
[c] admirans Q

confiscate his property, he went overseas to the king. He approached him himself, without making use of the services of an intermediary, and found him in the chapel of his new castle at Château Gaillard hearing high mass, on the feast of the great doctor St Augustine,[1] and immediately greeted him. The king was on a royal throne near the entrance, and the two bishops of Durham and Ely [2] stood at his feet. When the bishop greeted the king he did not reply, but having frowned at him after a little while turned his face away. The bishop said to him ' Lord king, kiss me.' But Richard turned his head even further and looked the other way. Then the bishop firmly gripped the king's tunic round his chest, and shook it violently, saying again, ' You owe me a kiss, because I have come a long way to see you.' The king answered 'You deserve no kiss from me.' He shook him more vigorously than before, this time by his cloak which he held firmly, and said boldly 'I have every right to one,' adding, ' Kiss me.' The other, overcome by his courage and determination, after a little while kissed him with a smile. There were present two archbishops, and five bishops standing between the king's throne and the altar. These were anxious to include the bishop amongst themselves after his victory over the king and made a place for him near the king. He, however, passed them by and took up his position on the step at the side of the altar, and with eyes firmly fixed on the ground, he concentrated only on the sacrifice of the mass. The king looked at him almost all the time with great curiosity.

---

[1] 28 August 1198
[2] Philip of Poitiers was bishop of Durham 1197-1208 ; Eustace, chancellor since 1197, was bishop of Ely 1198-1215.

Cum igitur, ad trinam inuocationem Agni qui tollit peccata mundi, iam pacis osculum sacerdos dedisset cuidam archiepiscopo, qui regi de more pacem erat allaturus, rex usque ad gradus ei obuius processit, sumptumque ab eo signum accepte pacis per immolationem celestis Agni, cum humili reuerentia episcopo Lincolniensi per oris sui osculum porrexit. Ita princeps *a* illustrissimus uenerationis obsequium, quod sibi archiepiscopus parabat deferre, ipse potius episcopo sancto studuit exhibere. Nam ad ipsum alacriter perrexit ; et nil tale suspicanti set attentius Domino supplicanti, honorem ipsi, Domino id utique disponente, impendit ; ut impleretur quod Dominus ait, ' Glorificantes me glorificabo.' [1]

Capitvlvm VI

Qualiter regem rationibus superatum et sedatum de suis excessibus increpauerit. Quantum sibi honoris rex ipsa mox die aduentus sui ad ipsum detulerit. Et quid honoris cito post hec regi retributum a Domino fuerit.

Quam etenim *b* instanter, inter quelibet leta et tristia, inter cuncta prospera et aduersa, Domini semper gloriam quesierit, cum tota indesinenter uite illius series docuerit, etiam id quod sub articulo huius *c* diei gessit luce clarius patefecit. Nam cum post terrores multiplices ac uexationum plurimarum acerbitates ei diutius intentatas, subito et insolito eum honore sublimitas regia dignata fuisset, soliditas pectoris eius neutro temptationis iaculo uel ad momentum cessit, quo minus, calcata funditus humani fauoris gloria, hoc indeclinabiliter

---

a + ille X   *b* Quoniam Hugo X
c + de quo loquimur X   [1] 1 Kings 2: 30

When it came to the ' Agnus Dei qui tollit peccata mundi ' which is repeated three times, the celebrant gave the kiss of peace to one of the archbishops, who, as was customary, was intending to bring the ' Pax ' to the king ; but he advanced to the step to meet him, and having received from him the pledge of peace conferred by the sacrifice of the Lamb of God, he humbly and reverently passed it on by himself kissing the bishop of Lincoln.   Thus, the noble prince took special pains to transfer to the bishop of Lincoln the mark of deference which the archbishop was preparing to pay to himself. He came to him suddenly when he was completely unaware of his intention, being absorbed in prayer.   God had so arranged that he should receive this tribute, that his own word might be fulfilled, ' I will glorify those who glorify me.' [1]

Chapter VI

How he rebuked the king, now completely placated and won over by his arguments, for his sins.   The very great favour shown to him by the king on the day of his arrival, and how shortly afterwards God bestowed great honour on him as a reward.

Even if the whole course of his life had not demonstrated how in good or evil fortune and in prosperity or adversity he sought only God's glory, the events of that day would have been proof positive of that fact.   His equanimity was not even temporarily shaken, either by a long period of constant anxiety and persecution, or by the sudden and unexpected marks of the royal favour which followed it, for being utterly indifferent to men's

exequeretur, quod profuturum ad Dei gloriam sagacissimo mentis acumine peruidisset.[a]

Explicito namque superius memorato sacri altaris officio, ad regem accessit ; super indignatione ipsius contra se, citra meritum suum [b] excitata, pauca set fortia expostulauit ; et quod in illum nichil penitus aliquando deliquisset, euidentissima ratione propalauit. Quibus rex cum in contrarium nil referre potuisset, crimen huius offense in Cantuariensem retorsit Archiepiscopum, qui sibi multotiens sinistra de eo litteratorie suggessisset. Que simul uniuersa ueritate uacua fuisse, promptissima rationum facillitate conuincens episcopus, ' Saluo,' inquit, ' honore Dei, et salute anime mee ac tue,[c] utilitatibus tuis numquam prorsus uel in modico obuiaui.'

Ita regia indignatione sedata, regiis exeniis episcopus honoratur ; [1] et a rege hospitandi gratia in castellum quod uocitabat Portum gaudii, quod ipse recenter construxerat in quadam insula non procul sita, destinatur. Rogabat uero ut etiam die sequenti ad se ueniret, et ita cum gratia et fauore suo ad propria, post iteratum cum eo colloquium, remearet. Quod ille gratanter audiens se in crastino reuersurum promisit. Verum de [d] salute anime ipsius pastorali sollicitudine pie curiosus, apprehensa eius manu, a sede sua ipsum eleuans pertraxit seorsum usque ad locum prope altare ; ibidemque sedere eum monens cum et ipse pariter sederet, sic eum secretius alloquitur, ' Noster,' inquit, ' parochianus es,[2] domine rex ; nobisque incumbit [e] ratione pastoralis cure, pro anima uestra, quam uniuersitatis Dominus proprio redemit cruore, in tremendo ipsius iudicio respondere.

---

[a] preuidisset X
[c] O rex . . . saluti . . . tuis utilitatibus X
[e] oportet X
[b] + excusaret X
[d] pro X

praise, he only sought whatever his natural intelligence suggested would redound to the glory of God.

When the holy sacrifice of the mass which I have already described was ended, he approached the king and remonstrated with him in a few forcible words for his recent wholly undeserved anger with him, giving him some very good reasons to show that he had never failed in his duty to him. The king could not contradict him and laid all the blame on the archbishop of Canterbury, who had so often misrepresented him in his letters. The bishop by his ready explanations was easily able to convince him that it was all completely untrue. He said : ' Except for the honour of God and the salvation of my soul and yours, I have never up till now opposed anything however trivial which was to your advantage.'

The king's indignation was thus dispelled. He made royal gifts to the bishop,[1] and sent him to lodge as his guest at Portjoie which he had recently constructed on a certain island not very far away. He asked him to come back to see him on the next day so that after another interview he might return home assured of his favour and friendship. He heard this thankfully and promised to return on the morrow. As his spiritual father, however, he felt his responsibility for the welfare of his soul, and so, taking his hand, he made him get up from his chair and drew him apart to a place near the altar. He asked him to sit down, and sitting down himself, spoke thus to him in private. ' You are our parishioner,[2] Lord King, and because of our priestly office we shall have on the terrible Day of Judgment to

---

[1] One of these presents was a pike for the bishop's dinner, appropriate for one who did not eat meat (cf. Giraldus, *Vita S. Hugonis*, pp. 105-6).

[2] Thus called because he was born at Oxford, in the diocese of Lincoln.

Volo igitur michi dicas *a* qualiter se habeat status interior anime uestre ; ut ei consilium uel auxilium, prout superna iuuerit *b* aspiratio, efficaciter possim adhibere. Iam enim anni unius spatium elapsum est ex quo uobis alias locutus fui.'

Cui dum rex diceret conscientiam sibi bonam esse fere in omnibus nisi quod *c* odio laboraret hostium, quos iniuriosos pateretur et nequiter infestos, episcopus ait, ' Si per omnia Dominatoris omnium gratie placueris, facile tibi inimicos tuos aut pacatos efficiet aut expugnatos subiciet. Verum summo opere tibi cauendum est ne tu, quod absit, Auctori tuo in aliquo iniuriosus existas, aut etiam in proximos quippiam iniquum committas. Dicit enim Scriptura quia " Cum placuerint Domino uie hominis, etiam inimicos conuertet ad pacem ; "[1] cum e contra de aliis dicat, " Pugnabit pro eo orbis terrarum contra insensatos ; "[2] et iterum de Domino uir sanctus dicit, " Quis umquam restitit ei et pacem habuit ? "[3]

' De te uero, quod quidem mestus loquor, iam publicus rumor est quia nec proprie coniugi maritalis thori fidem conseruas, nec ecclesiarum priuilegia, in preficiendis maxime siue eligendis earum rectoribus *d* illibata custodias. Dicitur enim, quod sane nimium piaculare *e* crimen est, quia pecunie seu fauoris interuentu quosdam ad regimen animarum promouere soleas.[4] Quod procul dubio si uerum est, pax tibi a

---

a dicatis X   *b* innuerit B[2] ; adiuuerit X
c nisi quod] non quidem B   *d* pastoribus X
e peculiare QX
[1] Prov. 16: 7   [2] Wis. 5: 21   [3] Job 9: 4
[4] Richard's reputation for marital infidelity is shown by Howden's account (III, p. 288) of his resumption of marital relations with Berengaria, with whom he had not lived since his return from his Crusade, after a serious illness at Easter 1195 which caused a temporary reformation in his way of

answer for your soul, which the Lord of the world redeemed with his own blood. I ask you therefore to tell me the state of your conscience, so that I can give you effective help and counsel as the Holy Spirit shall direct me. At least a year has passed since I spoke to you about it on another occasion.'

The king answered that his conscience was clear in almost everything except his hatred for his enemies, because of their relentless and persistent attacks on him. The bishop replied ' If you were to try and please the merciful God who rules the world in all things, he would enable you to be reconciled with your enemies or to defeat them. You must, however, take special care to see that you do not yourself sin against your Maker, which God forbid you should do, and that you do not injure your neighbour. The scriptures say, " When the ways of a man are pleasing to the Lord, he shall make his enemies wish for peace." [1] On the other hand it says of those who displease him, " The whole earth shall war on his behalf against the froward." [2] Again a holy man has said concerning the Lord " Who ever opposed him and had peace ? " [3]

' Concerning you, indeed, and I speak in sorrow, it is generally reported that you are not faithful to your marriage bed, and do not keep inviolate the privileges of the Church, especially in the matter of the appointment or election of bishops. It is even said that you have been wont to promote people to the rule of souls from motives of friendship or because they have paid for it, and this is a very heinous sin. [4] If it is true, undoubtedly God will not grant you peace.' The king listened

---

life. Howden also gives a contemporary epigram on his immorality and other vices (IV, p. 84). Richard's sale of offices, including bishoprics, before and after the Crusade was notorious.

Domino concedi non potest.' De hiis itaque regem pro tempore admonitum diligenter et instructum, et de aliis quidem se penitus excusantem, de aliis opem intercessionis sue sedulo flagitantem, cum benedictione dimisit ; qui *a* ad hospitium regia sibi prouisione delegatum letus secessit.

Rex interea de eo cum suis loquens et uirtutem animi eius multa laude *b* concelebrans, ' Vere,' inquit, ' si tales qualis iste est, essent passim et ceteri episcopi, nullus contra eos regum aut principum attollere presumeret ceruicem.'

Tunc ei a suis suggestum consiliariis fuit quatinus per eum in Angliam litteras destinaret *c* quibus a magnatibus terre alicuius modi subuentionis auxilium flagitaret. Quas ea de causa illum ferre *d* potissimum consulebant, quia procul dubio a cunctis fauorabilius exciperentur, si per tantum sibi nuntium allate fuissent. Nonnulli etiam hoc episcopum libentius sperabant executurum ut inde regio fauori ulterius commendari potuisset. Verum, ut ait sapiens, ' Frustra iacitur rete ante oculos pennatorum.' [1] Protinus siquidem per regis domesticos sibi omnia hec innotuerunt.

Suggerentibus autem sibi clericis quatinus in re tam facili pareret alacriter regie uoluntati, ille cum magna aspernatione uerba eorum respuit, dicens, ' Absit,' inquit, ' hoc a me. Nec enim proposito set neque officio meo istud congruere potest. Non est meum portitorem fieri regalium litterarum. Non enim, inquam, meum est exactionum huiuscemodi uel in modico existere cooperatorem. Num latet uos quia semper uelud nudato supplicat ense iste potens ? Et hec presertim potestas iugiter cum petit premit.*e* Angli

a et Xp   *b* *om* B
c dirigeret, in X   *d* deferri X
e premitur Q

attentively to his exhortations and counsels, denying in some cases that he was guilty, and imploring the assistance of his prayers in others. After receiving his blessing he sent him away, and Hugh thankfully set out for the lodging which the king had chosen and provided for him.

The king in the meantime discussed him with his attendants and commented with much appreciation on his holiness. ' Indeed,' he said, ' if the other bishops were such as he, no king or ruler would dare raise up his head against them.'

His councillors then suggested to him that he should send a letter by him to England to ask the magnates of the kingdom to provide him with an aid of some sort. They advised that he should take it, chiefly because a more favourable answer would undoubtedly be made by everyone, if it were brought by such a messenger. Some of them hoped that the bishop would willingly undertake the commission in order to advance further in the royal favour. However, as the sage says, ' The net is spread out in vain before the eyes of the birds '.[1] The king's attendants immediately laid the whole matter before him.

When his clerks suggested to him that in such a trivial matter he could readily do what the king wished he rejected their advice with considerable acerbity. ' In no circumstances ', he said ' could I do this.' The suggestion is an insult to my office. It is no business of mine to act as a royal messenger, and I will not participate in any way in such exactions. Surely, it must be obvious even to you that when a great man begs he always does so at the sword's point, and this particular one when he begs pushes the sword home. Our English kings first

---

[1] Prov. 1: 17

nostri blandis quidem salutationibus primum alliciunt *a* quos demum asperrimis coactionibus, non ad quod ipsi uolebant set ad quod sibi placuerit conferendum impellunt. Sepe etiam inuitos exequi cogunt quod semel ultroneos aut ipsos aut eorum predecessores fecisse nouerunt. Non me contingat talibus immisceri quibus, cum dispendio proximi, gratia comparatur regis terreni, et indignatio succedenter incurretur *b* omnipotentis Dei.'

Monet igitur regis consiliarios ut procurent ne sibi talia iniungantur, unde, contradicendo regie deliberationi, ipsius denuo gratiam ipsum necesse sit aliquatenus demereri. Que ut regi innotuerunt, statim mandauit ei quatinus ad suam cum Dei benedictione ecclesiam rediret ; nec ad se ueniendi mane, ut condixerant, laborem assumeret,*c* set pro eo ad Dominum bono animo indesinenter oraret. Sic ille in nomine Domini a curialium laqueis liberatus, Dominum magnifice cum suis omnibus benedicens, ad sua cum gaudio remeauit.

Non autem uidetur supprimendum silentio quod diuinitus ad consolationem sociorum eius contigisse interpretati sunt, qui cum eo ad regem, ut prefati sumus, pariter uenerunt. Cum enim ad primos gradus capelle, ubi missarum sollempniis rex intendebat, uenisset episcopus, chorus prosam de beato Augustino decantans, hunc uoce altissona uersiculum incepit,*d*

' Aue inclite presul Christi, flos pulcherrime.' [1]

Hec enim primum uox ingressis fores castelli ab editiori loco emissa, stuporem simul et confidentiam sociis intulit Christi presulis. Que licet de alio prolata esset presule, hanc tamen, quasi de suo in tali hora

a Angli . . . alliciunt] Verbi gratia nostis quia blandis quidem sollicitationibus X : sollicitationibus Q
b incurritur X   *c* sumeret X
d decantabat X

ensnare with flattery and blandishments those whom
finally they forcibly constrain to give not what they
themselves are willing to but what the kings demand.
They often compel men to do unwillingly what they
have discovered that they or their predecessors did on
one occasion voluntarily.   May I never be one of those
people who would win the favour of an earthly ruler by
doing injury to their neighbour, and afterwards bringing
on themselves the wrath of Almighty God ! '

He urged the king's councillors to arrange that he
should not be asked to do such things, since by resisting
the royal plan he must necessarily again lose his favour.
They informed the king, who once again sent word to
him to return with God's blessing to his church, and not
trouble himself to come and see him on the morrow as
they had arranged, but to pray diligently to God for his
spiritual welfare.   Thus, by God's favour he escaped
from the snares of the courtiers, and he and all his
company set out joyously for home, blessing and
magnifying the Lord.

It does not seem right to pass over in silence an
incident which his companions on the journey to the
king, which I have described, interpreted as a sign of
divine assistance.   When the bishop reached the first
step of the chapel where the king was hearing mass, the
choir was chanting the prose for blessed Augustine, and
had just begun at the top of their voices the versicle

' Hail renowned bishop of Christ, and fairest flower.' [1]

These words coming from the higher part of the

---

[1] cf. Sequence *Adest nobis dies alma* used for St Cuthbert at Durham,
for Confessors at Sarum and Rouen and for Martyrs at Westminster.

profiteretur *ᵃ*antistite, ipsius comites pro bono acceperunt omine.

Auxit letitiam huius presagii alius continuo uersiculus, sub ingressu eorum in capellam decantatus. Sic enim ingredientibus illis ad regem, uoce consona ab uniuersis intropositis episcopis et clericis fortius est proclamatum,

' O beate, O sancte Augustine, iuua cateruam hanc.' ¹

Ita illi, geminata consolatione animequiores effecti, a nimie formidinis *ᵇ* deiectione in spem superni iuuaminis ceperunt respirare. Nec enim iniuste quidem formidinis causam talis ira principis eis uidebatur incussisse, cum iuxta dictum sapientis, ' Sicut fremitus leonis, sic et ira regis.' ²

Terruerat quoque eos, cum recenti exemplo Saresbyriensis episcopi innumeris contumeliis et dampnis afflicti duorum precipue nobilium uirorum, comitis uidelicet Willelmi cognomento Marescalli et comitis de Alba Mara, relatio.³ Hii namque, tertia antea die apud Rothomagum accesserant *ᶜ* ad episcopum ; et per quantas iniurias furor regis in dominum Saresbyriensem efferbuisset, quanta etiam Lincolniensi minatus fuisset illi exponentes, supplicabant quatinus eis que uiderentur expedire ad sui ipsius commodum, regi per eos intimanda ad eius animum mitigandum, de causa sua uel negotio

---

ᵃ proferretur X
ᵇ fortitudinis B
ᶜ accesserunt X
¹ See Note 1, p. 106
² Prov. 19: 12
³ William the Marshal (1146?-1219), son of John Fitz-Gilbert hereditary Marshal of England, earl of Pembroke and Striguil through marriage with Isabella, heiress of Richard Strongbow, was in the service of the young king Henry, and after his death in that of Henry II. He was an associate justiciar under Longchamp and Walter of Coutances during Richard's Crusade and captivity and, according to his biographer, after the king's death won over Hubert Walter to support John's claim to the throne. The general respect for him as the ideal feudal knight is shown by his being

building, and heard by the companions of Christ's
bishop just as they passed through the doors of the castle
filled them with wonder and confidence for although
they referred to another bishop, they seemed so completely applicable on this particular occasion to their
own bishop, that they took it as a good omen.

Another verse, sung almost immediately afterwards
just as they entered the chapel, raised their hopes in
connection with this portent even further. As they
entered the king's presence the united voices of all the
bishops and clerks within lustily proclaimed,

' Blessed and holy Augustine assist this congregation.' [1]

This double encouragement raised their spirits from
great dejection and anxiety, and they began to breathe
again owing to their confidence in the divine assistance.
To have incurred the wrath of such a ruler did not seem
to them an unreasonable ground for alarm, since,
according to the saying of the wise man, ' The wrath of
kings is as the roaring of a lion.' [2]

In addition to the recent case of the insufferable
rudeness shown to the bishop of Salisbury and the
losses he had sustained, they were further alarmed by
the report given by two men of exceptionally high rank,
the Earl Marshal and the earl of Albemarle.[3] These
two had met the bishop at Rouen three days earlier, and
had told him how the hot indignation of the king had
found vent in the penalties inflicted on the bishop of

---

sent with Langton as envoy to the rebel barons in April 1215 and the choice
of him as regent after John's death. He won the battle of Lincoln and conducted the negotiations with Louis VIII and the rebel barons. St Hugh
would have known him well as he was sheriff of Lincoln from 1190-1194
(cf. *Histoire de Guillaume le Maréchal* (ed. P. Meyer), Société de l'Histoire de
France 1891-1901 and S. Painter, *William Marshal*, Oxford 1933).

insinuare dignaretur. Asserebant enim sub iureiurando quia mallent totis facultatum suarum uiribus pacem ei redemisse, quam eueniret ut iuxta motum furoris sui regia in eum immanitas debacharet.*ᵃ* 'Nec solum,' inquiunt, 'quia uos fidelissime diligimus, talia prosequimur ; uerum etiam quia tam nobis quam domino nostro regi et suis omnibus non mediocriter in hoc casu timemus. Nulli dubium esse potest quin ipsum quam celerrime celestis ultio percellat si uestram, quod Deus auertat, indignis exagitare iniuriis presumpserit sanctitatem. Erimusque et nos et amici nostri in obprobrium et direptionem *ᵇ* dimicantibus aduersum nos inimicis nostris.'

Talia prosequentibus episcopus statim responderat,*ᶜ* 'Gratias quidem immense beneuolentie quam habetis erga nos referrimus toto mentis affectu. Optime uero noui quia pre ceteris in sua presenti uexatione, cui satis compatimur, domino nostro regi estis necessarii ; bene *ᵈ* etiam noui quia uobis pre ceteris ad compensationem tenetur impensi seruitii. Nolo igitur ut pro me, cui adeo irascitur, aliqua uerba faciatis, ne si uobis duriora responderit, in eius obsequio *ᵉ* reddamini segniores ; aut si uos pro me exaudierit, sese magnum pro uobis quid gessisse reputans, ad retribuendum uobis bona que meremini ipse inueniatur aliquatenus remissior. Id tantum, si uidetur, ei dicere poteritis quia ut eum inuiseremus in partes istas uenimus ; cui si libuerit ut ipsum uideamus, per quemlibet ex suis nobis significet quo loci *ᶠ* debeamus occurrere ei.'

Hiis uero *ᵍ* dictis, nobiles uiri *ʰ* prudentiam simul et magnanimitatem eius admirantes, plurimum edificati

---

ᵃ deseuiret X   *ᵇ* deiectionem X
ᶜ respondit Q   *ᵈ* unde X
ᵉ B omits these three words   *ᶠ* loco X
ᵍ ab eo QX   *ʰ* + illi QX

Salisbury, and in terrible threats against the bishop of Lincoln. They urged him to discuss his case and business with them and decide what would be in his best interests, that they might report it to the king in order to appease him. They swore that they were ready to do all they could to bring about a reconciliation, rather than expose him to the full force of the king's fury. ' We would act in this way,' they said, ' not only because of our sincere affection for you, but because we fear that the affair will end badly both for us and for the lord king and all his people. It is obvious that the vengeance of Heaven will speedily fall on him, if he dares to inflict uncalled-for injuries on your reverence. We and our friends would suffer shame and loss at the hands of our enemies.'

When they had finished the bishop answered at once, ' I thank you with my whole heart for your great good-will towards me. I know well that you are more indispensable than anyone else to the lord king in his present plight which greatly grieves me, and I am also aware that he is more indebted to you than to others because of your faithful service. I do not therefore wish you to put in a good word for me with whom he is so angry, lest he should rebuff you so rudely that you would become less devoted to his interests, or, if he forgave me at your request, he would think he had done you a great favour, and be less ready to reward you as you deserve. If it seems good to you, tell him only this, that we have come to these parts to visit him, and that, if it is his pleasure for us to see him, let him send someone to inform us where to meet him.'

When they heard this, the two magnates were filled with admiration for his discretion and generosity, and went away much impressed. They told their master everything, and he also was not a little amazed at his

abierunt ad dominum suum, hec omnia ei renuntiantes. Qui et ipse non parum hec illius uerba miratus et animo repente per omnia fere erga illum nutu diuino immutatus, protinus iubet ei renuntiari quatinus sequenti die tertia apud castrum superius memoratum occurreret ei. Quod ordine pretaxato etiam factum est.

Vix autem episcopo in Angliam reuerso, cum nec-dum ad ecclesiam suam peruenisset, idem rex contra regem Francorum prope Gisortium impetu facto, captis pluribus optimatum illius, ipsum in fugam coegit.[a] Tunc etiam comes Niuercensis in fossatum castelli deiectus, aquis enectus interiit.[1] Huius autem triumphi seriem mox Lincolniensi episcopo significans, et ut pro eo sicut ceperat orare dignaretur suppliciter exorans, nomina quoque et numerum uirorum fortium[b] quos ceperat litteratorie expressit, scribens inter cetera et asserens quod etiam rex Philippus satis de fossato bibisset in quod cecidisset quidem fuga precipiti, set cita suorum ope subuectus[c] euasisset interitum. Hunc autem honorem atque tropheum ei celitus concessum meritis sancti presulis multi etiam suorum affirmabant, quem ipse pro domino, pristina simultate omissa, decreuerat impensius uenerari.[d]

---

[a] egit Q
[b] om B
[c] + non o
[d] supplicare X

words, and by the divine dispensation his mind was suddenly almost completely changed about him. He immediately ordered that a message should be sent to him, that he should meet him three days later at the castle I have already mentioned, and there everything happened in the way I have described.

The bishop had only just returned to England and had not yet reached his cathedral, when the king attacked the king of the Franks near Gisors and put him to flight, many of his nobles being taken prisoner. On this occasion the count of Nevers fell into the moat of the castle, and was drowned in its waters.[1] Richard sent an account of his victory to the bishop of Lincoln, and begged him to continue his prayers on his behalf. He also put in the letter the number of distinguished men whom he had captured and their names. Amongst other matters he described how King Philip too would have drunk his fill of the water of the moat into which he had fallen in his precipitate flight, if he had not been immediately rescued by his men and so escaped death. Many of his own men declared that this notable victory had been granted to him by God through the merits of the holy bishop, since, forgetting his first rage, he had decided to treat him with great deference as his lord.

---

[1] Fought between Courcelles and Gisors on 28 September 1198. The flight of Philip II and the French caused the breaking of the bridge at Gisors, with the result that Philip narrowly escaped drowning. For Richard's letter to Philip of Poitiers, bishop of Durham, describing the battle and his own feat of unhorsing three French knights with one lance and giving the names of his more distinguished prisoners, cf. Howden IV, pp. 55-59. According to Wendover (*Flores Historiarum* I, pp. 278-80) the king wrote to all his friends in England, so St Hugh would presumably have received a copy of the same letter.

CAPITVLVM VII

De factiosa quorumdam machinatione contra episcopum et eius clerum. De litteris iniquis archiepiscopi,
cum eorum baiulo, spretis ab episcopo. Et de regiis
executoribus terras eius inuadere ad iussionem regis
formidantibus.

Contabuit inter hec in seipso collisus serpentis liuor
antiqui, et de gloria fidelis serui Dei emulorum eius
fraudulenta molitio confusa erubuit. Ea quidem indoluit
uictam se in machinationibus suis deciuisse ;[a] nec
machinari tamen, spe quidem uincendi iterum, pretermisit, unde cum auctore suo diabolo desperabilius denuo
uinceretur. Iam uero metuens ex desperatione concepta
in ipsum adeo eminentissime sanctitatis uerticem insidi-
arum suarum directe et euidenter laqueos suos intendere,
per sibi coherentium saltem membrorum intricationem
ad illius nititur lesionem nouis et exquisitis fraudium
cuniculis prorumpere.

Excogitato itaque uersute subtilitatis irrefragabili, ut
putabat, uauframento, suggerit[b] regi plurimos esse inter
ecclesie Lincolniensis canonicos qui, redditibus innumeris locupletes, auro etiam uel argento prediuites,
citra grauaminis iacturam non modicas pecunias suis
quiuissent scriniis inferre. ' Huiusmodi uero ingenio
eas,' inquiunt, ' facile erit ab eisdem extorqueri. Scribat
dominus noster rex Cantuariensi archiepiscopo ut de
gremio Lincolniensis ecclesie duodecim uiros prudentia
et consilio preminentes, eloquentia etiam preditos, quos
ipse nouerit uestro seruitio esse ydoneos, ad uos destinare
festinet ; qui rebus oportunis sufficienter instructi, uestra

[a] defecisse X
[b] ut . . . suggerit] ut putabatur, machinamento suggeritur Xp

Chapter VII

How some people maliciously intrigued against the bishop and his clerks, and how the bishop treated with contempt the archbishop's hostile letters and his messenger. How the royal officials feared to seize his lands in pursuance of the king's orders.

Whilst these events were taking place, the malice of the ancient serpent withered away to his own detriment and to the glory of God's servant, the unscrupulous intrigues of his enemies merely causing shame and confusion to themselves. They were grieved that they had been defeated and caught in their own devices, but did not cease from further efforts in the hope of succeeding this time. However, they and their master the devil were again even more decisively defeated. Their desperation now made them afraid obviously and directly to make a person of such pre-eminent holiness the centre of their plots. They therefore strove to wound him by making those most closely connected with him the object of their new and subtle schemes.

Having devised a stratagem which they believed left no loopholes, and must be successful, they suggested to the king that many of the canons of Lincoln were so wealthy and well endowed with gold and silver, that without much loss to themselves they could bring a considerable amount of money into the treasury. 'It will be easy,' they said, 'to take it from them by a device of this kind. Write, lord king, to the archbishop of Canterbury that he make haste to send you from the Lincoln chapter twelve men with a high reputation for discretion, prudence and eloquence, whom he considers well qualified to serve you. These having a sufficiency

possint negotia propriis illorum sumptibus in curia
Romana, in Alimania atque Hispania, necnon et alibi
quo eos censueritis destinandos, competenti sollertia
expedire.'

Quid pluribus immoremur ? Venit tandem nuntius
archiepiscopi ad episcopum presentans ei ex parte illius
duodecim paria litterarum, totidem ecclesie sue personis
eminentioribus porrigenda, sigillo archiepiscopi inclusa.
Attulit etiam speciales episcopo litteras in quibus predictarum tenor litterarum iuxta formulam superius
comprehensam exprimebatur. In earum uero calce,
regia pariter auctoritate et sua mandauit ᵃ quatinus
litteras singulas illis ad quos erant scripte mitteret
quos ad suam quoque presentiam destinaret paratos ᵇ
iuxta formam regii mandati, ad ipsum quamtocius regem
transferre.ᶜ

Hiis cognitis, illi specialius turbabantur, qui tunc
ibidem presentes inuenti, ad inuisam se audierunt
expeditionem accersiri.ᵈ At episcopus ad audita nichil
respondens, erat enim hora prandendi,ᵉ ad mensam
accessit iam paratam. Clerici inter prandendum inuicem
musitantes, timere se asserunt ne duriora episcopus
nuntio responderet, cum non pontificali seueritate set
potius lenitate summissa, in casu tam formidoloso opus
esset ; experiendum primitus, si forte blandiente
supplicatu dominus Cantuariensis posset deliniri qui, si
uellet,ᶠ consilium istud in melius facile commutaret.

Hec illis mutuo conferentibus, aduertit citius uir
robusti pectoris formidinis eorum diffidentiam. Vnde
nullius eorum super formanda responsione consilium
expetiuit ; set continuo ut surrexit a discubitu, ad
nuntium qui uenerat hec est prosecutus.

ᵃ mandauerit B   ᵇ destinatos B   ᶜ transfretare X
ᵈ accersiti B   ᵉ prandii X   ᶠ uelit oX

of what is chiefly needed, can promote your interests at their own expense at the Curia, and act on your behalf efficiently and conscientiously in Germany or Spain or wherever you decide to send them.'

What need to dwell on this? The archbishop's envoy finally arrived and presented to the bishop from him a packet sealed with the archbishop's seal, containing twelve letters for him to deliver to the twelve most important dignitaries of his chapter. He brought also a special letter for the bishop giving the gist of these letters which I have already described. At the end, he directed him in the king's name and his own to send the letters to the persons to whom they were written, and dispatch them to him, ready, in accordance with the royal command, to go immediately to the king.

When their contents were known, those who were there present were greatly disturbed on learning that they had been summoned to make this unexpected journey. The bishop made no comment, and as it was the hour for dining and the meal was ready, went to dinner. During the meal the clerks conversed together and expressed their fear lest the bishop should answer the messenger too bluntly. So critical a situation required suavity and submission, and not episcopal censures. The first course was to try the effect of supplication on the archbishop, since he, if he wished, could easily think better of the plan.

Whilst they discussed the matter together, this man of high courage soon got wind of their misgivings. For this reason, he did not consult them about his answer, but immediately after rising from table, addressed the messenger as follows :

'Noua,' inquit, 'nec uspiam hactenus sunt audita, tam ea que auctoritate regia quam et illa que sua nobis uoluntate iniunxit dominus noster.[a] Sciat tamen me numquam litterarum suarum portitorem fore uel fuisse, nec clericos nostros regiis aliquando seruitiis obligasse aut obligaturum esse. Prohibui sepe clericis etiam alienis in episcopatu nostro beneficiatis ne in publicis functionibus, ut est in distrahendis forestis [b] et aliis in hunc modum administrationibus, sese seculari clientele obnoxios auderent efficere. Quosdam etiam in hoc minus obedientes salutaribus monitis nostris beneficiorum suorum diutina priuatione castigauimus. Qua igitur ratione de intimis ecclesie nostre uisceribus euellere debemus quos ad regia obsequia mittere iubemur? Satis sit domino nostro regi quod, certe in periculum salutis anime sue professionis sue officio pretermisso, negotiorum illius executioni sese archiepiscopi iam ex integro deuouerunt. Quod tamen si parum ei uidetur, ueniet cum suis en iste episcopus; ueniet, inquam, audire iussa eius ex ore eius; ueniet etiam iuxta eadem iussa illius quod iustum fuerit promptissime executurus.[c]

'Tu uero tuarum duodenarium litterarum quas nobis attulisse te dixisti, tecum asporta, inde quod libuerit actitaturus. Hec uero uniuersa que tibi loquor domino nostro archiepiscopo seriatim enarra, ad postremum uero dicturus ei quia si ad regem hoc ordine ituri sunt clerici nostri, cum eis pariter et ipse ibo. Nec enim ipsi sine me modo ibunt, nec sine ipsis alias iui ego. Hec enim pastoris boni ad oues suas, et bonarum ouium ad pastorem suum ratio est, ut nec iste illas incaute exponendo dispergat, nec ille istum temere fugiendo aberrent.'

---

[a] + archiepiscopus X   [b] forestariis X   [c] exequetur X

' The royal commands and the wishes of our archbishop which he has intimated to us are something
entirely new and unheard of up till now. He must know
that I have never been and never will be a distributor of
letters. I have never constrained my clerks to serve the
king, nor will I do so. I have often forbidden even clerks
not in my service who hold benefices in my diocese to dare
to oppress the laity in pursuance of their administrative
duties, by making distraints under the forest law or in
any other way. I have even punished those who ignored
my just commands by sequestrating their benefices
for long periods. Why ever therefore should we
remove from the heart of our church these people and
send them to serve the king in obedience to his
commands ? Let it content our lord the king that the
archbishops, certainly to the danger of their souls and
forgetful of their profession, have wholeheartedly devoted
themselves to the promotion of his business. If this does
not seem enough to him, this bishop will accompany
his clerks, he will come, I say, to hear his orders from his
own mouth, he will come in obedience to these orders,
ready to do whatever is right.

' You can take away with you your twelve letters,
which you have told me you have brought to me, and
do what you like with them. Tell our lord and archbishop in full everything I say to you, and finally inform
him that if my clerks go to the king as instructed I shall
go with them. They shall not go without me now, nor
have I gone without them on other occasions. The
relation of a good shepherd to his flock and theirs to him
means that he should not lose them by exposing them
to danger, nor should they stray or dare to run away
from him.'

Iras ad hec spirabat litterarum baiulus. Erat enim curialis clericus ; in hoc ipsum, ut tali fungeretur legatione, de industria assumptus. Erat quoque, ut dabat intelligi, fastu innato tumidus set tumidissimus ex afflatu spiritus curialis. Qui cum pararet minas euomere quas, anhelitu pre cordis tumore intercluso, uix sufficiebat proferre, intercidit uerba uirosa episcopus, recedere eum quamtocius iubens. Qui protinus ita perturbatus et confusus abscessit.

Misit uero quosdam ex suis uiros prudentes episcopus ad archiepiscopum, rogans et monens quatinus premetiri dignaretur et precauere in edictis huiuscemodi, ecclesiastice *a* immunitatis quam tueri tenebatur euidens preiudicium, nec sue in talibus ullatenus preberet auctoritatis assensum. Quorum ille precibus siue rationibus specietenus potius quam medullitus flexus, rancore parumper dissimulato, quem palam ex inobedientia ut dicebat suffraganei sui se concepisse memorauerat, cum auctoritas simul et ratio certa prescribat numquam debere per obedientiam malum fieri, cum debeat interdum bonum intermitti,*b* spopondit se prouisurum quatinus, salua utilitate *c* regia, licuisset ut presens negotium ad pacem domini Lincolniensis aut sopiretur funditus aut moderatius ordinaretur.

Verum non in longum locum habuit quies pacis repromisse. Emissis enim cito post ista publicis edictis, iubentur possessiones episcopi in manus recipi regalium exactorum. Quod ut audiuit episcopus, ' Nonne,' inquit clericis suis, ' uere dixi uobis quia uox quidem hominum istorum uox Iacob est, set manus manus sunt Esau ? ' [1]

Verum ut ea que gesta sunt summatim percurramus, illi quibus fuit demandata executio edicti tyrranici pre

---

a ecclesie Q   *b* omitti X   *c* uoluntate X

The bearer of the letter almost foamed at the mouth. He was a Chancery clerk, who was specially employed as a messenger in cases of this type, obviously full of his own importance and one whose insolence had been greatly increased by his position at court. His indignation made him almost speechless, and when he was beginning to use threats, the bishop cut short his insolent words by abruptly ordering him to go, which he immediately did in a state of perplexity and confusion.

The bishop, however, sent some of his wisest councillors to the archbishop, asking and advising him to deign to weigh well and consider the obvious threat to the liberties of the Church, which he was bound to defend, contained in orders of this kind, and in no circumstances to give to them the support of his authority. Although not really deeply impressed he made a semblance of being appeased by these prayers and arguments. Hiding the anger which had been roused in him at what he described as open defiance on the part of his suffragan, although both the scriptures and reason declare that one should never do wrong out of obedience but only sometimes postpone a good action, he answered that he would do his best to ensure, if the interests of the king allowed him, that the present business should either be dropped altogether, or conducted with more moderation for the sake of the bishop of Lincoln.

The promised peace was of short duration. Soon after this a proclamation was made ordering that the possessions of the bishop should be seized by the royal officers. When the bishop heard of it, he said to his clerks, ' Surely I told you the truth, that the voice of these men is that of Jacob, but their hands those of Esau.' [1]

To deal briefly with what ensued. Those who had been ordered to carry out this tyrannical decree, at first

---

[1] Gen. 27: 22

nimia formidine primo supersedere mandato, sug-
gerentes regi quanti esset periculi tam iubentibus quam
exequentibus quicquam unde incideretur in maledictionem uiri illius attemptare, manifestissimum *a* siquidem esse quod cuicumque ille maledixisset malediceret Dominus et maledictio, ut ait propheta, citius
deuoraret illum.[1]

Erat tunc in exercitu quidam Rutariorum princeps
uocabulo Marchadeus,[2] homo per omnia belluine seuitie
et perdite conscientie, uir ad quodlibet scelus et sacrilegium preceps. Rex igitur, nichil aut parum motus ad
meliora, per ea que a suis executoribus crebro ei
suggerebantur, ' Meticulosi sunt,' inquit, ' Anglici isti.
Mittamus itaque Marchadeum qui ludere norit cum
Burgundiensi illo.'

Cui statim quidam amicorum suorum ait, ' Necessarius est, domine rex, Marchadeus guerre uestre.
Ceterum opera illius et obsequio certissime fraudabimini
si efficitur *b* anathema Lincolniensi episcopi.' Quod rex
sibi nequaquam expedire affirmans, plusque ipsius
periculum quam suum proprium reformidans, illum
quidem *c* mittere supersedit, set unde ipsemet exitialiter
periclitaretur committere non precauit.*d*

Cuidam igitur officiali *e* suo nomine Stephano de
Turneham,[3] uiro utique fideli et timorato, nostro etiam
pontifici satis deuoto, dedit in mandatis ut sicut uitam
suam ac menbra diligeret, bona Lincolniensis episcopi

---

a manifestum X   *b* efficiatur X   *c* + ne periret QX
d non expauit nec precauit X   *e* om B
[1] cf. Is. 24: 6
[2] Richard's celebrated mercenary captain, after whom the bridge
Makade at the king's new castle at Andély was named. He is reputed to
have been responsible for the torture of Richard's slayer, and was himself
murdered at Bordeaux in 1200. The mercenaries, routiers or Brabançons
were excommunicated by the Church, and were the ' scum ' of the military
profession. Their cruelty was regarded by contemporaries as one factor in
the decline of loyalty to the Angevins which made Philip II's conquest of

postponed its execution out of panic, pointing out to the king the great danger both to its initiators and executants of doing anything which would cause their excommunication by the bishop. It was abundantly clear that divine retribution fell on anyone he had excommunicated, and in the words of the prophet the curse soon destroyed them.[1]

At that time there was with the army a mercenary captain called Mercadier,[2] who was in every way more like a savage beast than a man, completely pitiless and notorious for every crime and sacrilege. The king whose better nature was hardly, if at all, roused by the frequent representations of those he had ordered to carry out his decree, said, ' You English are too scrupulous. We will send Mercadier who will know how to deal with this Burgundian.'

Some of his friends immediately replied, ' Lord King, Mercadier is essential in your campaign. You will lose his services if he falls under the malediction of the bishop of Lincoln.' The king then declared that this would be disastrous for him, since he feared for Mercadier's safety more than for his own. He therefore refrained from sending him, but did not dread doing something equally fatal to himself.

He therefore gave written instructions to one of his officials Stephen de Turnham,[3] a faithful and godly man and devoted to our holy bishop, that if he valued his life and limbs, he would at once confiscate the possessions

Normandy an easy matter (cf. F. M. Powicke, *The Loss of Normandy* (Manchester 1913), pp. 336-43).

[3] Stephen de Turnham, one of Richard's companions in Syria, who escorted Queen Berengaria and her sister-in-law, Queen Joan of Sicily back from the Holy Land. He acted as an itinerant justice in Essex, Surrey and Hertford during the last years of Richard's reign, and must have attended St Hugh's funeral as he was one of the witnesses of the homage of the king of Scots at Lincoln in 1200. In 1213 he had the custody of the future Henry III.

absque dilatione in manus suas reciperet.*a* Qui tandem regio metu coactus, misit quosdam ex suis ad terras uel quecumque mobilia *b* reperissent, cum uillis et castellis ipsius occupandas. Quibus primum ad recipiendum opidum Lafford tendentibus occurrit forte non longe a burgo sancti Petri comitatus episcopi. Cuius illi occursu territi, diuerterunt paululum de uia ; et accersitis quibusdam e clericis, exposuerunt eis quanta minatus fuerit *c* dominus rex domino ipsorum quia distulisset *d* episcopum desaisire, et quia inuiti metuque supremi discriminis astricti, ad id exequendum modo irent. More igitur quinquagenarii tertii a rege perfido missi ad Helyam,[1] isti quoque humiliantes se supplicabant obnixius ut, illis mediantibus, misereretur animabus eorum uerus ille seruus Dei, ne propter eius *e* offensionem quam timebant incurrere, ultio celestis consumeret eos. Orant ut regiam potius mitigare festinaret animositatem ne detrimenta cumularentur undique, etiam insontibus et a merito contentionis inter regem et pontificem mote prorsus alienis. Spondent interim se pro uiribus illibatas seruaturos res illius, petunt [ut] *f* suspendat ad tempus sententiam excommunicationis, qua et regem amplius exacerbari et suam eorum proueniret innocentiam periclitari.

Hec ubi episcopo innotuerunt, ' Non est,' inquit, ' istorum seruare res nostras. Eant *g* tamen ; et res non tam nostras quam domine nostre sancte Dei genitricis Marie, ut eis uidebitur, tractent et inuadant.' *h* Hec dicens, protulit e sinu fimbriam stole linee qua collo suo, dum iter ageret, semper appensa utebatur sub

---

a recepisset B
c fuerat X
e *om* B
g Extant X

b + episcopi X
d distulit B¹
f quatinus Xp; *om* B
h inuadent B

of the bishop of Lincoln. He at length, constrained by his fear of the king, sent some of his men to seize the estates with his castles and manors and whatever goods they found. These when they were journeying to take over the town of Sleaford happened to meet near Peterborough the bishop's company. Terror-stricken by this encounter, they withdrew a little way from the road, and then approached certain of his clerks, and told them of the terrible threats of the lord king against their master for his delay in disseizing the bishop, and how they themselves much against their wills and constrained by fear for their own safety, had now come to carry this out. Like the fifty-three sent by the wicked king to Elijah,[1] these urgently and humbly implored them, that through their intercession the faithful servant of God might have compassion on their souls, lest on account of his wrath which they dreaded to provoke, the divine vengeance should destroy them. They begged that he would take immediate steps to placate the king's anger, lest, owing to it, innocent people quite unconcerned in the dispute between him and the bishop might be involved in its serious consequences. They undertook meanwhile to do their best to keep his possessions intact, but asked that he would suspend his sentence of excommunication for the present, since it would merely exasperate the king still more and ruin both them and himself, in spite of their innocence.

When they reported this to the bishop, he said, ' It is not for them to preserve our possessions. Let them go their way and seize and treat as they think right what is not our property but belongs to our Lady Mary, the holy mother of God.' As he spoke, he drew out the

[1] cf. 4 Kings 1: 9-15

capa sua ; eamque manu agitans, ' Hoc certe,' inquit,
' filulum restituet nobis usque ad extremum obolum
quicquid isti duxerint rapiendum.'

Veniensque in uillam suam Bugdenam appellatam,
ubi et litterarum archiepiscopalium supradictus portitor
ad illum uenerat, ubi quoque de tuenda libertate
ecclesiastica per clericum quemdam diuini oraculi
premonitionem, ut dudum supra commemoratum est,
acceperat ;[1] iussit continuo litteras fieri quibus pre-
cipiebat *a* archidiaconis et decanis locorum in quibus
constitute fuerant possessiones sue quatinus, adunatis
secum uicinarum ecclesiarum presbiteris, mox ut in
partes illorum peruenirent executores memorati, pulsatis
campanis accensisque candelis, omnes illos subicerent
anathemati qui res ecclesie sue uiolenter contingere et
iniuste occupare, precipiendo seu obsequendo presumpsissent.

Hiis in hunc modum dispositis, cum omnes pene sui
metu et perturbatione uehementi fluctuarent, ille demum
lectulo exceptus ac si nichil inquietudinis pertulisset,
suauissimum extemplo menbra *b* laxauit in soporem.
Nec enim ista ad intima cordis eius umquam pene-
trabant. Ea quoque nocte, ut constaret eum, corpore
etiam soporato, Deo uigili mente iugiter inherere,
' Amen ' continuis fere per interualla momentis ipsum
audiuimus resonare. Faciebat hoc cunctis prope *c*
noctibus, quod dictu mirum est, nichilque aliud ab ore
dormientis aliquando insonuit. Hac uero nocte crebrius
solito et intensius ac uelud cum spiritus uehementiori *d*
impulsu ' Amen ' iterat, iterare non desistebat.

a precipiebatur X
b menbra] *om* B ; laxauit] laxatur B²
c pene X
d uehementis X

fringe of the linen stole which he always wore round his neck under his cloak when on a journey, and fingering it, said, ' This fringe shall restore to us down to the last halfpenny whatever they think fit to rob us of.'

He came to his manor at Buckden, where the bearer of the letters of the archbishop had come to him as I have already described, and where he had received from a clerk a divine message to defend the liberties of the Church, as I mentioned a long way back.[1] There he immediately ordered letters to be written, in which he commanded the archdeacons and the rural deans of the districts where he had property that, having at once assembled the priests of the neighbourhood as soon as the escheators I have already mentioned came into those parts, after ringing the bells and lighting candles they should excommunicate all those who dared to order the illegal and violent seizure and occupation of his possessions and those who obeyed them.

When these arrangements had been made which caused fear and alarm to almost everyone, he went to bed as if there was nothing to worry him and immediately fell sweetly asleep. His inner serenity seemed quite unaffected by these happenings. That night, however, although his body rested, his soul seemed to be intent upon God, for we heard him every moment saying Amen. He did this almost every night, but, wonderful to relate, no other sound ever came from him as he slept. This particular night, however, as if he were under the domination of some intense feeling, he kept on repeating Amen, more frequently and earnestly than usual, and never stopped doing so.

---

[1] pp. 85-92

CAPITVLVM VIII

De duabus feminis, quarum alteram a phitonico, alteram ab incubone eripuit demone.

Iam uero quod pretereundum non fuit,[a] in capitulo Lincolniensi ad regem se pro communi necessitate trans mare iturum predixerat. Iam filiis suis benedictione ad missas ritu sollempni data, illa scilicet qua benedicere iussi sunt filiis Israel sacerdotes in lege per Moysen, quam ille in benedictionali suo scribi fecerat[1] ; commendatus orationibus singulorum atque libato inuicem sancto pacis osculo, uniuersos commendauerat uerbis apostolicis Deo et uerbo gratie eius.[2] Inde ut premissum est directo calle ad manerium peruenerat supradictum.

Vbi cum paucis maneret diebus, suggeritur ei a decano uicini loci mulierculam quamdam in decanatu suo que spiritum uideretur habere phitonicum, plurimas ad se diuinando turbas pertrahere populorum. Indicabat enim passim furta, a quibuscumque admissa, et occulta queque retegebat[b] maleficia. Si uero ab ipso, ut idem aiebat decanus, seu a quouis discreto et litterato uiro conueniebatur super hoc aut corripiebatur, mox inportuna lingue uolubilis dicacitate arguentem eam quasi stupidum reddebat et elinguem ; sicque omnes uerbositatis affluentia opprimebat ut nullus eam euincere aut ei silentium ualeret imponere.

Ad hec statim episcopus ' Iam,' inquit, ' non post multos dies Londonias adituri, cum per fines uestros transitum faciemus, adduces illam in loco oportuno in occursum nostri.' Quod et factum est. Descendit

---

[a] pretermittendum X . . . est Q   [b] detegebat QX

Chapter VIII

Of two women, one of whom he delivered from a familiar spirit which prophesied, and the other from being plagued by the devil.

It should not have been omitted that he had declared in the chapter at Lincoln that on behalf of the whole community he would go to the king across the sea. At mass therefore he gave his sons the solemn pontifical benediction prescribed by Moses in the law for the priests of Israel, and which he had had copied into his Benedictional.[1] Then having asked for the prayers of each one of them, and exchanged the holy kiss of peace, he commended them all in the words of the apostle to God, and to his gracious favour.[2] Then as I have related he went to Buckden by the shortest route.

When he had been there a few days, the rural dean of the neighbouring district told him of a certain woman in his deanery who was reputed to have the spirit of prophecy and drew large crowds by her prognostications. He alleged that she had frequently revealed thefts, no matter who had committed them, and exposed concealed crimes of every kind. The dean further said that if she was taken to task and rebuked by himself or any other pious and learned man, the flood of abuse soon rendered the rebuker dumbfounded and speechless. Indeed, her flow of words overwhelmed everyone, and no-one was able to quell or silence her.

The bishop immediately replied, ' When a few days from now, I shall be passing through your district on my way to London, bring her to meet me at a convenient

---

[1] cf. Num. 6: 24-26   [2] Acts 20: 32

itaque, uisa muliere, de equo suo episcopus. Astabat
uero ibidem populi frequentia cum paruulis qui manus
impositione erant confirmandi. Muliere igitur sibi
presentata, uir Domini quasi cum indignatione obbuccans
non tam miseram illam quam eius inhabitatorem
occultum demonem, ' Age iam o infelix,' inquit, ' quid
nosti diuinare nobis ? ' Proferens autem clausum
dextere sue pugillum implicitam in eo tenens extremi-
tatem stole sue, ' dic,' ait, ' sodes, siquidem nosti quid
habeat inclusum manus ista.' [a] Hoc eo dicente, statim
uelud exanimis corruit ad pedes eius muliercula, paulo
ante procax et ceruicosa, nunc autem subito ad uocem
uirtutis tante, nec modo fandi set etiam standi impotens
effecta. Aufugerat enim internus agitator [b] qui eam
male uegetauerat, et illa remanserat sub manu sanantis
medici salubriter debilis, que sub impetu perimentis
morbi extiterat prius letaliter fortis. Cum ergo ad
uestigia eius inclinata aliquamdiu iacuisset, precepit
eleuari eam. Tunc decano interprete usus, ignorabat
enim linguam rusticane mulieris, inquiri iussit qualiter
diuinationis peritiam accepisset. Que tenui et submissa
uoce, cum fuisset sepius interrogata, respondit, [c]
' Nescio,' inquit, ' diuinare, set misericordiam imploro
sancti huius episcopi.' Iterumque defixo in terram
uultu procidit ad pedes eius. Cumque, imposita manu
capiti eius, pro ea breuiter orasset, data benedictione,
precepit eam ad priorem Huntedinensem,[1] illarum
uidelicet partium penitentialem [d] adduci, dans ei in

---

[a] mea Qv
[b] habitator QX, and B²
[c] dixit Q
[d] penitentiarium X

[1] The Augustinian priory of St Mary's Huntingdon was founded between
1086 and 1092 by Eustace the Sheriff (de Lovelot). Its most famous
colonies were Hexham (Northumberland) 1113, Merton (Surrey) 1114,

place'. Thus it was done. When he saw the woman, the
bishop dismounted. There was there a crowd of people
with their children for him to lay his hands on and
confirm. When she was brought to him the man of God
angrily scoffed not so much at the wretched woman herself as at the demon by which she was possessed. ' Show
now, wretch, what you can reveal about us.' He held
out his clenched right fist with the end of his stole held
tightly in it. ' Tell me,' he said, ' I pray you, if you can,
what is enclosed in my hand.' As he said this, the woman
fell down in a faint at his feet, and she who before had
been swollen-headed and stubborn, now suddenly at the
voice of authority, was able neither to speak nor stand.
The familiar spirit which had before possessed her for
evil purposes, deserted her, and she, who had before been
fatally strong, but in the clutches of a mortal disease,
was left weak but curable in the hands of the skilful
doctor. When she had lain at his feet for a little while,
he ordered them to raise her. Then with the rural dean
as interpreter, for he could not understand the woman's
dialect, he asked how she had acquired skill in divination.
When she had been repeatedly asked, she replied in a
low and quiet voice, ' I cannot soothsay, but I beg this
holy bishop to have pity on me.' Then with her face to
the ground, she fell again at his feet. He laid his hand on
her head and, having prayed for her a little while, he
gave her his blessing and ordered her to be taken to the
prior of Huntingdon [1] who was then penitentiary in that
region, to whom he sent written instructions, that after a

Embsay (afterwards Bolton Abbey, Yorks.) 1120-1, and Aldgate. The prior
mentioned here was either John who resigned in 1225 (*Rotuli Hugonis de
Wells*, ed. F. N. Davis, C. and Y. Society, London 1908, III, p. 54), or his
predecessor. The office of penitentiary to give absolution in cases reserved
to the bishop was rare till the 4th Lateran Council of 1215.

mandatis quatinus ueram ageret, premissa confessione
purissima, de omnibus peccatis suis penitentiam. Quod
etiam ut postmodum accepimus fideliter impleuit.
Preceperat enim ᵃ ei ne ulterius presumeret aliena
maleficia diuinare, set propria assuesceret indesinenter
mala lugere et accusare. Que ex hoc tempore adeo
modesta apparuit et taciturna cum prius garula nimis
extiterit et procacissima ut hoc ipsum loco ingentis
miraculi haberetur penes uniuersos qui mores illius
pristinos agnouerunt.

Huic loco pro causarum necnon et personarum
similitudine, alterius ab infestatione demoniaca ereptionem mulieris, uirtutibus huius uiri iuste annumerandamᵇ
reseruauimus exponendam, licet tempore diuerso celebratam. Intimauerat ei quodam tempore uir eximie
eruditionis et doctrine Bartholomeus Exoniensis presul,[1]
quia quidam demon in specie iuuenis abuti consueuerit ᶜ quadam infelici muliercula in sua diocesi
constituta. Quam etiam asserebat tam sibi quam et
aliis uenerabilibus personis detestabilis huius passionis
sue erumpnam flebili sepius confessione propalasse, et
consilium quo eriperetur ab obsceno oppressore studiosius inquisisse ; ieiuniis insuper et uaria carnis
maceratione illam memorabat peccatricia menbra sua
fere usque ad internicionem perdomuisse ; hec uero
simul omnia nichil sibi contra odiosum et improbum
amatorem contulisse. In talibus quoque non paucorum
iam curricula temporum eam dixit protraxisse.

Hic ᵈ uenerabilis pater Hugo, pudoris pariter et
pietatis instinctu compatiens miserabili femine et

ᵃ vero (erased) B ; + ipsa X   ᵇ admirandum X
ᶜ consueuerat QX   ᵈ Hinc Xp
[1] Archdeacon of Exeter 1155, and bishop 1161-84, he supported first
the king and then the archbishop in the Becket controversy. His fame as a
canonist caused Alexander III to employ him frequently as a judge-

full confession, she should do fitting penance for all her sins, which as I afterwards heard she faithfully carried out. He also commanded her never again to dare to reveal other people's misdoings, but unceasingly to confess and bewail her own. From that time forth she who before had been so garrulous and arrogant became silent and humble, which in itself seemed a great miracle to all who had been conversant with her former behaviour.

Owing to the similarity of the cases and the persons, I have decided to describe here his rescue of another woman from the attacks of a demon, which is rightly to be reckoned among his miraculous acts, although it took place at quite a different time. Bartholomew, bishop of Exeter,[1] a man of exceptional learning and holiness, once told him that a demon in the shape of a young man was constantly molesting an unfortunate woman living in his diocese. With many tears she often confessed to him and other devout men how horrible and hateful his attacks were, and sought their counsel as to how to escape from her filthy seducer. He related how she had almost killed herself by fasting and by the austerities to which she subjected her sinful body, but none of these things availed against her horrible and shameless lover. According to him, she had endured this for a long time.

Our venerable father Hugh's own purity and compassion made him both pity the poor woman and detest

---

delegate. He was a friend of John of Salisbury and archbishop Baldwin, to whom, when abbot of Ford, he dedicated his *De Libero Arbitrio* and his *Dialogus contra Iudaeos*. A hundred of his sermons are in MS Bodley 449, and his popular penitential is printed by Dom A. Morey in *Bartholomew of Exeter* (Oxford 1937), pp. 164-300. Adam's story is probably apocryphal as Bartholomew died two years before St Hugh became bishop of Lincoln. Giraldus Cambrensis included him with St Hugh amongst the six model bishops whose lives he wrote.

indignans impuritati demoniace, ' Iam,' inquit, ' si ista, ut asseritis, contra peccatum suum contritione cordis, confessione oris et corporis afflictione erigitur, nil aliud demum superesse uideo nisi ut oretur pro ea instantius apud clementiam piissimi Redemptoris.' Episcopus autem Exoniensis hoc se secumque alios innumeros iam diu fecisse, set nil profecisse palam commemorans, ipsum quoque ut pro ea dignaretur orare suppliciter flagitabat. Cui ille, ' Hec,' inquit, ' non ego tantum set quisque fidelium deuotissime facere debebit.'

Post hec digressis ab inuicem episcopis, cum sibi occurrissent iterum aliquanto tempore iam elapso, inquisiuit sollicitus iste animarum liberator episcopum illum superius memoratum qualiter res se haberet circa ouiculam gregis sui quam pestifer ille lupus tam immaniter laniauerat. Cui pontifex non solum eius ereptionem set ereptionis quoque ordinem satis mirabilem exposuit in hunc modum.

' Adiuta,' inquit, ' orationibus uestris, dudum illa euasit probrose seruitutis iugum. Cum enim die quadam incestus ᵃ ille demon incredibili eam libidinis furore delusam exanimem pene reddidisset, ille abscedens euanuit et illa in conclaui suo nimio dolore et merore ᵇ addicta remansit. Cum ecce in alterius specie iuuenis alius, ut ei uidebatur, spiritus ingrediens ad eam, unde adeo mestos gereret animos sollicitari ᶜ cepit. Qua respondente nil, ait ille, " Scio uereque noui quia nequam ille afflixit te, set non mirum, est enim peruersus et malignus admodum. Verum si desideriis meis et consiliis prestare uelis assensum, numquam de cetero is ad te habebit accessum."

' Ad hec illa plurimum exhilarata confestim respondit, " Nichil est," inquit, " sub celo facultati mee possibile

---

ᵃ infestus X   ᵇ dolori et merori Qv   ᶜ sciscitari QX

the unclean spirit. ' If she,' he said, ' has combated her temptation with heartfelt sorrow, confession and bodily austerities, I do not see that anything more can be done except to pray earnestly for her to our merciful and compassionate Redeemer.' The bishop of Exeter, however, said that he and very many other persons had long done this but with no apparent result, nevertheless he prayed and besought him to be so good as to pray for her, to which he replied, ' Not only I, but all the faithful ought to do this most fervently '.

After this the two bishops parted. When they again met a little while later, this healer of souls inquired anxiously of the bishop just mentioned how things were with the ewe of his flock whom the wicked wolf had so mercilessly attacked. The bishop described not only her rescue, but gave the amazing story of this rescue in detail.

' By the assistance of your prayers,' he said, ' she has now been freed from the burden of that shameful bondage. One day when the licentious demon had by the terrific force of his assault nearly killed his victim, he vanished, and she remained alone, overcome by grief and misery. Suddenly, she seemed to see another spirit in the shape of another young man approaching her, who asked anxiously why she was so sad. As she did not answer, he said, " I know and understand that it is because you are tormented by an evil spirit ; and it is not surprising, for he is obstinate and cruel. If, however, you are willing to follow my wishes and counsels, never from henceforth shall he approach you."

' She was greatly gladdened by these words and immediately replied, " There is nothing on earth within my capacity, that I would not willingly do or undergo if only I could be spared his approaches." " Do not," he

quod non libens facerem seu perferrem dummodo ab
ipsius accessu perinde saluari potuissem." " Mecum
ergo," ille ait, " amoris non dubites fedus inire. Ego
siquidem quecumque poposceris aut optaueris tibi
prestabo, nichil a te tuis contrarium uotis exigam, nichil
non delectabile siue amabile tibi inferam." Spondet
illa hec et alia pollicenti assensum dummodo experiatur
promisse liberationis effectum. Tunc ille eduxit eam ad
proximum domui sue locum et herbam eminus suc-
crescentem illi demonstrans, " Istam," inquit, " herbam
tolle et in sinu tuo reconde ac circumcirca in domo tua
sparge. Experimento disces dum hec feceris, me in
promissis ueridicum extitisse." Fecit illa quod fuerat
edocta. Venitque post hec in nota effigie demon
uersipellis, astansque prope fenestram qua intrare
solebat et exire et intro aspiciens, dixit ad mulierem,
" Quidnam istud est horridum et putridum quod in hac
ede sparsisti ? Proice quamtocius longe a te et a domo
tua inuisum gramen quod imprudens tibi applicuisti."
Illa dissimulante monitis obtemperare maligni, cepit
ille nunc minis nunc blanditiis agere ut herbam eiceret
quam se exhorruisse dicebat. Qui ut se contempni
uidit ab ea, post morulas aliquot recessit furibundus et
minax. Nec paulo tardius affuit alter ac quasi aggrat-
ulans dilecte ait, " Verane esse didicisti que tibi locutus
sum ? Nunc ergo dum ego tecum secretius loquar,
amouebis parumper a te herbam nostratum uniuersitati
odiosam. Post meum uero discessum resumes arma-
turam graminis tui qua illesa conseruaberis ab insidiis
hostis uirosi. Nequaquam enim furcifer ille ad te
presumet ullatenus accedere dum sentiet me tecum
presentem esse." Ad hec illa, " Venies," inquit, " si uelis
et si possis ad me, nec enim promissioni mee debeo
contraire. Ceterum herbam istam, uita comite, num-

answered, "have any misgivings about making a love
pact with me. I, for my part will give you whatever you
ask or desire, and will require nothing from you which
is contrary to your wishes and will do nothing to you
which you do not find pleasing and delightful." She
agreed to this and to his other offers, on condition that
she should really be set free. He then led her to a place
near her dwelling and showed her a plant growing hard
by saying, " Take this plant and hide it in your bosom,
and scatter it all round your house. You will see for
yourself when you have done so that my promise has
come true." She did as she had been instructed. The
disguised demon came in his usual shape and standing
at the window by which he was accustomed to enter and
depart, said to the woman, " Whatever is this disgusting
and stinking plant which you have scattered about your
house. Cast away at once as far as you can from you
and from your home this horrible herb with which you
have imprudently surrounded yourself." When she
refused to obey the command of the Evil One, he began
to threaten and cajole her to throw away the plant to
which he said he had an aversion. Finding she took no
notice, he left after a short delay, in a rage and using
threats. A little later the other appeared and as if trying
to woo his beloved, said, " You've now proved for yourself, have you not, that what I told you was true. Now,
therefore while you and I have a nice little tête-à-tête,
do move away from you for a bit our plant which everyone detests. After I've gone you can once more use it
as a protection to keep you safe from the assaults of a
persistent enemy, for this rascal will never dare molest
you whilst he knows that I am with you." She answered,
" You can come if you wish, and if you can, for I ought
not to break my promise, but, as long as I live, never

quam reiciam a me, que sola michi potuit contra impurissimum oppressorem securitatem prestare." Quid plura ? Et iste sicut ille prior, post diuturnas *a* preces, post minas et blanditias frustra protractas, circumuentum se a muliercula diu multumque deplorans, in auras inanes demum euanuit. Mulier uero iam fide et deuotione ac bona conuersatione melius quam herba illa armata, uitam ducit *b* in Dei timore honestam et quietam.

'Hec autem omnia, ut a nobis narrantur, ego ab illius ore cum ad me demum iam curata penitentie modulum et absolutionis beneficium susceptura uenisset audiui.' Et hec quidem Exoniensis episcopus episcopo retulit nostro, que ipse frequenter nobis, plurimis presentibus,*c* referebat. Si cui autem ista forte minus uidebuntur esse credenda, legat Bedam in explanationem *d* Luce euangeliste, et hiis similia que suis temporibus acciderunt, a tanto doctore ibidem conscripta reperiet.[1]

Mulier uero prefata, dum orationis gratia *e* multa peragraret sanctorum loca, peruenit demum Cantuariam. Vbi dum a uiris religiosis orationum inquirit suffragia, cuidam monacho sancti Augustini herbam illam e sinu suo prolatam *f* ostendit. Quam ille nobis, nos ipsam episcopo postmodum demonstrauimus, nam eatenus eam minime agnouerat. Elapso autem tempore unius anni, retulit nobis idem monachus qualiter iuuenis quidam necnon et puella de prouincia Estsexie per talem herbam, ipso eam prebente eis et demonstrante, a prestigiis demonum eis uisibiliter colloquentium erepti fuerint et defensi. Set de hiis plura referre non est temporis aut operis huius. Ipsam uero herbam Greci

---

a diurnas B   *b* duxit X   *c* *om* B
d explanatione Qv   *e* *om* B   *f* *om* B

will I cast away from me this plant, which is my only defence against my lascivious seducer." To be brief, just like the former, after long and vain prayers, threats and blandishments, and great and protracted lamentations that he had been cheated by the woman, he at last vanished into empty air. The woman, however, lived a quiet, chaste and God-fearing life, finding faith, piety and good conduct a better defence than any plant. All that I have described, I heard from her own mouth when she came to me already cured to receive a slight penance and absolution.'

What the bishop of Exeter related to our bishop, he often repeated to us and to many other persons. If it seems incredible to anyone, he should read Bede's Commentary on the gospel of St Luke. There he will find described by an eminent theologian similar incidents which occurred in his times.[1]

The woman of whom I speak, having visited and prayed at many shrines, came at last to Canterbury. There when asking for the prayers of the community she took that plant out of her bosom and showed it to a monk of St Augustine's. This he showed to us, and we afterwards showed it to the bishop, for up to that time he had been unable to identify it. After a year had passed, the same monk told us how a young man and girl from the county of Essex when he showed and exhibited that plant to them, were cured and protected from the attacks of demons who were seen conversing with them. It is not, however, the time or place to say any more about this. The common name of the plant is Ypericon in Greek, and in Latin either the perforated plant or St-John's-wort. Amongst other properties

---

[1] cf. P.L. 92, 438

Ypericon, Latini herbam perforatam siue herbam sancti Ioannis appellare solent. Que preter alias satis utiles potentias quas phisici assignant, uenenum specialiter consumere perhibetur, siue bibitum siue alio modo sumptum, aut etiam morsu uirulenti animalis inflictum aut infusum, si trita et aquis temperata patienti detur in potum. Nec forte putamus esse absurdum si munere Creatoris *a* estimetur percepisse contra spiritualium nequitias serpentum que materiale extinguit uenenum. Legimus namque etiam quasdam gemmas set et aliarum rerum certas species, fantasias euacuare laruales ; dum nichil in orbe reliquit sine remedio competenti, quod ledi ualeat hostis liuore *b* maligni, propitia miseratio cuncta saluantis Dei. Sic enim magis deicitur superbi illius arrogantia spiritus, dum rebus abiectis et uilibus malignitatis sue uirtus eneruata reliditur.

Capitvlvm IX

De homine furioso a demone liberato. Et de furis ereptione ad suspendium destinati.*c* Et qualiter barronibus scaccarii Hugo sit locutus.

Exigit casus recens ut sollempne miraculum, Domini uirtute patratum per fidelem ipsius famulum iam nunc recenseamus. Id quidem paulo superius, temporis ratione quo gestum est, debuisset exponi, si omnia que de tanto summi Patrisfamilias operario innotescere necesse,*d* nostro crederemus obsequio posse euolui. Verum nos, ut prefati sumus, ea potius que edificant

---

a + uires X
b quo . . . liuor B²
c destinato B
d + est X

ascribed to it by the doctors it is alleged to be a sovereign remedy against poison, whether administered in a drink or in some other way, even if this is due to the bite of a poisonous animal, provided it is crushed, and infused in water and given to the patient as a drink. We do not judge it ridiculous to suppose that a bodily remedy for snake-bite should not by God's mercy have been effective against the assaults of the ancient Serpent. We have read moreover that some gems and certain other kinds of things can dispel ghastly nightmares, for nothing in the world which can be hurt by the malice of the treacherous enemy has through the gracious mercy of our Saviour been left without an adequate remedy. Thus the arrogance of that proud spirit is the more humbled when his power and malice are rendered harmless by petty and trivial objects.

Chapter IX

Concerning the madman out of whom a demon was driven, and the thief saved from the gallows. Hugh's interview with the barons of the Exchequer.

A recent event makes it necessary for me to recount a stupendous miracle wrought by God through the agency of His faithful servant. This should have been described a little earlier according to the time when it took place, if I had believed that it was my essential duty to make known every work of this great servant of our heavenly Father. But, as I have already said, being anxious to select from so great a model of the virtues acts

ad emulationem uirtutis quam ea que excitant ad
plausum admirationis de tanto uirtutis exemplari prelibare cupientes, istud cum aliis satis innumeris sub
silentio pene preteriuimus. In quo tamen opere plus
eminet quod deuotum prouocet ad uirtutem quam quod
curiosum excitet ad stuporem.

Itaque nuper contigit ut cum uenerabili uiro domino
abbate Walthamensi Ricardo per uillam uocabulo
Cestrehunte, abbatie sue proximam, transiremus. Cuius
ut plateas ingressi sumus, reuocauit nobis in memoriam
presentia locorum hoc quod ante circiter annos tredecim
ibidem conspeximus gestum. Eo siquidem temporis
articulo, quo regie insectationis procella quam modo
describimus,[a] in Lincolniensis ecclesie pastorem, semetipsum pro ouibus suis exponentem, primum efferbuit, id
accidit quod referrimus. Ea namque tempestate isdem
peruigil ouilis Dominici custos Londonias adierat cum
archiepiscopo ceterisque regni optimatibus super tanto
negotio tractaturus. A quibus id solum consilii reportauit
ut pecunie ingentis summam a clericis suis exigeret,
quam, ad sedandum regis [b] auari furorem, ei per quemlibet ex suis celerius destinarit. Ait namque archiepiscopus : [c] 'An nescitis, domine episcope, quia ut
ydropicus aquam, ita dominus rex sitit pecuniam?'
Cui citius more suo ille responderat, 'Plane etsi ipse
ydropicus est, set ego aqua non ero quam ille [d] deglutiat.'
Discedens itaque a Londoniis, ad suam festinus repedabat
ecclesiam, unde proponebat, dispositis omnibus, ad
regem, ut supradictum est, uelocius [e] transfretare.

Mane igitur die quadam Dominica, per uillam
memoratam quam Cestrehuntam antiquitas nominari
instituit, agebat iter. Cumque iam pene totus comitatus

---

[a] descripsimus X	[b] *om* B	[c] + illi X
[d] ipse uel ille B	[e] citius Q	

which should be a spur to the imitation of his goodness rather than those which merely arouse wonder and admiration, I had been on the point of omitting it as well as very many others. However, this incident ought to be a stimulus to virtue and not merely a cause of curiosity and amazement.

It happened lately that in company with Richard, the venerable abbot of Waltham, I was passing through the vill of Cheshunt which is near his abbey. As we entered the village square, I remembered what I had seen take place there about thirteen years earlier. What I am going to relate happened at the time when the storm of the king's wrath first broke on the shepherd of the church of Lincoln, sacrificing himself on behalf of his sheep. It was just about the time when this watchful guardian of the Lord's sheepfold had been to London to discuss the matter with the archbishop and other important personages in the government. The only advice they could give him was to raise an immense sum of money from his clergy, and send it quickly to the avaricious king by one of his household in order to appease his anger. The archbishop added, ' Surely you are aware, lord bishop, that the lord king thirsts for money like a dropsical man for water.' To this he replied with his usual ready wit, ' Even if he has the dropsy, I will not be water for him to swallow.' He left London, and returned hastily to his church, where, having made the necessary arrangements, he determined, as I have already mentioned, to go abroad immediately to the king.

At dawn one Sunday he was journeying through the vill I have already mentioned, which has since the olden days been called Cheshunt. Most of his people had gone on ahead, and when he with a few attendants reached

illius precessisset, ipse cum paucissimis sociis uille medium ingressus, magno uulgi lamentantis clamore subito uallatur. Exoratur denique a populo confluente ut quemdam conuicaneum suum, a seuissimo possessum demone, sacre consignatione dextere dignaretur benedicere. Quem ut uidit, aperto domus sue hostio, interius iacere ligatum mox spiritu totus infremuit; nec contentus illum ut erat a remotis benedicere, equo quem sederat descendit, ita dicens, ' O proh nefas ! hec utique non se recte habent.' Cernebat namque demonis captiuum supinum iacere, caputque ad postem, manus singulas ad singulos hinc inde paxillos humo altius defixos habentem religatas. Pedes quoque pariter uincti palo erant astricti. Ipsius autem oculi miserabiliter [a] rotabantur in girum ; os nunc in hanc, nunc illam in partem, miserabili rictu contorquebatur. Nunc linguam in immensum protendebat ab ore, nunc dentibus stridebat ; nunc hiatu faucium immanissimo, patulum gutturis meatum ac si quiddam ingens baratrum et intuentibus horridum, demonstrabat.

Ad quem presul uelociter accurrens, facto super eum sancte crucis signo, inclinauit se, et dexteram aliquamdiu prope os illius tenebat obpansam,[b] euangelicum interim capitulum, scilicet, ' In principio erat Verbum ' [1] uoce suppressa percurrens. Cernebat inter hec miserum capud quod huc illucque indesinenter agitare consueuerat, immotum habere et quietum, et ut solent canes cum ictus timent castigantium, oculos subaspiciendo cum quadam formidinis nota in partem uariam meticulose dirigere. Percurso itaque euangelio usque ad locum ubi dicitur ' Plenum gratie et ueritatis ' erexit se episcopus et patientem aliquamdiu tacitus

[a] mirabiliter QX
[b] ob pausam B

the centre of the vill he was suddenly surrounded by a throng of people giving vent to loud lamentations. They rushed up to him, and besought him to bless with the sign of the holy cross one of their neighbours who was possessed by a terrible demon. The door of his house was open, and when Hugh saw him lying bound inside, he groaned in spirit, and not content to bless him from a distance, he dismounted from his horse, exclaiming 'Alas, this is not as it should be.' He saw the possessed man lying prostrate with his head tied to a post and each of his hands to great stakes fixed in the ground. His feet also were bound to a beam. The unhappy wretch was rolling his eyes, and his mouth kept twisting now in this direction and now in that with a ghastly leer. At one moment he stuck his tongue out, and at the next he gnashed his teeth, and then opening his mouth wide he showed the whole back of his throat which appeared to the spectators like some horrible cavern.

The bishop hastened to him, and after signing him with the cross, bent down, and kept his outstretched right hand for a little while over his mouth, at the same time reciting in a low voice the chapter of the gospel 'In the beginning was the Word'. [1] Whilst this was happening he saw that the poor fellow was holding his head still and motionless, which had been turning all the time this way and that, and like dogs when they fear a beating, was moving his eyes fearfully and furtively in various directions. Having continued the gospel up to the words 'full of grace and truth', the bishop raised himself and looked silently at the sufferer for some time, who suddenly turned away his face from him and derisively put out his tongue. Then the valiant assailant

[1] John 1: 1

considerabat. Qui repente in partem alteram uultum ab illo declinans, linguam more subsannantis produxit ab ore. Tunc indignatus ille strenuus potestatis aduerse debellator, aquam et salem ecclesiastico ritu celerrime benedicens atque commiscens, aspersit super illum. Iubensque circumstantibus ut de illa aqua ei in os mitterent, et dans omnibus benedictionem *a* equum ascendit atque discessit. Benedicebant uero illum uniuersi et singuli, asserentes quod suus episcopus paulo ante eadem uia descendens, cum uidisset demoniacum nimio actus pauore, equum cui insederat calcaribus urgens, non solum absque subuentione miserum per-transierit *b* set tamquam ipsemet furiis ageretur, equo currente aufugerit. Vir autem ille, ex tunc liberatus a demone, suam in posterum uitam in omnibus studuit emendare ; uacansque diutius per loca sanctorum peregrinationi pie, cum annis aliquot uixisset deuote, fine tandem bono quieuit in pace.[1]

Hec de consummatione illius in uilla prefata nuper a uicinis suis, qui et interfuisse se dicebant curationi memorate, accepimus. Vbi quoque didicimus qualiter a demone correptus fuerit, cum scilicet mane die quadam in naui dormiret prope Londonias, quo nauali uehiculo adduxerat ligna uenalia ; ubi mox in eum spiritus malignus intrauerat, tam socios suos nautas quam et menbra propria dentibus manibusque discerpere et laniare aggressus est ; uix multorum auxilio tentus et uinctus ac in naui ad trabem magnam astrictus, inde ad propria reuectus est.

Set redeundum est ad ceptum iter pontificis nostri uersus regem, stilo iam currente exponendum. Cum igitur, ut diximus, expulso spiritu phitonico a muliere,

a om B
b pertransierat X

of the powers of darkness waxed indignant, and rapidly mixed water and salt and blessed them in the form prescribed by the Church, and sprinkled it upon him. He ordered the bystanders to put some of the water in his mouth, and after giving them all his blessing, mounted his horse and rode away. They one and all blessed him, declaring that the demoniac's own bishop had passed that way a little while before, and when he saw him had in panic dug his spurs into his horse and had not merely passed by the sufferer without helping him, but galloped away as if pursued by the Furies. The man, who was from then onwards delivered from the demon, did his best to reform his life in every way. He spent much time in pious pilgrimage to the shrines of saints, and after living devoutly for some years, finally made a good and peaceful end.[1]

I learned about his death recently from his neighbours in the vill I have mentioned, who said they had been present at his cure. There I also heard how he came to be possessed by the demon. Early one morning he was sleeping near London in a ship which had brought wood to be sold. Suddenly the evil spirit had entered into him, and he had begun to tear and rend his fellow sailors and his own limbs with his hands and teeth. It was only with difficulty and the assistance of a large number of people that he was secured and tied to a great beam in the ship, and so brought home.

I must now resume my narrative of our bishop's journey to the king. The day after he had, as I have related, expelled the soothsaying spirit from the woman,

---

[1] This miracle was described by Adam to the canonisation commission in 1219, and was confirmed by the abbot of Waltham and a canon of London. It took place in late 1198, or early 1199. See Introduction, vol. I, p. xii. For other examples of reading a Gospel over the sick cf. H. Thurston, *Life of St Hugh of Lincoln*, London 1898, pp. 407-8.

die sequente territorium sancti Albani fuisset *a* ingressus,
ecce occurrit ei cum apparitorum turba quidam
dampnaticus, qui ob commissum furtum, reuinctis post
terga brachiis, ad meritum protrahebatur *b* suspendium.
Ceteris igitur, ad benedictionem pontificis expetendam,
de more suppliciter accurrentibus, ingessit se ui qua
potuit etiam uinctus ille ; ruensque primum ad ceruicem
caballi eius ac statim sub pedibus eius procidens,
misericordiam flebilibus uocibus inclamabat. Tunc
episcopus, reductis *c* confestim habenis, quisnam ille
esset uel quid sibi uellet inquisiuit. Cui dictum est a
suis, rem ut erat agnoscentibus, ' Non uestrum est
domine de isto plura inquirere, quin potius sinite eum et
pertransire.' *d* Dicebant ista metuentes ne illum in sui
omnium *e* penes regem periculum temptaret eripere.
Set ipse eo magis causam inquirens misericordiam
interpellantis, ut eam plenius agnouit uoce alacri
dixit, ' Eya, benedictus Deus !' Tunc ait ministris qui
eum ducebant *f* ad supplicium, ' Redite, filii, nobiscum
in uillam ; et nobis istum dimittentes, maioribus uestris
et iudicibus nos eum uobis abstulisse renuntiate. Nos
enim uos securos faciemus.' Qui resistere non ausi,
hominem ei dimiserunt. Quem mox ille solutum a
uinculis elemosinario commendauit suo. Qui ut hospitium est ingressus, conuenientes ad eum clerici sui et
ministri monebant instantius et exorabant quatinus
permitteret iudices quod sui esset officii exequi circa
reum suum. Dicebant namque, ' Hactenus, domine,
nullam contra uos siue rex siue alius quis qui uobis
insidiatur, aut iustam aut iuste similem potuit reperire
causam. Si uero sententiam forensium iudicum iam

---

a om B   *b* promeritum trahebatur QX
c reluctis B   *d* pertransite QX
e et omnium suorum X   *f* deducebant Q

he entered the lands of St Albans, where he met a
condemned thief who, with his hands chained behind
his back, was being taken by a band of sheriff's officers
to the death he richly deserved. When the rest hurriedly
approached to pray the bishop to give them the customary
blessing, the fettered man exerted what strength he had,
and hastened first to the horse's head and then falling
at his feet wept and implored him to take pity on him.
The bishop reined up his horse and asked who he was
and what he wanted. His attendants when they had
found out answered, ' My lord, do not bother any more
about him, but leave him and pass on.' They said this
out of fear that he would try and save him, and embroil
all of them with the king. This merely made him more
curious about the petitioner. When he had full
information he ejaculated fervently, ' Blessed be God ! '
Then he said to the beadles who were taking the man to
execution, ' Return, my sons, with us to the vill, and
leave him in our charge. Tell your superiors and the
justices that I have taken him from you, and I will
protect you.' They did not dare to protest and left
the man with him. He immediately had his fetters
removed and put him in the charge of his almoner.
When he reached his lodging, his clerks and household
officials came to him in a body and begged and implored
him earnestly to let the judges carry out their duty in
the case of their own prisoner. ' Up to the present, my
lord,' they said, ' neither the king nor anyone else who
is lying in wait for you, can give any good reason or
even a plausible one for their attacks. If, however, you
use your episcopal authority to set aside a sentence
passed by secular judges when it was about to be carried
out, your enemies will say that you have shown contempt
for the royal office, and are guilty of high treason.'

latam, iam executioni demandatam, uestra duxeritis pontificali auctoritate irritandam, dicetur ab emulis quod in ipsam regis coronam deliqueritis et quasi in *a* reatum incideritis lese maiestatis.'

Quibus ille, ' Noui,' inquit, ' magnanimitatis uestre confidentiam. Set accersiantur ad nos huc iudices isti,' iam enim foris aderant *b* querentes loqui ei, ' et audietis,' inquit, ' illorum sermones et nostros.' Quibus ad suum consessum admissis, sic eis est locutus, ' Nostis, o uiri prudentes, hanc sancte matris uestre *c* ecclesie ubique terrarum prerogatiuam esse ut cuiusque periculum dampnationis declinantibus, et ad eam confugium facientibus, securitatem prestet et incolumitatem conseruet.' Quibus id se bene scire idque iure obseruari debere respondentibus, adiecit ille : ' Si istud scitis, illud,' inquit, ' nichilominus scire debetis quia ubicumque fuerit episcopus *d* cum simul adunatis Christi fidelibus ibi est et ecclesia. Qui enim materiales lapides ecclesie suo consueuit ministerio Domino dedicare, qui et lapides uiuos, ex quibus uerius constat ecclesia, per singula sacramenta, ut Dominica templa ex hiis fiant, habet sanctificare; iure debet, ubicumque fuerit, ecclesiastice dignitatis priuilegio gaudere et periclitantibus cunctis iuxta illius formulam subuenire.'

Quod iudices illi gratanter accipientes, antiquis etiam Anglorum legibus [1] hoc ipsum recolentes fuisse expressum, set nunc modernorum uel pontificum desidia uel tyrranide principum esse aboletum, habito super hoc

---

a om B
b stabant X (*cf.* Mt. 12, 46)
c nostre X
d episcopo B

[1] This bold claim of the extension of the right of sanctuary finds some support in a Glastonbury charter attributed to king Edgar ; cf. William of Malmesbury, *Gesta Regum*, I, p. 171 : ' should the abbot or any monk of that place on his journey meet a thief going to the gallows or to any other punishment of death, they shall have power of rescuing him from impending

'I am impressed,' he replied, ' by your courage and boldness ; now go and bring those judges to me, (for they were already outside, seeking to speak to him) and you shall hear what we have to say to each other.' When they had been admitted to his circle he addressed them thus. ' You must know, good sirs, that it is the right of holy mother Church everywhere in this land to give sanctuary to and protect anyone taking refuge with her to escape from the peril of any sentence.' They answered that they were well aware that this law must not be broken ; to which he made this rejoinder, ' If you know this, you ought also to know that wherever there is a bishop and a company of the faithful servants of Christ, there is a church. He who as part of his pastoral office is accustomed to dedicate the inanimate stones of a church to God's service, has the duty through the different sacraments to sanctify the living stones, which are the Church in an even truer sense, that the Lord's temple may be erected from them. Such a man is bound wherever he is to exercise the rights of his office and protect those who are in danger in accordance with her traditions.'

The judges thanked him, and recalled that this was an ancient English law[1] which had fallen into disuse

---

danger throughout my kingdom '. The same privilege was granted to the abbot of Battle by William I (cf. *Chronicon Monasterii de Bello*, London 1846, p. 24), and it was successfully claimed in 1364 (cf. Lower, *Battle Abbey Chronicle*, p. 204). In the later Middle Ages the same privilege was exercised by cardinals in different parts of Europe (cf. W. Ullmann, *A Disputable Consuetudo contra legem in the Later Middle Ages*, in *Butterworth's South African Law Review*, 1956, pp. 85-94). But it should be noted that all these are privileges, not the common law of the land. There is nevertheless a certain justification for Adam's assertion in the Laws of Æthelstan (cf. F. Liebermann, *Die Gesetze der Angelsachsen*, I, p. 172, law 6, 1 e 2), but this concerns a temporary respite, whose duration varies with the dignity of the ecclesiastical or civil magnate concerned.

tractatu ad inuicem, locuti sunt ei in hanc formam,
'Domine,' inquiunt, 'filii et parochiani uestri sumus,
uosque pater et pastor noster. Nec igitur contra
priuilegium uestrum uenire uel disputare nostrum erit ;
nec erit, si placet, uestrum in nostri periculum quippiam
attemptare. Proinde si istum liberatis, nos minime
resistemus, set uobis, si placet, ne erga dominum
regem periclitemur prospiciendum relinquimus.' ᵃ Tunc
ille, ' Bene,' inquit, ' et recte locuti estis. Ego igitur
istum de manibus uestris tollo. Pro qua uiolentia ego
ubi oportebit sufficienter respondebo.' Sic reus letum
letus euasit, liberque Londonias cum episcopo uenit et
inde quo libuit indempnis abiuit.

Episcopus autem ad proceres regis scaccario presi-
dentes accessit ; eosque ut indempnitati ecclesie sue sub
eius presertim absentia benigne prospicerent amicabiliter exorauit. Qui ei reuerenter assurgentes, et quod
petierat obtemperanter se facturos pollicentes, com-
pulerunt eum multis precibus ut secum uel ad momentum
resideret. Quibus ille uix adquiescens sedit tandem.
Vnde illi exhilarati, ' Iam,' inquiunt, ' triumphaliter
gaudere ualebimus qui diem uidimus quo ad regis
scaccarium Lincolniensis sedit episcopus.' Ad hec ille
locum ᵇ erubescens, continuo surrexit, osculumque porrexit uniuersis dicens : ' Iam,' inquit, ' et ego de uobis
triumphabo, si post libatum pacis ᶜ osculum quicquam
in ecclesiam meam admiseritis minus pacificum.' Quod
illius factum et dictum illi nimium admirati, mutuo
loquebantur, ' O mirabilem prudentiam uiri huius !
Ecce quam de facili prescripsit nobis ut neque iussi a
rege sine magno dedecore ei debeamus molesti existere.'

ᵃ reliquimus B   ᶜ om B
  ᵇ *iocum* (in which case the translation would be, ' Blushing at this
pleasantry ') makes better sense than *locum* which, however, is the word in
the manuscripts.

either owing to the negligence of the bishops or the royal tyranny. Having discussed the matter together they answered him to this effect, ' Sir, we are your sons and parishioners and you are our father and bishop. It is not for us to attack or to question your rights, nor, by your leave, ought you to do anything to bring us into danger. Therefore, if you release this man, we shall not interfere, but will leave it to you, if you please, to ensure that we are not held to account by the king.' He replied, ' A shrewd and excellent answer. I remove him from your hands, for which violence I will willingly answer wherever I ought.' So the lucky thief escaped the gallows, and came with the bishop to London as a free man. From there he got safely away to the place of his choice.

The bishop went to the barons of the Exchequer and asked them courteously to do him the favour of protecting the rights of his church, particularly during his absence. They rose out of reverence for him, and readily promised to do what he requested. By dint of much persuasion they induced him to sit with them at least for a short time. He finally did so, but very unwillingly. They were highly delighted. ' Now,' they said, ' we shall be able to rejoice over our victory, who have seen the day when the bishop of Lincoln has sat at the king's Exchequer.' This made him blush to realise where he was, and he got up at once and kissed all of them saying, ' I too will crow over you if you after receiving the kiss of peace, commit the smallest act of hostility against my church.' They were greatly impressed by his words and behaviour, and said to each other, ' The craft of the man ! How adroitly he has made it impossible for us to injure him in any way, even by order of the king without its redounding greatly to our dishonour.' Having given

Quibus ille benedictione data recessit ; et regem adire disponens, post hec citius in Normaniam transfretauit.

CAPITVLVM X

Qualiter transfretauerit regem aditurus. Et de consolatione per uisionem diuinitus ei facta. Et qualiter regi defuncto dissuadentibus suis occurrerit, cuius etiam sepulture interfuit.

Circa id temporis rex iam expeditionem direxerat aduersus comitem Engolismensem, cui iniustum ut dicebatur bellum parabat inferre. Inter ipsum uero et regem Francie ab armis interim quiescendum prescribebant legales *a* treuge, quas indixerat initiate iam tempus Septuagesime. Cum igitur peruenisset episcopus in Neustriam, in terra illa, ob presentiam maxime legati domini pape qui in illis partibus erat, tribus fere septimanis moratus est. Inde circa principium Quadragesime Andegauiam profectus, in quodam manerio sancti Nicholai non longe ab urbe Andegauensium non minori *b* temporis spatio perhendinauit, regis prestolans reditum a locis remotioribus in quibus ipsum bellicis uacantem tumultibus adire nimis uidebatur importunum. Interea a uiris rogatus religiosis ordinis *c* Grandimonstensis[1] qui in uicino degebant loco, ordines apud ipsos celebrauit. Qui dum obnixius *d* peteretur ab archidiacono Oxenofordensi nomine Waltero Map

---

a regales X   *b* minoris QX
c om B   *d* obnoxius B

[1] This small Order, somewhat similar to that of the Carthusians, was founded c. 1076 at Muret in the diocese of Limoges by St Stephen of Muret, after whose death it was transferred to Grandmont. It was a favourite Order of Henry II, who contributed generously to the building

them his blessing he departed, and immediately afterwards crossed to Normandy, intending to go to the king.

CHAPTER X

How he crossed the sea in order to go to the king, and the divine consolation received by him in a vision. How, after the king's death in spite of the opposition of his attendants, he went to him and was present at his burial.

At that time the king was conducting a campaign against the count of Angoulême, a war which it was alleged, he had embarked upon without any justification. The formal truce made between him and the king of France, to begin at Septuagesima had ended their hostilities for the time being. For this reason when the bishop reached Normandy, he remained in the duchy for almost three weeks, chiefly on account of the presence there of the papal legate. From there at the beginning of Lent he set out for Anjou, and stayed for some time at the manor of St Nicholas, not far from the city of Angers. He was awaiting the return of the king from distant parts, into which as he was engaged in a campaign it seemed very imprudent to go. During his stay at the request of the monks of a Grandmontine house [1] in the neighbourhood he held an ordination at their monastery. There he firmly rejected the earnest request of Walter

---

of the church there. He visited it several times and in 1170 expressed a wish to be buried there. Although two-thirds of the 140 houses founded in the 12th century were in Henry II's territories, the first English priory Grosmont in Yorkshire was not founded till 1204. The other two houses, Craswall and Alderbury-on-Severn were founded c. 1225. Henry left the Order some money in his will (cf. R. Graham, ' The Order of Grandmont and its houses in England ' in *English Ecclesiastical Studies* (London 1929), pp. 209-246).

quatinus iuuenem satis ut uidebatur ydoneum, notum quoque episcopo et carum, familie ipsius archileuite prepositum, ad gradum promoueret subdiaconatus, nulla ratione adquieuit, set pro eo intercedentes non sine motu quodam indignationis compescuit. Quod tunc quidem mirati sunt uniuersi qui aderant ; set paulo post eodem clerico, culpis suis exigentibus, lepre contagione terribiliter perfuso, rei euentum considerantibus satis claruit uirum Dei quid ei futurum esset in spiritu preuidisse, in quo noluit benedictionem sacre ordinationis deperire.

Manente autem episcopo in loco prenotato,^a audiebatur passim regem in contemptores suos minari grandia et seua moliri, unde et comitem predictum euertere penitus festinabat. Perhibebant etiam nonnulli quod Lincolniensem episcopum simul et clerum inter illos computaret, quibus ob sui contemptum grauia queque rependere quamtocius maturaret. Talia de ferocissimo homine audientes clerici non mediocriter timebant sibi.

Erant sub ipso tempore apud urbem Andegauensium ex clericis Herefordensis ecclesie preminentiores quedam persone presentes pro eligendo episcopo ad regiam uenire disponentes. Erat unus ex hiis memoratus Walterus,[1] qui et archidiaconus et canonicus erat Lincolniensis episcopi ^a et prebendatus etiam in ecclesia Herefordensi. Quem dum in episcopum eiusdem loci quidam prefici ^b exoptarent, metuebant ne simultate presenti qua aduersus Lincolnienses regius ^c intumuerat animus, sui desiderii prepediretur effectus.

^a ecclesie X   ^b preficere X
^c aduersus ecclesiam Lincolniensem regis X

[1] Walter Map (b. c. 1135), a Welshman from a Hereford family of some standing who had served Henry II before and after 1154, studied theology or canon law at Paris and then won patronage from the bishop of Hereford

Map, archdeacon of Oxford, that he would raise to the subdiaconate a young man who seemed eminently suited, being steward of the archdeacon's household, and well known and esteemed by the bishop, and sharply rebuked those who intervened on his behalf. This caused general surprise, but when a little later this clerk was found to be badly infected with leprosy, a just retribution for his sins, those who thought about the case fully realized that the man of God had foreseen what would come to pass, and so had refused to profane the sacrament of ordination.

Whilst the bishop was in the place I have mentioned there was a widespread rumour that the king was devoting all his energy to putting into effect the terrible threats he had made against those who defied him, for which reason he was determined to encompass the complete ruin of the count of Angoulême. Some even said that he included the bishop of Lincoln and his clergy amongst those upon whom as rebels he had decided to take vengeance as quickly as possible. His clerks, on hearing this about such a violent man, were not a little alarmed for themselves.

At this time some of the most prominent clergy of the diocese of Hereford were in the city of Angers, intending to go to the king in order to elect a bishop. Amongst them was this Walter [1] who, besides being an archdeacon and a canon of Lincoln also held a prebend at Hereford. Him they wished to be promoted as bishop of that diocese, but were afraid lest the present bitter

---

and the king. He was often in attendance at the court and entertained on the king's behalf St Peter of Tarentaise (see I, 38-40 and Walter Map, *De nugis curialium* (OMT 1983), 134–41). He was also canon of Lincoln from 1183, chancellor from *c.*1186 and precentor *c.*1189-1196 or 1197, when Hugh made him archdeacon of Oxford. Twice he expected a bishopric (Hereford 1199, St Davids 1203), but twice he was disappointed. He died an archdeacon in 1209-10.

Communi igitur consilio Herefordenses cum
Lincolniensibus, assumptis secum decano et precentore
Andegauense necnon et aliis quibusdam ipsius *a* ecclesie
canonicis, ad episcopum pariter conuenientes, summis
ei nisibus conati sunt persuadere quatinus pro malitia
presentium dierum, ut suus archiepiscopus crebro
premonuerat, tempus redimendo nuntios ad regem
destinaret, eique in auxilia sumptuum certam pecunie
summam se daturum sponderet ; ac tali compendio
seipsum, a labore dispendioso et sollicitudine anxia
absolutum, ad suam quamtocius sedem reuocaret.
' Iam,' inquiunt, ' non modo regna set et regiones
singulas bellicus hinc inde fragor concutit ; turbantur
populi, urbes et uicos metus inuadit. Nichil iam tutum,
non ciuitas ad inhabitandum, non ager publicus ad
uiandum. In breui, nec manere in hiis locis securum
erit nec abscedere liberum.'

In talibus totum pene diem usque ad uesperam
consiliarii nostro Iob non parum onerosi decreuere.*b*
Nam et isti a tribus locis conuenerant ut hec illi con-
sulerent et hiis eum quasi consolarentur. Hic uero solus,
non contra tres solum homines set contra totidem
hominum turmas indefense *c* repugnans, rationes eorum
uacuas ratione ostendebat. Hoc enim non, ut illi
sentiebant, tempus redimere set tempus perdere et
quidem turpissime astruebat ; ubi dignitas et libertas
ecclesie laicali *d* adeo substernitur *e* satellitio ut nec
personis nec possessionibus ecclesiasticis ecclesiastica
quies et tranquillitas concedatur, nisi pretio inportabili
pro laicorum arbitrio hodie pax redimatur que crastino
rescindatur. Et ille quidem talia de redemptione tali
sentiebat et proferebat.

Nobis uero iam satis factum est conspicabile quid

---

a *om* Bt *b* detriuere X *c* indefesse Q ; indesinenter X
d locali B *e* substerneretur X

anger of the king against the canons of Lincoln should prevent them from obtaining their desire.

The Hereford and Lincoln clergy consulted together, and came to the bishop with the dean and precentor of Angers and other canons of the church. They did their best to persuade him that, owing to the evils of the present days about which the archbishop had often warned him, he should redeem the time by sending messengers to the king, to promise him a fixed sum of money as financial assistance. Such a simple proceeding would save him considerable hardship and much anxiety and enable him immediately to return to his see.

' At present,' they said, ' not only does the tumult of war resound in this realm, but in every province ; the population is panic-stricken, and every city and village a prey to fear. There is safety nowhere, neither for the inhabitants of cities, nor for travellers on the roads. In short, it will not be safe to stay here, nor will you be free to depart.'

These councillors wasted almost the whole day until evening like this, and were very tedious to our Job. They also had come from three places, on the pretext of advising and consoling him. He, however, without help, vigorously resisted not three men alone, but three groups of men, and showed by his arguments the fatuousness of theirs. This would not be, as they thought, to redeem the time, but a shameful waste of time. The rights and liberties of the Church were now being so much brought into subjection by the secular authorities that the clergy and their possessions could only enjoy a temporary peace and security at an impossible price, and on the lay power's own terms, as, what it accepted today, might be annulled tomorrow. Such were the

per huiusmodi exactiones ille spiritu Dei plenus preuiderit in ecclesia Anglicana paulo post euenturum ;
qui inpresentiarum uidemus expulsis et in exilium trusis
monachis *a* et clericis, episcopis etiam et archiepiscopis,
non partem quamlibet set uniuersitatem pariter bonorum
suorum laicorum cessisse rapinis. Cum igitur uehementius imminerent *b* consiliatores memorati ut, procrastinatione remota, statim adquiesceret consilio iam
diutissime reprobato ; ille, nimio affectu tedio, quia
cernebat eos quantum in proposito *c* pertinaces tantum
nisi eis morem gereret animo implacabiles, inuisum
tandem colloquium ita conclusit.

' Iam,' inquit, ' fratres, ista quoad presens sufficiant :
mane inspirante Domino in unam et bonam con-
ueniemus sententiam quam ipse ad nominis sui gloriam
nouit uberius profuturam. Nox enim habet consilium,
ut frequentius experimento docti sumus.' Illis post hec
recedentibus, ipse afflictus et spiritu anhelus confitebatur se uix umquam in tam breui tantum tedii
pertulisse. Sedit uero meditabundus aliquamdiu, omnipotentem Dominum intimo cordis affectu exorans ut sic
perplexitatis tante nodum *d* effugeret, quatinus et illum
minime offenderet et amicos ac filios nequaquam uelud
aspernando eorum sententiam scandalizaret. Laxatis
autem menbris demum in soporem, cordis eius intima
Deum *e* sompniare ceperunt. Tunc, post longas uisionis
almiflue delicias, hanc celitus emissam uocem audiuit,
' Mirabilis Deus in sanctis suis, Deus Israel ipse dabit
uirtutem et fortitudinem plebi sue ; benedictus Deus.' [1]
In hac uoce ille sompno excitus *f* stratum deserit,

---

a + religiosis X
b insisterent B²
c + suo Q
d modum B
e *om* B
f exutus Q : excitatus X

feelings he expressed about the kind of ransom which they had suggested.

It is now plain to us that God had fully revealed to him what would befall the English church a little later as a result of these exactions, for we now see that regulars and seculars, and even bishops and archbishops have been driven out and exiled, and not only a portion but all their goods have fallen a prey to the greed of the laity. When, therefore, the councillors I have mentioned urgently pressed him to hold out no longer, but at once accept the advice which he had rejected for so long, he, being completely worn out and realizing how obstinately they adhered to their opinion, and how determined they were that he should give way to them, finally put an end to the wearisome argument with these words.

' My friends,' he said, ' we have had enough of this for the present ; tomorrow morning God may enable us to agree on the course of action which He knows will most fully redound to His glory and honour. We have learned by frequent experience that night brings counsel.' After they had left him, he was so depressed and worn out, that he admitted that he had scarcely ever been made so tired in so short a time. For a little while he sat lost in thought and praying fervently to Almighty God that he might find a solution to his harassing problem, and neither sin against Him, nor annoy his friends and sons by rejecting their advice. When at last his body was relaxed in slumber, he dreamt of God in the depths of his soul. Then after a long enjoyment of the delightful vision he heard a heavenly voice repeating, ' God is exalted in his saints, the God of Israel will give courage and strength to his people : blessed be God.' [1]

---

[1] Ps. 17: 36

solitoque citius ad confessionem quam die qualibet
Sabbati faciebat, accessit. In qua sese uehementer
reprehendebat super quantulacumque titubatione he-
sterna, qua uel specietenus continentie *a* sue noxia
consulentibus prerogasset.*b* ' Spero tamen,' inquit,
' ut confitenti sibi *c* et deflenti iniquitatem meam
propitietur michi Dominus noster clemens et pius, et
iuxta omnia mirabilia sua eruat nos a presenti angustia.'

Ecce autem in breui post hoc uenit ad eum uenerabilis
abbatissa de Fonte Ebraldi,[1] indicans ei secretius regem,
telo baliste percussum, ancipiti sorte inter confinium uite
et leti fluctuantem, dies iam aliquot in nimiis doloribus
protraxisse. Quantum uero recolere possumus, rex
ipsa die iaculatus est ictu letali qua episcopus adeo
cruciatus fuit importunitate *d* sinistri consilii. Eo autem
interstitio temporis quod ictum et nuntium intercessit
regii *e* uulneris, nemo etiam, unde mirabamur, ei
quicquam loquebatur super diffinitione tam ardui
tamque urgentis negotii. Ipse uero sub silentio presto-
labatur salutare Dei.[2]

Decanus interea et canonici Andegauensis ecclesie
rogabant eum quatinus instanti die Dominica Palmarum
diuinum apud eos exequeretur officium, quia suus
pontifex a curia necdum redierat Romana quo nuper
episcopalem perceperat consecrationem. Quibus ille
adquiescens, cum iam precedenti sabbato ad urbem
tenderat memoratum, medio itinere occurrit ei clericus
quidam nomine Gilbertus de Laci, uerbis certissimis
annuntians regem mortis iam debitum exsoluisse, quem

---

a spem conuenientie Q, continentie X   *b* prorogasset X
c om B   *d* importunitatibus Q   *e* regis Q

[1] Fontevrault was founded by Robert of Arbrissel in 1101. Like the
Order of Sempringham it was a double Order, of which however the head
was an abbess, who acted as visitor of the daughter houses. The stores,
books and money were also in the charge of the nuns. On his deathbed the

Being roused from sleep by these words he left his bed, and made his confession as he was wont to do every Saturday, but earlier than usual. He accused himself bitterly of his slight wavering on the preceding day, by which he might even in appearance have conceded to his evil counsellors a foothold against his own determination. ' I hope, however,' he said, ' that our merciful and compassionate Lord will forgive me as I have repented and confessed my sin, and by His almighty power will deliver me from my present straits.'

Shortly afterwards, the venerable abbess of Fontevrault [1] came to him, and privately informed him that the king had been wounded by a shaft from a crossbow, and had passed some days in great pain. His condition was critical and it was doubtful whether he would live or die. As far as I can remember, the king had received his fatal wound on the very day that the bishop had been so harassed by the importunity of his evil counsellors. During the time which elapsed between the wounding of the king and the messenger's arrival, to our amazement no one conferred with him how this serious and difficult affair should be conducted. He indeed quietly awaited ' the salvation of God '.[2]

In the meantime the dean and canons of Angers asked him to officiate at mass on Palm Sunday, as their bishop had not returned from the Curia at Rome where he had recently been consecrated. He had consented when, on the Saturday before, while he was on his way to the city, a clerk named Gilbert de Lacy met him on

founder recommended that his successor should be a woman who before her conversion had had experience of temporal matters. The Angevin connection began with the second abbess, Matilda, the aunt of Henry II. He, Eleanor of Aquitaine (who died there aged 81 in 1204) and Richard I were all buried in the abbey church.
[2] cf. Lam. 3: 26

et die sequenti ad uestigia patris sui apud monasterium Fontis Ebraldi tradendum innotuit sepulture.

Hiis uero *a* auditis, altius ingemuit ; seque ad locum designatum in obsequium funeris mox suis intimauit esse iturum.   Quod ne faceret eorum pene uniuersitas dissuadere temptauit.   Vbi autem peruenit ad urbem, agnouit iam circumquaque hos percrebuisse rumores, passimque uiantibus uiolentias inferri et rapinas undique exerceri.   Nam et suorum quidam qui ab Anglia ei sumptus afferebant, in manus predantium inciderunt, qui eis quadraginta marcas argenti abstulerant.

Suadebant igitur amici una cum domesticis suis ne seipsum et suos talibus exponeret tumultibus ; quin potius in ciuitate resideret quousque regi defuncto princeps legittimus succederet, per quem uiolentorum nequitiam comprimi eueniret.   Asserebant namque plurimi tantam eorum esse peruersitatem quod non magis deferrent pontifici quam persone cuilibet laicali. ' Quid uero,' aiebant, ' uobis suppeteret consilii si, quod Deus auertat, in remota solitudine uecturis et uestibus uos per istos contingeret spoliari ? '

Ad hec ille, ut uere iustus, qui sicut leo confidens absque terrore in omni terrore fuit,[1] immo et illato semper terrore constantior, infit, ' Satis utique patet quanta in hoc itinere timenda set timidis occurrere possunt. Verum michi multo *b* magis timendum existimo ne domino quondam et regi meo meam ignauiter uidear in tali articulo subtrahere presentiam, nec fidem uel gratiam mortuo reseruem quam uiuo semper deuotus exhibui.   Quid enim si nobis molestiam intulit dum sibi a malignis adulantium consiliis minus cauit ?   Certe set presentiam meam numquam non *c* cum summo excepit

----

his way, and put the king's death beyond a doubt for he informed him that on the morrow he would be taken to be buried with his father at Fontevrault.

On hearing this news he groaned aloud, and immediately told his attendants that he would go to the place I have mentioned to attend the funeral. Almost all of them tried to prevent his doing so. When, moreover, he came to the city, he heard rumours from all sides that everywhere travellers were being attacked and robbed. Some of his own people, who were bringing him money from England, fell into the hands of freebooters who took from them forty silver marks.

His friends and servants both urged him not to expose himself and his companions to these risks, and to stay in the city until the dead king's rightful successor had succeeded in repressing the violence of wicked men. Many of them alleged that their wickedness was so great that they had no more respect for a bishop than for a layman. ' What ', they said, ' would you do, which way would you turn, if, which God forbid, in some lonely spot you should be despoiled of your horses and garments ? '

He who, like the just man, was as brave and confident as a lion,[1] and indeed became more fearless in the face of danger, replied to this as follows : ' It is abundantly clear how many things there are to alarm nervous travellers on this journey. What, however, seems to me much more to be feared is that I, like a coward, should deny my attendance to my former lord and king on this occasion, and fail to pay to the dead the honour and homage I always faithfully rendered to the living. Suppose he did injure me, because he was not sufficiently on his guard against evil councillors and their flattery ?

---

[1] Prov. 28: 1

honore, numquam me inexauditum dimisit cum ei proprio ore super negotiis meis aliqua suggessi. Si quid in absentem deliquit, obtrectantium liuori non sue id debuit prauitati seu malitie ascribi. Reddam igitur uicem pro uiribus meis michi sepius ab eo impensis honoribus, nec per me stabit quin eius obsequiis deuotus existam.ᵃ Si pergenti predones occurrant, si equos tollant, si uestes auferant, eo expeditius pedes incedent ᵇ quo fuerint uestium sarcine leuiores. Si et pedes ᶜ constringantur et incedendi facultas denegetur, tunc primo legittime excusabitur absentia corporalis, cum non suo uitio set alienis fuerit remota obstaculis.'

Hec dicens, relictis in ciuitate sociis et uniuersa pene supellectili sua, uno tantum ex minoribus clericorum suorum et uno cum paucis ex clientibus monacho secum pergentibus, ire cepit. Audiens uero reginam Berengariam¹ in castro morari quod Beauford appellatur, diuertit a uia publica et per horrida siluarum loca, ut eam super uiri sui consolaretur interitu, ad memoratum opidum peruenit. Locutusque ad cor uidue merentis et usque ad animam pene consternate, miro modo spiritum eius deliniuit. Quam optimis sermonibus ad habendam in aduersis tolerantiam, in prosperis cautelam informans, celebrata ibidem missa ac benedictione sollempni regine cum aliis ᵈ qui aderant multa ex deuotione impertita, recessit continuo. Peruenit autem ipsa die ad opidum quod Samur dicitur, exceptusque cum letitia et ᵉ occursu festiuo ab oppidanis illis, apud predictum Gilbertum de Laci, tunc ibi ᶠ scholis uacantem,

---

ᵃ assistam Q ᵇ incedam X : incedet O
ᶜ + compedibus X ᵈ + matronis que X
ᵉ in Q ᶠ ibidem QX

¹ Queen Berengaria, daughter of Sancho VI of Navarre, married Richard in Cyprus in 1191. In 1230 she founded the Cistercian monastery of Espan (Maine), where she was buried.

To be sure he did ; but when I was with him he always treated me with the utmost respect, and granted my requests whenever I approached him personally about any matter concerning myself. If he treated me badly in any way when I was absent this should be put down to the malice of my traducers and not to any ill-will of his own. I will therefore do my best to make some return for his frequent unsolicited acts of kindness, nor will it be my fault if I do not render my services at his funeral. If I encounter robbers on my way, and if they take away my horses and my garments, my feet will get me there all the more quickly, if they have been relieved of the weight of my clothes. If they also tie my feet together and deprive me of any power of motion, then and then only will my bodily absence be excusable, being due not to my own fault but to the obstacles imposed by other people.'

After he had said this, he left most of his companions and almost all his baggage in the city and set out, taking with him only one of his least important clerks, a monk and a few of his servants. Hearing, however, that Queen Berengaria [1] was staying in the castle of Beaufort, he left the highroad and journeyed through a wild forest region to that town, in order to comfort her for the death of her husband. His words went straight to the soul of the sorrowing and almost heart-broken widow, and calmed her grief in a wonderful way. He spoke to her most beautifully on the need for fortitude in misfortune and for prudence in happier times, and after celebrating mass, and giving the queen and those with her his solemn blessing most devoutly, he at once departed. That day he reached a town called Saumur, where the townsfolk came joyously to meet him. He yielded to the earnest entreaties of the Gilbert de Lacy I have already

nimiis eius deuictus precibus mansit. A quo liberalissime exhibitus, sequenti mane, Dominica Palmarum die, uenit ad monasterium Fontis Ebraldi, obuiosque habuit in ipsis foribus ecclesie regii funeris portitores. Quo demum honorificentissime iuxta magnificentiam͞regiam tradito sepulture, rediit denuo ad hospitium pretaxatum. Inde per triduum continuatim ad monasterium pergens suprascriptum, missarum et psalmorum replicatione, tam regibus ibidem sepultis quam fidelibus cunctis in Christo quiescentibus, ueniam implorabat [a] et lucis perpetue felicitatem.

Capitvlvm XI

Quomodo Ioannes agnominatus Sineterra, in locum fratris sui regis Ricardi succedens, circa primordium principatus sui se habuerit, siue quo ad reuerentiam episcopi seu quo ad notabile presagium sui.

Feria uero quarta iam dilucescente, frater regis Iohannes cognominatus Sineterra susceptus est apud Chinonem a proceribus quibusdam Anglorum castrum ipsum seruantibus, ut preesset omnibus loco sui fratris. Familia quoque regis defuncti ibidem constituta se ad ipsum contulit eadem die. Prestiterat enim sollempne iuramentum quod testamentum regis defuncti fideliter exequeretur, quod preterea legitimas priorum consuetudines iustasque terrarum siue populorum leges quibus erat proficiendus inuiolabiliter conseruaret.[b] Rex quidem, modico ante obitum suum tempore, terris omnibus quas habuit [c] ipsum destituerat, eo quod accepisset eum cum rege Francorum in sui proditionem

---

[a] implorauit X   [b] obseruaret X   [c] habuerat Q

mentioned, who was attending the schools there and stayed with him, where he was most hospitably entertained. At dawn the following day, which was Palm Sunday, he came to the monastery of Fontevrault, and met at the very door of the church the bearers of the king's coffin. When he had been most honourably buried with royal pomp, the bishop at last retired to the lodging assigned to him. From there for three whole days he used to go to the monastery and by the repetition of masses and psalms, prayed for pardon and the bliss of everlasting light for the souls of the kings buried there and of all the faithful who had fallen asleep in Christ.

Chapter XI

How John, surnamed Lackland, who succeeded his brother King Richard, behaved just after his accession, and the amazing foresight of the bishop for all his deferential attitude towards him.

On Wednesday early in the morning, the king's brother John, surnamed Lackland was received at Chinon as his successor by certain English magnates who held the castle there. The household of the dead king was also there and joined him on that very day. He had taken a solemn oath faithfully to fulfil the provisions of the will of the dead king, and also to preserve in their integrity the ancient and lawful customs and just laws of the lands and peoples over whom he was to rule. The king, however, a short time before his death had deprived him of all his lands, because he had learned that he had plotted against him with the king of France. At the time of the king's death he was with his nephew

conspirasse. Qui sub ea tempestate qua rex occubuit apud nepotem suum Arturum in Brittania fuit. Fratris uero nece audita, Chinonem uenit cum paucis ; misitque statim ad episcopum, in burgo supradicto consistentem, et repatriandi commeatum prestolantem, suppliciter *a* exorans quatinus suam ei celerius exhibere dignaretur presentiam. Ad cuius sibi occurrentis in uia conspectum, ille gaudio gauisus immenso, admisso equo, ei relicto comitatu uniuerso obuius processit ; eumque ueneratus rogauit ut ab eo minime discederet set pariter secum reuersurus in Angliam, in partibus transmarinis contubernium sibi exhiberet indiuiduum. Quod ille se nequaquam facturum prolatis rationibus insinuans, uenit tamen cum eo usque Samur, cum prius uisitassent apud Fontem Ebraldi busta regalia, patris scilicet et fratris illius.

Vbi que tunc gesta sunt, cum sint notitia et imitatione digna, non uidentur desidioso silentio supprimenda. Cum enim nouus ille tantarum gentium dominus, plurima stipatus nobilium turma, ad hostium chori manu propria diutius pulsans ingredi uellet, ut sepulchra uideret predictorum seque orationibus sancte illius commendaret congregationis, responsum accepit a duabus reuerende grauitatis sanctimonialibus quia nulli mortalium liceret aut conuentum inspicere aut septa interiora adire nisi sub presentia abbatisse sue. ' Illius,' inquiunt, ' reditum operiri *b* uos oportet que mox de itinere speratur reuersura. Nec durum reputet excellentia uestra quod nec illius intuitu ordinis nostri statuta infringimus. In hoc potius diue *c* memorie genitor uester uobis imitandus censeatur qui in uiris religiosis id quam maxime uenerabatur si tradita sibi maiorum

Arthur in Brittany. On learning that his brother had been killed, he came to Chinon with a few attendants, and immediately sent a message to the bishop who was in the same town, awaiting his companions in order to return home, begging him that he would soon do him the honour of visiting him. When they met in the street, as soon as he caught sight of him he showed immense pleasure and, spurring on his horse, he left all his companions behind and came towards him. He asked in most respectful terms not to think of leaving him but to return with him to England, and give him his company whilst he was on the continent. Hugh gave many reasons why it was impossible for him to do this, but nevertheless went with him to Saumur, after they had visited the royal tombs of his father and brother at Fontevrault.

It would be wrong to pass over in silence what occurred there, as it is memorable and worthy of imitation. When the new ruler of so many peoples, accompanied by a vast throng of nobles, himself knocked at the door of the choir which he wished to enter in order to see the tombs and commend himself to the prayers of the devout community, two nuns of mature age answered that no human being could see the convent or enter its enclosure unless the abbess were present. ' It is hoped that she will shortly return from a journey,' they said, ' and you must await her return. Your highness must not be offended that we do not break the statutes of our order at your wish. Rather your father ought to be imitated in this matter, since what he especially admired in monks was that they should observe strictly and with undeviating devotion the customs handed down to them by their founders.' With these words, these wise virgins repelled and shut out the prince who had knocked, and

instituta rigida et inuiolabili deuotione obseruarent.'
Hiis ita *a* prolatis, uirgines ille prudentes pulsantem
principem compescunt et excludunt ; clausisque diligenter foribus ad socias reuertuntur.

Is uero ad episcopum conuersus, rogabat eum
quatinus petitionem suam pro suffragiis illarum apud
Deum optinendis ancillis Christi exprimeret, plurima
etiam bona que eis conferre disponebat eisdem pro-
palaret. ' Nostis,' inquit, ' quia satis auersor omne
mendacium ; cauebo igitur michi ne labiis *b* promissa
uestra enuntiem nisi hoc certissime a uobis implenda *c*
presumam.' Iurat ille se non modo que tunc promittebat
impleturum set pro tempore et loco hec se habundantius
cumulaturum. Quod episcopus sanctimonialibus, ipso
astante, exposuit ; eiusque auspicia precibus illarum
meritisque commendans, data uniuersis benedictione, una
cum ipso discessit. Cui plurima iam de pietate in Deum,
de clementia in subditos, de iustitia in uniuersos disseru-
erat.*d* Qui ad omnia se paratum, animoque pronum
ac deuotum contestans, ei tamquam patri et preceptori
se ex integro semper pariturum affirmans, totius sui
moderationem eius sanctitati attentius commendabat.

Cui etiam, inter amice confabulationis uerba, productum e sinu lapidem inclusum auro et collo suo
appensum ostenderat, asserens hunc cuidam suorum
progenitorum cum tali fuisse celitus pollicitatione dona-
tum, quod numquam priuaretur auite dominationis
amplitudine quisquis *e* successorum suorum ipsum
meruisset possidere. Ad hec uero episcopus confestim
responderat, ' Non,' inquiens,*f* ' in lapide insensibili
fiduciam ponatis set tantum in lapide uiuo et uere
celesti, domino Ihesu Christo. Huic fundamentum
cordis uestri, huic spei uestre anchoram firmissime

a itaque Q *b* + meis X *c* impendenda X
d deseruerat B *e* si quis X *f* inquit X

having shut the doors carefully returned to their companions.

John turned to the bishop, and asked him to beg the handmaids of Christ on his behalf to pray to God for him, and express his intention of conferring many favours on them. ' You must know,' he replied, ' my hatred of lies. I will not therefore allow my lips to make promises for you, unless I can be certain that you will fulfil them.' John swore, not only that he would carry out what he now promised, but, time and place permitting, would do even more. The bishop, whilst he stood by, informed the holy nuns of this, and besought their prayers and good works for his welfare, and left with him, after giving his blessing to the community. He spoke to him for a long time about the fear of God, mercy towards his subjects and justice to everyone. John protested that it was his wish and intention to do all these things, and declared that he would obey him in everything as his father and director, and be at pains always to be guided by his holy counsels.

Whilst they were speaking confidentially together in this way, he drew from his bosom a stone set in gold which was hanging round his neck and showed it to him. This he declared had been given to one of his ancestors, and that God had promised that none of his descendants who were fortunate enough to possess it should ever lose any part of their vast domains. The bishop immediately answered him, ' Do not put your trust in an inanimate stone, but in the living true and heavenly stone, our Lord Jesus Christ. Make Him the centre of your soul, and anchor all your hopes on Him, for He is the firm and living stone which will shatter all who resist Him, and will not suffer those who trust Him to slip, but will

imprimatis. Hic enim solidus et uiuus lapis, ut omnes sibi resistentes conterit, ita sibi innitentes defluere non sinit, set ad altiora semper attollens, ipsos etiam ad ampliora promerenda dilatando extendit.'

Cum uero ad porticum iam peruenissent ecclesiam ingressuri, ubi species seu ymago extremi examinis quo electi a reprobis secernuntur, eleganter satis pro modulo humani exprimitur artificii opere sculptoris, episcopus comitem futurum in proximo regem manu protraxit ad leuam Iudicis ubi reges cum suis insignibus inter dampnatos, audituri, 'Ite maledicti in ignem eternum,' [1] a gehennalibus tortoribus rapiuntur in Tartarum. Tunc ait episcopus 'Horum eiulatus et interminabiles [a] cruciatus uobis indesinenter animus representet ; hec perpetua supplicia uobis ante cordis oculos assidue uersentur : horum malorum sedula recordatio doceat uos quanto sui dispendio aliis ad tempus modicum proficientur regendis hominibus, qui seipsos male regendo [b] sine fine cruciandi demoniacis subiciuntur spiritibus. Hec dummodo uitare licet semper expedit formidare, ne cum non licet iugiter postmodum contingat tolerare.' Dicebat quoque celaturam seu picturam huiuscemodi in ipsis ecclesiarum aditibus congrua satis ratione pretexi, quatinus intraturi et pro necessitatibus suis Dominum rogaturi hanc summam et supremam necessitatem suam esse sciant, ut impetrent ueniam pro delictis ; qua impetrata securi permaneant a penis et gaudeant in deliciis sempiternis.

Et quidem episcopus talia prosecutus est. Set o utinam, o Iohannes, qui usque in diem hunc quo annus iam quartusdecimus elabitur ex quo ista dicta et facta sunt, omnia uidetur obliuioni tradidisse [c] que illa die

---

[a] + dolores et X   [b] regentes X
[c] dedisse X

raise them always to higher things, and will exalt and promote them to a loftier destiny.'

When they reached the porch of the church and were about to enter, there was over it a representation of the Last Judgment showing the separation of the elect from the damned, a magnificent example of the human sculptor's art. The bishop led the count, who was so soon to be a king, to the left side of the Judge where there were kings in full regalia amongst the damned, about to hear the words, ' Go ye cursed into everlasting fire '.[1] These were being carried off, by their demon tormentors into Hell. The bishop then said, ' Fix your mind always on their howls and perpetual torment, and let your heart dwell upon their unceasing punishment ; by frequently recalling their misfortunes you will learn the great risks those incur who for a short space of time are set over others as rulers, and who by not ruling themselves are eternally tortured by demons. This fate ought always to be dreaded whilst there is time to avoid it, lest it should have to be endured forever when it is too late.' He said also that such sculptures or pictures were at the entrances to churches for a very good reason, namely that those about to enter and pray to God in their need, should understand what would be their last and final extremity and so would pray for forgiveness for their sins. By such prayers they would be secure from torment and enjoy everlasting happiness.

The bishop continued in this strain. Would that John who, during the fourteen years which have elapsed since the day on which such things were said and done, seems to have forgotten what he saw, heard and promised then, would remember at this late hour what

---

[1] Matt. 25: 41

uidit, audiuit, promisit, et dixit : o, inquam, quod tunc
fecit et dixit utinam uel nunc sero recordetur, et licet
id penitus a pluribus desperetur, ad euadendum
perpetuum interitum tandem animetur ! Cum enim in
Deum et proximum, cum in clerum et populum tanta
commiserit ut esse uideatur plaga eius incurabilis et
excessus irreparabilis, ipse tamen, oculo mentis obturato,
nec que presentialiter patitur sentit, nec que post
modicum pati meretur intelligit, confusionis sue atque
deiectionis certa dispendia. De quo, iam teste toto pene
mundo, impletur illud quod dicit Scriptura, ' Impius
cum uenerit in profundum malorum contempnit.' [1]
Vtinam uero imminens uexatio det ei intellectum ut
saltem tunc studeat eternam uitare calamitatem, cum
temporalem funditus amittit potestatem, et de sinistra
se in dexteram transferat supremi Iudicis, cum experietur
quid habeat ponderis iudicium quod paruipendit ecclesiastice seueritatis. Id enim se facturum in loco superius
memorato asseruit.

Transiens quippe et manu trahens secum episcopum
ad parietem oppositum eique ostendens reges, speciosis
insignitos coronis, angelico ductu in gaudium tendentes
superni Regis, ' Hos,' inquit, ' domine episcope, nobis
potius monstrare debuistis, quorum exemplum atque
consortium sequi et assequi habemus in uotis.' Tam
uero in gestu et affatu, paucis post hec diebus, humilem
se ostendebat et submissum ut uideretur excedere modum.
Occurrentibus sibi ob iter [a] mendicis ac fausta impre-
cantibus, corpore incuruato et capite altius demisso
gratias diligenter referebat ; salutantes se pannosas
etiam aniculas mitissime resalutabat. At uero post
triduum letificatos non mediocriter ex hiis, tam epis-

---

[a] ob iter] *om* B

he on that occasion professed and did ! Although many would deem it impossible, by this means he might be roused at last to do his best to avoid damnation ! The wrongs and enormities committed by him against God and his neighbour and against clergy and laity appear indeed irremediable and irreparable. He however, owing to his darkened mind, does not realize or understand the reason for his present misfortunes, or what he will justly have to suffer after the short span of this life, or the certainty of his shame and damnation. In his case, almost the whole world can observe the fulfilment of the text, ' The wicked man takes no heed, however great the evils which befall him.' [1] Would that the troubles which threaten would give him understanding, and that the complete loss of his temporal power would cause him to take pains to avoid eternal damnation, so that when he has experienced the heavy weight of the Church's censures which he makes so light of, he may endeavour to transfer himself from the left to the right hand of the supreme Judge, as he declared he would do at the place I have mentioned above.

Drawing the bishop with him, he crossed over to the opposite wall and pointed out to him kings, made conspicuous by their splendid crowns, conducted joyously by angels to the king of Heaven. ' My lord bishop,' he said, ' you should have shown us these, whom we intend to imitate and whose company we desire to join.' For the next few days both in speech and action he made a parade of meekness and humility. When the beggars he met wished him prosperity, he bowed to them and thanked them most assiduously, and graciously returned the greetings of ragged crones. After three days, how-

---

[1] Prov. 18: 3

copum quam et alios ista conspicientes, ex aliis gestis et
dictis incongruis multo amplius contristauit. Ex quibus,
gratia compendii plurima supprimentes, pauca referrimus, ut coniciat prudens auditor ubi talem perpenderit
radicem, qualem estimare liceat secuturam fructuum ex
eadem arbore fertilitatem.

Cum igitur die sacratissimo resurrectionis Dominice,
oblaturus ex more ad manus accessisset episcopi altario
assistentis, aurea ei numismata a cubiculario suo, sicut
mos regius exigebat, bissena dabantur in palmam ; hec
ille, stipatus undique haut modica turba nobilium, cum
staret ante episcopum, diutius intuens et quasi ludendo
exagitans, tam diu offerre distulit quousque omnes eum
intuentes mirarentur. Tandem presul, motus ob huiusmodi *a* eius gestum tali hora et in tali loco, ' Quid ita,'
inquit, ' respicis ? '   Qui ait illi, ' Istos sane aureos
intueor mecum reputans quia ante dies paucissimos si
tenuissem eos, non uobis illos offerrem set mee potius
crumene inferrem ; uerumptamen iam modo accipite
illos.' Indignatus ad hec uir Dei et uice illius uehementer
erubescens, ut erat mentis pie et cordis generosi, pro-
tensum ad se retraxit brachium suum nec illius aurum
contingere passus, nec suam dexteram ore tam auaro
sustinens osculari ; fremens uero in semetipso et capud
suum mouens in eum, ' Iacta,' inquit, ' ibi quod tenes et
recede.' Qui in peluim argenteam in quam oblata
congregabantur, nummos ipsos proiciens abscessit.

Nichil uero sibi de oblatione quisquam eorum qui
episcopo adherebant in aliena umquam ecclesia, nisi
forte ubi ecclesias dedicaret, retinere presumpsit, dicente
sepius ipso satis iniustum uideri ut ab ara alterius illi
quicquam temporale asportent qui de gratia locum

a huius QX

ever, his completely different words and behaviour grieved the bishop and others much more than they had been pleased at what they had previously witnessed. Most of this I shall not describe for the sake of brevity, giving only a few examples, to enable the intelligent reader to judge for himself what sort of fruit could be expected from a tree with such a root.

On the holy feast of the Resurrection of our Lord he approached the altar to make his offering, as was the custom, to the bishop who was assisting there. His chamberlain placed in his palm the twelve gold pieces which are the customary oblation of kings. Surrounded by a large crowd of nobles, he stood in front of the bishop, gazing on these coins and playing with them, and delayed making his offering for so long a period that everyone gaped at him in amazement. At last, the bishop, annoyed at such behaviour at this particular time and place, said, ' Why do you look at them so intently ? ' He answered, ' I am looking at these gold pieces and thinking that if I had had them a few days ago I would not have delivered them to you, but have pocketed them ; but now you can take them.' The holy and generous soul of the man of God was outraged, and, blushing with shame on his behalf, he drew back his arm, and refused to touch the gold, or let such greedy lips kiss his hand. He groaned and shook his head at him, saying, ' Put down what you are clutching, and go away'. Throwing the money into the silver basin for oblations, he withdrew.

None of the bishop's clerks dared to retain for him any oblations made in a church which did not belong to him, unless he was consecrating it ; for he often said that it seemed to him very unjust that those who through the favour of the pastor of that church were receiving

ipsum custodientis spiritualem mentium alimoniam
ibidem percipiant.[a] Hoc quoque tam in propria quam
in aliena ubique diocesi obseruari a suis faciebat. Nec
de ista ergo suorum quilibet oblatione quicquam accepit.
Videbatur autem tunc quibusdam quia Dominum in hoc
imitaretur [b] fidelis et prudens seruus eius. Vt enim
Dominus ad Chaim et ad munera eius olim non respexit,[1]
ita modo seruus Domini, quia muneris oblatorem non
inmerito improbauit, uel eius munus tangere contempsit.
Qui uerbum Domini astantium multitudini predicare
exorsus, cum de bonorum seu malorum principum
moribus et premiis postfuturis multa dissereret, dum ab
aliis deuote acclamaretur sibi, memoratus principum
ille primus qui mane comedunt,[2] tam materiam quam
moram sermonis non eque ferens, tertio [c] misit ad eum,
flagitans obnixe ut sermoni metam ponat, diuina cele-
bret, quatinus sibi post tanta ieiunia uesci concedat.
Set fortis euangelizator noster qui super montem
excelsum conscenderat, uota et mandata ipsius longe
despiciens, quin et uocem fortius exaltans, multitudinem
maximam auditorum tam diu pane spiritualis doctrine
cibare non destitit, donec cunctis acclamantibus plurimis
quoque illacrimantibus, ad digne percipiendum panem
sacramentalem, qui de celo descendit et dat uitam
mundo,[3] eos sufficienter pro tempore informaret. Princeps
uero ille, utriusque refectionis, uerbi scilicet [d] et sacramenti expers, carnem suam carnibus saturare festinans,
mentis ieiunia non curabat. Neque enim ipso die
Pasche set nec sequenti festo Ascensionis Dominice,
quando in regem promotus est, sacre communionis
misteria percipere adquieuit. Ferebatur quoque a

[a] participant QX
[b] miraretur B
[c] ter X
[d] cibi scilicet doctrine X

spiritual benefits there, should carry away any temporal profit from an altar which belonged to another.   He made his clerks keep to this rule both in his own and in other dioceses.   Certain persons considered that on this occasion the prudent and faithful servant followed the example of his Lord.   Just as the Lord had rejected Cain and his gifts,[1] so his servant rightly rebuked the donor of this gift and refused to let his own hand touch it.   He began to preach the word of God to this large congregation, discoursing much on the characters of good and bad rulers, and their future reward.   The rest of the company were greatly edified, but the prince I have already mentioned, the first royal person to eat early in the day,[2] disliked both the theme of the sermon and its length. He sent someone to him three times to implore him earnestly to wind up his sermon and celebrate mass, as he wished to eat after such a prolonged fast.   Our determined gospeller who had alighted on a lofty hill, took no notice of his wishes and messages, and merely raising his voice continued to feed his vast audience with the meat of sound doctrine, until all were applauding and many were in tears, and he had prepared them sufficiently for the time being to receive worthily the sacramental bread which descended from Heaven and gives life to the world.[3]   The prince, however, rejecting both foods (I mean—the word and the sacrament), was eager to fill his belly with meat, and cared not at all for the emptiness of his mind.   Neither on Easter day, nor the subsequent feast of the Ascension, the day of his coronation, did he receive the sacraments.   His intimates

---

[1] cf. Gen. 4: 5
[2] cf. Eccles. 10: 16
[3] cf. John 6: 33

familiaribus eius quia ex quo discretionis annos attigit, illius numquam particeps extiterit.

Post hec, octaua die Pasche, dum apud Rothomagum intra sacra missarum sollempnia ducatus susciperet insignia, cum sollempni more ei daret archiepiscopus lanceam in manus, uexillum preferentem quo duces Neustrie honoris sui inuestituram solebant percipere; ille, audito tumultu applaudentium et pueriliter cachinnantium adholescentium quondam sodalium suorum, ut erat diuinis animo parum intentus, ad eos post tergum leuitatis instinctu conuersus, dum iocantibus et ipse arrideret, hastam quam minus firmiter apprehenderat decidere permisit in terram. Quod sibi ominis fuisse signum infausti, consona pene uniuersorum qui aderant interpretatio asserebat. Iam uero rei huius presagium clarius enitescit dum illo eneruiter lasciuiente, non solum ducatus Normannici, immo et cum aliis prouinciis et comitatibus Aquitanici etiam ditionem amisit. Supremo nimirum omnium Rectore id iuste disponente ut qui ad ipsum usque in presens cor suum dirigere et spem in eo figere neglexit, nec ipse manu ualida sibi commissos regere nec eorum subiectionem sibi diutius quiuerit uendicare.

Verum de principis huius principiis, hominis uidelicet qui non posuit Deum adiutorem suum,[1] hec ita summatim perstrinxisse sufficiat. Restat uero ut ad retexendum finem uite hominis, habitantis iugiter in adiutorio Altissimi et in protectione Dei celi finaliter commorantis,[2] in aliis remota [a] iam nimium hec nostra qualiscumque recurrat oratio.

[a] remorata X

declared that he had never done so since attaining to the years of discretion.

Later, on the octave of Easter, at Rouen during the celebration of high mass, he received the ducal insignia, the archbishop placed the lance reverently in his hand with a pennon, the customary investiture of the dukes of Normandy. He, however, hearing the bursts of applause, and the childish laughter of his former youthful companions, and his attention being very little absorbed by the rite, turned round out of levity, and whilst he and they were laughing together, the lance which he was not grasping firmly enough fell on the ground. Almost the whole assembly declared that this was a bad portent for him. Their forebodings were abundantly justified, when owing to his wanton inertia he lost not only Normandy, but also his other counties and territories, including even Aquitaine. It was an exceedingly just dispensation on the part of the Ruler of all things, that one who has refused up till today to turn his heart and fix his hopes on Him, should not be able to rule his subjects successfully for long, or maintain his sway over them.

The little I have said about the first days of the reign of this king, a man who did not make the Lord his helper,[1] is quite sufficient. It remains to relate the end of the life of the man who, living always with the help of the Almighty, now dwells in the presence of the king of Heaven.[2] After this long digression I shall therefore continue my narrative.

[1] cf. Ps. 51: 9
[2] cf. Ps. 90: 1

CAPITVLVM XII

Quomodo apud uicum qui Fleche dicitur, missas sollempniter celebrando, uiolentiam predonum, equos diripentium et sarcinulas suorum euaserit. Itidemque Cenomannis, ymnos matutinarum protractius cantando, armatorum insidias eluserit. Et demum cum gaudio triumphali ad suos in Anglia redierit.

Cum enim stili uelocioris impetum usque ad lectoris tedium effluere pertimescimus, de gestis insignibus dictisque memorabilibus uiri beatissimi satis innumera ex consulto preterimus. Quod eo confidentiori animo facere presumimus, minusque suppresse ueritatis fraude nobis metuimus, quo a nobis omissa, sicut supra memorauimus, ab aliis commodius dicta scriptoque indita esse certissime speramus. Cursim igitur ea que restant usque ad felicem excessum ipsius perstringimus, ne aliunde iam tenentibus aut postmodum percepturis potiora, hec nostra non modo superflua set etiam uideantur onerosa. Ne uero ut etiam presumptuosa condempnentur, eorum arbitrio relinquimus prouidendum quorum sumus imperio compulsi ad scribendum.

Sciendum itaque ipsum uere mundi exulem et celi ciuem, ex tunc quam maxime presentis incolatus sui dispendia exhorruisse, celestisque habitationis desiderio flagrasse, ex quo plenius animaduertit optatam a quibusdam regni mutationem ad deteriora uergere et speratam status ecclesiastici meliorationem in aduersum cedere. Ad ecclesiam ergo suam quamtocius censuit repedandum quatinus saluti commissarum sibi[a] sollertius prouideret animarum, sibique liberius ex

---

[a] *om* B

CHAPTER XII

How, by celebrating high mass in the village of La Flèche, he escaped from the clutches of freebooters, who had stolen his horses and baggage, and again, at Le Mans by his protracted singing of Matins, he avoided a surprise attack. How he at last returned in joy and triumph to his flock in England.

Since I have feared to weary my readers by letting my pen run away with me, I have purposely omitted very many of the remarkable deeds and memorable sayings of this most saintly man. I have had the courage to do this, and also fewer scruples about the deliberate suppression of facts, because, as I have already said, I have every confidence that what I have omitted, has been much better described by other writers. I will therefore pass rapidly over the remainder of his life up to his happy death so that those people who either now possess or subsequently find a fuller account elsewhere may not regard mine as both unnecessary and tedious. I refer any critics of my presumption in undertaking the work to those who commissioned it from me, and in obedience to whom I was compelled to write it.

It must be understood that this exile on earth and citizen of Paradise, from now onwards hated more than ever the trials of this present world and longed passionately for his heavenly home, from which he now sees even more clearly that the change in the kingdom desired by certain persons has been much for the worse, and that instead of the hoped-for improvement in the Church's position there has been a marked deterioration. He therefore thought he should return as soon as he could to his Church to provide more carefully than ever

uberiori fructu pietatis omnimode ad superna gaudia exquireret commeatum.

Valedicens itaque memorato principi, recessit ab eo secunda feria Pasche. Cumque peruenisset ad uillam quamdam in qua hospitari decreuerat, quam incole Fleche uocant, ingressus ecclesiam missas *a* celebrare parabat. Et ecce, illo necdum sacris uestibus induto, turbati ad eum occurrunt ministri sui, nuntiantes equos et redas ipsius ab illius loci custodibus retineri, quosdam etiam ex sagmariis suorum a predonibus abduci. Erant uero in comitatu ipsius dominus Gilebertus Rouecestrensis [1] episcopus et clerici diuersorum locorum quam plurimi. Qui omnes unanimiter *b* rogabant eum quatinus pretermissa ob tante necessitatis et perturbationis euentum missarum celebratione, euangelium sibi legi contentus foret utque se et suos expediret a tantis periculis animum intenderet. Qui nil turbatus ex hiis que a raptoribus gerebantur set nec motus ex hiis que a comitibus suggerebantur, ut surdus et mutus ad audita ceptis tantum insistebat. Nec simpliciter et plane sacrum contentus officium peragere, immo sandaliis, tunica et dalmatica cum ceteris insignibus utens, utque uniuersos diuino presidio melius communiret, pontificalem benedictionem agendis interserens, missam more sollempni quam deuote peregit. Omnibus ergo rite completis, dum sacris se exuit induuiis,*c* accurrunt ipsius loci magistratus in ecclesiam, suppliciter et obnixe ueniam petentes quod impedire suos uel turbare *d* presumpsissent. Spondent quoque obsequia si dignetur pernoctare in loco, sin autem duxerit ulterius procedendum, conductum ex suis *e* ad loca tutiora pollicentur.

---

a missam X   *b* *om* B   *c* indumentis QX
d perturbare Q   *e* ex suis] *om* B
[1] Gilbert Glanville, bishop of Rochester 1185-1214, had been one of Becket's scholars and was summoned to Germany by Richard I in 1193.

before for the souls committed to his care, and gain for himself by an even more intense concentration in every pious exercise a more ready access to the joys of Heaven.

Therefore bidding farewell to the aforementioned prince, he departed on the Monday after Easter. When he reached the village where he had decided to stay, which was called La Flèche by the natives, he entered the church and made preparations to celebrate mass. Before he had finished vesting, his servants came to him and in a state of great agitation told him that his waggons and horses had been impounded by the garrison and that some of his pack-horses had been seized by robbers. He had then in his company Gilbert, bishop of Rochester [1] and very many clerks from different dioceses. They all begged him to give up the idea of celebrating mass because of their critical and dangerous situation and content himself with the reading of the Gospel, and consider how he and his companions could best escape from their perilous position. He remained unperturbed by what the marauders had done and, taking no notice of the reports and representations of his companions, merely went on with what he had begun as if he were deaf and dumb. He was not satisfied with an ordinary mass, but putting on sandals, tunic, dalmatic and the other vestments, he celebrated high mass with deep devotion, so as to commend the whole company more fully to the divine protection and gave his pontifical blessing to those present. When every part of the rite had been completed, and he was taking off his vestments, the bailiffs of the town hurried into the church, and begged him humbly and earnestly to pardon them for daring to hold up or molest his people. They offered him their services if he would honour their town by passing the night there, but, if he thought it better to go on,

Quos ille satis hilariter allocutus, ut erat spirituali
iocunditate ac *a* celesti repletus conuiuio, conductum
illorum non respuens, continuo ab eis recessit. Ipsaque
die cum uniuerso comitatu ad monasterium sancti
Petri ¹ in suburbio constitutum Cenomanensi peruenit.

Sequenti diluculo, dum matutinale Deo *b* exsoluit
officium et longas *c* more solito recitari facit lectiones,
tumultus ingens a menibus ciuitatis increpuit. Milites
namque cum manu armata, directi a comitissa Brittanie
et eius filio Arturo, insultum fecerant *d* ut Iohannem
prenominatum caperent, qui nocte quidem ipsa illuc
aduenerat, set presentiens insidias sibi paratas, ante
lucis exortum urbem clanculo pertransierat. Hec ut
primum agnouit Girardus, quidam ex clericis episcopi,
turbulenter satis et anxie ei studuit que didicerat
nuntiare, orans instantius ut officium quod agebat
breuiatis *e* lectionibus percantaret, quatinus discur-
santium manus armatorum dubia adhuc sub luce facilius
declinando, cum sociis qui iam precesserant instantem
tutius perageret dietam. Verum ille, ut hunc quoque
turbinem impauidus excepit, sic tranquille cum omni
diligentia debitos Deo ymnos persoluit. Nec plane ad
insipientiam sibi. Nam dum moratur *f* affuit eiusdem
loci abbas, qui illum eques precessit *g* et per semitarum
compendia illesum deduxit ultra ciuitatis suburbia.
Ex hiis uero qui ipsum precesserant plures intercepti
atque detenti sunt hostili uiolentia. Reliquit autem
ibidem in custodia predicti abbatis redas duas cum
equis aliquibus et uaria supellectili. Que simul omnia
prefata comitissa, ad ciuitatem ipsam sequenti die
adueniens, ad ipsum deduci fecit, orationibus illius

---

a ab B   *b* *om* B   *c* + ex X
d fecerunt QX   *e* breuitatis B   *f* moraretur X
g precesserat o   ¹ later called Notre-Dame de la Couture.

they undertook to escort him to a safer spot. He spoke to them very cheerfully, being full of spiritual joy after his heavenly banquet, and, accepting their escort, at once left the town. That day he and all his company reached the monastery of St Peter [1] in a suburb of Le Mans.

The next day at dawn, whilst he was in the middle of Matins, and was having the long lessons recited as was his custom, an immense and growing noise was heard from the ramparts of the city. A band of armed knights sent by the countess of Brittany and her son Arthur, had attacked in order to capture John, who had arrived there that night, but suspecting the trap prepared for him, had left the city secretly before it was light. One of the bishop's clerks, Gerard, first discovered this, who being exceedingly disturbed and alarmed at what he had found out, hurried to tell him. He urgently implored the bishop to use the shorter lessons for the office which he had begun to chant, so that whilst the light was still faint he might more easily avoid encountering the soldiers and more safely accomplish the journey which lay before him together with his companions who had gone on ahead. He, however, was unmoved amid this panic, and calmly continued the recitation of the hymns in honour of God. Nor was his foolhardiness misplaced, for owing to this delay the abbot of that place came to his aid and went before him on horseback, conducting him safely by bypaths beyond the boundaries of the city. Many of the people who had left before him were waylaid and taken prisoner by the enemy. He left there in charge of the abbot two carts and some of his horses and a varied assortment of baggage, all of which was dispatched to him by the countess of whom I spoke on her arrival at the city the following day, accompanied by an

seipsam et filium suum studiose commendans. Ipse uero Sagiensem tendebat ad urbem.

Acceperat quoque relatione plurimorum abbatem de Perseni optimis esse studiis preditum probisque moribus ualde insignitum. Audiens quoque illius cenobium non procul a uia qua pergebat esse constitutum, cupiens uiri Dei notitiam sibi comparare eiusque orationibus seipsum commendare, nec temporis inquietudine nec itineris potuit longitudine reuocari quin ad ipsum inquirendum alacri deuotione properaret. Per deuios itaque suisque omnibus ignotos calles, cum paucis suorum ad diu quesitum demum peruenit monasterium, reliquis serui-entibus et sociis recto itinere ad urbem premissis, quo erat ipse hospitium subiturus. Cum agnouisset uero abbatem tunc esse absentem, celebrata missa discessit, totum uidelicet expendens pie deuotionis unguentum in ipso iustorum capite et domino Ihesu Christo, quod participare decreuerat cum menbro ipsius et seruo fideli admodum et *a* honesto.

Iam uero post hec, omni sublato cuiuscumque difficultatis obstaculo, ecclesie sue gremio letus excipitur, pacem exoptatam filiis reportans multo quidem sudore set multipliciori *b* honore partam et toto uite ipsius spatio duraturam. Occurebant uero *c* undique non modo ex ciuitate et in ciuitate uel diocesi sua turbe letantium et applaudentium   tamquam   duci   eximio   sublimiter triumphanti ; uerum plurimi quoque in Normania, in Anglia ex populo et ex clero prorsus innumeri, unani-miter ei conclamantes *d* ' Benedictus qui uenit in nomine Domini.' [1] Ipse uero totum Deo et nichil sibi tribuens benedicebat Dominum qui semper in omnibus triumphat suos in Christo.[2]

---

a *om* B   *b* multiplici X
c + ei X ; + illi p   *d* conclamabant X

earnest request for his prayers on behalf of her son and herself. He himself went to the city of Seéz.

Very many persons had informed him of the high reputation of the abbot of Persigny, for learning and holiness. When he discovered that the monastery was not far from the road along which he was travelling, neither the disturbed times nor the length of his journey could deter him from giving effect to his desire to meet the saintly man and obtain his prayers. By a circuitous route unknown to any of his companions, after a long search he eventually came with a few attendants to the monastery, sending the rest of his servants and companions by the direct road to the city where he was proposing to stay. He found, however, that the abbot was away and left after celebrating mass, thus lavishing all the precious perfume of his generous devotion, part of which he had intended to bestow on his righteous and faithful servant and member, on Christ Jesus our Lord, the head of the elect.

After this, to the great joy of his church he returned to it with all his difficulties solved and, bringing to his sons the peace they had desired, which, although obtained by immense efforts, enhanced his reputation even more greatly, and was to last all the remainder of his life. Not only in the cities or outside them, or in his own diocese, but everywhere in Normandy and England large crowds of clergy and people came to meet him. These cheered him joyously as if he were a leader who had won a great victory, crying out with one voice, ' Blessed is he who cometh in the name of the Lord.' [1] He indeed giving all the honour to God and none to himself, gave thanks to the Lord who always gives victory to his people through Christ.[2]

[1] Matt. 21: 9   [2] cf. 2 Cor. 2: 14

Capitvlvm XIII

Quod anno sequenti, pace reformata inter reges, Iohannem scilicet Anglorum et Philippum Francorum, Cartusiam adire ceperit. Et itineris illius incidentia usquequo perueniretur ad sanctum Antonium.

Expleto iam uno post regis [a] coronationem anno, ad petitionem illius transfretauit iterum episcopus, ut interesset colloquio ipsius cum rege Francorum in quo demum pax reformata est inter eos.[1] Videbatur sibi tunc oportunum tempus inuenisse uir Dei ut domum inuiseret Cartusiensem. Habuerat sane iamdiu in uotis ante uite presentis excursum locum semper amatum adire statumque ordinis presentialiter intueri et gregis illius quam pusilli tam et sanctissimi, aspectu et affatu interna sua desideria ab externis tumultibus aliquantulum respirando uberius refouere. Optauerat [b] profecto sarcine etiam pastoralis cure ex integro si daretur facultas renunciare, ne mundanis litibus decidendis [c] sub pretextu spiritualis officii, ordine ut memorabat prepostero totis ferme diebus cogeretur inseruire. ' Iam,' inquit, ' urbium pretores uel presides et ecclesiarum presules eo fere solo distare cernuntur quod isti continuis,[d] illi diebus interpolatis, forensibus uacant litigiis. Illis interdum licet rei familiaris sue utilitatibus consulere, isti ipsa etiam animarum suarum negotia uix quandoque permittitur tractare.' Sollicitauerat iam secundo uel tertio aures summi pontificis per internuntios super

---

[a] + Iohannis X   [b] Optabat X   [c] diffiniendis X
[d] cernuntur . . . continuis] dicuntur . . . continue X
[1] Peace of Le Goulet, 22 May 1200. John did homage and paid a relief of 20,000 marks for the Angevin possessions, surrendering the Norman Vexin and Evreux to Philip. The disputed lordships of Issoudun and Graçay in Berry were to be the dowry of Blanche of Castille, whose marriage to the future Louis VIII was part of the terms. John also undertook not to support his nephew Otto of Brunswick's candidature for the Empire. In

Chapter XIII

How, next year, when peace had been made between the two kings, John of England and Philip of France, he visited Chartreuse, and what befell on his journey up to the time of his arrival at St Anthony.

A year having elapsed since the king's coronation, the bishop went abroad again at his request in order to be present at the conference between him and the King of France where at last peace was made between them.[1] It seemed to the man of God that this would be an excellent opportunity for him to visit Chartreuse. He had long desired before the end of this present life, to go to the spot he had always loved and see for himself the state of his order and taking a short breathing-space from the troubles of the world abundantly refresh his soul by seeing and conversing with that small and saintly flock. He had indeed longed to give up entirely the burden of his episcopal duties, if he were given an opportunity, lest he should be constrained to spend almost all his days deciding secular lawsuits by reason of his spiritual office which he used to declare meant putting last things first. ' Now,' he would say, ' almost the only difference between the governors or bailiffs of towns and the prelates of the church, is that the former are deciding cases every day and the latter on alternate days. The former at times are allowed to attend to their own wordly affairs, whereas the latter are scarcely permitted occasionally to attend to their spiritual welfare.'

---

return his succession to the Angevin territories including Brittany was recognized and Arthur became his vassal. Hence St Hugh's exhortations to the latter to live at peace with his uncle.

huiuscemodi cordis sui proposito ; set ille nullatenus
adquiescens, non modo petitionem eius repellebat set et
petitionis mediatores durius obiurgabat. Omnium sane
difficiliores ac magis arduas negotiorum decisiones quas
inter fines totius Anglie auctoritate uentilari *a* contingebat apostolica episcopo delegabant *b* Lincolniensi
quotquot suis temporibus ecclesie presiderunt Romane
pontifices summi.[1] Persone queque nichilominus et
mediocres et infime, quantum de meritis presumebant
cause sue tantum coram eo contra suos aduersarios
optabant litigare. Illos enim, siue uiribus niterentur,
siue armarentur dolis, sub examine iudicis iustissimi et
ueritas facilius conuincebat et equitas citius percellebat.
Nam et hoc quoque donum acceperat a Deo ut sicut eo
nemo equi et recti tenacior, ita nemo inueniretur de
facili qui eo uideretur uelocior siue acutior in discussione
ueri et falsi. Quod in eo attendentes hii qui peritiores in
iure et in uentilationibus forensium siue ecclesiasticarum
causarum exercitatissimi habebantur, miraculis ascribe-
bant dum ille talium insuetus et quasi legum nescius
omnium precederet *c* acumina et ingenia preuolaret
iuris peritorum.

Vidimus quemdam in Londoniensium ciuitate pre-
potentem, Iordanum de Turri uocitatum, quem
auctoritate litterarum domini pape in ius traxerant
pauperes et pusilli *d* duo, sub tutoribus adhuc agentes
orphani, super iniqua detentione quarumdam domorum,
hereditaria successione ipsis competentium. Causam
ipsam in forum ecclesiasticum titulus cui dicebatur
inniti adduxerat usurarum. Hic die sibi prefixa, non
quasi litigaturus set quasi litis progressum descisurus, ad

---

a discuti X   *b* delegabat Bp
c precelleret X   *d* pupilli X

On two or three occasions he made representations through other people to the pope concerning his heart's desire, but he would not hear of it, not only rejecting the petition but sharply scolding those who brought it. All the popes who ruled the church during his episcopate delegated the most complicated and most delicate cases of appeal throughout the whole of England to the Bishop of Lincoln.[1] Moreover, persons of medium and low rank, if convinced of the justice of their case, were exceedingly anxious to implead their opponents before him. Whether they relied on force, or used trickery as their weapon under the examination of the most just of judges, the truth was easily elucidated and justice quickly triumphed. He had received this gift from God, that just as he was unequalled in integrity and uprightness, so no-one displayed the same acuteness and speed in sifting truth from falsehood. Those with much more knowledge of law, and practice in dealing with secular and ecclesiastical suits, when they observed this, thought it miraculous that he who was unversed in such business and had very little legal training should excel skilled lawyers in shrewdness and penetration.

I saw a leading London citizen named Jordan de Turre, whom two poor and unprotected orphans suing through their guardians had brought into court after an appeal to the pope, alleging the unjust detention of certain houses which they had inherited. The reason for bringing the suit into the ecclesiastical court was that it raised the issue of usury. This man appeared before the bishop on the day fixed, not like a litigant but like a judge, and accompanied by a great band of men who

---

[1] These were Urban III (1185-7), Gregory VIII (1187), Clement III (1187-91), Celestine III (1191-8), Innocent III (1198-1216). See Introduction, vol. I, p. xxx-xxxii.

episcopum, plurimo stipatus agmine propugnatorum potius quam aduocatorum, accessit. Cui dum litteratorie simul et uiua uoce inhibitiones precesque obtulissent stipatores sui, tam ex parte domini regis quam et aliarum sublimium potestatum necnon et ciuium communiter Londoniensium *a* ne in causa procederet, quia si faceret hoc, ut asserebant, in sue urbis preiudicium redundaret ; cum assessores ac domestici sui subsistendum esse in causa unanimiter decernerent, ille intra semetipsum paululum deliberans, hac demum uoce oppressorem opprimit pupillorum. Meminerat enim pius ille pater orphanorum scripture dicentis, ' Pupillo tu eris adiutor.' [1]

Ait itaque, ' Reuera, Iordane, quamquam nobis extiteris *b* carus, nullatenus tamen contra Deum tibi deferre ualemus. Verum quia niti contra tot et tantos fautores tuos, non modo paruulis istis immo et nobis ipsis nostrisque coniudicibus constat esse inutile, quod sumus acturi nolumus te latere. Pro me ipso tamen loquor, liberabo animam meam. Scribam igitur domino pape quia tu solus in terris istis eius iurisdictioni contradicis eiusque auctoritatem solus tu euacuare contendis.' Hac illa sententia ac si Partica sagitta feriretur precordialiter tactus, nimirum intelligens quanti foret ponderis relatio ista in auribus summi pontificis, presertim emissa ab ore uiri tanti nominis, tractare cepit incontinenti cum suis super restitutione facienda destitutis. Nec enim exitum alias inuenit. Verba quippe uiri iusti, sicut stimuli et quasi claui in altum defixi,[2] non dico cedere set nec attingi quidem rationibus aut blanditiis quiuerant uiri in generatione sua prudentissimi.[3] Mox igitur conquerentibus ad condignum

---

a Lincolniensium B
b extiteritis X

seemed more like professional champions than advocates. His supporters brought with them and read aloud letters of prohibition and also requests from the king and other persons of importance and the whole body of the citizens of London that Hugh should not continue the case. They asserted that if he did so it would redound to the injury of the city. His assessors and household were all in favour of stopping the case, but he after a short period of deliberation, finally crushed the despoiler of the defence-less. The compassionate father of orphans had remembered the words of holy writ, ' Thou wilt be the helper of the fatherless.' [1]

He spoke as follows, ' Indeed, Jordan, although you have been our friend, we cannot on any condition favour you against God. As it is generally thought that it would be useless not only for these children but even for us and our fellow-judges to oppose your numerous and powerful supporters, I do not wish to conceal my intentions from you. I speak for myself only, and as my conscience dictates. I shall write to the pope that you alone in this land defy his jurisdiction and try to make his authority ineffective.' This statement like a Parthian shot pierced him to the heart, for he realised very well the effect of such a report on the pope, especially when made by a man so universally respected. He immediately began to discuss with his friends how best to make restitution to his victims, since he could find no other alternative. The words of the righteous man ' as goads or as nails fixed on high ' [2] could not be gainsaid or even weakened by the arguments or persuasions of a man wise in his generation.[3] He soon therefore indemnified the plaintiffs, and with, as he declared, the loss of the

[1] Ps. 9: 14
[2] cf. Eccles. 12: 11
[3] cf. Luke 16: 8

satisfecit, nec sine enormi, ut asseruit, dispendio sumptuum quos in fundo ipse expenderat. Sic una breuisque
uiri iusti optinuit allegatio quod uix umquam crederetur
optinere causidicorum quantalibet multitudo.

Licet uero in similibus persepe casibus naufraganti
subsidium prestaret innocentie seu ueritati, indignam
tamen pontificis opera reputabat sollicitudinem, que
magis circa terrena et transitoria quam erga celestia et
eterna sepius uersaretur. Portabat uero set in angaria
crucem huiusmodi actionum de solius *a* merito obedientie, excusationis potius suffragium quam premium rei
commendabilis expectans.

Verum hec innumeris uerborum necnon et gestorum
eius non est necesse astrui documentis que tamen
scribenti ad manum satis occurrunt, cum talis animi ea
sit in eo irrefragabilis approbatio quod ad proprium
scaccarium siue compotum reddituum uel expensarum
suarum numquam residere, numquam huiuscemodi
domus proprie ratiociniis dignatus sit intendere. Quod
uero episcopum domui sue debere esse bene prepositum [1]
monet apostolus ita implendum docebat et ita implebat,
ut uiris fide et discretione opinatissimis *b* hec opera
imponeret ; *c* de quibus tamquam de seipso *d* confideret
dum irreprehensibiliter se haberent, secus uero agentes,
quod diu quidem latere non poterat, incontinenti
amoueret. Nec enim priuato erga quemlibet eorum
quibus dispensationes rerum crediderat, amore tenebatur ; quos fides et industria poterat commendare, non
queuis artior necessitudo ad perperam quid agendum ut
assolet animare.

Verum iter eius uersus Burgundiam prosequamur.
Licentia igitur a rege et archiepiscopo apud castrum de

a solo o   *b* optimatissimis o
c imponerentur Xp   *d* ipso B

immense sum of money he had expended on the property. One short speech of this just man thus obtained what a whole multitude of advocates could scarcely have succeeded in getting.

Although in a large number of similar cases he supported the cause of innocence and truth when they were in peril, he regarded such work as unworthy of the attention of a bishop, because it often was more concerned with worldly and earthly matters than with the spiritual and eternal. These lawsuits were a cross and penance undertaken solely from motives of obedience, for which he expected pardon and indulgence, rather than the reward due for a good work.

It is, however, quite unnecessary to quote any of his words or deeds as proofs, although innumerable examples occur to the author. The incontrovertible proof of his attitude towards such matters is his refusal ever to be present at his own exchequer or the audit of his revenues and expenses, and even at the examination of his household accounts. He interpreted the counsel of the apostle [1] that a bishop should be a good steward of his household as meaning that he should lay this task on men renowned for their honesty and prudence, and acted up to this. He had the same confidence in such men as in himself, as long as they did not abuse his trust, and those who did otherwise, a fact which could not be long concealed, he immediately dismissed. Personal friendship had nothing to do with the choice of those to whom he committed his affairs ; he appointed those whose probity and energy recommended them, and not those whose close relationship would tempt to act wrongfully as is usually the case.

[1] 1 Tim. 3: 4

Andeli petita et accepta, prima *a* die mensis Maii que fuit quarta feria Pentecostes, proficisci cepit. Quod uero impetus eum non carnis et sanguinis, ut quidam uaniloqui garriebant, set reuera Spiritus ageret, ut in ipsis iam primum feruescentis ardoribus estatis tanti laborem itineris aggredi non timeret, hinc satis claruit ; *b* quod loca sanctorum reliquiis aut religiosis seruorum Dei conuentibus celebria, nec solum in ipso itinere presentia uel itineri etiam contigua, uerum quoque plurimum remota deuotus adiuit. Quia enim tempus instabat iam colligendarum frugum, quod ille annis singulis sancte uacationi dicare consueuerat, ut dum alii materiali fructu frumenti, uini et olei suas exteriores satagerent replere apothecas, ille interius spiritualibus horum bonorum copiis multiplicari potuisset ; decernit modo totum illius temporis spatium in religiosa fatigatione expendere, et sicut consueuerat ad ecclesie sue, agri uidelicet Domini, culturam et sationem tempore iaciende sementis redire.

Imprimis itaque apud Meollentum sanctum adiuit Nicasium.*c* Quem suppliciter ueneratus, auro etiam ei oblato, de capite ipsius os insigne quod manibus extraxit propriis cum ingenti letitia consecutus, iturus inde Parisiis, ad beatum diuertit Dionisium. Sane cum niteretur aliquem ex dentibus beati Nicasii, cuius nudum in manibus tenuerat capud sanctissimum, auellere et sibi pro benedictione retinere, nec id efficere potuisset, misit digitos in nares illius que semper bonum Christi

---

a ultima vp Whitsunday, 1200, was on May 28. *D gives a marginal correction of this primitive error.*

b Quia uero ut in ipsis iam primum feruescentis ardoribus estatis tanti laborem itineris aggredi non timeret, eum non impetus carnis et sanguinis, ut quidam uaniloque garriebant, set reuera Spiritus ageret, hinc satis claruit ; X

c + archiepiscopum quondam Remensem X

Let us now continue his journey to Burgundy. At the castle of Andely he obtained from the king and the archbishop the permission he had asked for and on the Wednesday after Pentecost which was the last day of May he began his travels. His willingness to embark on such a strenuous journey at the beginning of the summer heat was due to the inspiration of the Holy Spirit and not, as some scandalmongers aver, to the ties of blood and friendship. This is clearly proved by his visits out of devotion to famous shrines and monasteries, including not only those on or near his route, but many a good distance from it.

It was near the time of harvest which he was wont every year to devote to contemplation, that whilst others worked hard to fill their outward storehouses with earthly corn, wine and oil, he could increase the abundance of his interior spiritual graces. He decided now to spend the whole time in religious exercises, and return, as was his custom, to the cultivation of the field of the Lord, that is his church, at seed-time.

First, therefore, at Meulan he came to the shrine of St Nicasius, where, having prayed with deep devotion and made an offering of gold, he acquired a large bone, which he removed with his own hands from the head. This acquisition caused him immense joy. Whilst on his way to Paris he turned aside to go to St Denys. Although his attempt to extract one of the teeth of St Nicasius whilst holding the holy head uncovered and keep it as a blessed relic was a failure, he did manage to put his fingers in the nostrils which had always breathed the good odour of Christ, and easily removed a delicate little bone which had separated the martyr's two eye-sockets. This he received with fitting devotion as a precious gift and pledge of God's favour, and with

odorem spirare consueuerant, et summa cum facilitate
unum eduxit oscillum ualde speciosum quod martiris
geminos oculorum orbes interiectu sui discriminare
consueuerat. Hoc pignus adeo pretiosum, auspicato [a]
Deitatis munere susceptum, digna cum deuotione
complexus, spem concipit uberiorem quia in uiam pacis
et salutis dirigeret eum Dominus, prosequente sese
fauore pariter tanti pontificis, qui sibi hoc dignatus est
de suis intimis artubus prerogare, quod ipse numquam
ante destitit inter sacratissimos oculos fixum habere.[1]

Cum uero apud sanctum Dionisium, ut dicere
ceperamus, haut breues protraxisset moras, dum ad
singula que sibi ostendebantur sacra, necnon ad uniuersas
ibi quiescentium sanctorum memorias, larga fundit [b]
orationum libamina, iam uicum illum egresso innumere
occurebant clericorum turme. Cateruatim namque
ruebant de ciuitate, in obuiam uniuersali scholarum
consultori, ut de illo quidam uersificator insignis ait,
uniuersarum pene nationum scholastici, coram cernere
cupientes per quem, post sanctum Nicholaum, incom-
parabilia erga clericos agnouerant exerceri beneficia.
Cunctis itaque aduenienti in nomine Domini applaudentibus, hiis osculo et alloquio, illis aspectu solo cum
benedictione illius glorianter perfruentibus, a nonnullis
ad hospitium urgentissime inuitatur. Set dum omnibus
in hoc satisfieri non posset, uni tantum qui pridie
sollicita prece hoc impetrare satagerat, sese in hospitem
non negauit. Erat hic ipsius, ut dicebatur, cognatus
nomine Reimundus, uir multa honestate conspicuus, ab
ipso in canonicum Lincolniensem ac demum in archi-
leuitam Leircestrensem promotus.[2] Qui ne a tam nobili
stemate generosi sanguinis degenerare uideretur, ut

---

[a] auspicantis X
[b] fudit X

renewed hope that the Lord would lead him along the way of peace and salvation, with the assistance of this renowned bishop who had condescended to bestow on him a part of his very frame which had always until then remained between his most blessed eyes.

When he came as I have already mentioned to St Denys he did not stay there long. On leaving the township, after praying assiduously not only before the relics displayed for his benefit, but also at all the shrines of the church, large bands of clerks were assembling to greet him. The scholars of almost every nation had hastened from the city in a body to meet the man whom a famous poet has described as their especial patron. They were anxious to see the person whom with the exception of St Nicholas they regarded as their chief friend, and hailed him as one who came in the name of the Lord. Some could exultingly boast of having received his kiss and spoken with him whilst others had to be content with seeing him and receiving his blessing. Certain of them pressed him to be their guest. Being unable in this matter to gratify everyone, he accepted the hospitality of the man who had on the previous day earnestly and repeatedly requested this favour. This was his kinsman, Reimund, a man with an outstanding reputation for integrity, whom he had made a canon of Lincoln and finally promoted to be archdeacon of Leicester.[2] He, fearing to be unworthy of his illustrious ancestry, always tried to imitate the generosity of spirit which he had marked in his patron. At the time of the

---

[1] Nicasius, bishop of Rouen, was martyred *c.* 340. At the Norman invasions his relics were removed to Meulan, which later became a priory of Bec. In the twelfth century his feast was kept in England as well as in France. He is not to be confused with St Nicasius of Rheims (died *c.* 407).

[2] Reimund, made archdeacon of Leicester, 1195-1198, occurs as witness to Lincoln charters (cf. C. W. Foster and E. K. Major, *Registrum Antiquissimum*, II, p. 330).

semper emulatus fuerat libertatem spiritus quam in tanto
agnouerat patrono, longe post decessum uiri beatissimi,
cum tempore interdicti Anglicani omnes fere ecclesiarum
rectores, quos tamen in exilium barbaricus regis furor
minis *a* coegerat, interueniente pecunia bona sua
redimerent a manu laicali, ipse pene solus spontaneum
potius elegit et diutinum subire exilium quam sponse
Regis eterni, sancte uidelicet ecclesie libertatem, ad
nutum regis terreni indigne quantum in se fuit subicere
seruituti. Cui tamen, iuxta fidei et deuotionis sue
meritum, nutu diuino pie retributum est ut qui diuitias
multas amplumque honorem pro iustitia postposuit,
absque nota dedecoris et obligatione criminis, diuitias et
honorem quem habuit continue retinuerit, honore
quidem in inmensum cumulato ex tam honorabili facto,
et diuitiis suis minus sibi quam cuiuis residentium et
male redimentium sociorum suorum hactenus inminutis.
Quas ille quoque exulibus liberaliter communicans,
sicut omnibus imitande uirtutis exemplum, ita compluribus necessarie stipis prestitit adminiculum.

Quod nos de hospite, tanti hospitis susceptore, nemo
quasi per excessum breuiter commemorasse succenseat,
cum nos quoque sub eadem tempestate, dura exulandi
necessitate constrictos, ipsius liberalitas trimenstri ferme
dierum circulo humanissime fouerit, multisque in suo
secum precibus detentos hospitio honorifice exhibuerit.*b*
Non possumus itaque sicut nec debemus, quam uidimus et
experti sumus bonitati eius minime perhibere testimonium. Set nec ista scribendo longius recedimus a
proposito, qui magistri recolentes insignia, discipuli
pariter recensenda estimamus preconia. Gloria siquidem
patris est filius sapiens, et laus discipuli refunditur in

---

a minime X
b exhibuit X

Interdict, when the holy man had long been dead, and when even in their exile the savage fury and threats of the king compelled the greater number of the prelates of the English Church to pay money for the redemption of their possessions from the secular power, he was almost the only one who of his own free will chose a long exile rather than be responsible for the cowardly betrayal of the liberty of Holy Church, the bride of the heavenly King, to the dictation of an earthly ruler. His loyalty and devotion in preferring righteousness to wealth and preferment were justly rewarded by divine providence, since he retained his riches and position, without the smallest slur on his honour, and added greatly to his reputation by his honourable behaviour. Up to the present time his revenues have diminished less than those of his colleagues who remained at home and made this shameful bargain. He shared them generously with the exiles, thus not only setting everyone an example to be imitated, but supplying very many of them with a modest provision in their penury. No one can blame me for mentioning in passing the host of such an illustrious guest, since it was he, when I at that time was an exile and in want, who most kindly and generously befriended me for a period of almost three months, and constrained me by his many prayers to accept his munificent hospitality. Having seen and had experience of his goodness I can and must bear witness to it. In writing this I am not abandoning my plan, for I consider that when describing the splendid acts of the master, I should also commemorate the virtues of his disciple, since a wise son is the glory of his father and the praise of the disciple redounds to the credit of the master. Thus, a valiant archdeacon brings honour to his bishop, as for example

magistrum. Sic et archileuita strenuus suum exornat episcopum, ut Sixtum Laurentius, Valerianum *a* Vincentius, Pontius quoque Ciprianum.[1] Revera set nec Hugoni gratior umquam gratia ulla fuit quam uidere filios suos ambulare in ueritate, maxime si parati inuenirentur pro ipsa ueritate aduersa equanimiter tolerare, et usque ad mortem pro ea uiriliter decertare.

Set iam ceptam de episcopo historiam prosequamur. De archidiacono hec ita tetigisse sufficiat. Qui theologis uacabat auditoriis ea quidem tempestate in supradicta Parisiaca ciuitate, sic et postea quando cum eo morati sumus in prefata nostra relegatione.

Venit autem in hospitium illius inuisere episcopum illustrissime indolis adholescens, regis Francorum filius et heres Lodowicus, qui proximo sumpserat in coniugium regis Anglorum neptem ex sorore, Hispaniarum uidelicet regina[m] nomine Candidula[m].*b* Venit autem secum nepos prefati regis Arturus, Galfridi comitis Brittonum quondam filius, tunc annos circiter quatuordecim natus. Hos pariter complexus Hugo pius cuique illorum congrua sibi monita saluberrima dulciter instillabat. Lodowicus uultu placidus que dicebantur auide intendebat ; Arturus aspernanter id maxime admittebat quod eum de dilectione et pace ad patruum suum regem Anglorum habenda admonebat.

Interea Lodowicus pontificem orat ut nouam nuptam quam duxerat inuisere dignaretur. Quod ille benigne annuens, ita pedibus suis ad proximum regis palatium iuit. Afflictamque quodam recenti casu adholescentulam uerbis paucis in tantum exhilarauit ut statim, merore postposito quo diebus aliquot lugubris incedebat, et uultum de cetero et animum gereret letissimum.

---

a Valerium X
b Candidam Q Blancha X

Lawrence to Sixtus, Vincent to Valerian and Pontius to Cyprian.[1] Moreover, nothing pleased Hugh more than to see his sons walking in the paths of justice, especially when he found that they were ready to bear misfortune patiently for righteousness sake, and to strive manfully for it even to death.

I will now resume the story of the bishop, having said quite enough about the archdeacon. The latter at that time attended the theological lectures in the city of Paris, and even did so later when I was staying with him during my exile to which I have already referred.

Whilst the bishop was staying there Louis, the son and heir of the king of France, a charming and promising youth, who had recently married Blanche, the niece of the king of the English, the daughter of his sister, the queen of Spain, came to visit him. He brought with him the king's nephew Arthur, the son of Geoffrey the late count of Brittany, who was then about fourteen. Hugh kindly embraced them both, and gently gave them valuable and useful counsel. Louis appeared pleased and listened intently to what he said, but Arthur obviously greatly disliked his advice to live at peace and amity with his uncle the king of England.

Louis later begged the bishop to honour his newly-wedded bride with a visit. He gladly agreed to do so, and set out on foot for the royal palace which was quite near. The maiden was saddened by a recent loss, but a few words from him cheered her up so much, that she immediately forgot the grief and depression under which she had laboured for some days, and her happiness was reflected in her face.

---

[1] Pontius (died 260) was the biographer of St Cyprian. Vincent of Saragossa, spokesman of Bishop Valerian of Valencia, was martyred there in 304. Lawrence, Rome's most famous martyr, suffered, like Sixtus II, in 258.

Post hec cum Trecensem iam preterisset comitatum uenit ad eum uir quidam, uoce miserabili misericordiam illius implorans. Fatebatur enim se, culpis suis exigentibus, excommunicationis sententiam ab ipso excepisse, unde cum metu continuo finalis interitus, crebris iugiter infortuniis urgebatur.

Sententie causa ista fuit. Fuerat idem *a* custos quarumdam uillarum comitis Leircestrie quo tempore fur quidam in ecclesiam confugit uille que uocatur Barkeleia *b* cuius ipse uillicus fuit. Est autem fundus ipse in episcopatu Lincolniensi. Dominus fundi precipuus habitus fuit in bellicis rebus, linea uero sanguinis generosi potioribus regni proceribus iungebatur. Hinc regis fauore comitatus, non minus suis quam sibi nonnulla preter ius usurpandi fiduciam uendicabat.*c* Officiales itaque illius, contra Scripture monita dicentis 'Noli esse iustus nimium,' [1] in hominem querentem ecclesie misericordiam seuam exercentes iustitiam, ipsum dolo productum de Christi asilo *d* suspendio peremerunt.

Tunc uero episcopus in transmarinis agebat. Vnde reuersus et quod factum erat agnoscens, sententiam *e* generalem in auctores et complices huius malefacti promulgauit. Reliquis uero qui super huiusmodi sacrilegio cauteriatam gerebant conscientiam, ecclesiastice humiliter se subicientibus discipline, hic satisfactionis abhorrens districtionem et relinquens Angliam, ad dominum suum confugerat in Neustriam.

Siquidem compulsi sunt illi qui necem intulerant fugitiuo, necnon et illi qui proditione illum de septis ecclesie protraxerant, omnibus exceptis femoralibus uestibus nudi, iam putrefactum hominis cadauer effodere

---

a + aliquando X *b* Brackeleia Q
c uendicabant Bo *d* ecclesia X
e + excommunicationis X

After this when he had just passed through the county of Troyes, a man came to him who with groans implored his compassion. He confessed that he had been excommunicated by him, as he richly deserved, for which reason he was haunted by the dread of eternal damnation besides having had to endure almost continuous misfortune.

The cause of his excommunication was as follows. Whilst he was bailiff of certain vills belonging to the earl of Leicester, a thief had taken sanctuary in the church of the vill of Brackley of which he was reeve. The manor was in the Lincoln diocese. The lord of the manor was a great warrior, of noble blood, and related to the best families of the kingdom. Being high in the king's favour he and his men confidently usurped rights which were not legally theirs. His officials, contrary to the instructions of holy writ, ' Be not just to excess ',[1] had exacted the full penalty from one who had sought the Church's protection, whom they hanged, after luring him from Christ's sanctuary by a trick.

The bishop was at that time abroad, and learning of the outrage on his return, he promulgated a general excommunication of the perpetrators of the crime and their accomplices. The rest, being conscience-stricken about the sacrilege, humbly submitted to the discipline of the Church, but he, shrinking from the shame of penance, left England and sought refuge with his lord in Normandy.

In fact, those who had caused the death of the victim, or had by treachery removed him from the precincts of the church, naked except for their breeches, had been compelled to dig up the already putrid corpse

---

[1] Eccles. 7: 17

feretroque impositum a suspendii loco humeris ita nudis
in uillam per unius fere milliarii spatium reportare. Ad
omnium quoque limina ecclesiarum ipsius uici, a cunctis
illius capituli presbiteris uerberati, circumportati corporis
menbra, iam a putredine tabefacta, propriis manibus et,
ut dictum est, nudis semper corporibus, in cimiterio
basilice unde uiuum eduxerant sepelire sunt coacti.
Post hec Lincolniam nudis pedibus adire ac pre foribus
singularum tante ciuitatis ecclesiarum latera flagellis
exponere, et hiis similia hyemali presertim tempore ad
tolerandum satis aspera iussi sunt perferre.

Hec iste de quo agitur, cum unus esset ex illis, ferre
non sustinens, Angliam maluit exire quam angelis ex
condigna penitentia gaudium exhibere.¹ Ceterum iuxta
sententiam beati Iob, ' Qui timet pruinam, irruet super
eum nix ',² et sepe periclitatur morbo qui non patitur
aspere tractari a medico. Nec dissimiliter huic ex suo
cessit consilio. Qui enim reatus sui noluit sustinere
correctionem dum adhuc status integritatem potuit
retinere, ingruentibus hinc inde super eum aduersitatis ᵃ
procellis, eo usque dampnis affectus est et uariis in-
comodis ut, sicut asserebat, eum tederet uite sue.
Domini quoque sui cui prestare obsequium se arbitratus
est dum contra episcopum recalcitrare nisus est, adeo
sibi gratiam senserat ex hoc ipso sublatam ut eum in suo
nec obsequio sineret permanere nec in suo aspectu
libenter eum uellet apparere. Qui reuersus tandem in
se, quem censuit fugiendum medicum iam credidit
expetendum. Quem anhelus et anxius demum inuenit,
a quo et medelam iam in remotis posito uix perceperit ᵇ

ᵃ aduersitatum QX   ¹ cf. Luke 15: 7
ᵇ percepit QX   ² Job 6: 16

of the man, and placing it on a bier to carry it on their
bare shoulders from the place of execution to the village,
a distance of almost a mile.   After taking the body and
limbs which were now in a state of corruption round
all the churches of the district, and being beaten outside
each of them by all the priests of the chapter, they were
finally compelled to bury it with their own hands,
still naked as I have described, in the cemetery of the
church from which they had removed the man when still
living.   After this they were ordered to go barefoot to
Lincoln, and outside all the churches of that immense
city bare their backs for the scourge and perform other
similar penances which were particularly severe in
winter time.

The man about whom I am speaking, although he
had been one of them, refused to submit, and preferred
to leave England rather than make the angels rejoice
by a fitting show of penance.[1] However, as blessed Job
says, ' Who fears the frost, the snow falls upon ',[2] and
the illness of those who reject the unpleasant remedies
prescribed by the doctor is often fatal.   This man's
obstinacy had a similar result.   Being unready to accept
punishment in spite of his guilt, at a time when he could
still have kept his position in society, from henceforth
he was buffeted by the storms of adversity and sustained
such losses and misfortunes, that he declared his life
became a burden to him.   He had believed that his
endeavours to defy the bishop would have his lord's
support, but he fell so much under his displeasure that
he dismissed him, and desired never to see him again.
At length having recovered his senses, he decided that
he should search for the doctor from whom he had
thought to escape.   He found him at last after a hectic
and anxious search, and received from him with

quam in uicino sponte oblatam percipere contempsit. Subiit iam letus septennis sarcinam penitentie qui breuiorem contempserat adimplere.

At heremita noster, suos cupiens coheremitas inuisere, congruo satis ordine nobilem illum heremitarum principem, beatum dico Antonium, orationis gratia primo studuit *a* in suo quo celeberrime colitur oratorio expetere, et postmodum Christi militum cohortes, huius instar ducis eximii obseruantes uastissimas heremi stationes adire. Diuertit itaque dierum trium itinere a uia que ducebat Cartusiam, ad montem utique Dei ; uenitque ad montem Antonii, ubi ignea lux incendii gehennalis, dum uisibiliter extinguitur, quodam uelud nature sue inuisibili preiudicio assidue cancellatur. Ibi uno intuitu non miraculum unum aut duo, immo non centena set innumera perspeximus miracula, omnibus ubicumque a nobis antea uisis miraculis plus stupenda. Vidimus enim iuuenes et uirgines, senes cum iunioribus [1] per sanctum Dei Antonium saluatos ab igne sacro, semiustis carnibus consumptisque ossibus uariisque mutilatos artuum compagibus, ita in dimidiis uiuentes corporibus ut quasi integra uiderentur incolumitate gaudentes. Concurritur siquidem a totis mundi finibus a quibusque laborantibus hoc malo quo nullum deterius, ad hunc locum quo beati Antonii cineres sacratissimi tunica Pauli primi heremite adhuc obuoluti seruantur, qui omnes fere infra diem septimam diuinitus curantur. Nam si quis sub hoc dierum spatio corporis sanitatem non recipit, a corporis colluuione, salubrius ut pie presumitur, morte intercedente confestim excedit ; tantique patroni suffragio

---

a + uisitare et X
[1] cf. Ps. 148: 12

difficulty in distant parts the cure which he had con-
temptuously rejected when it was freely offered him at
home.   Now he submitted joyfully to a seven-years'
penance, having previously scorned a shorter one.

Our hermit desired to visit his fellow hermits and
appropriately determined first to seek out their venerable
patron, I mean St Antony, and to pray at the most
famous of his shrines ; and then go to the bands of the
soldiers of Christ, who after the example of their
renowned founder had formed settlements in the wilderness.   He therefore left the road to Chartreuse, the mount
of God, for a three-days' journey and came to the mount
of Antony, where the fiery light of the flames of Hell is
visibly extinguished and as though by a certain invisible
damage done to its very nature is all the time being
annulled.   There on one visit alone we witnessed not
merely one or two or even a hundred but innumerable
miracles, all of which were more amazing than any we
had seen anywhere else.   We saw young men and girls,
old men as well as younger ones [1] healed by Antony the
saint of God from the devastating fire, which had
already half eaten away and consumed their flesh and
bones, and had deprived them of various limbs, leaving
them to live with mutilated bodies, for which they were
as thankful as if they were intact.   From every part
of the world the victims of this disease, which is more
horrible than any other, come in throngs to this spot
where the holy remains of blessed Antony, wrapped in
the tunic of Paul the first hermit, are still preserved, and
almost all of them are cured by God's mercy within
seven days.   Indeed, those who do not recover their
bodily health within this period, are immediately and,
one may piously hope, happily released by the intervention of death from the infection of their body, and

quem fide non ficta expetiit ad perhennis uite sospitatem attingit.

Est autem in ipsis miraculis hoc insignius miraculum. Igne namque restincto [a] in membris patientium, caro et cutis uel artus quisque quos morbus uorax sensim depascendo exederit, minime quidem restaurantur. Verum quod est mirabilius nudatis ossibus que truci incendio superfuerint, sanitas et soliditas cicatricibus ipsis residui corporis tanta confertur ut uideas plurimos in omni etate et sexu utroque, brachiis iam usque ad cubitos aut lacertis usque ad humeros absumptis, similiter et tibiis usque ad genua uel cruribus usque ad renes aut inguina exustis funditus et abrasis, tamquam sanissimos multa alacritate pollere. Adeo uirtus sancti perditarum in eis partium dampna retentarum firmitate compensat, ut nec uiscerum teneritudo intima cum ipsis interdum costarum obicibus cute spoliata et carnibus, frigoris aut alterius molestie iniuria de facili pulsetur ; permanentibus in mirum plagarum uestigiis [b] preter dolorem uulnerati ad honorem medici et testimonium morbi, cunctis [c] inspicientibus, ad materiam timoris necnon et incitamentum deuotionis.[1]

Perlatus est autem insatiabilis hic solitudinis amator et inhabitator a Constantinopoli ad illius deserti regiones circa id temporis quo uiri doctissimi et, quod pluris est, in sancta religione precellentissimi, magister Bruno cum collega sua Lauduino et aliis quinque electissimis, ad

---

[a] extincto X
[b] permanentia nimirum plagarum uestigia X
[c] + pretendunt ; *om* ad X

[1] The disease of St Anthony's fire, accurately described by Adam, was really a form of ergotism due to the use of diseased grain in bread. Epidemics of it were not uncommon in medieval France and Germany : a sporadic case occurred in Suffolk as recently as 1762, affecting a whole family who recovered from it after the loss of some limbs. The cures described may well have been due to a change of air and especially improvement in diet

by the assistance of so mighty a patron, whom they had approached with sincere faith, attain the repose of eternal life.

One very amazing feature of these miracles is that when the fire has been quenched in the limbs of the sufferers, the flesh, skin, or limbs which the devastating disease had attacked and consumed are never restored. It is even more remarkable that although the bones which have survived the devouring fire remained completely uncovered, so much health and well-being is given to the rest of the body in spite of these scars that you can see very many persons of all ages and both sexes, with their arms already scarred or wasted away as far as the elbows or even the shoulders, or with their legs burnt away or amputated in the same way at the knees, thighs, or even at the loins or the groin, with as much vitality as the completely healthy. The power of the saint was so great that the sound condition of the parts which survived made up for those they had been deprived of, so that neither the fragile internal organs, nor the exposed ribs where the skin and flesh had been eaten away were easily affected by the cold or any other type of hardship. The marks of the wounds remained in a wonderful way without causing pain to the victim as a testimony to the disease [1] and to the fame of the doctor, arousing fear and encouraging devotion in all who beheld them.

This fervent lover of and dweller in the desert was brought from Constantinople to this lonely place about the time when those most learned men, and what is more important, unsurpassed in their holiness, Master Bruno,

---

(cf. H. Thurston, *The Life of St Hugh of Lincoln*, London 1898, pp. 478-83). For the relics of St Anthony mentioned, cf. P. Noordeloos, *La Translation de S. Antoine en Dauphiné*, *Analecta Bollandiana* LX, 1942, pp. 68-81.

spirituale tirocinium commilitonibus eorum in montibus
uicinis sacra Cartusiensis ordinis fundamenta iacere
sunt agressi. Qui more suo hereticorum contubernia
perhorrescens, maumeticolas fugiendo dilectam olim
deseruerat Egyptum urbemque memoratam quo se
transferri permiserat multa insignia miraculorum gloria
aliquot annis decorauerat. Set neque in istis beneplacitum erat ei, in quibus fermentum non uniforme set
error plurimorum totam pene massam corruperat.
Congratulans uero uelud subite cuidam resuscitationi
inolite sibi conuersationis, perferri se disposuit in partes
illorum quos etiam specialius in unitate Catholice
matris ecclesie edere nouit pascha Dominicum in asimis
sinceritatis et ueritatis.[1] Verum ne languidis ope suo
indigentibus aut ipse deesset aut solitarie degentibus ex
confluentium multitudine importunus existeret, non
presentiam sui set uiciniam dilectis sibi accolis heremi
condonauit ; fauoris tamen et amoris uite quondam sue
professoribus eximium prerogauit indicium, dum suas
peculiariter reliquias uiro reuerentissimo [a] priori Cartusie
Gigoni tangendas et exosculandas indulsit. A quo ipsas
transponi etiam ac in nouam, quam idem uir de taxeis
compegerat tabellis,[b] reponi uoluit capsam et sollerti
deuotione recondi. Teca namque uetus, in qua diutius
quieuerunt ossa beata, non tam uenustate quam longa
terra marique gestatione dissuta fuerit et conquassata.
Auro autem uel argento aut metallo quolibet seu lapide
pretioso contegi, ornari siue colligari cistam suam num-

and his colleague Landuin and five other chosen souls
embarked upon their spiritual warfare and laid the
foundations of the holy Carthusian order in the neighbouring mountains. Shunning the society of heretics, as
was his custom, to escape from the followers of
Mahommed he had formerly left his beloved Egypt, and
permitting himself to be removed to the town I have
mentioned, made it renowned in a few years by many
striking miracles. He was not, however, well pleased with
those in whom the leaven did not work evenly and the
errors of the majority had corrupted almost the whole of
the dough. Rejoicing, however, at the sudden and unexpected revival of the way of life of which he had been
the founder he decided to be moved to a land where he
knew for certain the inhabitants celebrated the Lord's
Passover with the unleavened bread of sincerity and
truth[1] and in communion with the Catholic church, our
mother. Yet in order not to fail the sick who needed
his help, and to prevent those who dwelt in seclusion
from being vexed by the crowds of pilgrims, he did not
settle amongst his beloved disciples but in their vicinity.
Nevertheless, he gave especial proofs of his favour and
love for those who professed his former way of life, by
permitting the most venerable prior of Chartreuse,
Guigo to handle and kiss his sacred relics. He was even
willing that he should translate them, and place them
carefully and reverently in a new casket, which he had
fashioned from yew wood, for the old case in which his
blessed bones had rested for so long had become dis-
jointed and damaged not so much from age as from its
long journeyings over land and sea. He would never
allow his shrine to be made of gold, silver or any other

---

[1] cf. 1 Cor. 5: 8

quam permisit ; nec clauus in ea de materia huiusmodi potuit infigi, ut uel ad momentum inhereret, adeo ambitionis in eo odium et paupertatis inolitus amor hodieque perseuerat.

Ad huius itaque sacratissimam aram Hugo noster, episcopus quidem officio set heremita proposito, diuina quam deuotissime celebrauit. Tecam sane tam inestimabilis thesauri consciam eminus trabi suppositam uidimus, nec prope altare prominentem ᵃ set parieti adherentem, et preter morem sacrorum scriniorum quasi cuiusdam abditi latibula fouentem.

Capitvlvm XIV

De aduentu illius atque receptu apud Gratianopolim, Cartusiam, Belensium atque Alueriam ᵇ et apud alia inter hec loca ; et incidentia plurima singulorum locorum.

Debitis ergo uotis patrono tanto solutis, cum et xenodochium ipsius loci uisitasset et in solatia uictualium pecuniam custodibus largiri precepisset ; grandis quippe debilium multitudo, quos ante curationem morbus uariis menbris priuauit, ibidem consistit ;[1] Gratianopolim proficisci instituit. Inde namque ad Cartusiam per ardua montium et aspera rupium iter expeditius et locorum natura et commeantium frequentia patefecit. Inspeximus quoque arces et castella secus uiam qua itur

---

ᵃ preminentem X
ᵇ Aualon X
[1] This hospital was founded at St Didier de la Mothe by Gaston of Dauphiné in gratitude for his own cure from St Anthony's fire. There was already a church there dedicated to St Anthony. The community in charge of the hospital wore a black habit with the blue cross of St Anthony shaped

metal, or to be decorated or banded with these, or precious stones, nor could a nail of such material be hammered into it without immediately falling out, for his hatred of this sort of display and his ingrained love of poverty still survived.

Our Hugh, a bishop by profession but a hermit at heart, celebrated mass with much devotion at his holy altar. I myself saw the chest which contained these priceless relics resting upon a beam high above. This was fixed in a wall not overhanging the altar so that unlike most reliquaries it seemed to cover the hiding place of a recluse.

CHAPTER XIV

Concerning his arrival and reception at Grenoble, Chartreuse, Bellay and Avalon and other places, and what took place on each visit.

After he had paid due reverence to so great a saint, he visited the hostel attached to the shrine, where he ordered that a generous sum of money should be given to the guardians for the provision of nourishing food, for there were large numbers of sick folk there, already crippled by the disease before their cure,[1] and then he started for Grenoble. The route from there to Chartreuse, although it went through steep mountains and rocks and crags, was made easier and clearer by the character of the district and the crowds of visitors. Along the road to St Antony's we saw castles and fortresses, the lords of

---

like the Greek T. It became monastic in 1218 and adopted the rule of the Canons Regular in 1297. There were houses in France, Spain and Italy. It was suppressed at the French Revolution.

ad sanctum Antonium, fulmine cum dominis suis pessumdata eo quod peregrinis eius iniurie fuissent in eis illate. Optinet namque precipuus hic morum et sanctitatis Helye successor prerogatiuam pariter uirtutis sui decessoris. More siquidem Helye uerbo citius in contumaces ignem deicit ad uindictam quem in supplicibus extinguit ad medelam.[1]

Subtrahere [a] possemus copiam exemplorum ni iudicium mereretur [b] lectoris de frequentiori excessu digressionum. Hec tamen uel succinte de uirtutibus sancti, cunctis qui post ipsum floruerunt sanctis semper imitandi, iccirco memorauimus quia magnalium que cotidie operatur memorie posterorum nichil, ut ibidem accepimus, a quoquam stili beneficio destinatur. Quod in tantum displicuit Hugoni nostro ut ei potius quam Antonio nos arbitremur prestare obsequium, ista itineris sui occasione breuiter perstringendo.

Cuius iam aduentus mox ut Gratianopolitis innotuit, uniuersi pariter in obuiam ruunt uiro in partibus illis uotis omnium exoptato.[c] Quem, suo cum antistite uiro admodum uenerabili extra urbis menia susceptum, per urbem mediam floribus et palliis olosericis uarioque decore ob eius specialiter reuerentiam splendidius coronatam,[d] usque ad sancti Iohannis Baptiste ecclesiam cathedralem cum canticis letitie et sollempni deducunt processione. Erat autem natalitius dies eiusdem, post unicam mundi dominam Dei genitricem tam ordinis Cartusiensis quam et episcopi nostri specialis aduocati, precursoris Domini.

Missam maiorem maxima cum deuotione Hugo celebrauit. Post euangelium sermonem fecit ad populum mire suauitatis nectare conditum. Sicque geminatam

---

[a] Subtexere X   [b] mereremur X
[c] expectato X   [d] ornatam Q

which as well as they themselves had been struck by lightning for their maltreatment of pilgrims. This was the work of the renewer of the way of life of Elias who shared his predecessor's holiness and especial powers. Like Elias he called down swiftly in vengeance on the rebels the same fire which he extinguished when he healed those who besought his aid.[1]

I could cite innumerable examples if I did not fear criticism from my readers for my frequent digressions. I have, however, made this brief mention of the virtues of the saint who has been a perpetual inspiration to all the saints who have flourished since his day, because, as I learnt there none of the miracles taking place every day have been recorded for posterity by any pen. This so much vexed our Hugh, that I feel I am doing a service to him rather than to St Antony by making his journey the occasion for this brief account.

As soon as his arrival was known at Grenoble all the people hastened out to meet the man they most wished and desired to see in those parts. They and their bishop, a very venerable man, received him outside the ramparts of the city and led him in solemn procession and with songs of joy through the city which was hung in his honour with flowers and silken cloths of different colours to the cathedral of St John the Baptist. It was the birthday of the forerunner of Christ who after the sole queen of the world and mother of God is the especial patron of the Carthusian order and of our bishop.

Hugh celebrated at high mass with fervent devotion. After the gospel he preached to the people in words of a wondrous honeyed sweetness. The charm of his elevating discourse increased the double pleasure caused

---

[1] cf. 4 Kings 1: 9-14

letitiam, et annue sollempnitatis et prime post episcopatum sue uisitationis, ciuibus quondam et fratribus suis
salubris alloquii gratia cumulauit ut pane lacrimarum
uniuersos pene cibaret, dans eis potum in lacrimis set
in mensura.[1] Tanta denique cum humilitate talique ex
deuotione suffragia orationum ab uniuersis expetiit,
exiguitatem sui et indignitatem exaggerans, quem
superna dignatio de stercore eleuatum collocasset in
sublimi,[2] ut ab oculis omnium exitus aquarum educerent
lacrimis distillantes oculi sui.

Baptizauit quoque ipsa die puerum iam septennem,
filium militis strenuissi Willelmi de Aualun fratris sui,
quem de sacris fontibus presul Gratianopolitanus suscepit.
Cumque patruus ipsius pueri uehementer instaret ut
nomine suo, quod est Petrus, uocari debuisset ; sug-
gerente presentium scriptore, respondit ei Hugo, ' Nequaquam, set uocabitur Iohannes,[3] preiudicat enim tibi
et loci et diei presentis patronus.' Hunc nichilominus
Iohannem, mire indolis puerum, hic itidem scriptor in
ecclesia Belensi, posito alphabeto super altare sancti [a]
Baptiste, prima paulo post elementa perdocuit litterarum.
Peregimus autem tante sollempnitatis diem cum eiusdem
ciuitatis episcopo, a quo tam splendide nobis exhibita
sunt quecumque iura hospitii exigebant ut uideretur
modus ipse excedere modum ; diceres tunc dapsilitatem
Burgundionum ipsum quoque uicisse luxum effusionis
Anglicorum.

Inde, summo mane sequentis diluculi, tendentibus
nobis Cartusiam, maiorem pene itineris partem pedibus
conficere cogebantur [b] quos equi uehebant. Ascensus
enim continuos per ardua et confragosa montis latera
equi sessore uacui uix explicabant ; burdones uel asini

[a] + Iohannis X
[b] cogebamur X

by the annual feast and his first visit since he became a bishop so greatly that he almost fed them with the bread of tears and gave them tears to drink in good measure.[1] Finally with the greatest earnestness and humility he besought the whole congregation for the help of their prayers, unduly stressing his own weakness and unworthiness and the divine condescension which had raised him from the mire and exalted him to the heights.[2] The tears which flowed from his own eyes caused everyone else to weep copiously.

On that day he baptised a boy already seven years old, the child of his brother William of Avalon, a very valiant knight, to whom the bishop of Grenoble acted as godfather. The boy's uncle insisted that he should be named Peter after himself, but at the suggestion of the writer of this book Hugh replied, ' No, his name shall be John,[3] for the patron of this place, whose day it is, has a better claim than you '. This John was certainly a very intelligent child, to whom the same writer a little while afterwards gave his first reading lessons, the alphabet being set out on the altar of St John the Baptist in the church at Bellay. We spent this important saint's day with the bishop of the city, who discharged every obligation of hospitality so magnificently that all bounds were exceeded. It might almost be said that the courtesy and kindness of the Burgundians surpassed even the lavish generosity of the English.

From there, at dawn on the following day, we set out for Chartreuse, and those who rode were forced to walk for the greater part of the way, for horses even without their riders could scarcely make the continuous ascent along the steep and precipitous mountain side. The

---

[1] cf. Ps. 79: 6   [2] cf. Ps. 112: 7   [3] Luke 1: 60

hunc liberius permeant callem.[a] Episcopus, necessitate suadente, conuersus in peditem, nimio licet sudore lassesceret, spiritu tamen promptus et alacer, socios meando lassabat.

Id tamen sollicitus prouidebat ut dormientibus tempore meridiano fratribus ad ipsos perueniret; cauebat summopere ne suus aduentus quietem illorum saltem modice infestaret. Mansit apud eos, immo inter eos, tribus continue [b] septimanis quasi unus ex eis, horis maxime nocturnis psallentium numquam choro fratrum absens. Dormiebat in cella solitaria semper solus. Quo etiam tempore quantum ibi hauserit quantumue sparserit ex uicaria collatione uirorum sanctorum dulcedinis spiritualis, nemo a nobis expectet litteris explicari. Id namque ne uerbis quidem posset effari uel ipsemet qui rebus id ipsum meruerat experiri.

Veniebant illuc gratia uisendi eum episcoporum nonnulli, clerici quoque et laici quamplurimi. Pauperes in uicina commanentes parochia, quasi ad olim conclamatum et iam rediuiuum parentem proprium, confluebant certatim ad eum. Quos ille non impari affectu complexus et deosculans, amicabiliter cognoscentes se recognoscebat et factis.[c] Cum quibus et familiaria miscens colloquia, paruulo ille se docebat et factis et uerbis consimilem, quem magister mitis et humilis suis proposuit in euangelio imitandum discipulis.[1] Cumulabat uero affabilitatis gratiam manus munere non parca, quia uigebat in eo pariter et lingua eucharis et dextera liberalis.

Mansit quoque apud inferiorem, ubi conuersi morantur, habitationem diebus aliquot, ut ipsos etiam

---

[a] calcem B
[b] commune B
[c] et factis] om QX

path is easier for the sumpter mules and asses. Necessity
compelled the bishop to walk and although the exertion
tired him considerably, his energy and high spirits made
it difficult for his companions to keep up with him without getting tired.

He had taken care to arrange that he should arrive
at the time of the brethren's midday siesta; for he was
very anxious not to disturb their peace in any way by
his coming. He spent three whole weeks with them, or
rather amongst them as one of themselves, making a
point of never being absent when the brethren were in
choir chanting the night office. He always slept alone
in his solitary cell. No one must expect me to describe
how much spiritual consolation he received or how much
he gave in his conversations with these holy men during
this period, for even someone who had himself deserved
to experience it could not express it.

Several bishops and large numbers of clerks and lay
folk came there to see him. The poor of the neighbouring parishes came in crowds to him, as if he were their
long lost father now returned from the dead. He kissed
and embraced them with equal affection, welcoming in
return those who gave him such a friendly welcome. By
his behaviour, and the informality of his intercourse
with them he showed himself both in word and deed like
the child, whom the meek and humble Master gave in
the gospel as an example to his disciples.[1] His gracious
friendliness was accompanied by large gifts, for his kind
words and generosity were both equally remarkable.

He spent some days at the lower house where the lay
brothers dwelt in order that they might enjoy to the full
his words of exhortation, and he in his turn might feast

[1] cf. Matt. 18: 1-5

satiaret ab uberibus consolationis sue, et ipse uicissim ex eorum colloquiis et moribus disciplinatis epularetur quasi ab introitu glorie gentium.[1] Horum enim nonnulli a lata mundalium actionum uia digressi illamque artam et arduam uiam que ducit ad uitam ingressi, spe felici expectabant aditum paradisi. Hiis preterea diebus, certis horis sese pauperibus ad uisendum eum confluentibus exponebat, cum quibus ita socialiter uerba conserebat [a] ut inter eos residens solo monstraret habitu monachili quod non esset aliud [b] quam unus ex ipsis.

Insinuauerat ei episcopus Geneuensis quanto eum suus consul preiudicio annis iam ter quaternis depressisset, unde uinculo anathematis ipsum ab olim innodauerat. Ob cuius etiam metum propriam ciuitatem ingredi non audebat. Nam, si nos memoria non fallit, asserebat tria iam effluxisse annorum lustra ex quo sedem sue cathedralis ecclesie prohibitus est adire.

Tunc fortis ille noster et fidus, ut de illo quidam uersificus cecinit ' Pastorum baculus ',[2] plurimum consolans et coroborans fratrem afflictum et mestum, misit quamtocius priores duos ex ordine Cartusie, ut comitem corporis diutino languore maceratum exhortarentur, quatinus patri suo episcopo et ecclesie matri sue reconciliari festinaret ; posuitque uerba in ore,[c] id precipue dicendum ei inconculcans [d] ut patris gratiam flagellantis satageret inquirere ne, morte citius irruente, fieret extorris a filiorum hereditate. Hos uero ille ad se loquentes aspernanter quidem presentes audiuit ; set postquam recesserunt, obtentu uiri Dei ut ipse perhibebat, in se reuersus ac medullitus ad uim uerborum que illi mandauerat compunctus, ecclesie quam leserat satisfecit.

[a] conferebat o
[b] alius Q
[c] + eorum Xp
[d] inculcans QX

on their conversation and disciplined manner of life as if it were the anteroom of the kingdom of God.[1] Some of them, moreover, had abandoned the broad highway of worldly activities, to set out on the strait and narrow road which leads to eternal life and were awaiting their entry into the joys of Heaven. During these days, also, he devoted certain hours to the poor who flocked to see him, with whom he mingled so informally, that when he was with them only his monastic habit showed that he was not one of themselves.

The bishop of Geneva confided to him, how greatly he had suffered at the hands of the count during the last twelve years, for which reason he had long ago excommunicated him, and did not dare enter his own city because of his fear of him. Indeed, if I remember aright, he declared that he had been barred from his cathedral church for fifteen years.

Our valiant and faithful bishop, whom a certain poet extolled as the ' staff of pastors ',[2] greatly comforted and encouraged his depressed and afflicted brother. He immediately sent to the count, who had for a long time been suffering from an illness, two priors of the Carthusian order to exhort him to reconcile himself speedily with his father and bishop and with Mother Church. He told them what they should say, insisting especially that he should do all he could to seek the forgiveness of the father who was punishing him lest, death intervening, he should be excluded from the inheritance of the sons of God. He, indeed, whilst they were with him treated their words with scorn, but after they left, through the intervention of the man of God, as he alleged, he came to himself, and being softened and moved by his message,

---

[1] cf. Is. 66: 12
[2] cf. infra, p. 232

Sicque absolutus primum a sententia, deinde a carnis sarcina, in pace quieuit.

Post spatium autem trium ebdomadarum, episcopus sciens esse scriptum ' Relinquet homo patrem et matrem et adherebit uxori sue ',[1] ad ecclesie curam quam olim desponderat redire disponens, preter alia donaria, pignora inestimabiliter pretiosa ecclesie a cuius uberibus in uirum perfectum coaluerat, iam ultimum ei ualefaciens iamque discedens, in perpetuam sui memoriam dereliquit. Habebat in scriniis suis capsulam argenteam quam in basilicarum dedicationibus circumferebat in manibus, numerosis sanctorum sanctarumque reliquiis plenam. Has uel ipsemet uel ipsorum custos scriniorum, monachus et capellanus suus, plerisque in locis adquisiuerat. Set episcopus a se perquisitas uiro religiosissimo Cartusiensi sacriste coram priore et fratribus tradidit, in loco illo conseruandas. Monacho[a] suas dimisit ad proprium monasterium apportandas.

Verum quia de sanctorum reliquiis fecimus mentionem, non uidetur otiosum si ad gloriam sanctorum uel edificationem legentium de hiis breuiter adhuc aliqua referamus.[b] Iusserat episcopus anulum sibi fieri ex auro purissimo et lapidibus pretiosis, habentem in parte que digitum exterius ambiebat quasi monile quoddam concauum, quod repositorium esse uoluit sanctarum reliquiarum. Erat autem receptaculum ad quatuor fere digitorum mensuram undique latum. In hoc portiones congesserat sanctorum pignorum ad numerum usque tricennarium.

Cum uero ex maxima deuotione sollicitudinem gereret super adquisitione tam salubris thesauri, institit[c]

---

[a] + autem suo Xp
[b] X omit two pages
[c] instituit B
[1] Gen. 2: 24

he made reparation to the Church he had injured, and first being freed from the excommunication, and then from the burden, of the body, died in peace.

The bishop, who knew the text, ' A man shall leave father and mother and cleave to his wife ',[1] when three weeks had elapsed, decided to return to resume the care of the church which he had formerly espoused. On his departure from the church by whose milk he had grown into the full stature of a man, in addition to other gifts, he left it as a last farewell token and as a perpetual memorial of himself, a bequest of inestimable value. He had amongst his treasures a silver casket which it was his custom to carry in his hands when he consecrated churches. This contained innumerable relics of saints of both sexes, which had been acquired in very many different places either by himself or his monk chaplain who had the custody of his treasury. The bishop gave those he had obtained himself to the very devout sacrist at Chartreuse in the presence of the prior and brethren, to be preserved there, and handed over to the monk his own acquisitions to take to his own monastery.

Whilst I am on the subject of the relics of the saints it would not be amiss to give certain anecdotes which contribute to their glory and to the edification of the reader. The bishop had ordered to be made for him a ring of the finest gold set with precious stones, which had in the part which encircled the outside of his finger a kind of hollow jewel which he intended to use as a repository for relics. This receptacle was about the width of four fingers, and in it he had collected thirty relics of the saints.

Although he tried with deep devotion and earnestness to acquire these priceless treasures, he wanted most of all

magnopere quatinus de corpore magni Christi confessoris precipuique monachorum ducis et legislatoris Benedicti aliquid optineret. Super tali quoque desiderio suo litteras direxit affectuosas uiris uenerabilibus, abbati et monachis cenobii Floriacensis, ubi sanctissima tanti patris ossa requiescunt, scribens eis per quemdam eorum fratrem et monachum, custodem quarumdam suarum quas secus Lincolniam optinent possessionum, petensque obnixius quatinus sibi dignarentur aliquid impertiri de copia suarum in hac parte diuitiarum. Quid multa? Rediit tandem litterarum baiulus, attulitque uiro desideriorum[1] desiderii sui precisque effectum, unum uidelicet ex dentibus sancti, cum palle[a] qua erant inuoluti cineres beati non modica portione. Habuitque in manibus reciprocas eorum ad quos missus fuerat litteras, quibus et tanto patri debite salutationis rependebant obsequium, et muneribus transmissis indubitatum ferebant testimonium. Quibus tandem lectis et acceptis, uir Dei miro gestiens gaudio, iussit extemplo accersiri aurificem suum qui manebat in castro ipsius Banebiria nuncupato. Ad tempus uero illud quo hec gesta sunt, consistebat episcopus in manerio suo quod Dorcacestria dicitur, quod distat milliaribus fere triginta a castro prenominato.

Interea, dum instruitur nuntius, qui erat aurifabrum adducturus, quatinus et instrumenta ipsum iuberet secum afferre quibus aperire conuenienter potuisset iterumque recludere anulum sacramentalem episcopi, (sic enim cognominabat eum quia in ordinum et consecrationum celebrationibus ad deuotionis incentiuum illo frequentius utebatur) ecce subito qui iubetur inquiri artifex[b] adest, tamque inopinatam quam exoptatam sui presentiam gaudentibus pariter et stupentibus affert.

[a] palla B¹   [b] aurifex Q   [1] cf. Dan. 9: 23

to obtain a portion of the body of that great confessor of Christ and patriarch and lawgiver of monks, Benedict. This ardent desire caused him to dispatch a pleading letter to the venerable abbot and monks of the monastery of Fleury where the most holy corpse of the saintly father reposes. He sent this by one of their own monks and brethren, the warden of certain estates held by them near Lincoln, beseeching them earnestly to give him some portion of their immense treasure. The sequel was that the bearer of the letter returned at last, and brought to the man of desires [1] the reward of his prayers and longings, namely one of the teeth of the saint and a large portion of the cloth in which his remains had been wrapped. He also brought a letter in reply from those to whom he had been sent, in which the greetings and compliments of the venerable bishop were courteously returned, and sure proof was furnished as to the genuineness of the gifts which had been dispatched. Having received and read these, the man of God was filled with gladness, and immediately summoned his goldsmith who lived in his town of Banbury, since when these events took place the bishop was at his manor at Dorchester, which is almost thirty miles from the place I have just mentioned.

Lo, whilst he was giving instructions to the messenger who was to fetch the goldsmith, to tell him to bring tools with him in order to open and then close up again the bishop's sacramental ring (he gave it this name because he often used it at ordination and consecration ceremonies as an incentive to devotion), the craftsman he was sending for suddenly arrived. This unexpected and wished-for arrival equally amazed and rejoiced the company. When questioned why he had come he related how about midnight a person had

Requisitus uero aduentus sui causam, affirmabat dormienti sibi circa noctis medium quemdam astitisse qui iuberet eum mox ad episcopum festinare, ' " Sunt enim," inquit, " ei transmisse reliquie pretiosissime quas te oportet in anulo eius recondere. Surge ergo uelociter, iterque ad ipsum aggredere." Ad hanc uocem excussus a sompno, ita suspensos gerebam animos ut nil cuiusquam operis tractare possem, quousque ad uos ista dicturus, et utrum uera essent que audieram probaturus, uenirem. Ecce igitur ego et *a* utensilia mea : uos utimini artificis opera sicut scitis.' Hec siquidem artificis *b* reuelatio atque relatio et certitudinem roborauit et cumulauit letitiam omnibus qui presentes ista cognouerant. Partitus est autem quibusdam abbatibus et aliis qui interfuerunt uiris religiosis homo liberalissimus, portiunculas de palla quam susceperat ; dentem suauissime sepius deosculatum in anulo recludi fecit.

Apud Fiscamni quoque insigne monasterium, de osse brachii *c* beatissime Christi dilectricis Marie Magdalene duo mordicitus *d* excussit frustra. Ipsum autem os nullus tunc presentium uel abbas uel monachus aliquando inspexerat tegmine nudum. Erat enim duplicibus pannis sericis et lineo simplici artissime insutum. Cuius inspectionem dum episcopo flagitanti exhibere nullus auderet, ille a quodam notario suo scalpellum arripiens, fila festinanter dissecuit, atque inuolucrum illud dissuens, sacratissimum os ori et oculis suis reuerenter applicuit. A quo dum impressione digitorum nil quiuisset excutere, prius incisiuos deinde molares dentes apposuit, quorum uiribus duas inde citius portiones abrupit quas dextere ista scribentis intulit, ita dicens, ' Serua nobis hec *e* peroptime.'

---

a + ecce o *b* aurificis o *c* om B
d mordicus Q *e* hoc B

appeared to him in his sleep who ordered him to go at once to the bishop. ' Some very valuable relics have been sent to him which you must insert in his ring. Get up immediately and start your journey to him.' ' Being awakened by these words, my mind was so disturbed that I could not concentrate on work of any kind but had to come and tell you these things to find out for myself whether what I had heard was true, so here I am with my tools, make what use you please of my skill.' All those who were present and heard the goldsmith's account of his vision had their faith strengthened and their joy enhanced. The bishop, out of his unbounded generosity, distributed small fragments of the cloth which he had received to the abbots and monks who were there. He frequently kissed the tooth with deep devotion before having it placed in his ring.

When he was at the celebrated monastery of Fécamp, he extracted by biting two small fragments of the bone of the arm of the most blessed lover of Christ, Mary Magdalen. This bone had never been seen divested of its wrappings by the abbot or any of the monks who were present on that occasion, for it was sewn very tightly into three cloths, two of silk and one of ordinary linen.

They did not dare to accede even to the bishop's prayer to be allowed to see it. He, however, taking a small knife from one of his notaries, hurriedly cut the thread and undid the wrappings. After reverently examining and kissing the much venerated bone, he tried unsuccessfully to break it with his fingers, and then bit it first with his incisors and finally with his molars. By this means he broke off the two fragments, which he handed immediately to the writer, with the words, ' Take charge of this for me with especial care '.

Cernentes uero hec abbas ^a et monachi, iampridem stupentes et pauidi, nunc uero seuientes et irati, exclamant, ' O, o, proh nefas ! Credebamus episcopum uenerationis obtentu expetisse hec sacra reuerenda, et ecce ritu canino hec dentibus tradidit lanianda.' Quos talia prosequentes ille blandis sermonibus deliniuit, dicens inter cetera uerbum memorabile, ' Si,' inquit, ' ipsius Sancti sanctorum paulo ante corpus sanctissimum digitis licet indignis contrectauimus, dentibus quoque uel labiis attrectatum ad interiora nostra transmisimus, quare non etiam sanctorum eius menbra ad nostri munimen et ipsorum uenerationem atque memoriam nobis impensius conciliandam, fiducialiter attrectamus et debito cum honore seruanda, nobis cum facultas datur adquirimus ? '

Alio quoque tempore apud burgum sancti Petri, de brachio gloriosi regis et martiris Oswaldi, quod adhuc cum ossibus et pelle in carne cruenta tamquam recenter de corpore uiuo excisum monstratur, neruum qui prominebat lentumque et mollem ductu contrectanti prebebat, cultello exscidit, seruandumque omni cum reuerentia sibi retinuit. Hoc ^b itaque cum aliis que enumerare longum est sanctis reliquiis, in anulo composuit sepius memorato. Cum ^c autem uice quadam a partibus transmarinis uenisset Lincolniam, hunc anulum more sollempni in munus optulerat super altare beate Virginis, finaliter ibi conseruandum. Cuius post ^d oblationis immemor, ipsum quoque totiens memoratum anulum Cartusiensibus cum ceteris dari reliquiis imperauit. Cum uero ad memoriam reduxisset ^e monachus suus, ipsorum sacrorum custos, factam ab eo pridem donationem, anulum iussit ecclesie Lincolniensi restitui.

---

^a abbates B
^d postea X

^b Hec Q
^e + ei X

^c X *resume here*

When the abbot and monks saw what had happened, they were first overcome with horror, and then became exceedingly enraged. They cried out, ' What terrible profanity ! We thought that the bishop had asked to see this holy and venerable relic for reasons of devotion, and he has stuck his teeth into it and gnawed it as if he were a dog.' He mollified their anger with soothing words. Part of his speech is worth recording. ' If, a little while ago I handled the most sacred body of the Lord of all the saints with my fingers, in spite of my unworthiness, and when I partook of it, touched it with my lips and teeth, why should I not venture to treat in the same way the bones of the saints for my protection, and by this commemoration of them increase my reverence for them, and without profanity acquire them when I have the opportunity ? '

On another occasion at Peterborough where the arm of the glorious king and martyr Oswald is displayed with the bones and skin, and flesh still bloody as if recently severed from a living body, he severed with a knife a protruding sinew which was pliable and flexible enough to be drawn out by whoever handled it. This he kept and preserved with great devotion. It and other holy relics which it would take too long to describe he placed in the ring I have mentioned so often. Once, returning to Lincoln from abroad, he solemnly offered the ring at the altar of the blessed Virgin, as a final bequest. Afterwards he forgot this oblation, and ordered that the said ring should be given to the Carthusians along with the rest of his relics. When his monk who had the custody of them reminded him of his previous gift, he ordered the ring to be restored to the church of Lincoln. He had sent to them, however, as a present the golden casket studded with precious stones which was in his treasury at Lincoln so that they could keep in it the collection of

Capsulam uero ex auro et gemmis fabrefactam, que apud Lincolniam fuit in scriniis ipsius, eis mittendam dedit ; in qua reponerentur collate ipsis *a* reliquie sanctorum. Quod eodem monacho satagente, post excessum uiri sancti impletum est.

Expleta uero largitione prefata, episcopus ad inferiora conuersorum habitacula continuo descendit. Die postera, Cartusie Dei benedictionem imprecans et suam largiens, corporetenus discessit a loco in quo iugiter corde permansit et animo.

Rogatus autem sepius instantissime a uiro deuoto et strenuo, priore sancti Domnini *b* quatinus domum quam regebat uisitare *c* presentie sue dignaretur accessu, ad eius cellam diuertit. Qui eum *d* una cum fratribus suis suscipiens obuiatione sollempni uelud angelum Domini, egit cum eo diem sollempnem in cordis letitia et exultatione spirituali.

Disponebat uero episcopus inuisere quoque Villam Benedictam, sic enim uocatur cella in qua religionis sacre libauit primordia. Dictante uero ratione itineris, perrexit prius ad castellum quod fuerat patris sui, in quo mansiones habebant et non modicam dominationem duo ipsius germani, Willelmus uidelicet et Petrus. Hii semper Hugonem utpote milites strenui, ita ad uirtutis cursum incitare gaudebant ut solet admisso subdi *e* calcar equo. O quotiens isti non tantum episcopo set con-siliariis quoque ipsius, et presentes suggesserunt et absentes mandauerunt ne in falsorum fratrum seu crudelium dominorum persecutionibus animo lassaretur ! Asserebant malle se natum ipsum non fuisse quam eum contra natales ingenuos ad depressionem libertatis ecclesiastice uel ad momentum animo degenerante cessisse. Ad hos igitur hospitandi gratia ueniens, non istorum solummodo set nobilium, mediocrum et in-

---

a ipsius X   *b* + et sancti Maximi X
c letificare X ; *om* B   *d* enim B   *e* subdere X

the relics of the saints which he had given them. This was done after the death of the saint, owing to the efforts of the same monk.

After making the gift I have mentioned, the bishop immediately descended to the house of the lay-brethren. The next day, after praying for God's blessing on Chartreuse and giving it his own, he withdrew his physical presence from the place, but left his heart and mind there.

The zealous and holy prior of St Domninus had often earnestly begged him to honour the house over which he ruled by a personal visit. He therefore turned aside to go to that cell. The prior and his monks came out to meet him and welcomed him with as much reverence as if he had been an angel of the Lord. They spent a memorable day with him, with hearts full of gladness and spiritual joy.

The bishop intended to visit Villarbenoît, the religious house in which he had the first taste of the religious life. His route made it inevitable that he should go first to a castle of his father's, where his two brothers William and Peter now dwelt and had large estates. These two valiant knights greatly enjoyed encouraging Hugh to act bravely, just as they pricked their steeds with the spur. When present they very often urged not only the bishop but his councillors, and when absent sent to them, that he should not lose heart on account of the persecutions of false brethren or tyrannical rulers. They declared that they would prefer him not to have been born, rather than that in a moment of cowardice he should belie his noble birth, and compromise the freedom of the Church. When he came to stay with them he was welcomed not only by them and the nobility but equally warmly by people of all ranks

fimorum loca uicina *a* incolentium, uniformi con-
gratulatione suscipitur, a quibus et biduo ibidem
detinetur. Die demum tertia ad canoniam *b* peruenit
Ville Benedicte, quam loci incole Vilarbenerth uulgari
appellant nomine. Nec est dictu facile quantum suus
aduentus prestitit tripudium non solum eiusdem loci
incolis, immo et omnibus circumquaque uicinis. Dedit
autem ecclesie illi bibliotecam, decem comparatam
marcis argenti.

Inuisit et cellulam, cuius ut supradiximus prioratum
quondam adholescens gesserat, que nominatur ad
sanctum Maximum. In hiis uero locis uallabant eum
uiri decrepiti et senes cano capite, anus etiam incurue et
mulieres annis prouecte. Ab hiis Hugoni applaudentibus,
Hugonis rudimenta inter eosdem uelud lilium quondam
germinantia miris attolluntur preconiis. Asserebant
ipsa quoque illius prime adhuc etatis initia quadam
insite uirtutis lingua, future sanctitatis in eo prenuntiasse
insignia. At ille castrum repetens *c* denuo prenotatum,
una ibidem nocte quieuit.

Inde iam festinato in Angliam tendens, ad Belensem
altera metatione deuenit urbem. Ibi cratem dimidie
manus precursoris Domini cum digitis tribus, medio
scilicet et binis inferioribus, cute adhuc nitida uestitam,
suscipere meruit osculandam. Quam discooperire
nudamque uidere a pluribus retro annis nemo audebat.
Verum pedissequus et uernula ipsius Hugo, peculiari
flagrans amore sui patroni fiduciamque erga ipsum
nactus ulteriorem, hoc facere minime formidauit, con-
gaudentibus sane canonicis ipsius ecclesie quod uirum
reperissent tante puritatis qui hoc attemptare dignissime
potuisset. Premissa peccatorum confessione, absolutione

---

a + et Q 　　　　　*b* canonicam Q B[1]
c + de Aualon X

living in the neighbourhood. They persuaded him to stay for two days, and it was only on the third day that he came to the priory of Villarbenoît, a name which has been corrupted by the local inhabitants into Vilarbenerth. The joy which his arrival gave not only to the people there but to those of the surrounding regions cannot easily be described. He gave the church a Bible worth ten silver marks.

He visited the cell of St Maximus, where, as I have related earlier, he had been prior in his youth. Here he was completely surrounded by decrepit and white-haired old men and by bent women, well stricken in years who gave him an enthusiastic welcome, fondly recalling how he had passed his early years among them like a lily in bud. They declared that even in his youth his words had revealed his innate quality, and had been prophetic of his future holiness. He finally returned to the castle I have already mentioned, and rested there for one night.

From there he hastened back to England, making the city of Bellay the next stage in his journey. There he had the privilege of kissing the bones of half the hand of the precursor of Our Lord, and three of his fingers, the middle one and the fourth and fifth, with the shining skin still covering them. For many years past nobody had dared to see them uncovered. His faithful follower and servant Hugh, who had a peculiar affection for his patron and had acquired a complete confidence in him, had no scruples about doing this. The canons of the church were indeed exceedingly glad that they had found a man of such conspicuous holiness who was worthy to attempt this. After first confessing his sins and receiving absolution, and praying, he uncovered the venerable relic and displayed it so that all who were present could

et oratione subiuncta, reuerendum illud sanctuarium,
tegmine nudatum, cunctis presentibus *a* palam inspiciendum ostenditur. Ipsos quidem articulos qui tetigerant
sanctum Dei uerticem, ipse digitis tangere osculisque
lambere nequaquam uerebatur, data ceteris qui circumcirca proni adorabant benedictione, ipso in sublime
illos porrigente, nosque desuper in crucis modum eisdem
consignante. De quodam panno purpureo atque
uetustissimo qui diutissime huic sanctuario illud tegendo
inheserat, non modicam portionem incidit, quam suo
monacho summa cum deuotione amplectendam dedit.

In hoc autem itinere quatuor sui ordinis domos
inuisit et adiuit ; *b* Cartusiam uidelicet, Alueriam,
Louinium et Vallem sancti Petri. Alueriam cum esset
propter loca montuosa accessu difficilis et ab itinere
nostro remotior, hac specialiter de causa expetiit.
Belensis quondam episcopus, ex priore eiusdem domus
assumptus ad cathedram, onere iam pastoralis cure
abiecto, ibi denuo cellicolam se simplicem effecerat ut
celestibus desideriis liberius inseruiret.[1] Qui nostri
pontificis longo ex tempore exestuans desiderio, affatu
ipsius et aspectu cupiebat refoueri. Quod etiam per
internuntios eius *c* sepius innotuerat. Processerat quidem
uir *d* ille beatus in diebus suis, et mediante iam mundane
lucis occasu, ad interminabilis diei suspirabat ingressum.
Nec dissimiles animi, quamuis in etate dissimili, nostro
pontifici erant. Iam enim caduca omnia que ab annis
teneris semper uilipenderat, in graui etiam fastidio
habebat. Optato igitur uterque potitus colloquio, sue
singuli recessus conscientie, ex alterne sanctitatis fulgore,

---

a presidentibus B
b B *omits this clause*
c ei XP
d *om* B

examine it. He had no hesitation in handling and kissing the fingers which had touched the sacred head of God, and after giving his blessing to the worshippers, he raised it aloft, and made the sign of the cross over us with it. He also cut off a large piece of the ancient purple cloth in which for a long period the relic had been wrapped, and gave it to his monk who received it with deep veneration.

On this journey he visited and stayed at four houses belonging to his order, Chartreuse, Arvières, Lugny and Val S. Pierre. Although Arvières was not on our route, and very difficult to approach on account of its mountainous situation, he was particularly anxious to go there, because its former prior, who had thence become bishop of Bellay, had resigned his office, to live there as an ordinary monk, in order to devote himself without distraction to the consideration of heavenly things.[1] He had for a long time desired greatly the privilege of seeing and speaking with our bishop, and had often sent messages to this effect. The saintly man was in fact well advanced in years, and whilst awaiting the passing of this earthly light, was longing for his entry into eternal life. Although their ages were different, he very much resembled our bishop in temperament. From his early youth he had attached little importance to earthly things and regarded them with distaste. When the long-desired meeting took place, they revealed to each other their inmost thoughts, and each found the deepest recesses of their consciences were

---

[1] Arthaud, prior of Arvières in the diocese of Geneva founded by Amadeus count of Savoy in 1136, was bishop of Bellay from 1184 until his retirement to his monastery in 1190. He died in 1206. Lugny in the diocese of Langres was founded in 1170 by its bishop Walter, who became a monk there in 1179 and died in 1181. Val Saint Pierre, in the diocese of Laon, was founded in 1140 by Reginald de Rosoy (see map, p. 235).

dum sua uicissim occulta pandunt, splendidiores reddunt.

Qui tandem simul ad commune fratrum omnium uenere colloquium. Tunc a Lincolniensi dominus quondam Belensis formam pacis inter reges nostros inite sibi petiit coram fratribus retexi ; nam concordie illorum ipsum interfuisse cognouerat. Ad quam uiri tanti petitionem feruentissimus ordinis zelator haut modice contristatus, ita leniter et quasi iocando ait, ' O,' inquiens, ' domine pater, rumores audire et referre, etsi licet episcopis set monachis non licet. In cellas uel claustrum rumores ingredi non licet ; urbes deserere et in solitudinem rumores afferre non licet.' Hec dicens, ad spiritualis edificationis studium, postpositis rumoribus, uerba conuertit.

Capitvlvm XV

Relatio interpolata uie ipsius a Burgundia usque Londonias. Quo tandem egritudine pregrauatus appulit.

Set ecce dum uiri spiritualis imitabili uita, tamquam ligni frondosi atque fructiferi quod in paradiso ecclesie plantauerat Dominus ubertate amena, uehementer afficimur, extra proposite breuitatis compendium longius euagamur ! Dumque in legendis ex eo et recondendis in solatia amicorum, non solum pomis operum set et foliis uerborum delectabili studio insudamus, angustam cartalli exigui mensuram excedere uidetur adunate collectionis aceruus. Quod ea nobis de causa procul dubio accidit quia salutem pariter et refectionem legentium ex hiis procurari in magno paruitati ᵃ nostre

---

ᵃ paruitatis X

rendered clearer by means of the purity and holiness of the other.

Finally, they came together to converse with the community. Then the former bishop of Bellay asked the bishop of Lincoln to give the brethren an account of the peace treaty between our kings, since he knew that he had been present when it was made. This request from such a personage grieved the most devoted and zealous member of the order not a little, and he replied gently and almost jokingly, ' My lord and father, although it is legitimate for bishops to hear and relate such matters, it is not so for monks. It is not right to bring reports into the cloister or the cell, and to forsake the cities in order to discuss secular matters in the wilderness.' Having dismissed this business, he began discussing religious topics.

CHAPTER XV

The resumed account of his journey from Burgundy to London, where he at last arrived grievously ill.

My great interest in the exemplary life of this saintly man, who like a tree planted by God in the paradise of the Church brought forth abundant leaves and rich fruit, has caused me to abandon the limits I imposed on myself. The process of gathering and storing for the comfort of his friends both fruit and foliage, by which I mean his works and words, has caused the mass of material to exceed the narrow compass of a small work. This has undoubtedly happened because of my great desire in spite of my insufficiency to give both pleasure and profit to my readers, since I am certain that, in the words of the Apocalypse about similar matters, these

desiderio fuit. Confidimus namque, iuxta sententiam in Apocalipsi super huiuscemodi rebus expressam, hec et illa ad salutem gentium profutura[1] si cum deuotione sumantur fideli et pia. Verum in hiis per temporis aliquantulum nobis occupatis, messium iam et uindemiarum tempus elabitur; iustumque est ut cultorem atque custodem agri uineeque dominice, iuxta morem ut supra docuimus singulis pene annis ab ipso frequentatum, suis quamtocius procuratoribus et cooperatoribus restituamus. Nam et immutate uoces, gestusque subtristior alitum, nos quoque totis pene mensibus estiuis protractatam iam mutare uel potius terminare admonent cantilenam.

Montium ergo iuga, deuexa collium latera, uallium tractus atque camporum, uastosque pelagi sinus, celeri nunc lapsu quasi preteruolando transimus, que tunc cum illo ad suos remeante, laborioso commeatu peragrando et remigando transiuimus. Exigit quoque ratio ut qualiter ipse a mundana uarietate ad celestis patrie inuariabilem migrauerit stationem iam nunc succincte pandamus. Omittimus, ut innumera taceamus que referre quam omittere studiosis expediret, que tamen omittimus ne fastidiosis tedium exaggeremus;[a] omittimus, inquam, Cluniacum et quam deuote locum modernarum religionum fontem adierit, quam reuerentissime a tanta illius sancte multitudinis frequentia exceptus sit, quanta eiusdem congregationis instantia triduo secum morari, et uires post laborem sit compulsus resumere. Cuius loci disciplinam in choro, in claustro, in refectorio inter eos familiariter diuersans,[b] missas celebrans et cum eis pariter conuescens, cum plenius attendisset ac plurimum commendasset, sic demum ait, ' Vere, si locum hunc ut modo peruidissem cum necdum Cartusiam adamassem, suum me Cluniacus monachum fecisset.'

[a] ingeramus X   [b] conuersans X

things will be for the salvation of the nations,[1] if they are read devoutly and attentively. Whilst, however, they have engrossed my attention for a little while, the time for the harvest and vintage is slipping away. Therefore it is only right that I should return the cultivator and overseer of the field and vineyard of the Lord to his assistants and fellow-workers which, as I have already mentioned, was his usual annual custom. The changed note and lack of liveliness of the birds also warn me to change or rather end my song which has lasted almost throughout the entire summer.

Let me therefore now pass rapidly over as if flying the mountain peaks, the slopes of the hills, the stretches of the valleys and fields and the vast expanse of the sea, which we traversed with him on the long and laborious return journey to his friends. It is necessary now for me briefly to describe his departure from this transitory world to the stability of the heavenly kingdom. Just as I have already left out very many things which a conscientious writer would have inserted, lest I should weary the over-critical, so now I must omit Cluny, and the devotion with which he visited this cradle of contemporary monasticism, and the reverence with which he was received by the immense band of holy monks. Their great insistence forced him to spend three days with them to recover his strength after his labours. Celebrating mass and living and eating with the community as one of themselves he became conversant with the discipline of the monastery in choir, cloister and refectory and warmly praised it, finally declaring, ' Truly, if I had seen this place before I fell in love with Chartreuse, I should have become a Cluniac monk '.

[1] cf. Apoc. 22: 2

Quiddam inter cetera ibidem speciale uidit et laudauit, quod iccirco uel breuiter pagine inserimus quia a beato Benedicto institutum ab omnibus ubique locorum monachis neglectum miramur, et quasi obliuioni traditum. Agens namque de suscipiendis hospitibus in regula sua, beatissimus Benedictus inter cetera dicit, ' Legatur coram hospite lex diuina ut edificetur ; deinde omnis ei exhibeatur humanitas.' [1] Quod erga nos Cluniacenses hoc ordine compleuerunt. Post susceptionem eius cum processione festiua perceptamque illius benedictionem, episcopum dominus prior in locutorium deduxit, ubi cum eo sedit, assumptis pariter et senioribus de conuentu circiter duodecim. Vnus uero astantium [a] fratrum codicem regule pastoralis beati Gregorii pape, quem ad hoc ipsum manibus allatum tenebat, aperuit ; procedensque in medium, capitellum unum aperte et distincte ad intelligendum [2] percurrendo legit. Quo completo, innuente priore, finem lectioni fecit, et episcopus ad nutum prioris similiter, dicto Benedicite, loquendi licentiam presentibus dedit.

Set et Cistercium cursim [b] pertransimus. Quo diuertit ut missarum sollempnia in preclara festiuitate assumpte Dei genitricis celebrare potuisset. Gallia namque uniuersa preter quedam priuilegiata monasteria, ea tempestate sub interdicto fuit.[3] Deinde, uoti compos effectus, et fratrum loci illius orationibus commendatus, Claram Vallem quoque [c] uisitauit.

Miserat siquidem sancte recordationis Iohannes, Lugdunensium quondam archiepiscopus,[4] in occursum

---

[a] assistentium QX   [b] cursum B   [c] om B

[1] *Rule of St Benedict*, c. 53   [2] cf. 2 Esdras 8: 8

[3] This interdict was imposed by Innocent III after repeated efforts by him and his predecessor Celestine III to make Philip II take back his repudiated wife, Ingeborg of Denmark.

[4] John II, archbishop of Lyons, was an Englishman who had been treasurer of York, bishop of Poitiers 1162, papal legate and archbishop of

One special thing amongst the rest which he saw and commended, I am going to mention briefly because although established by the blessed Benedict it has been to my surprise neglected and almost forgotten everywhere by all monks. When providing in his rule for the reception of guests the most holy Benedict says amongst other things, ' Let the divine law be read to the guest for his edification, and then let every kindness be shown him '.[1] This our Cluniacs carried out in this way. After they had received him in solemn procession and received his blessing the lord prior took the bishop to the parlour, where he sat with him, about twelve of the senior monks being also invited. One of the brethren who was present opened a manuscript of the ' Pastoral Care ' of the blessed pope Gregory which he had brought with him for this purpose and was holding, and advanced into the centre of the room where he read straight through one short chapter clearly and distinctly enough to be followed.[2] When he had finished, at a sign from the prior the reading ended, and the bishop likewise after saying ' Benedicite ' with his consent gave the company permission to speak.

I will rapidly pass over Cîteaux, where he stayed in order to be able to celebrate high mass on the solemn feast of the Assumption of the Mother of God, since except for certain privileged monasteries all France was at this time under an interdict.[3] Then, having obtained his wish, and having commended himself to the prayers of the brethren of that house, he visited Clairvaux.

The former archbishop of Lyons, John[4] of blessed memory, had sent certain venerable men to him, begging

---

Lyons in 1182. He resigned his see c. 1195 and became a Cistercian at Clairvaux (cf. *Gallia Christiana*, II, c. 1180-1, IV, c. 130-3).

eius quosdam uenerabiles uiros, obnixe sibi supplicans quatinus in loco commoranti prenotato olim desideratam presentie sue copiam exhiberet. Qui *a* iam euo grauis, officio cure pastoralis renuntiauerat ; retentisque dumtaxat, iussu summi pontificis, insignibus pristinis, in illo sancto cenobio sacre contemplationi sedulus uacabat. Sciscitanti autem episcopo quibusnam scripturis meditationis sue negotia potissimum deuouisset, ita respondit, ' Psalmorum,' inquit, ' meditatio sola iam penitus totum sibi me uendicauit. Ex hiis cotidie recens et continue demulcens interioris hominis palatum, michi refectio indeficiens iugiter innouatur.'

Post hoc monasterium sancti Remigii secus Remensium ciuitatem situm, sanctitatis sue magnifice letificauit accessu. Vbi moratus per biduum,*b* librorum antiquorum copiam ibi repositam mirabatur ; modernorum desidiosam exprobrans incuriam, qui non solum patrum studia in condendis libris atque scribendis emulari detrectant, set neque relegere *c* seu reuerenter saltem tractare a patribus elaboratos codices sacros student. Hic uasculum quoque, per columbam celitus delatum beato Remigio, miratus et ueneratus est, in quo iugiter ad unctionem regum Francis sacri balsami copia rediuiua exuberat.

Cum autem peruenisset ad castrum sancti Audomari quod a portu Witsandie milibus decem abiungitur, ibi parumper a fatigatione diutina ante maris ingressum duxit respirandum. Erat inde haut procul situm monasterium ordinis Cisterciensis, Claramariscum ab incolis uocitatum. Instabat et post triduum gloriosa sollempnitas Natiuitatis perpetue Virginis, misericordie matris. Nolebat elongari a loci uicinia quo diuina *d* celebrari

---

a quo B   *b* triduum Q
c legere Q   *d* diutina B

him earnestly to gratify his longfelt wish to see him whilst
he was staying there. He, being now well advanced in
years, had resigned his bishopric, whilst retaining by the
pope's command his former rank, and was living a life
devoted to the contemplation of heavenly things at that
renowned monastery. When the bishop asked him what
part of the Scriptures he made the principal subject of his
meditations, he replied thus, ' Meditations on the Psalms
alone absorb me entirely. Going over these daily and
continually I find in them a perennial source of refresh-
ment, pleasing to the taste of the inner man.'

After this he greatly gratified the monastery of St
Rémi at Rheims by his holy presence. There he remained
for two days, and was amazed by the innumerable
ancient manuscripts stored in that place. He criticised
the indifference and neglect of this present generation,
which not only does not imitate the zeal of its predecessors
in composing and copying books, but does not even try
to read, or at least treat with care the ancient manuscripts preserved by their ancestors. Here he saw with
wonder and reverence the vessel brought from Heaven
by the dove to St Rémi, in which there is a new and
abundant supply of holy oil for the anointing of the
French kings.

When he reached the castle of St Omer ten miles
from the port of Wissant, he decided that after his
lengthy toils he would rest there for a short time before
embarking. Near at hand there was a Cistercian
monastery which the natives called Clairmarais. The
solemn feast of the Nativity of the ever-virgin Mother
of Mercy would take place in three days, and he did not
wish before so important a festival to be too far from a
place where mass was permitted to be celebrated, lest

licebat ante festum adeo preclarum, ne forte, aura dissentiente, in Angliam ad hoc celebrandum minus tempestiue occurreret. Ipsa igitur die qua sanctum Audomarum uenit, uenam sibi inscidi fecit ; quo liberius et alacrius, post explete obseruantie tempus quod in fleubotomia quies uendicare solet, desideratam percoleret celebritatem. Iam enim diebus aliquot in menbris singulis et corpore suo toto grauedinem cum lento *a* quodam dolore senserat accreuisse. Post minutionem uero adeo incontinenti hec ipsa molestia augmentata est, ut de mensa qua discubuerat, cum uix modicum quid gustasset, ceteris adhuc edentibus, abscedere et lectuli quietem adire sit compulsus. Quem mox ut ceruicem reclinauerat sudor infudit affluentissimus, qui die ipsa tota cum parte maxima noctis insecute fluere non cessauit. Tantum quoque cibi *b* fastidium mox incurrit ut per illud triduum uix quippiam gustauerit.

Circa uespertinas autem horas in uigilia festiuitatis memorate, profectus est ad cenobium prenominatum ; ibique, uno tantum monacho et conuerso uno ex suis secum retento, pernoctauit. Reliquos cum equis omnibus ad hospitium unde uenerant redire iussit, satis quoad licuit resistentibus abbate et fratribus ipsius loci et uniuersum illius comitatum secum summopere detinere certantibus. Episcopus in infirmaria quiescere preelegit. Deputati sunt in obsequium eius duo fratres qui nimia deuotione eius famulatui insistebant, a quibus, cum nichil esce sumere cogi potuisset, pedes sibi abluendos et officiosissime fouendos et extergendos compulsus est exhibere. Quorum ille benignitate satis delectatus, eis deuotionis sue uicem, Dei scilicet benedictionem et suam, gratissime rependebat. Nec

---

a acuto X
b om B

perchance, owing to unfavourable winds, he should reach England too late for its celebration. On the day he reached St Omer, he had one of his veins lanced, so that after the usual period of resting after a seynie he might be stronger and more vigorous for the ceremonies of a feast for which he had an affection. Already for some days he had felt an increasing heaviness and dull pain in his limbs and the whole of his body. His discomfort increased so much immediately after the seynie that during dinner he could scarcely eat anything, and had to leave the table and lie quietly on his bed, before the rest of the company had finished. Almost as soon as he lay down, the perspiration flowed from him, and continued to do so, all that day and for the greater part of the night. His disinclination for food was so strong that for those three days he hardly tasted a mouthful.

At the time of Vespers on the vigil of the feast he set out for the monastery I have mentioned, and spent the night there. He kept with him only one monk and one lay brother, ordering the rest of his attendants to return to their previous lodging with all the horses, although the abbot and monks did all they could to dissuade him, and were very anxious to give hospitality to the whole retinue. The bishop decided to rest in the infirmary. The two brothers who had been appointed to serve him showed him the greatest attention, and when they could not persuade him to eat, forced him to allow them to wash, dry and carefully rub his feet. Their kindness gave him much pleasure, and he repaid their services by giving them God's blessing and his own. Not long afterwards, by the divine favour, one became abbot and the other prior of the house. They treated me with great generosity when I stayed with them for a short

multum post alter eorum in abbatem, alter in eiusdem
loci priorem fauore diuino promotus,[a] nos, in exilii
nostri presentis excursu, ad eos parumper digressos
humane satis recognouere. In crastino antepenultimam
ibidem Christi pontifex celebrauit missam. Qua
deuotissime expleta, ieiunus a cibo corporali hospitium
suum repetiit in uilla sepe dicta.[b] Vbi rem prodigiosam
que tunc innotuit paucis explicamus.

Pistor quidam farinam die dominica consperserat,
triuerat atque fermentauerat, unde sequenti nocte panes
quoque uenales coxerat. Quos dum mane sequentis ferie
protraheret e clibano, panis quidam in pauimentum
fortiter allisus fracturam fecit, unde mox sanguinis riuus
qui panem circumquaque inficeret effluxit. Quo pistor
uiso, tale uehementer portentum expauit. Panem
denique cruentum frustratim comminuit et per singulas
fracturas cruorem liquidum stillare uidit. Fregit et
panes alios atque alios, et in omnibus cruorem fracturas
implentem aspexit. Conterritus itaque tam monstruoso
euentu, panes per unam fere ebdomadam, ne ab aliis
uiderentur, occuluit ;[c] set interim mercenarii seu
uicini eius id quod acciderat ad aures publicas detulerunt.
Quid plura ? Res demum oppidanis cunctis innotuit.
Vnus ex hiis panibus episcopo a conuicaneis exhibetur,
frangebatur a nobis, sequebatur mox cruor fracturam
ac si hominis seu uiui cuiusque animalis caro inscideretur.
Huius panis fragmentum [d] non modicum inde in sinu
nobiscum detulimus. Erat autem panis fermentatus.
Cocti pariter fuerant in clibano prefato panes asimi et
fermentati,[e] set panes asimi in sua puri qualitate
ostendebantur, nil prodigium [f] habentes ; fermentati

---

[a] + post mortem presulis Christi X
[c] occultauit QX
[e] B *omits these two words*

[b] supradicta X
[d] fragmen oX
[f] prodigiosum QX

time during my present exile. On the morrow Christ's
bishop celebrated there the last mass but one of his life
with great devotion and immediately afterwards, still
fasting, he went to his lodging in the town. I shall now
give a brief account of a miracle there, which became
known at that time.

One Sunday a baker wetted and kneaded his dough
and put the yeast in, and the following night baked the
loaves which he was going to sell. The next morning
when he took them from the oven, one of them fell on
the floor and was broken. A stream of blood soon
appeared which stained the crust of the bread. The
baker, seeing such an unusual occurrence, was exceedingly afraid. He crumbled up the bloody loaf, and saw
the blood oozing from each fragment. He then broke
the other loaves into pieces, and in every one of them
he perceived the blood filling each of the cracks. Being
terrified by such a horrible result, he hid the loaves for
nearly a week, lest anyone else should see them. In the
meantime, however, his workmen and neighbours
spread the news abroad, and as might have been expected
the whole town was finally informed of what had
happened. His neighbours showed the bishop one of
the loaves, and when I broke it, blood soon flowed along
the break, as it would have done if the flesh of a man or
animal had been cut whilst they were still living. I took
away with me in my bosom a large portion of this bread.
It was leavened bread. Both leavened and unleavened
bread had been baked in the same oven, but the unleavened remained unchanged, and no miracle occurred,
but blood issued from all the leavened loaves if they
were broken or cut.

omnes fundebant sanguinem si fractionem exciperent uel sectionem.

Hinc sentiebant nonnulli punitam fuisse tali casu hominis cupidi temeritatem, qui die dominica pre-parasset quod sequenti feria maturius distraheret ; dum panis asimus, post sacre lucis crepusculum conspersus et coctus, nil admisit horrendum, et ante uesperam contra religionis institutum in massam subactus et fermentatus non questui profuit set auctorem suum reum fecit constitui.*a* Plures siquidem ex hiis panibus per monasteria et ecclesias circumquaque missi sunt ad monumentum posteris, et presumptuosis sacrarum sollempnitatum uiolatoribus ad correctionis documentum diligenter conseruandi.[1]

At uero, matris misericordie ope, post celebratam, ut prefati sumus, in honore ipsius missam, famulus eius et uicarius deuotissimus egritudinis leuamen non modicum percepit. Exacta igitur sollempnitatis die cum letitia et exultatione, in crastino Witsandensem portum cum suis adiuit ; sequentis uero diei aurora ipsum nauim con-scendere uidit. Inuocata igitur summe Dei genitricis *b* matre, beatissima uidelicet Anna, aura que primo remissius spirauerat, carbasa repente impleuit. Solent quidem uniuersi marium transuectores sicut maris stellam Mariam *c* attendere ut cursum dirigant, ita Marie matrem precibus aduocare et muneribus corrogatis ambire, ut currere queant, cum subsidentium uentorum spiramina itineris commeatum negant. Huic uero semper, post ipsius natam, familiarius Hugo et deuotius

---

a ostentui QX   *b* + Marie Qv   *c* *om* Bo

[1] Here too Adam correctly reported the phenomena, but there is no need to posit a supernatural explanation of them (cf. also p. 160, *n.* 1). Matthew Paris (*Chronica Majora* II, p. 466) and Wendover (*Flores Historiarum* I, pp. 297-301) also both describe ' bleeding ' loaves, and there are well-

Some people felt that this calamity was a fitting punishment for the man's profanity and greed, for he had got it ready on Sunday, in order to be able to sell it earlier the next day. Nothing untoward happened to the unleavened bread since it had been prepared and baked after twilight on the holy day, but the loaves which had been set with the yeast in before the evening in defiance of the ordinances of holy Church, instead of bringing money to their maker, made his guilt manifest. Many of these loaves were dispatched to the monasteries and churches of the neighbourhood to be kept as a memorial to future generations and as a warning to those who dared to profane the Church's feast-days.[1]

However, after his celebration of the mass in honour of the Mother of Mercy which I have already mentioned, her devoted attendant and disciple perceived that thanks to her assistance he seemed much better. After a very happy and joyous feast, he and his attendants reached Wissant on the morrow, and dawn the next day witnessed his embarkation. After blessed Anne, the mother of the great Mother of God had been invoked, the wind which had before been slight, suddenly filled the sails. It is the custom of those who cross the sea to expect that Mary the star of the sea will direct their course, and for this reason when lack of a favourable wind prevents their journey they pray and make votive offerings to Mary's mother in order that they may be able to sail. Her servant Hugh's devotion to and

---

documented nineteenth-century examples. A bacillus in the yeast is the cause : it will be noted in Adam's account that the unleavened bread was normal. cf. H. Thurston, *Life of St Hugh of Lincoln*, London 1898, pp. 505-510.

dependebat uenerationis obsequelam. Que sibi *a*
uicissim in cunctis necessitatibus et periculis celerem
rependebat opitulationem. Tunc quoque inuocanti *b*
festina affuit, cursuque placidissimo litori optato celeriter
appulsum adeo exhilarauit, ut confestim post pressas
uestigiis arenas ecclesiam peteret, missarum sollempnia
de sacro ipsius puerperio celebraturus.[1]

Quo certe ex facto satis patuit quanta fuit in eo erga
Dominica sacramenta cordis deuotio, quem neque marina
iactatio nec cum morbida ualetudine inedie per multos
iam dies protracta maceratio a diuinorum celebratione
potuerit cohibere. Astruxit plane, continuata usque in
finem sacerdotalis officii executione, quonam instinctu a
primordio statim adepte discretionis tanto sacedotii
amore flagrauerit ut inquirenti, sicut et in premissis
retulimus, uiro quodam sancto ne *c* uellet sacerdos fieri,
uoce promptissima id magnopere uelle se continuo
responderet.[2] Quod sane non iccirco uoluit ut inde inter
homines quouis honore proficeret, set ob hoc tantum ut
eo magis magisque apud Deum et in Deum proficiendo,[3]
Deo tandem inseparabiliter inhereret. Vnde sicut
pridem monachus, quotiens de permissu ordinis licuit,
ita iam episcopus, quotiens possibilitati ratio concurrit,
missas celebrare nullo tempore pretermisit. Ex qua
precipue muneris sacri deuotissima frequentissimaque
perceptione, et singularem cordis munditiam et insupera-
bilem constantie ceterarumque firmitatem uirtutum,
optinere promeruit. Set et inuisibilium rerum et
spiritualium misteria secretorum inter ipsa reuerenda
canonis secreta ei diuinitus patuisse familiares ipsius *d*
non latuit.

a *om* B
b + eam Xp
c an X
d *om* B

veneration for her was only second to his for her child, and she in her turn gave him speedy assistance whenever he was in peril or need. On this occasion also, she gave such immediate help to her petitioner, that his gratitude for a calm and rapid voyage to the desired haven caused him as soon as he had disembarked to find a church, in order to celebrate mass in honour of her conception.[1]

The fact that neither the buffeting of the sea nor the discomfort of a fast, which had lasted for several days because of his illness, prevented him from offering up the holy sacrifice is certainly a striking proof of his heartfelt devotion to the Eucharist. His determination to perform his priestly function right up to the end shows plainly the survival of his great longing for it in his youth, which caused him as I have already described to reply eagerly to the inquiry of the holy man as to whether he would like to be a priest that it was what he desired most of all.[2] This, however, was not because he wished for honour from men, but only that by this means he might cleave ever more closely to God [3] and finally be inseparably united to Him. This was why he never missed an opportunity of celebrating mass, first as a monk whenever the rule of his order permitted him and later as a bishop on every possible occasion. His great detachment and his absolute integrity, his courage and his other virtues were due mainly to his frequent and devout reception of the holy elements. His friends were well aware, moreover, that in the holy mystery of the mass the hidden meanings of things invisible and celestial were made known to him by God.

[1] For this invocation of St Anne as patron of sailors cf. A. Wilmart *De obsequio in S. Annam testimonium e Vita S. Hugonis, Ephemerides Liturgicae* 42 1928, pp. 543-4.
[2] cf. *supra*, Bk. I, c. xi
[3] cf. *Rule of St Benedict*, c. 62

Aliquando capellanum suum quem pridie sanguinem minuisse sciebat, missam celebrasse cognouit. Quem tunc quidem blande corripuit. Set hoc iterum attemptantem durius increpauit, districte prohibens ne ulterius id facere presumeret. Et pericula ex tali presumptione non semel accidisse sibique innotuisse memorabat.

Verum, ut cepta procedat oratio, diem aduentus sui in Angliam apud Douram, ubi applicuit, una cum clericis aliisque domesticis et amicis suis, quorum ibidem turba non modica speratam et precognitam ipsius presentiam expectauerat, letam letus ipse cum letis exegit.

In crastino Doroberniam uenit. Ibi Christi basilicam mox urbem ingressus adiuit, in qua, primum ad Saluatoris aram, deinde ad singulas sanctorum in ea quiescentium memorias, maximeque ad gloriosi martiris Thome mausoleum diutissime set deuotissime orans, seipsum et suos diuino presidio et patrocinio sanctorum Dei attentius commendauit. Hinc priore multisque fratrum usque ad atrium exterius ipsum cum ueneratione deducentibus, ad hospitium suum diuertit.

Illic regis iustitiarii necnon et plerique optimates regni, quos ad locum illum nescio quis tunc casus asciuerat, episcopum certatim inuisere gaudebant, aduentui eius congratulando applaudentes, set molestie corporali qua illum affectum didicerant, nimio merore compatientes. Quos ille magnanimi cordis orisque constantia magnopere consolari studuit ; uultuque sereno, Dominica flagella seruis Domini dulcia esse debere et uerbis docuit et sui ipsius exemplo declarauit. Ceterum ille summus Paterfamilias, qui manum soluerat ut eum succideret, falcem non retraxit a culmi succissione, quem ad messem album iam uiderat, donec granum, celestis apothece sinibus recondendum, ab eius paleis

Once he discovered that his chaplain had celebrated mass the day after he knew that he had been bled. On this occasion he gently reproved him, but on his attempting to do so again he administered a sharp rebuke, and sternly forbade him to dare to do so again, telling him what dangers he himself had more than once incurred by such folly.

But, to continue my narrative, he spent the day of his arrival in England at Dover where he had landed, with his clerks and other attendants and friends. A great crowd of these knowing that he was expected were awaiting him there hopefully, and their joy at seeing him made him happy.

On the morrow he came to Canterbury. On entering the city he went at once to the cathedral, where he prayed long and fervently, first at the altar of our Saviour, and then at each of the shrines of the saints who are buried there, but especially at the tomb of the glorious martyr Thomas, devoutly commending himself and his friends to the aid and protection of God's saints. When he went from there to his lodging the prior and many of the monks respectfully accompanied him as far as the outer court.

The royal justices and many of the magnates of the realm who were in the city for some reason which I do not know, came eagerly and in large numbers to see the bishop. They showed great pleasure at his safe arrival, but were exceedingly grieved and saddened when they saw how ill he was. His brave and generous spirit made him do his utmost to speak reassuringly to them, telling them with a smile that the servants of the Lord ought to rejoice in His chastisements, and showing this by his own example. The Almighty Father, however, who had put forth his hand to cut him down, withheld not his

funditus excussum, ad horreum ab area transferret.
Quid uero necessitates corporee nisi palee, quid culmus
nisi corpus, quidue granum nisi spiritus iusti in messe
dominica intelligitur ? Eius quoque ager mundus est,
area eiusdem mundi pressura, horreum paradisus.

Huius sane prenuntia quedam messionis ei fuit
oculorum sensim *a* irrepens hebetudo que, pulueris et
caumatis continuato ingestu, memorate profectionis
tempore eorum aciem plurimum reuerberabat. Qui
crebro suggerentibus nobis quatinus uisui clarificando
alicuius opem medele sineret adhiberi, una semper et
eadem uoce respondebat, ' Satis,' inquiens, ' oculi nobis *b*
isti sufficient quamdiu fuerit usus ipsorum necessarius.'
Hiis igitur exterioribus parumper obtusis, nec tamen
pristino decore exterius priuatis, luminum interiorum
limpidior de die in diem claritas reddebatur.

Apud Cantuariam uero, ubi solent quorumdam
sepius leuari egritudines, ipsius adeo ingrauata est
egritudo ut inde Londonias non preter molestiam,
partim equitando partimque nauali uehiculo deporta-
retur. Nichil tamen hoc suis uotis aduersabatur, nec
precibus quas in Christi templo deuote libauerat, quod
ei accidit in aliquo obuiabat.

---

a sensum B   *b* nostri o

sickle from the corn which he saw was white already to harvest, until the grain had been separated completely from the straw, to be transferred from the threshing-floor to the barn in order to be stored in the heavenly garners.   What other interpretation can there be for the straw but bodily sufferings, for the sheaf the body and for the grain the soul of the righteous man in the harvest of the Lord, whose field is the world and His threshing floor its afflictions and His barn Paradise ?

An obvious sign of the approaching harvest was his gradually failing sight which during the journey I have described lost much of its keenness because of the dust and heat.   To my frequent suggestions that he should allow some remedy to be applied to improve his sight he always gave the same answer, ' My eyes will last for as long as I have to use them '.   Their beauty remained unchanged in spite of their being somewhat dimmed, and all the time the clearness of his inner vision became daily more brilliant.

At Canterbury, where so many cures usually take place, his malady increased so much that it was with difficulty that he was brought from there to London, partly on horseback and partly by ship.   He, however, desired nothing else, nor did what happened to him in any way conflict with the prayers he had so earnestly offered up in Christ's church.

Capitvlvm XVI

De languore ipsius apud Londonias. Et de transitu eius
ad Dominum. Et plurima de gestis uerbisque languentis,
recordatione perhenni dignissima.

Nam ubi proprium diuersorium quod secus Londonias
apud uetus Templum possidebat,[a] ingressus est, an-
helantia febribus menbra quies [b] lectuli protinus excepit.
Quod amicorum ipsius plurimi intuentes, mestitia
conficiebantur ; ipsoque audiente, diuinam exorabant
clementiam quatinus ipsum incolumem ecclesie sue
filiis, ad ipsius iam diu reditum ualde suspensis, restitui
iuberet.

Hos ille paucis blande consolatus, ait, ' Filiis nostris
in Christo karissimis siue presens corpore siue absens,
spirituali numquam presentia deesse ualebo. Verum
de ualetudine siue presentia mea corporali, immo et de
meipso toto, Patris solius [c] qui in celis est uoluntas
semper fiat.'

Transacta uero in eodem loco nocte una, postera die
hec ipsi qui scripsit ista locutus est, ' Hii qui nos,' inquit,
' temporaliter diligunt, immo et qui spiritualiter nos
amplectuntur, uitam meam temporalem, que michi
reuera fastidio iampridem esse cepit, satis cuperent
prolongari. Set nobis sententia longe distans est, qui
cernimus manifeste, quam in breui flebilis sit futurus
status Anglicane ecclesie. Melius itaque nobis mori est
quam uiuere et uidere imminentia gentis huius mala et
sanctorum.[1] Nam procul dubio in posteris Henrici regis
impleri necesse est quod Scriptura prelocuta est, " Spuria
uitulamina non dabunt radices altas " et " Ab iniquo
thoro semen exterminabitur." [2] Set et rex modernus

---

[a] + sanctus Hugo presul eger X   [b] quiete Bo   [c] filius B

Chapter XVI

Concerning his sickness at London and his departure to the Lord, and many words and deeds of his during his sickness which deserve everlasting remembrance.

When he reached the residence he owned in London near the old Temple he immediately rested his fevered body in his bed. His numerous friends were grief-stricken when they saw him, and in his hearing besought the divine Mercy to decree that he should be made whole and restored to his Chapter who had for so long awaited his return.

He spoke a few gentle words of consolation to them, ' My dearest sons in Christ, whether I am present or absent from you, I shall always be with you in spirit. My recovery, my life, and in truth my whole being is always solely at the disposal of our heavenly Father.'

After one night had passed in that place, the following day he spoke these words to his biographer, ' My earthly friends and even my spiritual sons seem exceedingly desirous of prolonging my life on earth, which I for my part have long found a burden. My own wish is exactly the opposite, for I clearly see how grievous the condition of the English church will shortly be. It is better for me to die than to live to see the evils which threaten this people and its saints.[1] The words of the Bible must inevitably be fulfilled in the case of the descendants of king Henry. ' Bastard shoots will not have deep roots ' and ' the offspring of an adulterous union shall be destroyed '.[2] The present king of the French will avenge his pious father Louis on the sons of the adulteress who

---

[1] cf. 1 Mach. 3: 59   [2] Wis. 4: 3; 3: 16

Francorum sanctum genitorem suum Lodowicum ulcisetur in sobole preuaricationis, que thorum cum eo immaculatum repudiauit eiusque emulo Anglorum regi impudica adhesit. Quamobrem Gallicus iste Philippus regiam Anglorum ita delebit stirpem quemadmodum bos herbam solet usque ad radices carpere. Nam a Gallis tres ipsius nati iam abrasi sunt, reges uidelicet duo, unus consul. Quartus qui superest curtam habebit pacem ab eis.

' Scis uero quia post biduum natale domini mei euangeliste et apostoli Matthei fiet. Dies illa mei quoque episcopatus natalitius erat ; in ea, ut scis, unctionem suscepi presularem. Sepius autem ab ineunte etate egrotaui nec tamen illam unctionem, que proprie dicitur infirmorum, hactenus percepi. Sola ex unctionibus que mee possent congruere persone, hec michi necdum est collata. Hanc igitur cras, in uigilia beati euangeliste, promereri exopto.

' Iam ergo modo faciem Domini preuenire debemus in pura et uera confessione, ut ipso Domino annuente, tam uenerabile sacramentum digne pro modulo nostro et salubriter pro dono suo nobis contingat suscipere.'

Hiis ita *a* memoratis, quicquid aliquando in se nouerat accusabile, uel quicquid in quolibet gradu etatis, ordinis aut professionis sibi de se potuerat displicere, cepit in conspectu Domini, sub testimonio eiusdem prius cui hec loquebatur, monachi et presbiteri sui, deinde adiunctis ei tribus reuerende honestatis sacerdotibus, sollicite confiteri. Quorum primus Lincolniensis decanus, secundus precentor qui cathedram ipsius post eum ascendit, tertius uero archidiaconus Norhamtonie erat, uir uita utique et doctrina clarissimus.[1]

In hac confessione nec illa omisit que innumeris

---

a itaque QX

forsook her lawful husband shamelessly for his rival, the king of the English. For this cause this Frenchman Philip shall wipe out the English royal stock just as the ox plucks up grass by its roots ; for already three of Henry's sons, two of them kings and the other a count, have been destroyed by the French, and they will allow the fourth who still remains only a short respite.

' You are aware that the day after tomorrow is the feast of my patron, the evangelist and apostle St Matthew, which is the anniversary of my consecration, when, as you know, I was anointed as a bishop. From my childhood I have frequently been ill, but nevertheless never until now have I received the unction which is reserved for the sick. Of all those which I ought to have had, this is the only one still lacking, and therefore tomorrow, the vigil of the feast of the blessed evangelist, I desire to be worthy to receive it.

' I ought, however, only to approach the presence of God after a full and sincere confession, in order that through his mercy and by his grace I may receive this great sacrament worthily and well as far as I am able.'

After he had said this he began very earnestly to confess every sin of which he felt himself guilty, and also whatever at every stage of his life and in all his different capacities might have been displeasing in the sight of God. This he did first to his priest and monk to whom he was then speaking, and later once more to him and to three good and revered priests, namely the then dean of Lincoln, the precentor, who afterwards succeeded him as bishop, and the archdeacon of Northampton, a man with a high reputation both for holiness and learning.[1]

In this confession he did not omit sins which he had

---

[1] The dean of Lincoln was Roger of Rolleston, the precentor was William of Blois (bishop of Lincoln 1203-1206), the archdeacon of Northampton was Richard of Kent.

pridem uicibus uiris deuotis compluribus fuerat con-
fessus. Horum quilibet fateri solebat quod neminem
quisque illorum eatenus uidisset qui sicut uir iste
semetipsum nosset accusare, sic a se omissa, sic indigne
commissa cum circumstantiis reatuum suorum prompte,
acute et plene sciret enumerare. In confitendo illud
semper replicabat, ' Mala,' inquiens, ' mea uera sola et
pura mala sunt ; bona, si qua sunt, non ita sunt set
malorum admixtione *a* inpura, malis undique concreta
et iccirco nec uera nec simpliciter sunt bona.'

Celebrata igitur per biduum huiuscemodi confessione,
circa horam tertiam in uigilia memorata, eukaristie ad
se delate obuiam, nudis plantis cilicio, tunica et cuculla
uestitus, processit a lectulo. Ante ipsum quoque
tremendum diuinumque sacramentum genua flectens et
suppliciter adorans, diutius orauit ; *b* commemorans
infinita beneficia Saluatoris humano impensa generi
illique gratias inde referens ac se, ut se dicebat nimis
culpabilem, eius misericordissime pietati commendans,
ipsius denique patrocinium et auxilium usque in finem
sibi affore, nec se umquam deserere flebiliter implorans.
Refectus denique uite eterne dabibus et extrema unctione
in peccatorum remissionem delibutus, gratias egit
Domino dixitque nobis, ' Iam medicis et morbis
nostris, ut poterit, conueniat ; de utrisque amodo erit in
pectore nostro cura minor. Ei me commisi, illum
suscepi, ipsum tenebo, ipsi adherebo cui adherere
bonum est, quem tenere beatum est, quem qui suscipit,
cui se qui committit, ualidus et tutus est.'

Admonitus autem postea dum languor ingrauesceret
ut etiam testamentum de more conficeret, ait, ' Tedet

a immixtione o
b adorauit B

confessed many times already to several devout men, each of whom used to say that until then they had never found anyone with such a sensitive conscience, or who took such pains to give so full and truthful an account of his sins and negligences. When making his confession he always reiterated, ' My evil acts are utterly and entirely evil, my good deeds, if there are any, are not completely good, but partly evil, because they have been contaminated by evil, and thus they are not really or thoroughly good '.

Two days having been spent thus over his confession, at about nine o'clock on the vigil which has already been named, he got out of bed to receive the Eucharist, clad in his hair shirt, habit and cowl and with his feet bare. He prayed for a long time, kneeling humbly in adoration before the holy and awesome sacrament, recalling the immense favours conferred by our Redeemer on mankind, and giving thanks for these. Although, as he said, he was a great sinner he commended himself to the abundant mercy and compassion of his Saviour, and besought him with tears never to abandon him, but to grant him his help and protection to the end. Finally, having partaken of the food of eternal life, and being anointed with the viaticum for the remission of his sins, he thanked God, and said to us, ' Now let the doctors and our sickness come to what agreement they will, neither from henceforth are of any consequence to us. I have committed myself to Him whom I have received, I will hold fast and cleave to Him to whom it is good to adhere, whom to possess is joy, for whoever receives Him and trusts Him is strong and secure.'

Afterwards when his sickness increased he was advised to make his will, as was the custom, and

me sane huius consuetudinis iam passim in ecclesiam traducte. Nam quo *a* ad animum meum, nichil omnimodis aut possedi umquam uel possideo quod censerem meum et non potius ecclesie quam regebam *b* proprium. Attamen, ne fiscus solito *c* rapiat si quid bonorum temporalium post meum obitum in episcopatu fuerit derelictum, iam nunc uniuersa que uideor possidere indigentibus eroganda delego Domino *d* Ihesu Christo.' Accitisque decano et duobus ecclesie sue archidiaconis, quecumque in possessionum facultatibus reperiri poterant, eorum prouisione dispertienda egenis ipsis contradidit.*e* Post hec orarium suum iussit afferri ; quod ceruici appendens, anathematizauit omnes illos qui de rebus suis aliquid fraudulenter supprimere, auferre uiolenter, liberamue facultatem exequendi quod iusserat predictis executoribus denegare temptassent.

Post susceptum uero munus extreme unctionis crescente indies ui febrium, duobus continuo mensibus lectulo decubuit ; cotidiana pene et quandoque sepius in die confessione repetita, leuissimos cogitationum motus ac uerborum excessus ' si quando anxianti eueniret ministrantibus indignari, purgare festinans. Orationi mens eius semper intendebat. Diuinum officium utroque tempore, noctis uidelicet et diei, studiose curabat horis statutis exsoluere ; quas, nec propter accessionem estus febrilis aut preterire patiebatur aut preuenire. Psallebat et ipse cum uires suppetebant cum psallentibus. Neglecte seu properanter legentes aut psallentes terribili mox uoce aut sonitu castigabat. Vtriusque rei summa ei cura toto semper euo precedenti fuit ut distincte *f* et debito tempore Creatori persolueret

---

a quod B¹   *b* regendam suscepi X
c solitus X   *d* + nostro Q
e tradidit X   *f* distincto B

answered, ' I find this practice recently adopted by ecclesiastics a burden, for upon my soul I have never possessed, nor do I possess anything of any kind which I did not consider to belong to the church over which I have been ruling and not to myself.   However, to prevent the usual usurpations of the Exchequer, any temporal goods left in my diocese after my death which might seem to be mine I leave to the Lord Jesus Christ for distribution to the needy.'   He then summoned the dean and two of his archdeacons and commissioned them to supervise the distribution to the poor of whatever goods they found in his possession.   After this he asked for his stole, and hanging it round his neck he ex- communicated everyone who tried fraudulently to conceal, or forcibly to carry off anything belonging to him, or to prevent his executors having complete freedom to carry out his instructions.

After he had received the benefit of extreme unction his fever perceptibly increased, and he remained in bed for two months, during which time he repeated his con- fession almost daily and on some days more than once, being anxious to receive absolution for the slightest irritability in thought or word, if occasionally he showed any temper towards those who were ministering to him. He prayed unceasingly and took particular care to recite the day and night offices at the proper times, and even during his bouts of fever would neither omit them nor anticipate them.   When his strength permitted he joined in when the psalms were chanted, and either by words or sounds showed strong disapproval of those who read or sang carelessly or irreverently.   One of his great preoccupations during the whole of his past life had been

laudes constitutas.[1] Vicissitudinem standi et sedendi inter psallendum quamdiu ualuit et ipsemet obseruabat et suos obseruare clericos compellebat ; ut dum unus sedendo fatigata menbra reficeret, alius stando diuine et angelice presentie reuerentiam exhiberet. Cum magnis interesset nobilium conuentibus aut descidendis preesset causantium litibus, sicut aliis moris est ad formandas interlocutorias interdum secedere, ita, cum exigerent momenta progresse lucis,[a] ad canendas diuertebat horas consuetas. In dedicationibus ecclesiarum, in celebrationibus ordinum, mos ei indissimilis fuerat.

Venit autem rex inuisere egrotantem. Cui ille nec modice quidem uisus est assurgere uel assidere, cum necdum adhuc uires ei deessent ad sedendum in stratu suo cum alimenta percipiebat. Rex ei compatientissime loquebatur, exponens ei semetipsum et sua ad beneplacitum ipsius exequendum. Illo autem, exclusis omnibus suis, ante iacentem diutius sedente et blandis sermonibus multa prosequente, episcopus fere nichil referebat [b] auditis. Res tandem suas et testamenti sui executores, cum tota pariter Lincolniensi ecclesia protectioni eius commendans, ipsi ualefecit. Desperauerat profecto iam de maneria illius ; quamobrem pauca ei loquebatur, ne perderet pulchros sermones suos.[2]

Metropolitanus quoque ipsius iacentem aliquotiens uisitans, quicquid humanitatis et benignitatis esset ei pro uiribus se exhibiturum pollicetur. Cui ad postremum suggerenti ut si quem forte uerbo aut facto minus iusto irritasset uel lesisset, ueniam ab offenso petere meminisset, ac demum profitenti quia suos sepius frequenter animos acerbissime prouocasset, qui pater spiritualis et primas eius haberetur, unde cordis penitudo uenieque necessaria uideretur postulatio, ita respondit :

<hr />

[a] litis X   [b] deferebat X   [1] cf. *Rule of St Benedict* c. 16   [2] cf. Prov. 23: 8

to render the praises due to his Creator [1] at the appointed times. As long as he was strong enough, he kept to the custom of alternately sitting and standing for the psalms and made his clerks do the same. Thus, whilst one sat down to rest his weary limbs, another stood up to show his respect for the presence of God and the angels. When he attended meetings of the Great Council or was acting as president in a lawsuit, it was his practice, when the light showed the time had come, to withdraw to chant the prescribed offices, just as others retired to frame their questions. This was also his custom at dedication ceremonies and ordinations.

When the king came to visit the sick man he did not rise or even sit to greet him, although he was still strong enough to sit up in bed to take food. The king was obviously much distressed and told him he was ready to do anything he wanted. He dismissed his attendants, and sat for a long time beside his bed, saying many kind words, to which the bishop hardly replied. Finally, before he bade him farewell, Hugh commended to his protection his property, his executors, and the church of Lincoln. He had already no illusions about John, and therefore spoke very little to him, knowing that his exhortations would be wasted.[2]

His archbishop also sometimes visited his sick-bed, and showed him marked kindness and consideration, promising to do anything he could for him. In the end he suggested that if he remembered he had angered or wounded anyone in word or deed without due cause he should ask their forgiveness, pointing out that Hugh had very frequently given him great provocation, and that since he was his primate and spiritual father, some expression of sorrow and a request for pardon would be fitting. He, however, replied :

'Sane, dum conscientie nostre abdita queque reuoluo, quia uos sepe ad iras prouocauerim euidenter inuenio. Quod tamen inde penitendum michi sit non perpendo ; set quia sepius et instantius hoc ipsum non egerim, michi dolendum scio. Set et crebrius solito, si diutius uobiscum uita ducenda restaret, id ipsum me facturum sub oculis cuncta inspicientis Dei firmissime propono. Memini namque quia, ut uobis morigerarer, ea que uobis tacere non debuissem, queque a uobis *a* si dicerentur equanimiter non audirentur, sepenumero ignauiter suppressi ; sicque mea culpa uestram potius quam Patris qui in celis est offensam declinaui. Ex quo accidit quod non solum in *b* Deum set, unde indulgentiam supplex inquiro, in uestram quoque paternitatem uel in primatum uestrum nec leuiter nec episcopaliter deliqui.'

Postmodum, imminente sibi iam post dies quindecim lucis huius die suprema, Gaufrido de Noiers, nobilis fabrice constructori quam cepit a fundamentis in renouanda Lincolniensi ecclesia erigere, Hugonis magnifica erga decorem domus Dei dilectio, talia idem est locutus : 'Quia dominum regem cum episcopis totiusque regni huius primoribus, Lincolniam in proximo ad generale colloquium conuenturos accepimus, accelera et consume quecumque necessaria sunt ad decorem et ornatum circa altare domini ac patroni mei sancti Baptiste Iohannis ; quia etiam per fratrem nostrum Rouensem episcopum, cum eo una cum ceteris aduenerit episcopis, uolumus dedicari. Nam et nos ipsi, denuntiati tempore colloquii, illic presentes erimus. Optabamus sane nostro illud ministerio consecrare, set quia Dominus aliter disposuit, uolumus ut priusquam illuc ueniamus,*c* occasione remota consecretur.' Hec ipsa

---

a nobis Qt   *b* *om* B
c perueniamus Q . . . excusatione omni X

' It is true that after making a thorough examination of my conscience I know well that I have often angered you. Yet, I do not consider that I should repent of this, but rather grieve that I did not do so more frequently and more earnestly. I am, however, firmly resolved under the eye of the all-seeing God to do so more often than before if I am spared. What I remember is, the number of times I weakly suppressed matters on which I should not have been silent, in order to appease you, because I knew you would not take it patiently if they were spoken about. My sin was that I preferred to offend my heavenly Father and not you. For this cause, I ask forgiveness for my serious shortcomings as a bishop not only against God but against you, my father and primate.'

A fortnight later, when his last day on earth seemed to be approaching, he said these words to Geoffrey de Noiers, the chief mason of the magnificent cathedral at Lincoln, which Hugh's immense zeal for the beauty of the house of God had caused him to begin to rebuild from the foundations : ' We have learnt that the lord king and the bishops and magnates of the whole kingdom will shortly assemble at Lincoln for a general council. Make haste therefore to finish whatever is needed for the beauty and adornment of the altar of my lord and patron St John the Baptist, which we desire to have dedicated by our brother the bishop of Rochester and the other bishops present. We also ourselves will be there at the time when the assembly is held. It was our wish to officiate at the consecration, but God willed otherwise. We desire therefore that it be consecrated without delay, before our arrival.' He made this request also to certain other people, enjoining upon his servants, and all the chief cathedral dignitaries that in the matter of food offerings and other services they should do their utmost

uerba et aliis quibusdam repetiit, dans in mandatis
seruientibus suis cunctisque maioribus personis ecclesie
sue, ut in xeniis uel obsequiis quantam possent deferrent
honorificentiam, non solum regi set episcopis aliisque
amicis Lincolniam aduenturis.

Vrgere eum interea languor uehementius cepit.
Geminatis cotidie paroxismis, in solida eius menbra
febrile seuiebat incendium ; uitalia et internorum
medullas dissenteria exhauriebat. Diebus aliquot ante
obitum suum, quecumque circa *a* exequias et sepulturam
eius uoluit expleri, nobis iterato insinuauit documento.
' Cineres,' inquit, ' sollempni ritu benedictos preparate,
quos in crucis modum spargetis super locum terre nude,
in quo ponetis me, cum instare uideritis horam supreme
expirationis mee. Cilicium enim more quorumdam, in
ordine nostro migrantibus nequaquam substernitur ; eo
quippe quilibet moriens apud nos contentus est *b* quo
pridem uiuens usus et indutus est.'

Hec quidem loquebatur cilicio et tunica indutus,
cuculla quoque superuestitus. Hiis inuolucris potius
quam indumentis, nullo egritudinis sue momento caruit.
Non ardor febris, non corporis tantus sudor, aliquid
horum ei detraxit. Cilicium bis aut semel mutari sibi
uix permisit, quod sudore ac si luto concretum et restis
more contortum, inter corpus et tunicam eius ex
laterum frequenti conuersione reperimus, quod etiam
ei cutem enormiter abrasisse nescio quot in locis
deprehendimus. Et quia nouimus apud Cartusienses
plurimum infirmis cilicia ex consuetudine tolli, dicebamus
ei, ' Domine, nimium ledit uos et exulcerat in continuis
iacentem sudoribus hispida uestis hec. Oportet uos
illam exuere et ea, iuxta morem ordinis, dum egritudo

---

a ante Q
b esse debet X

to give an honourable reception not merely to the king but to the bishops and other friends who would be visiting Lincoln.

Meanwhile he was growing worse and worse. Every day he had two paroxysms, and his whole body was consumed by the fever, and his internal organs were weakened by dysentery. Some days before his death he told us repeatedly what his wishes were about his funeral and burial. 'Have the ashes', he said, 'blessed and made ready, which you must scatter on the bare ground in the shape of a cross. Lay me on these when you see that my last hour has come, for the hair-shirt is not usually placed under those of our order when they are dying, because each of us who dies, desires to be clad in what he wore whilst he was alive.'

When he was saying this he was wearing his hair shirt, and tunic with his cowl over them. Never during his whole sickness were these garments or rather wrappings removed. Neither the heat of the fever nor the excessive perspiration caused him to lay them aside. Once or twice he reluctantly allowed us to change his hair-shirt which we found had become as stiff as mud because of the perspiration, and was twisted like rope between his tunic and his body because he tossed and turned so much. The scratches which I saw on his skin were too numerous for me to count. As we knew that often among the Carthusians it was the custom to remove the hair-shirt in sickness, we said to him, ' My lord, this hairy garment is tormenting you grievously, as you lie there, always perspiring, and is causing sores. It is only right that we should take it off, as it is customary in your order to be without it during serious illness.' He replied

infestat, penitus carere.'   Ad hec uero ille dicebat,
' Nolit Deus !   Absit istud ne fiat !   Non enim ledit set
lenit nos uestis hec, nec tam ulcerat quam iuuat.'

Precepit quoque scriptori presentium, dicens, ' Scio
equidem nec episcopum quemquam nec abbatem in hiis
locis reperiendum qui debitum commendationis officium
educende de carcere isto anime mee ualeat impendere.
Vniuersos namque huius terre prelatos edictum generale
protraxit Lincolniam.   Mittes igitur pueros cum equis
ad Westmonasterium, qui deducant inde septem siue
octo monachos ut celebrent uobiscum exequias nostras.
Ad decanum nichilominus sancti Pauli uerbis meis
mittens, mandabis illi quatinus ex clericis chorum
frequentantibus copiosam huc dirigat multitudinem.
Ita siquidem speciosas michi persoluetis exequias.   Cum
uero tempus fuerit ut corpus exanime pontificalibus
induatur ex more, sociabis tibi unum ex sacerdotibus
regularis habitus, qui tecum totum funus diligentius
abluat et extergat.   In ecclesia namque matrici sancte
Dei genitricis, non procul ab altari sancti Iohannis
Baptiste, habeo sepeliri.   Quamobrem exuuias corporis
huius mundissimas oportet exhiberi quas sudor tantus
multo iam squalore infecit.   Caue ne hac in parte
queuis obrepat neggligentia, qua loci reuerendi de-
honestetur dignitas sacrosancta.   Frater Petrus, conuersus
noster, limpham subministret abluentibus.   Preter uos,
trino in numero hoc michi munus exhibentes, nullus
omnino alius ubi hec fient intersit.

' Cum ad ecclesiam Lincolniensem perlatum fuerit
corpus meum, proferes ex scriniis nostris que ibi sunt
omnia uestimenta in quibus pontificalem suscepi consecrationem, a sandaliis usque ad mitram ; funusque
sepeliendum eisdem omnibus induetis.   Sunt namque
plana nec ambitiosa, que in usus istos hactenus con-

to this, ' God forbid that this should happen. This garment does not hurt me but soothes me, and heals sores rather than causes them.'

He gave these commands to the author of this present work : ' I know well that no bishop or abbot can be found to perform the rite of commendation by which my soul shall be released from its prison, for a general summons has sent all the prelates of this land to Lincoln. Therefore send servants with horses to Westminster to bring back with them seven or eight monks to assist you in performing our exequies. Also send a message on my behalf to the dean of St Paul's to request him immediately to send here a considerable number of the clerks of his choir. This will enable you to perform my exequies splendidly. When the time comes to clothe my dead body in its episcopal vestments as is the custom, select a monk in priests' orders to assist you in the task of washing and drying the corpse. I am to be buried near the altar of St John the Baptist in the church of the holy Mother of God, and therefore it is only fitting that every part of my body which the excessive perspiration has made very dirty should be thoroughly washed. Take care not to overlook any portion of it, so as not to dishonour so holy and venerated a spot. Our lay brother, brother Peter, will provide the washers with water. Except you three who are rendering me this service, let no-one else be present.

' When my body is brought to the church at Lincoln take from our wardrobe all the vestments there from the sandals to the mitre which I wore at my consecration, and array my body in them for its burial. These are plain and simple, and I have kept them for this purpose till now.' When his rings were brought to him, he gave me a gold one, set with an aquamarine which weighed

seruaui.' Anulis quoque suis ei presentatis, unum modici ponderis, aureum tamen habentemque saphiri aquatici gemmam uiliorem, nobis contradidit, ' Istum,' inquiens, ' dum episcoparer, digitus noster excepit ; istum dum sepeliar, dextera hec retinebit. Prospeximus nobis in hoc tunc, cum ad gradum istum accessimus, ut ordinatio et humatio nostra eisdem insignibus donarentur, que uidelicet uiuentem eisque utentem humilitatis admone-rent et circa extinctum tandem et tumulatum, hec fortuitu quempiam reperientem ad rapiendum ea sui pretio uel specie ^a minime prouocarent.'

Eo igitur hec prosequente, audientibus significatum est quod post sepulturam primam corpus eius trans-ferendum quandoque, ac proinde inspiciendum esse preuiderit ; quandoquidem primitus in sepulchro duplici, plumbeo scilicet et lapideo, utroque solidissime obserato recondendum, nec uidere illud quisquam, nec sua sibi ornamenta preripere ualuisset.^b

Ipsum uero sepulture sue ita designabat locum. ' Ante aram,' inquit, ' sepedicti patroni mei precursoris Domini, ubi congruentius uidebitur spatium, secus murum aliquem ponetis me, ne pauimentum loci tumba, ut plerisque in ecclesiis cernimus, importune occupet, et incedentibus offendiculum prestet aut ruinam.'

Cum uero durius ^c uexaretur doloribus immensis, huiusmodi sepius uerba orando repetebat, ' O pie Deus, requiem presta nobis. Bone Domine Deusque uerax, dona tandem nobis requiem.' Cui semel ita consolantis uoce diximus, ' Iam domine quiescetis,^d tactus nempe pulsus uestri finiri nunc innuit accessionem istam.' Ad hec ille, ' O uere,' inquit, ' beatos illos, quos uel extremi dies iudicii requie inconcussa donabit.' Ad quem uicissim dicentibus nobis, ' Huius diem iudicii illam Deo

very little. ' I wore this ', he said, ' on my finger during my episcopate, and shall wear it on my right hand when I am buried. At the time when I was made a bishop, I decided that the same signs of my rank should be used at my consecration and my burial, so that they might teach me humility when I used them during my lifetime, and when I was dead and buried their beauty and value should never by any conceivable chance tempt anyone to steal them.'

Whilst he was saying these things, his hearers realised that he had foreseen the translation of his body from its first resting place, and its exposition on this occasion, since he ordered that at the first burial it should be securely hidden in two coffins, one of lead and the other of stone to prevent anyone seeing it and robbing it of its ornaments.

He gave precise instructions about the spot where he was to be buried, saying, ' Place me before the altar of the patron saint I have so often mentioned, the precursor of our Lord, in any fitting place near a wall, in order that my tomb may not take up too much of the pavement and obstruct or injure those who pass by, as I have seen happen in a great many churches '.

When he was suffering terrible and excessive pain he often used to repeat this prayer, ' O merciful God, give me rest. Excellent Lord and true God, give me rest at last.' On one occasion I tried to comfort him by saying, ' Soon, my lord, you will be at peace, for when I feel your pulse it shows the crisis is ending '. He answered, ' How truly blessed are those to whom the day of the last Judgment shall give eternal rest.' I then said, ' God willing, your day of judgment will be when you

uolente habebitis qua istius carnis sarcinam deponetis',
ille e contra, ' Non,' inquit, ' recte sentitis. Non enim
iudicii set gratie et misericordie dies erit qua ego
defungar.'

Stupori presentibus magneque fuit admirationi,
inter multiplices cruciatus uiolentissimarum egritudinum,
inuicta semper animi eius fortitudo. Ita se in lectulo,
cum uellet, in latus aliud girabat ; ita robuste incedens,
cum secederet a lectulo quo esset necesse, ibat et redibat ;
ut congressum quemdam atque conflictum cum in-
firmitate corporis, uirtus animi eius iniisse putaretur.
Et dicebant medici, huiusmodi *a* gestus eius intuentes :
' Vere spiritus hominis istius sustentat infirmitatem
eius.[1] Vere cum apostolo insultare potest iste corpori
mortis huius et dicere, " Quando infirmor, tunc fortior
sum et potens ".' [2]

Vox quoque ita succo plena uirili ei fuit ut licet
submissior, subtilior tamen solito non satis audiretur.
Lectionem post martilogium de Iohannis euangelio,
ipsa quoque die qua discessit, proprie uocis sonitu ita
fecit terminari ut in crastino ibi coram funere eius ad
missam inciperet legi euangelium ubi pridie nutu eius
textus Scripture eiusdem desiit recitari. Quod postquam
aduertimus ut puta nemine procurante accidisse, glori-
ficauimus Deum qui pulchro miroque ordine omnia eius
opera uitamque totam usque in finem semper dirigebat.

Locus etiam scripture summe dulcedinis presagium,
ipsa rerum serie que geste fuerant, manifeste preferebat.
Erat namque de familiari confabulatione Saluatoris
nostri et Marthe ante suscitationem fratris eius Lazari,
qui ita contexitur, ' Dixit Martha ad Ihesum, " Domine,
si fuisses hic, frater meus non esset mortuus ".' [3] Cum

---

a huius Q

lay down the burden of this body,' to which he replied,
' You are wrong. The day of my death will not be one
of judgment, but of grace and mercy.'

Those present were amazed and greatly edified by
his unfailing courage amid the many terrible sufferings
caused by his illness. He turned over in bed whenever
he wanted to, and when he had to leave his bed he went
out and returned without tottering, so that it seemed as
if by a determined effort of his will he had declared war
on his physical weakness. The doctors observed his
behaviour and said : ' This man's spirit is not defeated
by his illness.[1] In fact, like the apostle he can mock at
the body of this death and say : " When I am weakest,
then am I strongest and most powerful." ' [2]

His voice was as vigorous as ever, but being lower
and softer than usual it was difficult to hear what he
said. On the very day of his death, after the martyrology, he ordered the lesson of St John's gospel to end
so that on the morrow the gospel read at mass before his
corpse began where the day before the reading of the
same passage had ended at his command. When we
afterwards understood this could not have happened by
any human contrivance, we glorified God who had always
ordered in so wondrous and marvellous a manner all his
works, and the whole course of his life right up to the end.

That passage from the scriptures was indeed a happy
augury in the very facts that it narrated. It described
the conversation between our Saviour and Martha
before the raising of her brother Lazarus and ran,
' Martha said to Jesus, " Lord if thou hadst been here,
my brother had not died." ' [3] Whilst every year he had

---

[1] cf. Prov. 18: 14
[2] cf. 2 Cor. 12: 10
[3] John 11: 21; this passage is still read at Masses for the Dead.

enim alias canonicas scripturas *a* temporibus statutis
tum ad matutinas tum ad mensam suam annuatim relegi
instituisset, quatuor euangelistarum totidem libros post
primam diei horam, premisso capitulo martirologii,
quatuor anni temporibus perlegi faciebat. Has enim
lectiones, etiam cum equitando iter ageret, nullatenus
omittebat. In quo religiosum eunuchi illius studium
equiparasse, aut etiam uicisse probatur, qui sedens
currum Ysaiam legisse, Philippumque cathezetam pro-
meruisse monitu angelico predicatur.¹ Quod enim ille
semel egisse commendatur in curru, hoc iste innumeris
uicibus equo tantum uectus continuo agebat usu.

Quem ut liquido innotesceret, nulla animi *b* deieccione
uel inter supprema uite discrimina, solite magnaminitatis
culmen deseruisse, hortatus est eum quidam ex amicis
suis, ad explendam peccatorum quantum sciret suffici-
entem confessionem, ita dicens, ' Quia domine, sicut
ipse melius nostis, efficacior Deoque acceptior est illa
confessio que specificat singillatim omnia, quam illa
que sub quadam generalitate includit singula, et uos
multo tempore ordinarius necnon et delegatus iudex
plurimorum extitistis ; quantum memoria recolit
satagite confiteri quos uel quot ob priuatum amorem
siue odium promoueritis, ut assolet, in negotiis suis, aut
depresseritis, minus uidelicet utendo legitime iudiciaria
potestate.' *c*

Ad hec ille uerbum protulit quod pluribus audientium
gaudio pariter et miraculo fuit. ' Odio,' inquit, ' seu
amore, set nec quidem spe uel timore, persone aut *d* rei
cuiuscumque, numquam a ueritate iudicii me scienter

---

a B² *adds* quatuor anni
b + eum X
c minus iuste X, *for these six words*
d seu Q

the other canonical books read to him at the appointed times both at Matins and at meal-times, he caused the four books of the gospels to be read in the four seasons of the year at Prime after the martyrology. He never neglected these readings even when journeying on horseback. In his study of holy writ he bore comparison with, if he did not excel, the eunuch, who is described as sitting in his chariot reading Isaias, and to whom as a reward an angel sent Philip as a catechist.[1] What the latter is praised for doing once in his chariot the former made it his practice to do on numerous occasions when he was only on horseback.

A striking example of the way in which even during the last crisis of his life his habitual serenity remained unclouded by any depression of spirit is his answer to a friend who had asked him to complete to the best of his knowledge a sufficient confession of sins. ' My lord,' he said, ' as you well know a confession which recounts each individual sin is more effective and more acceptable to God than one which groups sins into certain general categories. Since you have often been a judge ordinary and also a judge delegate of very many persons, try to confess as far as your memory avails how many people or cases you have on these occasions favoured or given judgment against out of personal love or prejudice, and thus abused your legal powers as a judge.'

Most of the spectators were equally pleased and amazed at his answer. He said, ' I do not recall ever knowingly to have given an unjust sentence, in connection with any person or case, from love or hatred, or from fear or expectation. If in delivering judgment I have

---

[1] cf. Acts 8: 26-31

exorbitasse memini. Si iudicando deuiaui a recto, hoc
proprie ignorantie aut certe assidentium crimen fuit.'

Nec pretereundum inconsulte uidetur quod *a* uir,
totius semper *b* uanitatis et superstitionis aduersator,
gustum potius carnium in extremis huius egritudinis *c*
quam esum pro bono obedientie nequaquam repudia-
uerit. Suggerentibus namque amicis et medicis
asserentibus quia, hyeme transacta, facilius curaretur
si esculentioribus cibis effectum iam corpus, et quartanis
algoribus post alias febres congelascens, foueri permisisset ; iussit archiepiscopus et in remissionem
peccatorum iniunxit ei ut in tali quoque dieta consilio
medicine parere debuisset. Ille uero prescriptum obiciens
ordinis Cartusiensis, quo in commune omnibus, morbidis,
sanis et moribundis esus carnium inhibetur, id sibi
illicitum fatebatur.

Set, ne multis immoremur, ad petitionem demum
clericorum suorum, de mandato quoque et sedula
monitione Cantuariensis archipresulis, susceptis per
dominum Robertum, tunc *d* quidem procuratorem ac
paulo post priorem Withamie,[1] fratrum *e* eiusdem loci
hortatoriis epistolis ut suo incunctanter archiepiscopo
in hac eius iussione obediret,*f* carnes, ab adholescentia
sua usque tunc nulla occasione a se prelibatas, in cibum
sumpsit. Dicebat uero nobis, ' Sciatis quia nec desiderio
nec remedio nobis aliquatenus esse poterit adeo suasus
iste carnium esus. Verumptamen, ne tot uenerabiles
uiros *g* scandalizemus, immo ne ab illius uestigiis uel in
morte iam positi recedamus, qui factus est obediens usque
ad mortem,[2] dentur nobis carnes. Hiis enim nunc
demum, pro fraterne dilectionis condimento, libenter

a quo B
c B *omits these four words*
e fratrem B
g om B

b *om* B
d *om* B
f pareret QX

swerved from justice, the fault was due to my own ignorance or that of my counsellors.'

It would be remiss not to mention that a man who had always disliked hypocrisy and scrupulosity did not in his last illness refuse to eat, or perhaps it would be better to say taste, meat when ordered to do so. On the advice of the doctors his friends suggested that when winter was over, he would recover more easily if he would allow his body, now chilled by quartan agues after the bouts of his fever, to be cosseted by more nourishing and sustaining foods. The archbishop there-fore commanded and enjoined upon him as he hoped for the remission of his sins to take the advice of his doctors about his diet. He, however, raised the objection that the Carthusian rule forbade meat-eating altogether and that this applied without exception not only to the healthy but also to the sick and the dying. However, not to make a long story of it, finally at the prayer of his clerks and at the order and energetic representations of the archbishop of Canterbury, supported by letters from Dom Robert, at that time procurator and later prior of Witham [1] and the monks there, exhorting him immedi-ately to obey the order of the archbishop, he consented to eat meat, which he had never tasted from his youth until now. He said to us, ' Please realise that neither my own inclination nor any hope of recovery would persuade me to eat meat. However, as I do not want to offend so many reverend persons, and still less when at the point of death not to follow in the footsteps of the One who was made obedient even unto death,[2] let meat be brought to me. Now at the last I will eat it willingly

---

[1] This prior Robert is also mentioned in the Witham chronicle fragment.
[2] cf. Phil. 2: 8

uescemur.' Sciscitantibus autem medicis quibusnam
carnibus uesci placuisset, ita respondit, ' Pedibus, si
uobis uidetur, suillis, quos infirmantibus a sanctis
quondam patribus legimus fuisse concessos.' Hos igitur
appositos, uixque primis dentibus attactos, iussit
amoueri. Similiter et de minutis uolatilibus minimum
quid gustauit.

Solebat, dum fuisset incolumis, quosdam uiros
religiosos maximeque rectores cenobiorum arguere qui,
preter consuetudinem regularem fratrum suorum, a
carnibus omnimodis ducerent abstinendum. Meminimus eum cuidam abbati abstemio talia quondam
dixisse, ' Tu,' inquit, ' frater, a quo solatium et exemplum
sumere debent subiecti tui, propter abstinentiam istam
extraordinariam in utroque peccaberis in eos. Tu *a*
ipse non delicias resecabis tibi, set mutabis et in hoc
quidem uanitatis crimen et superstitionis non facile
euadis. Tibi enim ab officialibus aut legumina peregrina
aut pisces carnibus pretiosiores, et uice sagiminis *b* uaria
condimenta, pigmentis et caris confecta rebus para-
buntur. Hoc discent exemplo subditi apposita sibi
fercula reicere et commentis cocorum nouis semper
inhiare. Qui uero nichil horum uoluerit aut ualuerit
querere, dum funditus apposita que carnes tetigere *c*
respuit, stomacho male conforato a mensis recedit.*d*
Quod dum sepius egerit, primo insompnietas, denuo
mentis torpor, postremo totius corporis imbescillitas, iam
ad omnia spiritualis uite exercitia inualidum possidebit.*e*
Quale uero solatium a te suscipere illi sperabunt qui,
diutino affecti tedio, numquam mense tue consortium

---

a + quoque X
b sanguinis od
c appositas carnes tangere X
d recedet QX
e inualidus permanebit X

with the love of my brethren as its flavouring.' The doctors then asked what meat he fancied, to which he replied ' If you recommend it, pigs' feet since I have read that the holy fathers formerly allowed the sick to eat them '. However, when it was produced, after one mouthful he ordered it to be taken away. Likewise when small birds were brought he hardly touched them.

When he was well he used to rebuke certain monks, particularly the heads of monasteries, who forced their monks to abstain from all sorts of meat, when this was not part of the rule. I remember what he said to an abbot who abstained from such food.

' Brother,' he said, ' you who should be a consolation and an example to your monks, by this unnecessary abstinence will sin against them in both these respects. You are not refusing delicate fare, but merely having a different sort and thus cannot easily be acquitted of hypocrisy and scrupulosity. Rare vegetables, fish which is much more costly than meat and a variety of sauces and highly spiced dishes will be prepared for you by your servants instead of meat. From your example your subjects will learn to criticise the food they are given, and always to long for new-fangled dishes. If unwilling or unable to get these, a man who absolutely refuses meat when it is set before him rises from table with his hunger unsatisfied. If he often does so, first sleeplessness, then torpor of spirit and finally bodily weakness will render him unfit for any of the exercises of the religious life. What relief can they hope for from you when they are well aware that to be invited to your table will be no relaxation from the dreary monotony of their daily routine ? The reason why I do not eat meat is because it is the rule of the order to which I submitted myself and

quicquam sibi recreationis allaturum certissime sciunt. Nam quod ego carnibus non utor, non tantum mei arbitrii est quantum ordinis decreti cui semel ceruicem subieci. Quamobrem et in leges suas ordo noster pauciores colligit, quia id quod ille instituerint *a* uarie complexionata multitudo non capit. Vos e diuerso, qui multitudinem regere suscepistis, sicut moribus multorum seruire iuxta legislatoris uestri sententiam debetis,[1] sic et multiplicibus eorum infirmitatibus condescendere et necessitatibus prouidere habetis.'

Et hec quidem ille dicebat. Verum de hiis sententiam uiri sapientis hoc loco preter historie cursum breuiter nos tetigisse, lectorem nostrum non pigeat, cum pariat quibusdam parum institutis non contempnendam formam necessarie discretionis.[2] Set iam que restant de boni doctoris nostri recessu a nobis, ut cepimus, explicemus.

Pridie quam migrauit a corpore, ut frequenter singulis prius septimanis consueuerat, uiaticum percepit corporis et sanguinis Christi. Sexto decimo kalendas Decembris, feria quinta, iam die aduesperascente, cum sentiret uires sibi magis magisque deficere, misit quosdam ex seruientibus ad priorem Westmonasterii, alios etiam ad decanum sancti Pauli, pro accersiendis, sicut pridem iusserat, clericis et monachis in obsequium funeris sui. Post hec, imposita diutius uertici nostro dextera sua, commendauit nos et uniuersos filios suos Deo uoce sua pene *b* suprema. Nam *c* percepta benedictione illius, diximus ei tertio, antequam uerbum aliquod ex ore eius elicere possemus, ' Rogate Dominum ut pastorem ecclesie uestre prouideat ei profuturum.' Ad quod tandem ait, ' Deus id faciat '. Hiis ab eo dictis, nudari

---

a instituit oX   *b* *om* B   *c* Nos autem Q

not because of my own wishes. Why my order has very few members is that its way of life is not intended for a large number of different temperaments. You, on the other hand, who have been set over a large community, are bound to consider many kinds of people [1] as your founder decreed, and thus it is your duty to have in mind their many weaknesses and provide for their needs.'

These are his very words. My readers should not take it amiss that I have made a slight digression in order to record the opinion on this matter of this wise man since it provides certain of the less discriminating with a very necessary golden rule not to be despised.[2] Now I shall resume my account of my dear master's departure from us.

The day before he died he received the last sacraments of the body and blood of Christ as he had earlier made a habit of doing weekly. On Thursday, November 16th when evening came he felt that his strength was waning and sent some of his attendants to the prior of Westminster, and others to the dean of St Paul's to summon the clerks and monks to perform the rites for the dying, as he had ordered some time before. Then laying his right hand for a long time on my head he commended me and all his sons to God. These were almost his last words. After I had received his blessing I said to him three times before getting any reply : ' Ask the Lord to provide a good pastor for your church '. He finally answered, ' May God so do '. After he had said this we uncovered the floor in front of him and arranged the ashes scattered over it in the form of a cross. He

[1] *Rule of St Benedict*, c. 2
[2] See Introduction, vol. I, pp. xx-xxi

fecimus pauimentum coram eo et crucis effigiem sparsis ibidem cineribus benedictis expressimus. Quam ille digitis e contra benedicens, capite demisso adorare nitebatur. Tunc, licet ab ore eius satis inuite tali hora secederemus, ne tamen minus plene die ultima diuinum audiret seruitium, cui adeo diligens studium omni pridem tempore consueuerat exhibere, ymnos qui ad complendum *a* dici solent cepimus decantare. Cumque ad illum psalmi locum ueniretur, ubi dicitur, ' Clamauit *b* ad me, et ego exaudiam eum ; cum ipso sum in tribulatione ; eripiam eum et glorificabo eum,'[1] illo ita fieri innuente,*c* expositus est in medio et cineri impositus. Psallentibus autem nobis festinantius, ille uultu placidissimo spiritum sensim colligebat, quem tunc in manus Conditoris tradidit cum Symeonis canticum psallentium chorus recitare cepit. Sicque tam prophetico quam et euangelico claruit testimonio quia tam crebro, ut prediximus, rogantem pacem sibi dari, Dominus exaudiuit. Probatum quoque et illud uerissime est quod ipse predixerat, quia dies defunctionis sue non sibi foret dies iudicii, ipsum qualibet amaritudine percellentis, set dies potius misericordie delictum omne clementer ignoscentis et gratie leniter in pace ipsum refouentis, prestante eo qui misericordiam et ueritatem eum diligere in omni uita sua fecit, quique ei gratiam et gloriam in uita et in morte sua dedit, Ihesu Christo Domino nostro, per quem gratia et ueritas facta est,[2] qui cum Patre et Spiritu Sancto uiuit et regnat, Deus benedictus in secula.*d* Amen.

---

a completorium Xp
b Clamabit vp (*&* *Vg.*)
c monente Q
d + seculorum X

raised his hand in order to bless them, and bending his head tried to genuflect. Then although we did not like leaving him at such an hour we withdrew to chant the usual compline hymns so that he who until now had . always been so conscientious about the divine office should on the last day of his life hear it in full. When we came to that place in the psalm which runs ' He shall call upon Me and I will hear him, I am with him in his tribulation, I will save him and will glorify him ',[1] at a sign from him, he was brought into our midst and laid on the ashes. We began chanting more rapidly, and he with an expression of deep peace, seemed concentrating all his forces, and when the choir began the ' Nunc dimittis ' he surrendered his soul into the hand of his Creator. Thus, prophecy and gospel were both strikingly apposite, for God heard the prayer of one who as I have related so often asked to be given peace. Another prophecy of his was also absolutely fulfilled, since the day of his death was not for him a day of judgment and dread, but rather one of mercy and of pardon for all his sins and of grace, sweetness, consolation and peace, through the assistance of the One who had caused him throughout all his life to love mercy and truth and gave him grace and glory in life and in death, Jesus Christ our Lord, the source of grace and truth [2] who liveth and reigneth with the Father and the Holy Spirit, God to be worshipped world without end, Amen.

---

[1] Ps. 90: 15
[2] cf. John 1: 17

Capitvlvm XVII

Quod multa consimiliter precesserunt et subsecuta sunt
beatorum episcoporum Martini Turonensis et Hugonis
Lincolniensis transitum.   Et alia quedam in modum
epilogi de rebus uariis Hugonis nomen contingentibus
scripta.

Cum duorum iam mensium spatio Lincolniensium
gloria Hugo artus febre iugiter, ut premissum est,
fatiscentes spiritui seruire coegisset, Martini Turonorum
gloriosi antistitis festiuitas ceperat imminere.   Huius
ille in omni uita sua cultor et emulator peculiaris
extiterat ; frequenter quoque in oratione sua *a* patroni
sui uerba usurpauerat ; omniumque uni uero Domino
hec cordis et labiorum suorum uota precator supplex
profuderat, ' Domine, iam satis est quod huc usque
certaui, et si parcis diutius anxianti, bonum est michi,
fiat, Domine de me uoluntas tua.   Cui si *b* non resultat
in hoc et uoluntas mea, fiat ut sub tempore festi domini
mei sancti Martini, optata post uarios et immensos
labores missio *c* concedatur michi.   Sub istius, si placet,
ducis et signiferi tui, o Rex glorie, festo triumphali, quo
de mundi huius principe triumpho potitus extremo ad te
peruenit, et me, licet immeritum, ad te iubeas accersiri.
Huius me, Domine, suffragiis commendatum et fultum
presidiis, a castris tuis ad palatium, a spe ad speciem
contuendam glorie tue, iubeas citius emigrare.'
    Talia non *d* semel, audientibus nobis, Hugo nec sine
multis gemitibus orando ingeminabat.   Nos quoque,
scientes quam deuota semper emulatione Martinum
coluisset, quam alacer in festiuitatum Martini celebrationibus extitisset, quam dulce habuisset uirtutes

---

a +et ipse X   *b* *om* B   *c* messio X   *d* + itaque X

Chapter XVII

The numerous coincidences preceding and following the deaths of the blessed bishops Martin of Tours and Hugh of Lincoln. And as an epilogue a description of various other events associated with the name of Hugh.

For two months now the glory of Lincoln, Hugh, had made his fever-ridden worn-out body obey the orders of his indomitable spirit when the feast of the glorious bishop, St Martin of Tours, approached. All through his life he had taken him as his special patron and model, and frequently when in prayer and supplication he had poured out aloud his whole heart to the one true God he had used the very words of his patron, which were, ' Lord, it is enough, that I have striven until this hour, yet if You spare my troubled soul for a longer time, to me it is good. Thy will, O Lord be done. If, however, my will is the same as Thine, grant that the death I long for after so many and great sufferings may take place at the time of the feast of my lord, St Martin. If it please Thee, O King of glory, command me, although unworthy, to come to Thee on that triumphant day on which my protector and Thy confessor gained his last victory over the prince of this world. Order me, Lord, through his intercession and protection to which I have commended myself, to pass swiftly from Thy camp to Thy palace and from hope to the vision of Thy glory.'

We heard Hugh frequently repeating this prayer with many tears and sighs, and remembering his emulation of and veneration for St Martin, and his eagerness to celebrate his feast, his pleasure in dwelling on his virtues and the pains he took to follow his example, we feared

Martini referre, imitari mores et studia sectari, satis
timebamus ne forte consequeretur sue *a* petitionis
effectum nosque desertos et desolatos morsibus exponeret
rapacium luporum.[1] Nec uero secus quam timebamus
euenit. Iustus namque Dominus iustitias dilexit [2] in iusto
suo et iniquitatum nostrarum meritis equitatem, quam
eis deberi uidit uultus eius, retribuit. Confisi tamen de
pietate iusti Domini, et opitulatione iusti serui sui,
uiciniora salutis demum consequi nullatenus despera-
uimus. Nam etsi ad momentum indignationis abiecit
nos, set non in finem affliget supplices suos, nec con-
tinebit in ira sua misericordias suas misericors et
miserator Dominus.[3]

Verum de tribulationum nostrarum premiis, iuste
quidem etsi minus plene iniquitatum nostrarum meritis
respondentibus, stilus interim sileat ; Hugonis potius,
ut cepit, uel barbarizando *b* triumphos explicet, narret
trophea,*c* ouationis insignia memoret. Hugonem namque Martino, de quo agimus, etsi per omnia conferre
fortassis pertimescimus, ipsum tamen ei in uita et in
morte multifaria ratione comparabilem claruisse aperte
uidemus. Quod expressius commemorare nobis quidem
non pigrum, lectori uero credimus fructuosum.

Igitur Martini ab infantia circa heremum aut
monasteria animus semper fuit, fuit et Hugonis.
Martinus in adholescentia, Hugo in pueritia, repudiatis
militaribus pompis, tyro Christi efficitur.[4] Martinus
uero ut militaret Christo, frementia militum castra
deseruit ; Hugo, ut expeditius adhereret Christo,
clericorum contubernia dereliquit. Martinus, ' signo

---

a *om* B
b ceperat . . . balbutiendo X
c + et beati Martini uirtutibus sancti Hugonis cognationis X

greatly that his prayer would be answered, and that we forsaken and desolate would be left to the attacks of ravening wolves.[1] Our fears were abundantly justified. The righteous Lord loved the righteousness of his faithful servant,[2] and inflicted on us the just retribution which he saw our sins deserved. Nevertheless, trusting in the mercy of the just God, and in the intercession of his holy servant, we do not despair of finally reaching the region of salvation. Although in his present indignation he has cast us off, the merciful and compassionate Lord will not afflict his suppliants nor continue his anger for ever.[3]

In the meantime, let my pen omit the salutary tribulations awarded to us by God, which are indeed less severe than our sins deserve, and continue to describe, albeit in homely language, the victory and triumph of Hugh and to relate and to record his spectacular success. Although I should perhaps beware of making Hugh resemble Martin in everything yet it does seem to me very obvious that there was a great resemblance between their lives and deaths. It is no hardship to me to dwell on this more fully since I think that it would edify my readers.

From their childhood both Martin and Hugh set their hearts upon either the eremetical or the monastic life, and the former in his early manhood and the latter in his boyhood renounced the glory of earthly warfare to become the soldiers of Christ.[4] Martin, however, abandoned the turmoil of barrack life to fight for Christ, whilst Hugh in order to adhere more closely to Christ left a community of clerics. Martin, without helmet or shield, but relying on the protection of the ensign of the

---

[1] cf. Sulpicius Severus, *Epistula III*, CSEL, I, p. 148
[2] cf. Ps. 10: 8   [3] cf. Is. 54: 8; Ps. 76: 10; 110: 4
[4] cf. Sulpicius Severus, *Vita S. Martini*, c. II, CSEL, I, p. 112-3 ; cf. also *supra* lib. I, c. 1

crucis, non clipeo protectus aut galea, hostium cuneos penetrauit securus ' ; penetrauit similiter armatos et Hugo cuneos euaginatos contra se uibrantium gladios, set non quidem semel, immo uicibus multis.[1] Martinus pontificatus arcem inuitus ac contradicentibus ascendit superbis, ascendit ordine pari et Hugo.[2] Martinus in conuiuio presbiterum pretulit regi superbo, sepulturam pauperum regibus regumque conuiuiis pretulit et Hugo.[3] Terrenum in diebus suis non extimuit Martinus principem, set neque Hugo.[4] Superstitiones ritusque sacrilegos longe lateque eliminauit ille ;[5] similiter eliminauit et iste. De quibus licet breuitatis gratia superius parce dixerimus, largius super hiis tractandum aliis relinquentes ; Norhamtonia tamen latronis,[6] Bercamestuda, Wicumbia et alia quedam loca fontium culturam, Hugone acriter decertante, postposuisse noscuntur. Martinus demonibus imperauit, imperauit et Hugo. Ille super falsis rumoribus et fama a demonibus septem conficta, ueritatem ab energumino studuit elicere ; iste ne phitonissa uera etiam diuinaret studuit inhibere.[7]

Martinus, quolibet pergens, oculos in celum semper figebat erectos.[8] Quod adeo mentalibus oculis agebat et Hugo, ut iter semper faciens ultra crinem equi cui insedisset rem prorsus aliquam corporeis oculis fere numquam uideret. Vnde constat quia hinc omni tempore contigerit, res quaslibet iuxta iter suum positas

---

[1] Sulpicius Severus, *op. cit.* c. IV, p. 114 ; *supra*, lib. IV, c. IV.

[2] Sulpicius Severus, *op. cit.*, c. IX, p. 118-9 ; *supra*, lib. III, c. I-IV.

[3] Sulpicius Severus, *op. cit.*, c. XX, p. 129 ; *supra*, lib. V, c. I ; Giraldus Cambrensis, VII, pp. 98-9.

[4] Ecclus. xlviii, 13 ; cf. Sulpicius Severus, *op cit.*, cc. IV, XX, pp. 114-116, 128-130.

[5] Sulpicius Severus, *op. cit.*, cc. XI-XIV, pp. 121-4.

cross advanced boldly into the ranks of the enemy, and Hugh, not merely once but on many occasions, advanced under the same protection against bands of men brandishing their naked swords.[1] Martin and likewise Hugh were unwillingly raised to the episcopate,[2] in spite of the opposition of the arrogant, and just as he at a feast served the priest before the haughty king, so Hugh esteemed the burial of the poor above kings and their banquets,[3] and neither he nor Martin showed any fear of the earthly rulers of their day.[4] Both of them also put down superstitious and magical abominations everywhere.[5] Concerning these I have said little for the sake of brevity, leaving them for others to describe, but it is common knowledge that Hugh after a bitter struggle put a stop to the veneration paid to a robber at Northampton,[6] and the offerings at streams at Berkhampstead and Wycombe and elsewhere. Martin and also Hugh were obeyed by demons. The former elicited the truth from the man possessed by seven devils who was spreading abroad lies and falsehoods, just as the latter forbade the woman with the spirit of divination to prophesy even the truth.[7]

Martin journeyed with eyes always raised heavenwards,[8] whilst Hugh when travelling was so lost in thought that he saw almost nothing beyond the mane of the horse he was riding. In fact it is well known that he never displayed the least interest in what he passed as he travelled, and like the holy man in whose biography it is

---

[6] cf. William of Newburgh, *Historia Rerum Anglicarum* (R.S.), Lib. IV, c. VIII, p. 311-2 ; for St Hugh's removal of the bones of Fair Rosamund from the choir of Godstow nunnery cf. Howden, *Chronica*, III, p. 170.

[7] Sulpicius Severus, *op. cit.*, c. XVIIII p. 127, where however there are ten (or sixteen) devils ; *Supra*, V, 8.

[8] cf. *Breviarium Monasticum*, 4th Lauds antiphon for St Martin : ' Oculis ac manibus in caelum semper intentus, invictum ab oratione spiritum non relaxabat, alleluia.'

nulla curiositate prospexisse ; set, quemadmodum de quodam scriptum legitur uiro sancto quia die pene tota secus ripam stagni cuiusdam equitans, ipsum stagnum minime uidisset,[1] ita et iste dum equitaret rem prorsus nullam nisi casu demonstratam ab aliquo oculis attendebat. Habebat iugiter ante se equitem, equuum suum precedentem et callium diuerticula que sequeretur meatu proprio premonstrantem.

Contigit interdum ut inter hos, presulem uidelicet eiusque ducem, quispiam commeantium medium immergens [a] se fortuitu, dum ad partem alteram inflecteret uectorem suum, animal pontificis de recto diuertentem tramite per deuia sequeretur. Quod ubi aduertebat preambulus eius, sepe stomachando aiebat, ' Improbe satis facit iste. En michi furatus est episcopum istum ! '

Set neque pedes uel eques, dum in uillis propriis diutius quandoque perhendinaret, delectandi seu, ut assolet, uti se res queque haberent, uisendi gratia aliquorsum pergebat, quin potius lectioni, orationi uel honestis et necessariis colloquiis uacans, euangelicum illud implere curabat, ' In quamcumque domum ingressi fueritis, ibi manete et inde ne exeatis.' [2] In aula, ubi semel finito mox prandio bibisset, nec ad momentum ulterius die illa residebat ; sumptis uero secum uiris honestioribus qui refectioni interfuissent, in cameram secedebat. Quos, dapibus ante et potibus quamlibet gratiose et splendide satiatos corporeis, splendidius tamen et gratius denuo reficiebat spiritualibus uerbis, et prolatis ex gestis aut dictis uirorum illustrium emulande probitatis atque uirtutis, pro statu audientium uariis exemplorum incitamentis.

---

[a] ingerens X

recorded that he rode for almost a day along the bank of a lake without being aware of it,[1] so he also rode without noticing anything unless someone chanced to draw his attention to it. It was customary for someone to ride just in front of his horse, to indicate any turnings in the route they were to follow by taking them himself.

Sometimes, one of his fellow travellers accidentally got between the bishop and his guide, and when the latter turned his horse another way, the bishop's mount would follow the one which had turned from the right road through byways. When the guide realized this, he used often to say angrily, ' That wretched fellow has purposely carried off my bishop '.

When he was spending a considerable time at his manors, he never went out on foot or horseback for pleasure or even, as is customary, in order to inspect his estate, but instead occupied himself with reading, prayer and edifying or necessary discussions, thus conscientiously obeying the gospel precept, ' In whatever house you shall enter there remain, and do not depart '.[2] In hall, he drank one cup after dinner, and spent no more time there that day, but withdrew to his chamber, taking with him the more distinguished of the company. These, whose bodies had already been well and abundantly refreshed by food and drink, then enjoyed an even more magnificent and attractive spiritual banquet, and were inspired by his accounts of the sayings and deeds of various types of famous men, selected with reference to his audience, to imitate their high-mindedness and virtues.

[1] This was St Bernard by the lake of Geneva.
[2] Luke 9: 4

Et in hiis quidem, immo et in aliis que enumerare
nimis longum est,[a] fuere similes sibi in uita et conuersatione Martinus et Hugo. Vnde non immerito diuinitus
actum est ut in morte quoque et in exequiarum decore,
uterque alterutri quam simillime responderet. Martinus
denique ' obitum suum longe ante presciuit, dixitque
fratribus dissolutionem corporis sui imminere,' [1] quia
indicauit iam se resolui ; hec quoque similiter prescire,
dicere et indicare datum est et Hugoni. Instante obitu,
Martinus [b] mergulos a flumine uirtute potenti uerborum
abegit ; Hugo, magna uirtute fretus meritorum, quosdam testamenti sui dilapidatores in reprobam quam
meruerant mortem, preueniens eos in maledictionibus
suis dedit. Cuius rei exempla licet historia hec preterierit,
tamen pincerne ipsius nomine Pontii exitus miserabilis,
quem Andegauis languens, tertio uenditus a predonibus,
demumque in doloribus nimiis expirans fecit, uera esse
que proferimus manifeste declarat. Possemus et de
aliis notissima huius rei testimonia proferre nisi fastidio
consulentes audientium plurima gestorum eius sub
silentio transiremus.

Hunc autem Pontium in principio egritudinis illius
grauiter apud sanctum Audomarum offendisse nouimus
episcopum, itemque Londoniis, morti iam uicinum,
tertio Lincolnie inhumane satis et auare in uenerabile
funus iam defuncti peccauit. Londoniis autem pro
superbia ipsius et contumacia, facie in faciem maledixit
ei sanctus Dei. At sanctus,[c] quia motum iracundie
usque ad labia progredi permisisset, ut delinquenti ex
malitia quamuis iuste malediceret, statim facta confessione penitentiam gessit. Quam tamen ut bene-

---

[a] *om* B   [b] *om* B   [c] + presul X
[1] Sulpicius Severus, *Epistula III*, CSEL, I, p. 147 ; cf. *supra*, lib. V,
c. XVI

In all these respects and in others which it would take too long to mention, there was a resemblance between the lives and characters of Martin and Hugh. Therefore it was only right that by God's providence their deaths, and the pomp of their funerals should be almost identical. Martin, indeed, foretold his death a long time beforehand, and informed his brethren that the dissolution of his body would soon take place, declaring that he was already dying.[1] It was also granted to Hugh to know and prophesy this. Just before his death the water-fowl left the river at Martin's command, and Hugh confident in the greatness of his own virtue and merits condemned the violators of his testament to well-deserved eternal torments, forewarning them of these by his malediction. Although this biography has proffered no examples of it, the terrible end of his steward Pons gives indubitable testimony to the truth of what I have just said. This man after being three times sold into slavery by pirates fell sick at Angers and finally died in agony. I could corroborate my statement by other notable examples if I had not decided to be silent about very many of his deeds so as not to weary my readers.

It was well known that this same Pons greatly angered the bishop at St Omer at the beginning of his illness, and also in London when death was already near at hand. Finally, at Lincoln when he was already dead his great and unnatural greed caused him to profane the venerated body. Whilst he was at London the saint of God had cursed him to his face for his presumption and disobedience, but because he had given vent to his indignation and had excommunicated his deliberately disobedient servant, although with justice, he immediately confessed and did penance, but nevertheless could not be persuaded to turn his malediction into a blessing,

dictione maledictionem sanaret, induci non potuit.
Vnde nos contristati uirum maledictionis hortari cura-
uimus ut ueniam delicti sui petere non tardaret. Set ille
pertinaciter salutis hortamenta deridens, episcopum suo
de cetero magis indigere seruitio quam se illius dominio
asserebat. Talia isto furiose prosequente, perpendere
pronum *a* fuit, quia equitas incommutabilis rationis
linguam regeret pontificis, qui licet seipsum de motu ut
putabat illicito reprehenderet, emisse tamen maledictionis iaculum quod iuste intorserat, illo perseuerante
in sua nequitia, reuocare non ualebat. Vbi et hoc
mirandum fuit quia eius pertinaciam licet absentis,
nemine indicante, per seipsum episcopus ipse cognouit.
Hic uero ex mendico omnique destituto amicorum
solatio, ad maximas excreuit diuitias in domo eius,
paulatim enim ad maiores officiorum prouectus honores,
ex puero seruientissimo iuuenis euasit superbissimus.

Set quid, ais, ad mergulos Martini, istius uel aliorum
testamenta diripientium mortuorum pertinet compara-
tio ? Multum, inquam, per omnem modum, si tamen
uerba pensentur que in auium illarum detestationem
protulit Martinus. ' Forma,' inquit, ' hec demonum
est : insidiantur incautis, capiunt nescientes, captos
deuorant, exsaturarique nequeunt deuoratis.' ¹

Peruagabant *b* totam insulam Anglicanam *c* merdi
siue mergi huiusmodi insidiantes egrotantibus, legata
ante mortem quoque testatoris rapientes set in eo quam
maxime formam sibi inducentes demoniacam quod cum
rapacem ingluuiem assiduis urgerent capturis, captis
tamen nequibant saturari. Verum Hugo beatus, horum

---

a promptum X
b Pernatabant X
c *om* B

which grieved me so much that I urged the man he had
cursed to ask immediately that his offence should be
forgiven. He, however, obstinately rejected my representations for his welfare, and asserted that the bishop
would suffer more from the loss of his services than he
himself would from losing such a master. His furious tirade
led me to believe that in spite of the bishop's repentance
for what he thought was unjustifiable anger, his rebuke had
been both just and reasonable, and that even he could
not destroy the effect of a well-deserved excommunication, when the offender remained obdurate. What was
amazing was that the bishop knew about his obstinacy
although he was not present and no-one had informed
him of it. The man from being practically a beggar,
and without any friends to help him, had acquired great
riches in his household and had risen gradually to a
position of great importance, with the result that from
being an exceptionally well-behaved boy he had become
a very insolent young man.

You will ask what has this, or the violators of the
testament of the deceased got to do with Martin's water-
fowl? I reply, that the comparison is in every respect
an apt one, if the words used by him to express his dislike
of those birds are considered. He said, ' They have the
shape of demons, who ensnare the unwary, and devour
the unsuspecting victims whom they have captured, and
are never satisfied with their prey '.[1]

England in all her coasts is haunted by this kind of
water-fowl, these birds of prey, who lie in wait for the
sick and snatch legacies even before the death of the
testator. They resemble demons especially because they
are never satisfied with the booty with which they stuff

[1] Sulpicius Severus, *ibid.*

semper more Martini aduersatus nequitiam, sepissime framea spirituali confregerat molas iniquorum et de dentibus eorum rapuerat predam.[1] Et summas post regem regni potestates ita sepe arcauerat [a] gladio Spiritus Sancti ut prone uestigiis eius prouoluerentur, ea que legatariis tulerant [b] restituere festinantes. Quorum insidias a rerum quas ipse legauerat contrectatione funesta cupiens arcere, proprio instinctu uinculo primum anathematis, ut supradictum est, illos innodauit qui tale quid ui siue fraude in ipsis rebus presumerent attemptare. Optinuit quoque tempore consequenti ut in concilio generali, quod eo uiuente adhuc apud Westmonasterium celebratum est, sollempnis innouaretur sententia anathematis, non solum in sui testamenti, immo et in cuiuslibet fraudatores legittimi testatoris.[c] Huic sententie rex ipse assensum suum, concilio cum archiepiscopo presidens, fauorabiliter acclamando dedit.[d]

Set ut et cetera de Martino et de Martini tunc famulo, nunc autem socio, sermo iste percurrat, bonam uirtutum suarum consummationem redditam ecclesie pacem Martinus reliquit ; Hugo nichilominus non solum Cantuariensi ecclesie, ut prefati sumus, set regno utrique Anglorum et Francorum, pro qua cis citraque mare pluries desudauerat, redditam pacem Martinus iste dereliquit. Martinus hinc migraturus, prope astanti [e] diabolo dixit, ' Nichil in me, funeste, reperies ; Abrahe me sinus recipiet.'[2] Nec diffidentius de se uel de suo receptu Hugo sentiens, constanter loquebatur, ' Non erit iudicii dies qua ipse defungar, set dies gratie et

[a] sepissime mulctauerat X
[b] abstulerant X
[c] testamenti X
[d] D *omits the next twelve pages*
[e] Assistenti X

their rapacious maw. Blessed Hugh, however, like Martin, always set his face against their iniquity, and frequently with his spiritual spear broke the teeth of these evil-doers, and snatched away their prey from their teeth.[1] With the sword of the spirit he often attacked the king's chief ministers with such vigour, that they fell at his feet and hurriedly restored what they had taken to the rightful heirs. Being desirous to protect his own bequests from their unscrupulous and malicious hands he, on his own initiative, as I have already related, laid his anathema on anyone who should attempt either by force or craft to appropriate them. Later, however, at a general council held at Westminster while he was still living, he got this solemn excommunication renewed, not only on his own behalf but on behalf of all those legally entitled to make wills. The king expressed warm approbation for this decree when he assented to it at a council presided over by himself and the archbishop.

To return to the other resemblances between Martin and his former disciple who is now his companion, the happy result of the holiness of the former was that he left his own church at peace, but the latter, on the other hand, by the unceasing labours at home and abroad which I have already described left not only the church of Canterbury but the two kingdoms of England and France at peace. Martin, when at the point of death, thus addressed the devil who was standing by him, ' Wretch, you have no hold over me, Abraham's bosom will receive me '.[2] Hugh felt much the same about himself and his reception, when he said confidently, ' The day of my death will not be for me a day of judgment,

---

[1] Job 29: 17
[2] Sulpicius Severus, *ibid.*, pp. 148-9

misericordie.' Vbi enim quid suum improbus ille exactor reperit, non permittitur immunis emigrare ad requiem alieni retentor debiti, citra agitationem equioris iudicii.

Ad puritatem uero et decorem funeris Martini, quibus et in morte ostensus est gemma sacerdotum,[1] id Hugoni ad funeris gloriam peculiariter auctum *a* est, ut uitro sicut Martinus purior et lacte candidior,[2] rosis quod de Martino tacetur uernantior, hominum innumeris millibus ostenderetur. Set de hoc inferius planius dicetur. Nam de pompa funeris eius quid digne dicemus ? Si de occursu monachorum et uirginum referre temptemus, neuter quidem sexus *b* uel ordo Hugoni defuit ; set numerus forte et multitudo, ratione locorum, huic inferior uel breuior quam Martino fuit. Verum si quid in hiis gradibus Hugo a Martino minus habuit, id ei supernus arbiter in dignitatibus potioribus suppleuit. Nam ut de inferioribus quos pre multitudine dinumerare nemo poterat taceamus, Hugonis funeri *c* aut sepulture interfuere archiepiscopi tres, presules quatuordecim, abbates amplius quam centum, comites plurimi, reges duo. Non enim contentus fuit prediues *d* Retributor ille bonorum, militis sui insignissimi tropheum regis solummodo Anglie et optimatum eius obsequiis adornari, nam et meritis eius hic honos impar extitisset. Qui etenim in exteris sepe nationibus officium sepulture peregrinus ipse indigenis studuerat exhibere, dignum certe fuit ut eius sepulturam non modo domestici et indigene, immo et externi et alienigene suis obsequiis perornarent. Et hoc quidem, iubente Domino, ei

---

a actitatum X   *b* *om* B
c funus B   *d* eternus X
[1] cf. *Breviarium Monasticum*, 10th Matins responsory for St Martin : ' Vivit in Christo gemma sacerdotum '.

but of grace and mercy '. Where, however, that harsh creditor finds anything belonging to himself, his debtor is not allowed to die in peace free from the fear of a just retribution.

The whiteness and brilliance of Martin's dead body, which showed him, even in death, to be the pearl of priests,[1] was reflected with much enhanced splendour by Hugh's. Like Martin's, it was clearer than glass, whiter than milk,[2] and—a thing we are not told of Martin's— redder than the rose, when it was shown to many thousands of people as I shall describe more fully later on. The grandeur of his funeral defies description. If I should mention the concourse of monks and nuns, although no sex or order was absent in Hugh's case, their number, owing to different circumstances, was possibly less than in Martin's. If, however, in this respect Hugh was inferior to Martin, the supreme Judge made it up to him by the presence of persons of higher rank. Hugh's funeral was attended by three archbishops, fourteen bishops, over a hundred abbots, many earls and two kings, not to mention a multitude which no-one could number of humbler folk. The munificent Rewarder of the righteous was not content that the triumph of His most valiant knight should only be graced by the attendance of the king of England and his magnates, for even this honour would have fallen short of his deserts. It was certainly fitting that one who as a stranger in a foreign land had so often made it his task to bury its inhabitants, should at his own funeral receive the homage not only of the natives of the country but also of foreigners. God indeed ordained that this should happen. Although the

---

[2] Sulpicius Severus, *Epistula III* (interpolated text), CSEL, I, p. 149 and note 19 ; cf. also F. M. Powicke, *The Life of Ailred of Rievaulx* (N.M.T.), p. 77.

adimpletum est. Verum istud etsi ad condignum uideretur sufficere pro exigentia factorum eius, set pro uoluntatis eius deuotione minus a condigno penitus extitisset si non a plurium quam ipse umquam ingressus fuisset regionum populis illud sibi munus rependeretur. Proinde, superna disponente clementia, preter Anglos, Normannos, Francos, Burgundiones seu aliarum quas ipse uidisset terrarum accolas, Sclaui quoque, Scoti et Hybernienses atque Galwedi celitus mandatas funeri eius detulerunt excubias. Nam Yberniarum unus et Sclauiarum archiepiscopus alius, cum principe Galwedie et Scotorum rege,[1] funebribus ei post agnitam eius migrationem ex more celebratis, demum funeri eius, in urbem Lincolniensem humeris suis, cum aliis magnatibus, ipso quoque rege Anglorum et archipresule Cantuariorum deportando, longius extra ciuitatem obuiam processerunt. Bis quoque officium quod pro nuper defunctis exsolui consueuit, in matrice basilica, ipsi uel pro ipso, cum tanta gloria Lincolnie solutum est ut, astante clero et populo cum nobilium infinita multitudine, lectiones soli episcopi uel archiepiscopi legerent, responsoria quoque uniuersa, iunctis sibi et aliorum graduum sublimibus personis, antistites precinerent uersusque decantarent. Quod tunc primo fecerunt quando ipsum obisse audiuerunt, iterumque sub presentia corporis eius, ubi in ecclesiam suam perlatum fuit, hoc idem facere addiderunt.

Verum hec interim de glorificati hominis gloria, qua glorificauit illum Dominus in uita et in morte sua transitoria, breuiter dicta sint ad laudem et gloriam sempiterne maiestatis Dei et hominis Ihesu Christi, qui cum Patre et Spiritu Sancto semper est et ubique in sanctis suis mirabilis. Cuius preconiis in conspectu omnis carnis magnifice accrescit ex eo [a] quod sanctos

---

[a] *om* B (*two words*)

former tribute might have been an adequate recognition of his actual deeds, only that of the peoples of regions he had never visited was sufficient recompense for the devoted spirit which had inspired them. Thus divine Providence so arranging it, in addition to the English, Normans, French and Burgundians and the inhabitants of the other lands he had visited, by a heavenly decree Slavs, Scots, and men from Ireland and Galloway kept vigil by his body as their final offering. An Irish and a Slav archbishop, the king of Scots and the prince of Galloway,[1] after his death was known and the customary funeral rites celebrated, met his body, which the king of England and the archbishop of Canterbury with the other magnates bore on their shoulders into the city of Lincoln, a long way from the city, and joined the procession. The usual rites for the lately dead were twice celebrated for him in the cathedral of Lincoln with great pomp, in the presence of a great crowd of clergy, nobles and people. Only archbishops or bishops read the lessons, and the prelates chanted all the responses and verses in conjunction with the most important personages of the other orders. They did this for the first time immediately after receiving the news of his death, and repeated it again over his dead body after it had been brought to his cathedral. I have given a preliminary and cursory account of the honours God vouchsafed to his saint during this transitory life and at the time of his death, for these redound to the praise and glory of our eternal and almighty Lord, Jesus Christ both God and man who together with the Father and Holy Spirit is

---

[1] The archbishop of Dublin was John Comyn (1182-1212) ; Bernard, archbishop of Ragusa from 1189, was in exile in England and became administrator of Carlisle in 1203 ; the king of Scotland was William the Lion (1165-1214).

suos, locis temporibusque plurimum distantes, fide tamen
et deuotione indissimili ^a ei famulantes, meritis et premiis
facit consimiles ; cuius regnum et imperium ^b inuariabile
permanet in secula seculorum.[1]

Capitvlvm XVIII

De trium uisionum reuelationibus, Hugonis glorie
astipulantibus.

Anno igitur gratie millesimo ducentesimo, sexto ^c
octauarum beati Martini die, breui interuallo post solis
occasum, ueri solis imitator, amator Martini, Lincolniensium lucerna Hugo,^d luci huius seculi ualefaciens,
solem adiit qui nescit occasum. Senario quippe uite
huius laboriose uiriliter exacto, requies illum eternalis
sabbati ueraciter excipiebat, octaua beate resurrectionis
feliciter numerandum. In cuius rei non incertum
argumentum, preter miraculorum signa que illius
obitum e uestigio subsecuta sunt, uisionum etiam
reuelationes plurime innotuerunt, ne suo Martino uel
in hac parte glorie Hugo uideretur inferior. Quis uero
non miretur ipsarum quoque uisionum seu reuelationum
modum consimilem, ut nec discors qualitas esset in rerum
signis, ubi tanta fuit parilitas in rebus ipsis ? Ne autem
imperitia nostra, que in ceteris doctissimum uite Martini
scriptorem nequit imitari, ab eius tamen uestigiis in

---

^a indissolubili X
^b cuius regnum est et imperium in secula seculorum. Amen. X
^c *om* B
^d + sexagenarius, annis pontificatus sui ter quinis et quinquaginta octo
diebus exactis, X

always and everywhere glorified in his saints. His name is greatly magnified in the sight of all flesh because he has given to his saints, who whatever their period or region have served him with the same loyalty and devotion, the same fame and reward, and his reign and kingdom shall remain unchanged for ever and ever, Amen.[1]

Chapter XVIII

Three visions revealing and testifying to the glory of Hugh.

In the year of grace 1200, on the 6th day of the octave of blessed Martin, shortly after sunset, the follower of the true Sun, and the disciple of Martin, Hugh the lantern of Lincoln, bade farewell to the light of this world and departed to the Sun which never sets. After sixty years of valiant endurance of the trials of this life, he was to enjoy the true repose of the eternal Sabbath and blissfully to be enrolled amongst the elect at the octave of the resurrection. Besides the miracles which took place immediately after his death, many visions completely corroborate the truth of this statement, lest Hugh's glory in this respect should appear less than his beloved Martin's. The resemblance between these visions and revelations should cause no surprise, for when their lives were so alike their miracles should be closely similar. Although owing to the insufficiency of our talent we

---

[1] Possibly this was the original conclusion of the whole work ; cf. Introduction, vol. I, p. xxi.

numero scribendarum aberret uisionum, tres tamen [a] sicut et ille suis, ita et nos nostris lectoribus duximus exponendas.

Harum uero prima, nocte illa quam ipsius transitus proxime subsecutus est, certo quodam casus imminentis presagio, superna clementia cuncta pie disponente, uni eorum qui secum positi erant preostensa est. Quam ille mane facto sociis manifestans, ea que in sollempnes exequias opus erant, die ipsa, medicis qui aderant sub-sannantibus et obiurgantibus eum, sollicitius studuit preparare. Nam phisici sanitatem ei usque in horam uite ultimam uitamque spondebant longiorem.

Erat autem huiusmodi uisus. Videbat, et ecce in uiridario quodam, parieti domus contiguo in qua iacebat episcopus, se putabat constitisse. Erat loci situs huius-modi. A parte boreali et ab occidua regione domorum septis claudebatur, ab oriente et austro cingebatur fossato, cui ex parte altera pomerium, ex altera cimi-terium adiacebat. Ipsum quoque fossatum dumis et uepribus succrescentibus obsitum erat. Ab ipso igitur parietis loco ubi caput lectuli episcopi decumbentis erat innexum, pirus proceritatis nimie et pulchritudinis immense, longe ultra illius uiridarii spatium porrecta uidebatur corruisse. Cuius uastum decorem decoramque uastitatem ille uehementer admirans, talia intra se cogitando tractabat : 'Quis umquam tam pulchram conspexit pirum ? O quanta nobilis materiei iactura erit,[b] si hoc in loco abdita putrescat speciosissima arbor ista, ex qua diptice tot possent excidi quot totius Anglie siue Gallie studiis scolasticis quiuissent sufficere.' Dum hec secum sopitus corpore set corde sollicitus ille pertractat, supposuisse lacertos stipiti iacenti repente se

***

[a] tantum X
[b] erat B

cannot copy the learned biographer of St Martin in any other respect, nevertheless we judge it right to follow his example and give our readers an account of three visions.

The first of these which was shown to one of those who was then with him on the night before his death, was certainly sent by the divine mercy which governs all things as a forewarning of an approaching doom. When the dawn came he related it to his companions, and during the day, in spite of the mockery and rebukes of the doctors in attendance took care to prepare what was necessary for the last rites. Even to the last hour of his life, the doctors guaranteed that he would recover and live for some time.

This was the vision. He saw, and thought that he was in a garden adjoining the wall of the house where the bishop lay. The situation was like this. On the north and west the garden was enclosed by the walls of houses, and on the east and south the boundary was a ditch, and on one side was an orchard and on the other a cemetery. The ditch was blocked by an undergrowth of thorns and briars. By the wall against which the head of the bed of the sick bishop had been placed was a remarkably tall and beautiful pear tree, which seemed to have fallen and to lie at full length far beyond the area of the garden. Being greatly impressed by such great beauty laid in ruin he thought to himself : ' Who can ever have seen such a magnificent pear tree ? What a terrible loss of fine timber if this splendid tree should decay whilst concealed in this spot, for enough writing-tablets could be cut from it to supply all the scholars of England and France.' Whilst his body rested and he was revolving such thoughts anxiously in his heart, he suddenly saw himself place his arms under the fallen

uidebat. Cuius dum molem leniter agitando per-
temptat, totum confestim lignum summa facilitate ab
imo subleuatum in brachiis, quasi ponderis penitus nil
haberet, huc illucque a se circumferri miratur. Interea
subito ramusculi eius ab ipso stipite deciderunt ; ipse
uero medius uectis, planus et enodis, in gestantis ulnis
permansit.

Cuius rei miraculo ille stupefactus pariter et iocun-
datus, sopore mox deposito, huiusmodi *a* cordi suo im-
pressam uisionis repperit coniecturam, ut etiam labiis et
ore talia secum loqueretur, ' Reuera in breui moriturus
est homo iste ; ipsum enim demonstrauit arbor hec
fructifera atque pulcherrima.' Que merito ad austrum
collapsa iacebat, iuxta illud uiri sapientis, ' Lignum in
quamcumque partem ceciderit, siue ad austrum siue ad
aquilonem, ibi erit.'[1] Siue enim ad amenitatem paradisi
homo ducatur, cum cadit in mortem, siue rapiatur ad
horrorem tartari, ibi erit ; quia inter Abrahe sinum et
infernum chaos magnum firmatum est, ut alterutrum
semel ingressus transire ad alterum siue transmeare
ulterius non possit.[2] Est namque inextinguibilis ignis
ille in quem mittitur arbor excisa que non facit fructum
bonum.[3] Que uero aliquando non desinit facere fructum,[4]
transplantatur super aquas ut estum nesciat, ut folium
non exuat, ut firmis imperpetuum radicibus subsistat.

Et talia quidem iste de sacramento uisionis sue se ad
presens intellexisse mane retulit quibus dignum duxit
ex sociis. Quid uero facilis illa arboris subleuatio
portenderit, non prius ad liquidum agnouit quam ista *b*
de uita illius atque uirtutibus ita, minus licet accurato,
facili tamen stilo digessit. Quecumque enim libellus
presens de uerbis aut gestis eius excerpta continet, ita pro

a huius QX
b *om* B

tree. On trying cautiously to move its immense bulk, he found to his amazement that he could lift it in his arms, and carry it about anywhere as easily as if it had almost no weight. In the meantime the branches fell off the trunk, and the main beam was left in his arms, planed and without any knots.

This miracle equally astounded and delighted him, and after he woke up, he found the dream had made so vivid an impression on his mind that he was repeating to himself out loud, ' He will certainly die very soon, for that fruitful and beautiful tree was himself.' Its fall southwards was appropriate, for according to the words of the sage, ' Wherever the tree falls, whether to the south or to the north, there it shall remain.'[1] When a man dies, whether he is conducted to the joys of paradise, or to the torments of hell, there he stays, for between Abraham's bosom and the infernal regions there is a great gulf fixed, so that once having entered either of them it is impossible to leave it or cross to the other.[2] The fire is moreover inextinguishable into which is cast the tree which is cut down because it bears no good fruit.[3] The perennially fruitful tree [4] on the other hand is transplanted beside the waters where it shall never wither or lose its leaves and where it shall remain rooted fast for ever.

In the morning he described to those of his companions whom he deemed worthy, his vision as far as he then understood it. The significance of the ease with which he lifted the tree was not clear until he had written this homely but unpolished account of his life and virtues. The selection in this little book must be

---

[1] cf. Eccles. 11: 3
[2] cf. Luke 16: 22-26
[3] cf. Matt. 3: 10
[4] cf. Jer. 17: 8

magnitudine uirtutum operumque uiri sancti estimanda
sunt ut frondes exigue facileque decidue ad uastissime
arboris conferri putentur robur immensum. Set neque
ad ea que memorie ista scribentis inseparabiliter de
magnalibus tanti uiri inserta, eius semper pectori
coherentia circumfert, hec ipsa que membranis tradidit,
aliter ualent comparari quam si leuium sarmentorum
fasciculos contiguis celo abietibus cedrisue sublimissimis,
quis duxerit conferendos.

Hec autem, licet peccatori hominumque indignissimo
de transitu uiri iusti preostensa sint, tamen quia funeris
eius obsequio profuerunt,^a cuius etiam rei gratia tantum-
dem innotuisse talia prescire non merenti noscuntur, illi
de Martini obitu reuelationi conferri apte merentur, qua
presulum sanctissimus Ambrosius, ad deferendum
exequiis ^b ipsius debite commendationis officium, celitus
meruit informari.[1] Nam et inter cetera ad similitudinem
frondium quos uiderat ab arbore mistica decidisse,
uniuersos pilos corone illius et barbe, ungues etiam pedum
et manuum, diligenter exscidi fecit et radi, postquam
uespere sequenti in mortem carnis cecidit idem dilectus
Domini.

Iam uero uti Martinus, postquam Seuero Sulpicio
cum libro uite sue reuelatus est, celos continuo uisus est
iter suum insequente discipulo eius Claro penetrasse,[2] ita
uiro ^c omnifaria laude dignissimo Ricardo Norhamtonie
archidiacono, ipsa qua decessit nocte demonstratur et
Hugo, per uiam speciosi tramitis et ardui ad regale
conuiuium properare. Qui cum miraretur in sompnis
curnam tantus pontifex contra morem iter illud solus

---

^a prefuerat X
^b obsequiis X
^c uero B

considered in relation to the amazing holiness and mighty works of this saintly man as a few faded leaves in comparison with the huge trunk of an immense tree. What the author has set down in writing about this astounding personality bears the same resemblance to the memories treasured in his heart as a bundle of light faggots does to the magnificent branches of a fir or cedar reaching almost to the sky.

This revelation concerning the death of the saint although made to a sinner and the most abject of men, owing to its significance in connection with his funeral, for which reason such matters have sometimes been revealed to the unworthy, merits comparison with the heavenly forewarning of Martin's death which enabled the most holy of bishops, St Ambrose, to make the right commendation at his burial.[1] Moreover, the leaves which he saw had fallen from the tree might symbolize the hairs round his tonsure and beard and his finger and toe nails which the man beloved of God had ordered to be shaved and pared the evening after his death.

Just as Martin after he had appeared to Sulpicius Severus with the book of his life was seen by him immediately to be caught up to heaven, with his disciple Clarus following him on his journey,[2] so on the very night of Hugh's death he was shown to Richard, archdeacon of Northampton, a man in every way highly esteemed, ascending rapidly along a brilliantly lighted path to the banquet of the King of Kings. In his dream whilst he was wondering at a bishop of such preeminence taking the unusual step of going on a journey

---

[1] cf. Gregory of Tours, *De Miraculis S. Martini*, lib. I, c. V (P.L. 71, 918). In reality St Ambrose had already died some months earlier (cf. *Analecta Bollandiana*, XXXVIII, 1920, p. 30).

[2] cf. Sulpicius Severus, *Epistula II*, CSEL I, p. 143

et incomitatus iniret, uidit repente unum ex capellanis
ipsius nomine Robertum, aliquantulum remotius
uestigia eius subsequentem.   Idem autem uir cui
ostensa sunt hec, tribus ferme diebus a loco aberat unde
episcopus ad mense celestis conuiuium meruit accersiri.
Predictus uero Robertus cognomento de Capella, satis
erat mansueti lenisque ingenii ; preterque ceteros mores
optimos quibus preditus fuit, quibuslibet afflictis erat
compatientissimus, cunctis uero in commune affabilis
et benignus ; fuerat quoque in orationibus et psalmis
deuotus admodum multumque assiduus.   Hic ea tempestate qua hec gesta sunt, Lincolnie morabatur.   Qui post
domini sui et magistri Hugonis episcopi decessum, nescio
quota die, acri febre correptus, ipsa die qua corpus
pontificis Lincolniam, ut inferius dicetur, intrauit ibidem
tumulandum, et ipse corporeis nexibus absolutum
spiritum *a* reddidit, in conuiuio Regis eterni epulis
immortalibus fruiturum.   De quo et illud memorasse
iuuat quia iugiter cum ad mensam resideret episcopi,
hospitum et aduenarum precipua illius animo cura fuit,*b*
quibus etiam remotius interdum discumbentibus fercula
mittebat et uina que illis credidisset sibi appositis
gratiora.   Super quo elemosinarius ei sepe infestus erat,
set frequenter obiurgatum numquam uidit emendatum.

De quo sane elemosinario, quia se mentio oportune
ut credimus obiecit,*c* rem obliuioni non tradendam
breuiter pagine nostre duximus inserendam.   Functus
est idem uir officio elemosinarii in domo episcopi omni
tempore ab exordio pontificatus sui usque ad unum
semis annum ante presulis excessum.   In quo strenuum
satis indigentium se procuratorem ostendit, prudenter
quibus et *d* quantum erogandum esset perpendens,

---

a + celo X   *b* om B
c quia merito optime, ut credimus, prefato Roberto se obiecit X
d om B

alone and unaccompanied, he suddenly saw Robert, one of his chaplains following a little way behind. The man who had the vision was almost a three days' journey away from the place where the bishop received his well-deserved summons to the heavenly feast. The Robert I have mentioned, who was surnamed de Capella, was a man of great sweetness and gentleness, and in addition to the other good qualities for which he was well known, had great compassion for suffering and was in fact kind and friendly to everyone ; he was moreover very fervent and devout over his prayers and over the recitation of the offices. At the time of these events, he was living in Lincoln. Some days after the death of his master and patron, bishop Hugh, he had a violent attack of fever, and on the very day that the body was brought to Lincoln for burial, as I shall relate later, his soul released from its earthly bondage departed to enjoy the delights of the banquet of the Eternal King. For the sake of edification it should be mentioned that he, when he dined with the bishop, took special pains to look after guests and strangers, supplying them, however far off they were sitting, with the dishes and wines he thought would most please them. This practice greatly enraged the almoner, whose frequent expostulations were, however, completely ineffective.

This allusion to the almoner seems to me most opportune, since I think I ought briefly to describe an incident connected with him which should not be forgotten. The office of almoner in the bishop's household was held continuously by the same person from the beginning of his episcopate to eighteen months before his death. He was exceedingly conscientious in his treatment of the needy, considering carefully who should be the recipients of his alms and how much each of them

fideliterque et deuote quod perpendisset impendens.
Qui tandem egritudine preuentus extrema, Hugonis
ministerio ultima institutionis Christiane percepit sacramenta. Nec multum post hec, episcopus consistens in
quodam municipio suo quod Lafford nuncupatum est,
uidit in sompnis se constitisse secus cellulam in qua
fratrem Morinum, hoc enim uocabulum uiro fuit,
reliquerat infirmantem. Qui introspiciens, columbam
niue candidiorem cernit ab angulo in angulum passimque per domum huc illucque uolantem et quasi exitum
anxie inquirentem. Quod ubi aliquamdiu miratus
aspexit, a sompno excussus surrexit iussitque paratos
adduci equos ut obuiam pergeret funeri fratris Morini,
quod de Stowa ubi exanimatum fuit ad Brueriam
depositum erat transferri ut sepeliretur ibi. Erat enim
idem Morinus de ordine militum Templi, eratque
Brueria quedam mansio insignis illorum subiecta ditioni.
Dum igitur sternuntur equi, et episcopus prime hore,
cum clericis suis quos fecerat accersiri, ymnos celebraret,
adest repente nuntius qui elemosinarium nocte media
indicat expirasse. Tunc episcopus quid uidisset et quia
ob ipsum uisum suum solito maturius surrexisset,
presentibus intimauit. Distabant ab inuicem Stowense
manerium, ubi ille obiit, et castrum Laffordense, ubi
eius obitum ex premissa reuelatione agnouit, fere milibus
uiginti. Aduenit autem obuius funeri ad locum memoratum, quod ibidem, pro requie fidelium diuinis ante
celebratis officiis et hostiis immaculatis,[a] deuotus huius
muneris executor Hugo sepeliuit.

Et hoc quoque incidenter retulimus, preter seriem
instituti tractatus quem prosequi ceperamus, in omnibus

---

[a] immolatis X

ought to receive, and showed great care and devotion in putting his decisions into effect. During his last illness Hugh administered the last sacraments of the Church to him. A little while later when the bishop was at Sleaford, one of his townships, he dreamed that he saw himself standing just outside the cell in which he had left brother Morinus, for this was the man's name, sick. Looking in he perceived a dove whiter than snow flying distractedly about the room from corner to corner as if desperately trying to find the way out. After he had looked at it with some surprise for a little while, he awoke and getting up ordered his horses to be saddled and brought round, so that he could meet the corpse of brother Morinus, which was being taken from Stow where he had died to Temple Bruer for burial. Morinus had belonged to the order of Knights Templars, and Bruer was one of their chief preceptories. Whilst the horses were being got ready and the bishop and his clerks whom he had summoned were chanting the Prime hymn, a messenger unexpectedly arrived to tell them that the almoner had died at midnight. The bishop then told the company what he had seen which had caused him to get up earlier than usual. The manor of Stow, where he had died, and the castle of Sleaford, where, through the vision I have described, his death had been made known to Hugh, were almost twenty miles distant from each other. He went to the place I have already mentioned to meet the body, and after the office and masses for the faithful departed had been duly celebrated, devoutly performed the task of burying it.

This digression from the main theme of our work is intended entirely for the reader's edification and not as a demonstration of the talent of the writer. It is moreover

hiis edificationem potius lectoris quam periti scriptoris
gloriam aucupantes ; in quo tamen a materia cepte
narrationis eo minus recessimus quo a funere ad funus,
ad uisionis reuelationem a consimilibus uisionibus
digressi sumus.   Set iam auxiliante Domino, ea que
parumper omisimus celerius explicanda repetamus.
Visionum igitur predictarum conspectores Seuero
Sulpicio sanctoque Ambrosio consimilia uidisse probantur.[1] Iam uero restat ut reuelationi beato Seuerino
Colonensi archiepiscopo de Martini gloria celitus
insinuate, aliquid non dissimile in medium proferatur,
quo ipsius sequipeda[a] Hugo olim preeuntis Martini
uestigiis irremote doceatur, ut in uia quondam laboris
ita et in tramite adeunde iam beatitudinis adhesisse.

Elapso siquidem post felicem eius transitum breui
temporis spatio, huiusmodi de Hugone cuidam suorum
ostensa est uisio.   Putabat se in quadam constitutum
basilica uastissime magnitudinis cum infinita populi
multitudine, prenuntiato sollempniter Hugonis episcopi
Lincolniensis aduentui suum prebuisse occursum.   Qui
dum repente inter eos media in ecclesia affuisset, tante
dulcedinis cantica circa eum audiri ceperunt ut in terris
nichil umquam eque iocundum et delectabile auditum
fuisse omnibus uideretur.   Horum uero, necnon et
eorum que inferius dicenda sunt auditor atque narrator,
ut turbam que confluxerat indefessis conatibus penetrauit, eminus episcopum quasi in lectica palliis olosericis
mirifice adornata iacentem uidit, que in medio basilice
substratis late per pauimentum tapetibus admirandi
decoris uisa est constitisse.   Subleuabat iacentis ceruicem

[a] sequipedo B

not really irrelevant to our narrative since we have proceeded from one death to another and to one vision from
very similar ones. Now, with God's assistance, we will
resume where we left off a little while ago in order to
finish quickly. The resemblance between the visions of
these men, and those of Sulpicius Severus and St
Ambrose has been shown,[1] and it now only remains to
describe one which is not unlike that seen by blessed
Severinus, archbishop of Cologne, of St Martin glorified
in Heaven. This will prove that just as Martin's
disciple Hugh had formerly during the toils of this life
taken him as his model in all things, so in his departure
to eternal bliss he followed the same path.

Shortly after his happy death one of Hugh's attendants had a similar vision. He thought he was in a huge
church where a great congregation had assembled, and
that he had come there to meet Hugh, bishop of Lincoln,
whose arrival had just been solemnly announced. When
he suddenly appeared among them in the centre of the
church, he began to hear a canticle of such great beauty
that they all agreed that so sweet and delightful a melody
had never been heard on earth. The man who saw and
narrated this and other matters which will be described
later, having pushed his way with great determination
through the surging crowd, saw the bishop some distance
from him, lying on a bed covered with costly silken cloaks
which seemed to be placed in the middle of the church,
the floor of which was covered with exceptionally fine
carpets. His head rested on a large cushion made of

---

[1] Gregory of Tours, *De Miraculis S. Martini*, lib. I, cc. IV-V, P.L.
loc. cit. (p. 211).

ceruical amplissimum, quod ex purpura et bisso, coccoque
bis tincto et iacintho satis operosa fuerat contextum.¹

Qui postquam intuentem se discipulum suum nec
propius accedere presumentem, clementi intuitu et ipse
conspexit, erecto capite in ipso gestario uisus est residere
ipsique discipulo, dextere manus indicio, ut ad se
ueniret innuisse. Quod turba circumposita que eminus
constiterat, nec loco appropiare quo ille iacuerat ᵃ
presumebat, mox ut aduertit, quasi ad salutandum eum
propius irrumpere festinauit. Quorum ille uelud
accessum interim declinando, capite reclinato in speciem
repausantis ᵇ menbra composuit. Tunc popularis
frequentia, importunum ei suum ad presens sentiens
accessum, retrocessit, seque ut prius in loco remotiori
reuerenter cohibuit. Turba quoque secedente, is etiam
qui accersitus fuerat, dans locum quiescenti, gressum
quo ad ipsum uenire ceperat fixit. Ipse uero secessisse
populum confluentem aspiciens, relicto gestario,ᶜ in
pedes se contulit, iterumque accersiens quem prius,
manu sua dextera leuam ipsius tenuit. Dehinc longius-
cule uersus altare quod eminus situm erat, ipsum
deducens, ei talia dixit, ' Noui ᵈ te sollicitum super statu
meo gerere animum, quamobrem te potissimum ut ea
que te mouent aperires accersiui. Tu nunc que te
sollicitant incunctanter proferre non differas.' Tum
ille, ' Hoc, domine, uotis omnibus antepono, hoc solum
pre ceteris omnibus nosse concupisco : qualiter uobis
ab hora recessus uestri a nobis actum sit, singulariter
audire desidero. Deinde quenam sint suauissima
cantica ista que tante dulcedinis melos auribus instillant
nostris, edoceri preopto.' Erat enim sonus canentium
mellifluus, uoces consimiles, uocum tamen discrimina
mira quadam uarietate distincta. Ad hec uero duo
unicum ille dedit responsum, ' Cantica,' inquiens, ' hec,

ᵃ iacebatX   ᵇ pulsantis B
ᶜ gestatorio X   ᵈ Non decet X

purple and fine linen in which scarlet and blue threads had been cunningly interwoven.[1]

He looked benignly upon his disciple who was watching him but not daring to approach any nearer, and then appeared to raise his head and sit up in his litter, making a gesture with his hand to invite him to come to him. As soon as the crowd, which surrounded him and had not ventured to draw near to the place where he lay, saw this, it rushed forward to greet him. He, however, as if disliking their nearness, lay down and stretched out his limbs as if about to go to sleep. The mob of people, realising that their proximity at this particular time was distasteful, withdrew and kept a respectful distance as they had done before. When the crowd retired, he, although he had been summoned, stopped at the place from which he had started in order not to disturb him. The bishop, seeing that the multitude had withdrawn, left his litter and stood up, and then after beckoning to him as he had done before, took hold of his left hand with his right. Whilst conducting him to the altar which stood a great way off, he spoke to him thus, ' I know that your heart is troubled about my state for which reason especially I have summoned you to enable you to speak freely with me about your fears. Do not be afraid but tell me frankly everything that is troubling you.' He replied, ' My chief wish, my lord, and what I desire especially to know and more than anything else to hear is how it was with you from the moment of your departure from us. Then I should like to learn what is this delightful melody which sounds so sweetly in my ears.' The sound of the singing was melodious, and the voices of the singers very much alike, yet they sang exquisitely in parts. He gave one answer

[1] Exodus 26: 1

ab hora illius quem dicis recessus mei a uobis, numquam michi defuerunt.' Quibus uerbis ita inquirenti satisfactum est ut de statu ipsius post mortem ultra nichil adesse posset tristitie ubi carmina tante letitie audiri potuissent.

Quiddam uero ab eo sciscitari studuit, unde plurimorum sepe inquisitionibus ipse tamquam pre ceteris episcopo familiarissimus pulsari consueuerat. Ait ergo, ' Domine, a pluribus referri audio, unde et mea sepius astipulatio flagitatur, cum ab ore uestro nil certum acceperim, quia uidelicet uobis quodam tempore sacra misteria celebrantibus, corpus Dominicum in specie uisibilis infantis in manibus uestris, contuente id uobiscum quodam clerico, monstratum sit et uisum.[1] Vnde et animus meus crebra stimulatur penitentia, quia os uestrum super huius rei ueritate *a* non interrogaui, cum totiens uobis adeo familiariter locutus fui.'

Hiis ille auditis ita uoce placida respondit, ' Etsi tunc, quando dicis, et alias frequentius hoc michi Dominus reuelare dignatus est, quid inde tibi uis ? '

Cum ad hec nec ille plura diceret nec amplius super hoc sermone iste eum percunctari auderet, adiecit ei confiteri cuiusdam formidinis scrupulum, qui eius ab annis puerilibus animo insederat, et dicebat, ' Quia domine, media uita in morte sumus,[2] dum mortis quandoque uenture ymaginem mentis conspectui sepius represento, horrore quodam immenso totus perfundor. Dum enim cogito quia a rebus cognitis ad eas quas nescio rerum species subito rapiendus, per illos etiam quos ignoro a notis omnibus abducendus sum, non sinor confusionis magne fluctibus non inuolui et tedii cuiusdam abysso funditus absorberi. Super huius uero

a ueritatem X

to both questions. ' From the time when you say I left you, I have never ceased to hear these melodies.' This reply completely satisfied the questioner that his state after his death must be one of absolute bliss, since he could hear the joyous songs.

He was also anxious to ask something about which he was always being questioned owing to his intimacy with the bishop. He therefore said ' Sir, I have heard it said by many persons, and I am often asked to confirm it though I have never learned the truth from you, that once when you were celebrating mass a clerk who was with you saw the body of the Lord in your hands in the likeness of a little child.[1] I have frequently reproached myself for not asking you whether it was true, since I have had so many opportunities of speaking with you in private.'

After hearing his request, the other quietly replied : ' What concern is it of yours, if on the occasion you have mentioned and on very many others, the Lord vouchsafed to manifest himself to me in this way ? '

He said no more about the matter, nor did his interrogator dare to question him further, but went on to confess to him a fear which had haunted him since his boyhood, saying, ' Sir, since in the midst of life we are in death,[2] why does a boundless horror overwhelm me whenever I picture my death to myself, as I often do ? When I think that I shall be snatched away from the world I know into the unknown, and taken by strangers away from my friends I cannot prevent myself from being utterly overcome and sunk in an abyss of despair and despondency. This terrible fear has begun to

---

[1] cf. *supra*, lib. V, c. iii
[2] The opening words of a Responsory for Lent and Septuagesima

incommodo, inordinato *a* ut bene iam sentire cepi
tormento, consilii uestri ope satis indigeo.' Ad hec ille
beneficus semper interpellantium se consultor responsione breui amplum contulit poscenti remedium,
'Tantum,' inquiens, 'sollicitus sis ante mortem bene
uiuere, et sollicitudinem eorum que mortem sub-
sequuntur Domino relinque.'

Hiis dictis, qui loquebatur, cum uisione memorata
repente disparuit. Qui uero hec uiderat et audierat,
gaudio plenus, de sompno excitus, super tribus articulis
supra memoratis ita sibi satisfactum medullitus quodammodo sensit ut omnem post hec dubietatis et timoris
scrupulum quoad predicta radicitus a suo pectore
auulsum esse, ipse quoque mirari consueuerit Deoque
et sancto ipsius famulo deuotas gratiarum actiones pro
tali consolatione indesinenter studeat referre.

Capitvlvm XIX

De multiplici decore funeris ipsius et de curatione
eiusdem. Et de hiis que obiter usque Lincolniam circa
corpus acciderunt. Necnon et de occursu regum duorum
et aliorum sublimium uirorum innumerabilium, qui
portando feretro humeros certatim supponebant.

Set iam tempus est ut celo receptum pro parte
potiore Martini pedissequum, terre quoque pro inferiore
sui portione monstremus commendatum. Qui licet hoc
gemino arcente receptorio, terra uidelicet et celo, uideri
a nobis ultra non possit, nobis tamen ille non deerit,
sicut ex premissis uisionum indiciis patuit, si amore
sequamur quo sequendum se docuit. Set nec solum

---

a incommodi inordinato X

torment me so much that I badly need your help and counsel.' The wise counsellor who never failed those who craved his assistance, in a few words provided the questioner with the remedy he needed. He said, ' Be anxious only to live well before you die, and leave the care for what shall follow after death to God.'

When he had said this, the speaker and the vision I have described immediately vanished, and he to whom it had been granted awoke full of joy, being so completely reassured about the three matters I have mentioned that all his doubts and fears in regard to them were absolutely and miraculously dispelled, for which great favour he always gave hearty thanks to God and his holy servant.

CHAPTER XIX

Concerning the grandeur of his funeral and the ceremony displayed at it and concerning the incidents which took place round his body on its way to Lincoln, and how it was met there by two kings and a host of other distinguished people, who vied with one another for the honour of carrying the bier on their shoulders.

It is now time to relate how after the immortal part of Martin's disciple had been taken up into Heaven his mortal remains were committed to the earth. Although this double reception into paradise and into the earth prevents us from seeing him any longer, yet, as the visions already described prove, he will not forsake us if we follow him with that love with which he taught us he must be followed. Indeed, he showed that he would never desert not only us who were his friends on earth but any of those who followed him with faithful hearts.

nobis quondam peculiariter suis, immo nec quibusque
fideli amore sequentibus se umquam defuturum ipse
ostendit ; qui mox celo receptus, terre uero necdum
commendatus, miris uirtutum insigniis eis se docuit
presentem et uiuentem, qui mortuum eum lugebant,
flebantque ueluti sibi absentem.   De hiis aliqua inferior
loquetur pagina.

Igitur, prout supra docuimus, postquam sub pacis
cantico pacis amator et reformator Hugo in pace in
idipsum obdormiens in Domino requieuit,[1] paucis suorum
astantibus, commendationis officium ei paruitas nostra
qua potuit deuotione exsoluit.[a]   Hinc ad lauandum,
sicut ipse disposuerat, corpus eius manus indignas
apposuimus.   Quod ubi nudatum est, supra quam credi
posset mundum multoque nitore conspicuum apparebat.
Ablutum uero et diligenter extersum pontificalibus
induimus insigniis.   Interea reuersi, quos ipse ut diximus
ad celebratores exequiarum suarum accersiendos desti-
nauerat, septem uel eo plures monachos et clericorum
copiosam adduxere [b] multitudinem.   Ab hiis tota ipsius
noctis spatia in ymnis et canticis spiritualibus expen-
duntur, posito in ecclesia sacro corpore et illis per girum
uotiuas excubias frequentantibus.

Celebratis in crastino missarum sollempniis, de
consilio medicorum, cum id penitus fieri non oportere
alii sentirent et assererent, exta corpori eius, quod
longius ad sepeliendum portari debuit, auferuntur.
Que in eadem ecclesia Beate Marie ad Vetus Templum
in uase plumbeo recondita et secus altaris crepedinem
sub lapide marmoreo honeste reposita, gloriosum
rediuiui corporis sui templum expectant, sub magne [c]
resurrectionis tempore feliciter subeundum.

---

[a] persoluit X   [b] deduxere Q ; adduxerunt X   [c] maxime Q

He had scarcely been received into heaven, and his body was not yet buried when wondrous cures showed those who wept and mourned for him as dead and absent that he was alive and present. Some of these I shall describe below.

When, as has already been described, Hugh the lover of peace and the peacemaker, being at peace with himself and God,[1] fell asleep in the presence of a few of his attendants, we performed the office of commendation as well and devoutly as our numbers permitted. After this my unworthy hands washed his body as he had directed. When I had stripped it its cleanness and whiteness were almost unbelievable. I carefully washed and dried it and arrayed it in its episcopal vestments. In the meantime, those whom, as I have mentioned before, he had sent to summon the persons who were to celebrate his exequies, had returned bringing with them seven or more monks and a large number of clerks. His body was laid in the church, and these forming a circle celebrated in turns the vigils of the dead, passing the whole night chanting hymns and spiritual canticles.

Solemn mass was celebrated on the morrow, after which by the advice of his doctors and in spite of strong opposition from others who felt that it was wrong, his bowels were removed from his body because it had to be taken a long distance for burial. These were placed in a leaden casket and honourably interred under a marble slab near the altar steps in the Temple church which is dedicated to the blessed Mary, there to await their reunion with his glorified body on the joyous day of the final Resurrection.

---

[1] cf. Ps. 4: 9

Hec autem licet inaniter et superflue quoad hominum prouidentiam gesta fuisse, ipsis mox uisceribus patefactis claruerit, diuinitus tamen ut ita fieret dispositum extitisse ad gloriam Dei qui semper est in sanctis suis [a] admirabilis, ad honorem quoque eiusdem serui sui uaria post hec ratione [b] innotuit. Et quidem tunc, ubi manu cirurgica ipsa interaneorum [c] secreta patuerunt, inuenta sunt nichil superflue collectionis, nil prorsus concreti, ut assolet, humoris intra se retinentia, set tali quodam purissimo nitore prelucebant ac si plurima cuiuslibet hominis diligentia abluta essent et undique purgata.

Erat profecto istud mirabile in oculis intuentium, set apud quosdam leuigabat pondus miraculi cum abstinentia temporis tanti uis dissenterie, qua diebus aliquot ante mortem uexatus, eius impetu credebatur ita potuisse funditus exinaniri. Quod tamen qualitercumque factum sit, hoc dicere ueraciter licet : quia exterius quidem lacte candidior, intus uero et extra uitro purior, corpore quoque monstratus est suo similis Martino, ut merito et ipse dici debeat in hac etiam parte ' gemma sacerdotum '. De cuius mirabili decore inferius loco competenti plura dicentur.

Conditum autem multis aromatibus a dormitionis sue loco Lincolniam eum ad sepeliendum cepimus transferre. Non est autem necesse, quia nec possibile nobis foret, fletus et gemitus occurentium undique describere populorum. Ciuitatis Londonie clerus et populus procul extra urbis menia cum crucibus et cereis feretrum prosecuti sunt. Ob iter [d] uero per agros et uillas uterque sexus, omnis conditio, gradus et ordinis cuiuscumque, in fines suos uenientibus obuiam confluebant sacri funeris portitoribus. Tetigisse feretrum palma

[a] om B   [b] narratione B   [c] internorum oV ; + uiscerum X   [d] obitum Bo

Although the precaution had appeared from the human standpoint quite unnecessary, once his bowels had been uncovered it was patent that God who is always magnified in his saints had ordained that this should be done for his own glory and that of his saint. When the hand of the surgeon made his internal organs visible no water or stool was found, and they were as clean and immaculate as if someone had already carefully washed and wiped them.

Those who saw it regarded it as amazing, though certain made light of the miracle, declaring that the abstinence, and the violent attack of dysentery which had troubled him for some days before his death would have acted as a purgative. However this may be, it can at least be truly asserted that his body resembled Martin's in that the outer skin was whiter than milk, and both it and the internal organs shone like glass, so that in this respect he can rightly be called ' the pearl of priests '. More will be said about its amazing beauty later on at a more opportune place.

Sweet spices were used to embalm his body, after which we began the journey from the place where he had fallen asleep to Lincoln where it was to be buried. It is neither necessary nor possible to describe the immense display of grief by the multitudes who met us everywhere. The clergy and people of London with crosses and candles attended us for a long way beyond the walls of the city. Everywhere whether in the villages or the open country, immense crowds of persons of both sexes, and of every rank, class and profession, collected when

suprema fuit. Quibus id negabatur pre constantium [a] turbarum multitudine, uel eminus adorasse et conspexisse non uile tropheum ducebatur.

In ipso itinere per iuge quadriduum, uno cotidie repetito uel potius continuato miraculo sanctum suum mirificauit Dominus. In manibus siquidem puerorum equitantium cerei quatuor iugiter ardebant, quos in morem facularum sub diuum expositos, nec uentorum spiramina nec interdum guttis densioribus rorantia nubium stillicidia extinguere preualebant. Pueri nunc ab equis descendentes, nunc cum uehementi impetu sellas uacuas reascendentes, cereos tenebant quos ignis inter hec non deserebat. Stupebant et pre admiratione in uoces exclamantium [b] prorumpebant, hec intuentium multitudines, asserentes nec inter manus clausum lumen a se teneri posse inextinctum. Vbi nullo contutati [c] uelamine, set Dei solius freti uirtute, flagrare non cessabant cerei, naturam propriam dediscente per merita sancti triplicis qualitate elementi. Flatus quippe aereus, humor aquaticus et splendor igneus triumphanti Christi militi iurata dependebant [d] obsequia.

Preter sacratiores uero aliorum de tantis omnipotentis Dei magnalibus sententias, hoc interim simplicium fidei commendasse sufficiat ; quia non immerito ipse tam iocundo luminis honore decoratus apparuit, qui ad decus matris ueri Luminis perpetueque Virginis, consueta ecclesie ipsius luminaria adiectione admodum numerosa cumulauit. Lincolniensi namque thesaurarie amplos in hoc ipsum assignauit redditus, ut ampla tante edis immensitas paribus propemodum inter nocturna officia cereorum micaret fulgoribus, ut interdiu radiis renitescebat solaribus.

[a] stipantium X ; constipantium Q   [b] exclamationum Q ; clamantium X
[c] concutati O ; contecti X   [d] impendebant X

the body was carried through their region. Everyone's great ambition was to touch the coffin, and those who were unable to do so on account of the mass of people surrounding it felt it no mean achievement to have seen and venerated it from some distance away.

On this four-days' journey, God glorified his saint each day by a miracle which was repeated or rather lasted all the time. The lighted candles carried by four servants on horseback, although exposed like torches to the air were extinguished neither by the strong winds nor by occasional heavy rain. When they dismounted, or hastily remounted their horses, they held the candles, which still remained alight. The crowds perceiving this broke into cries of amazement, asserting that even a flame protected by a person's hands would normally have been put out. That these candles without any shades, should through the power of God continue to blaze, was due to the change in the nature of three of the elements by the merits of the saint. Thus, air, water and burning fire did homage and fealty to God's victorious saint.

Whatever may be the other explanations given by scholars of this amazing miracle wrought by almighty God, this one should suffice for the faith of ordinary people, namely that these lights were an apt and just testimony to the glory of one who out of devotion to the mother of the one true light, Mary ever-virgin, had so greatly increased the number of lights in her church. He had assigned a large annual revenue to the treasury at Lincoln for this purpose, so that in spite of the immense size of the church the light of the candles during the night office was almost as strong as the light of the sun by day.

Crepusculo diei secunde postquam iter agressi sumus, ad uillam iuris episcopi Lincolniensis, Bikeleswad nuncupatam deuenimus. Vbi dum circa feretrum plangentium accolarum se turba conglomerat, in ipso ecclesie introitu qua per noctem illam uenerabile corpus quiescere debuit, hominis cuiusdam brachium ita confractum est ut crepitum ossis patientis fracturam illi etiam qui remotius constiterant clarius audirent.   Erat autem nomen uiri, qui etiam adhuc superesse dicitur, Bernardus. Quem sui ab ecclesie foribus semianimem rapuerunt et ad domum propriam delatum usque in mane patientie operam dare petierunt, tunc ei pollicentes subueniendum ope medicorum.   Sic ergo nec saltem colligatus nec quouis medicamine fotus, fracture adeo moleste locus plurimam noctis partem in doloribus magnis eum pertrahere coegit insompnem.   Qui demum in tenuem resolutus soporem, mox uidet episcopum brachium suum manibus piissimis contrectantem, dataque benedictione, a se post paululum recedentem.   Ceterum recessu indulte uisionis, collate benedictionis uirtus non recessit. Euigilans namque a sompno, ita penitus omni fugato dolore, os consolidatum et brachium sanatum inuenit, ut precedentem potius fractionem quam curationem subsequentem, per sompnum se suscepisse putaret.

Quarta profectionis dieta Stanfordiam uenimus. Ibi, dum agmine denso populi frequentia stipatur circa feretrum, et hinc uirginum Deo sacrarum [a] e uicino monasterio chorus,[1] inde circumiacentium uillarum accole populosis ipsius burgi turbis accrescunt, uix ante profunde noctis tenebras uicum ipsum ingredi ualuimus.

[a] sacratarum Xp

At twilight on the second day of our journey, we came to Biggleswade, a vill belonging to the bishop of Lincoln. At the entrance to the church where the saint's body was to rest for the night, the crowds of weeping villagers round the bier was such, that a man's arm was broken, and the noise made when the bone snapped was distinctly heard even by those who were some way off. The sufferer, who is said to be still alive, was named Bernard. He was carried by his friends half dead out of the church to his own home, where they besought him to try and be patient until dawn, when they promised that he should have the assistance of doctors. As the broken limb was not set, and no medicine was available to give relief, the fracture was so painful that he spent most of the night sleepless and in agony. When at last he fell into a light sleep, he saw the bishop touching his arm with his venerable fingers, who left him after a little while, having given him his blessing. The vision faded but the benefit of the benediction he had received did not ; for when he woke the pain had departed and he found that the bone had been set and that the arm was completely healed. Indeed, he felt that he had dreamed of the fracture and not of its cure.

On the fourth day of our journey we reached Stamford. There the dense mass of people round the coffin was swelled by a band of nuns from a neighbouring nunnery [1] and by the inhabitants of the surrounding villages in addition to the crowds from Stamford itself. As a result of this we were only able to enter the town

---

[1] The Benedictine convent of St Michael in Stamford was founded c. 1155 for forty nuns : it is mentioned in a charter of St Hugh, MS. DD Queen's College, Oxford, no. 286.

Istic uero, per merita serui sui tale Dominus miraculum patrare dignatus est, ut hoc mortuorum resuscitationi nemo iure dubitet preferendum.

Interfuit tanto occursui quidam uir innocentis uite bonisque per omnia studiis deditus, arte sutoria sibi sueque familiole uictum queritans. Hic, eminus conspecto glebe preciosissime gestario,^{a} cum accedere niteretur set pre turbarum densitate parum nitendo proficeret, multis audientibus in uoces huiusmodi prorupit, dicens, ' O bone Deus, quare non permittor ad optimi serui tui corpus accedere, ut uel fimbriam palliorum quibus tegitur osculari merear uel capud meum indignissimum sacris eius supponam reliquiis? O scrutator renum et cordium,[1] Ihesu Saluator benignissime, in hoc solo ^{b} desiderium meum adimple, ut feretrum quod conspicio corde et corpore prono ualeam subire, et sic de huius mundi colluuione animam meam tolle.'

Talia clamitans, nisibus indefessis, turbis quoque ad clamores eius attonitis paulatim cedentibus,^{c} immersit se sub feretrum tandem. Quod postquam attigit, et capite submisso adorauit, oculis et manibus in celum erectis, in hunc modum orare cepit, ' Gratias ago tibi, Pater misericordiarum et Deus totius consolationis,[2] quia misertus es mei, et in tantum consolatus es me ut, quod in hoc mundo super omnia concupiui, corpori sanctissimo serui tui corpus meum tot peccatis obnoxium quiuissem adiungere et ei qui fideliter seruiuit tibi meruissem approximare. Deprecor igitur te, omnipotens Deus, ut in hac nocte animam meam cum anima istius, cuius me corpus adire fecisti, in requie perhenni, ubi eam esse non dubito, iubeas collocari '. Hiis ab eo ita peroratis,

---

^{a} gestatorio oX ^{b} solum X ^{c} secedentibus Q

late at night. There, through the merits of his servant, God deigned to work a miracle, unquestionably even more remarkable than the raising of the dead.

In that immense crowd was a man of singular integrity and purity of life who maintained himself and his family by working as a tailor. He, having seen afar off the bier with its most precious dust, tried to approach it but with little success owing to the size of the crowd. In the hearing of many he expressed his feelings in this manner : ' Blessed God, why do you not permit me to draw nigh to the body of your holy servant, so that I may be allowed either to kiss the fringe of the cloths which cover it, or bear these holy relics upon my head ? Jesus, merciful Saviour, who knowest the inmost desires of all hearts,[1] grant me this my only wish which is that I can support this bier which I behold with both body and heart, and then take my soul away from this wicked world.'

Such was his prayer. His repeated efforts and ejaculations so amazed the crowd that it gave way little by little and at length he threw himself under the coffin. After he had reached it he reverently bent his head and then raising his eyes and hands towards Heaven, prayed saying, ' I give thee thanks, Father of mercies and God of all consolation,[2] that Thou hast had compassion on me, and consoled me so greatly, by allowing me what I desired above everything else in this world which was to be permitted to approach and touch with my corrupt and sinful body the body of Thy most holy and faithful servant. I therefore beseech Thee, Almighty God, that this very night Thou summon my soul to be with his soul whose body You have allowed mine to approach in the

[1] cf. Ps. 7: 10
[2] cf. 2 Cor. 1: 3

nos cum sancto corpore ecclesiam, in qua pernoctandum fuit, ingredimur ; ille suos subintrat penates, una sola strata interiacente, eidem ecclesie pene contiguos. Nec mora : irrumpunt uicini eius in ecclesiam, presbiterum turbatis uocibus inquirunt, repertum ad domum uiri, sumpto secum sacre communionis uiatico, celeriter properare compellunt. Quod ille in extremis iam positus, premissa confessione, percepta absolutione testamentoque legittime confecto, mox ut percepit, spiritum in pace emisit.

Habuerat uero sanctus in usu familiari, dum ad-uiueret, ut cum audiret quosdam intemperantius lugere quemcumque mortuum, inter alia consolationis uerba diceret eis, ' Et quid est istud quod agitis ? Per sanctam nucem ' (sic enim uice iuramenti ad firmationem uerbi interdum loquebatur), ' per sanctam,' inquiens, ' nucem, nobiscum male nimium ageretur, si mori numquam concederetur.' Miraculosam quoque mortuorum susci-tationem laudibus efferebat, set uiuorum ex hoc seculo miraculose aliquotiens factam ereptionem potius at-tollebat ; ut Petri subdiaconi [a] atque notarii beati pape Gregorii, et cuiusdam penitentis de quo agitur in miraculis sancti martiris et episcopi Proiecti, plurimorum quoque monachorum, ut legitur in uita beati Gemmeticensium abbatis Aichadii, necnon et illorum septem dormientium qui fuerant consobrini sancti Martini patroni Hugonis nostri.[1] Istorum seu et aliorum huiuscemodi dormi-tionem, quorumdam excitationi a mortuis censebat preferendam.

---

[a] dyaconi X

[1] For Peter cf. J. Mabillon, AA.SS. OSB saec. I, p. 497 ; for the miracles of St Prejectus, AA.SS. Boll., Jan. t.III, pp. 246-9 ; for St Aicard of

eternal rest where I know he assuredly is.' After he had finished his prayer, we carried the venerable body into the church where it was to remain that night, and he went to his house which was almost next door, there being only a street in between. Almost immediately, his neighbours rushed into the church, asking anxiously for the priest, whom they forced to go at once to the man taking the holy oils with him. He was already at the point of death, and after making his confession and receiving absolution, and making his will, his soul departed in peace.

During his lifetime, it was the saint's habit when he found people inconsolable in their sorrow for anyone's death, to say amongst other words of consolation, ' Why are you acting in this way ? By the holy nut,' an expression he used occasionally instead of an oath to make his words more emphatic, ' by the holy nut, it would be very hard for us if we were never permitted to die.' Although our Hugh spoke with admiration of the miraculous raising of the dead, he reserved his highest commendation for the occasional miraculous removal of the living from this world, as for instance of Peter the subdeacon and secretary of blessed Pope Gregory, and of a repentant sinner which is described amongst the miracles of St Proiectus, bishop and martyr, and of a large number of monks in the life of St Aicard, abbot of Jumièges, and of the Seven Sleepers, the kinsmen of his patron St Martin.[1] He thought their falling asleep and similar cases more edifying than examples of the raising of the dead.

Jumièges (whose feast was kept in some English monasteries), AA.SS. Boll., Sept. t. V, p. 101 ; for the Seven Sleepers of Tours, Gregory of Tours, *Vita Septem Dormientium*, P.L. 71, cc. 1107-18, especially 1116. In each case the prophecy of an unexpected death was fulfilled a few days later.

In hoc igitur miraculo a Martini sui uestigiis non recessit, set eius potius consors et sodalis apparuit ; dum ille septem, sub unius diei momento a uita mortali ad immortalem gloriam cognatos suos accersiuit, iste, uni quem fides sua et deuotio dignum fecit, aditum paradisi interuentu suo clementer aperuit. Hec quoque miracula eo stupenda quo rariora sunt,[1] eoque magis sunt appetenda quo probantur utiliora. Quis enim nescit utilius circa istum agi, qui beate mortis compendio miserabilem uitam, mortique sub sorte ancipiti semper esse obnoxiam euadens, ad uitam euolat mortis et miserie semper ignaram, quam circa quemuis alium, meritis reuocatam cuiuscumque sancti a tranquillitatis sinu feliciter quiescentium, ad repetendos uite huius erumpnose labores iamque euicte mortis experiendos rursum agones ? Talia igitur de hiis uir sanctus et sapiens sentiebat, qualia et ipse modo circa deuotum et ueridicum perhennis sue quam optinuit requiei testem et assertorem exhibebat.

Et hec quidem omnia sub ipso momento quo et gesta sunt, memorie pariterque intelligentie nostre, de dictis preteritis gestisque presentibus, presentis uite contemptoris et future amatoris Hugonis, occurrebant. Set iam et ut cetera que restant prosequamur, hoc in loco procuratores nostri lanternas corneas emerunt in quibus per diem candele iugiter circa feretrum lucerent. Cerei namque, motibus uariis equitantium et impulsibus uentorum irruentium exagitati, a facie ignis deuorantis nimium defluebant, manusque et indumenta gestantium continuis distillationibus molestius infundebant.

Set quia pretermissis duabus mansionibus, duas tantum alias, in quibus a Londoniis digressi requieuimus,

---

[1] cf. St Augustine, *Tractatus XXIV in Joannem*, P.L. 35, 1593

The miracle I have just described was no departure from the footsteps of St Martin, but an instance of their close resemblance to each other, for whilst the latter in the space of one day summoned his seven kinsmen from this transitory life to everlasting glory, the former by his intercession mercifully opened the gates of paradise to one individual as the reward of his faith and devotion. Such miracles are the more wondrous because of their infrequency,[1] and are the more to be sought for because of their obvious value. Who can deny that a person who by means of a holy death is removed from this wretched world, where the threat of death is always present, to a world where death and suffering are unknown, is better off than one who through the merits of some saint or other is recalled from the happiness of those resting in peace to the trials of this life and a second experience of the agony of death? Such was the opinion of the wise and holy man on this subject, which he put into practice for the benefit of this devout soul who bore such emphatic witness to his eternal rest.

All these things, at the very moment at which they happened caused us to remember the past sayings of Hugh, who had despised this world for love of the life to come, and to compare them with his present acts. To proceed now with what remains to be told. Our agents bought in that town lanterns of horn, for the candles which burned continuously throughout the day round the bier, for the movements of the riders and the strength of the winds caused the wax to melt so much owing to the fierceness of the flame, that the grease considerably injured the hands and garments of those who carried them.

My pen has passed over two of our halts and has described only two stages where we rested on our way

iam calamus expressit, cum in omnibus par nobis humanitas, summus uero sacro funeri honor delatus sit, uniuersas nunc breuiter et seriatim exprimemus, in quibus a Londoniis usque Lincolniam pernoctauimus. Prima igitur nobis cum monachis Heritfordensibus mansio fuit, secunda in Bikeleswald, tertia in Bugkedena, maneriis scilicet episcopalibus. In hiis tot eiulationibus *a* indigenarum et lamentis excipiebamur, ut meminisse horror, scribere uero superfluus labor sit. Metationem quartam Stanfordia, quintam *b* nobis Anacastria prefixit. Hinc miliaria bis dena computantur usque ad ciuitatem qua eramus uenturi.

Ad quam sexta profectionis die iam cominus aduentantes, cum ad descensum montis uno pene miliario extra urbem accederemus, obuios habuimus cum inestimabili multitudine cleri et populi, regem Anglie et regem Scotie, archiepiscopos, episcopos, principes,*c* abbates et proceres, quot uix umquam in Anglia pariter ante conuentum illum *d* contigit inueniri. Rex Scotie pre merore, quia nimis semper dilexerat uirum illum, in parte seorsum stans nec propius accedere ualens, lacrimis uacabat, cum sentiret magis esse gaudendum si rationem uis doloris admitteret.[1] Reliqui magnatum cum rege Anglorum humeros suos *e* supponunt oneri non ignobili. Nec parum sibi successisse gaudebat quisquis sua menbra illius corpori portando aptare meruisset, cuius merita obsequentium animas et corpora sustollere ad celestia et ab omni clade leuare potuissent.

a eiulatibus QX
b + mansionem X
c *om* B
d *om* B
e *om* B

from London, and although everywhere equal kindness was shown to us, and the greatest veneration for the holy body, I will merely record briefly and in order where we spent the nights between London and Lincoln. On the first night we stayed with the monks of Hertford, on the second at Biggleswade, on the third at Buckden, both of which were episcopal manors. The inhabitants of these received us with such a terrific display of grief that it is an unnecessary affliction to revive the tragic memory by writing about it. Our fourth halt was at Stamford and our fifth at Ancaster, which is reckoned to be about twenty miles from the city to which we were bound.

On the sixth day of our journey we were already near, and when we arrived at the foot of the hill almost a mile outside the city, we were met by the kings of England and Scotland, the archbishops, bishops, magnates, abbots and nobles and an immense crowd of clergy and people, such as had scarcely ever been seen in England before this gathering. The king of Scotland who had a deep affection for Hugh, was so overcome that he could not approach the coffin, but remained behind weeping bitterly, although if his sorrow had been less intense he would have realised that he had more cause for rejoicing.[1] The king of England and the rest of the magnates raised the illustrious load on to their shoulders. It was no small matter of congratulation for anyone to be granted the privilege of carrying the body of one whose merits could save from destruction the souls and bodies of those who rendered him this service and secure their admission into the kingdom of Heaven.

---

[1] St Hugh had escorted William to Canterbury when he came to do homage to Richard I in 1189, and had probably met him at the Council of Marlborough in 1186 (cf. Diceto II, p. 72). St Hugh's funeral is described with slight variation of detail by Giraldus, Diceto, Howden, Wendover etc. Adam was of course an eye-witness.

Capitvlvm XX

De scriptoris intentione qui ista digessit. Et quia
pontifex sanctus, delatus cum magna gloria in ecclesiam
suam, ibi subito facie immutata rubicundus apparuit.
De tribus que antequam sepeliretur ibidem patrata sunt
miraculis. De loco sepulture eius. Et de regis mitiga-
tione erga Cistercienses ob gratiam eius.

Sincerus rerum arbiter, in quo equitas iudicii uiget,
in litteris sacris non tam elucubrati sermonis ambitum
quam fructum utilitatis commendat. In causa scribentis
etiam quo affectu quoue instinctu articulos duxerit, non
quo atramento aut cuiusmodi chalamo scripturam
exarauerit, diligenter examinat. Id ipsum et nos, cum
diu iam uindemiando botros suauissimos uinee Domini
Sabaoth, uinee Soreth,[1] ueluti ad extremos peruenimus
antes,[a] te magnopere exoratum esse preoptamus, quicumque libanda duxeris ea que presenti libello, ac si
fructum saluberrimum uili insertum cartallo, tibi
presentamus. Nec modo qualiter sermonem dispositum
sensumue digestum reperierit, prudens et beneuolus
lector attendat, set potius quid utilitatis ex hiis que
imperite digessimus, reperire desideremus expetat.[b]
Nouerit nos imprimis Christi amore impulsos ut scri-
beremus,[2] meminerit subinde famuli sui honori, patrum
uenerabilium iussioni deferendo et fratrum plurimorum
piis petitionibus annuendo, arduo nos scribendi periculo
commisisse.

Nec tanti nobis constat hic iam consummati,
auctore Deo, laboris nostri prouentus, quo diutius hec in

---

[a] *Dimock's emendation.* aures B ; annos X   [b] eum perpendat X

CHAPTER XX

The writer's reason for this biography. How when our bishop was borne with great pomp into his cathedral, his pale countenance suddenly became ruddy. An account of the three miracles which occurred there before his interment, and the place of his burial and the king's concessions to the Cistercians out of devotion to Hugh.

The honest and fair-minded critic does not value the words of Holy Writ as much as its sense, and considers carefully the purpose and motives of the writer rather than the ink and pen he wrote with. I, who after gleaning the sweetest grapes for so long in the vineyard of the Lord of Hosts, the vineyard of Soreth,[1] have now come to the last row, make the same request of my readers, if anyone thinks it worth while to sample what he is offered in this book let him consider it as health-giving fruit in a cheap container. The discerning and well-disposed reader must not only notice the language and construction of the work but what is more important seek to learn the lessons which I desire to impart in my simple biography. Let him consider that my first motive in writing was love of Christ.[2] I would also remind him that it was only out of veneration for his servant that I yielded to the prayers and commands of many of his brethren and their venerable superiors and consented to undertake the arduous task of writing his life.

I value the work which with God's assistance I have now completed too little to wish it to remain for long in the form in which I have written it. Instead my dearest

---

[1] cf. Apoc. 14 : 18 ; Is. 5 : 2
[2] Sulpicius Severus, *Vita S. Martini*, c. 27, CSEL I, p. 137.

eo quo digesta a nobis uidentur optemus schemate permanere. Quin potius, sicut de innumerabilium passionibus gestisque sanctorum olim factum gaudemus, ut ea que prisca simplicium ruditas illepide conscripsit, nouorum eruditio elegantiori stilo illustrauerit, ita et de presenti opusculo quamtocius fieri in summis desideriis habemus. Tunc primum uotis successisse nostris ad plenum merebimur gloriari, cum ad Dei gloriam et laudem serui sui ea uenustate qui lecturus accesserit hec edita susceperit, ut rebus reuera gloriosis ignobilis carecter et inglorius minime obsistat, quominus in illum qui in sanctis suis gloriosus est, deuotione cordis et imitatione operis feliciter proficiat. Licet uero et alia suppetant innumera de uiro beato, cui omnia et opera et uerba in cognoscentibus et obseruantibus ea semper prosperabuntur, que fidelibus innotescere beneficio litterarum opere pretium constaret, nostre potissimum cure fuit ea que nobis, gratia familiaritatis ulterioris pre cunctis quos iam superesse nouimus, de illo comperta sunt et liquidius intimata, in unum uel aggerem, necessariam comportando materiem, futuri temporis impendio [a] quodammodo 'preparasse, non autem constructionem ipsius fabrice, insigniori opifici merito reseruandam, nobis usurpasse.

Igitur sicut dicere ceperamus, dum portando funeri tot se magnorum humeri uirorum certatim summitterent, ut nullius persone in globo tante multitudinis delectus esse potuisset, rex tandem et archiepiscopi siue episcopi ante urbis ingressum, pretiosam quam ferre susceperant, aliis quodammodo uiolenter diripientibus eam portandam cesserunt margaritam. Ita quibus uirium prestantior magnitudo feretrum subeundi copiam parauisset,

---

[a] impendia X

wish is that some more competent writer may soon
reshape this biography in a more literary form, a fate
which I know to my joy has befallen very many early
and badly written lives of saints and martyrs. My ardent
desire for the glory of God and the renown of his
saints would be fully realised, if I could truly say that
the would-be reader had my material so attractively
presented to him that a magnificent theme was not
spoiled by a poor and homely presentation of it, with the
happy result that the example of its subject would inspire
in him a heartfelt devotion to the One who is glorified
in his saints. Although it would certainly have been
exceedingly profitable to have committed to writing for
the benefit of the faithful very many other details about
this saintly man whose every word and deed was always
an inspiration to those who heard and saw them, my
chief aim was to limit myself to matters which owing to
my closer intimacy with him than anyone alive at present
I alone knew, or was fully informed of. My purpose was
merely to collect the material and make it available for
the labours of future generations, but not to undertake
the task of constructing an edifice, which should be left
to a more skilled architect.

As I was saying, so many distinguished people jostled
one another with such determination in order to have the
privilege of carrying his corpse on their shoulders, that
no choice was possible in so dense a throng. At the
entrance to the city, the king and the archbishops and
bishops yielded the precious pearl which they had been
carrying to the others who were determined to take
their place as its bearers. Those whose greater physical
force had secured for them the opportunity of carrying
the bier advanced triumphantly, some supporting it on
their shoulders and others with their hands. Their

nunc scapulis nunc manibus illud contingentes, gaudio pleni incedebant. Nec diutius tamen tripudio tali potiebantur. Repente enim ab aliis explosi, predam suam nouis raptoribus cedere compellebantur ; totoque itinere illo usque ad ecclesiam, quod non breui spatio tenditur, per singula fere momenta nouis noui succedebant baiulis baiuli ; nec numero pari, set tot erant portitores quot machina grabati admittere quibat *a* accedentes. Set nec alii quam sublimes uiri et preminentes istis se conflictibus inserere presumebant. Ita per plateas ex hyemalium proluuio aquarum luto altissimo plenas incedebant, frequenter suras, sepe etiam genua ceno immergentes. Qui accedere cominus non ualebant, nummos superiaciebant arche que corpus incluserat ; protensisque manibus eminus adorantes, sancto sese deuotius commendabant. Iudei quoque lugentes et plangentes ac uerum magni Dei famulum eum extitisse conclamantes, occursu pariter et fletu obsequium quod poterant ei impendentes, illam circa uirum Dei impletam esse sententiam nos aduertere compellebant qua dicitur ' Benedictionem omnium gentium dedit illi Dominus.' [1]

Sonantibus itaque per uniuersas totius urbis ecclesias classicis, cum ymnis et canticis spiritualibus sue tandem infertur gremio ecclesie. Hinc post modicum in secretiorem transfertur exedram, ipsis uestimentorum insigniis paruitatis nostre obsequio induendus in quibus olim pontificalem susceperat consecrationem. Erat uero tunc ibi uidere miraculum. Caro namque eius ita niueo quodam et uniformi candore nitescebat ut quoddam resurrectionis decus iam tot diebus extincta manifeste preferret.[2] Nichil in ea liuidum, pallidum aut sub-

---

a poterat XP

joy was not of long duration, for they were soon driven out by others, and had to yield their prey to new captors. Throughout the whole journey to the cathedral, which is not particularly short, at almost every moment new bearers replaced the former ones. The number was not always the same, but there were always as many bearers as the size of the coffin permitted. Only men of high rank and position dared to take part in the struggle. As the streets owing to the heavy winter rains were exceedingly muddy, the bearers as they advanced were often ankle-deep and sometimes even knee-deep in the mire. Those people who were unable to approach the coffin which contained the body of the saint, threw money on to it, and raised their arms in adoration, devoutly commending themselves to his prayers. Even the Jews came out, weeping to render him what homage they could, mourning and lamenting him aloud as the faithful servant of the one God. Their behaviour towards the man of God made us realise that the prophecy ' The Lord has caused all nations to bless him ' had in his case been fulfilled.[1]

The bells of all the churches of the city tolled as he was carried slowly to the chanting of hymns and canticles to the centre of his cathedral. A little later he was transferred to a side chapel where my unworthy hands performed the service of arraying him in the vestments he had formerly worn at his consecration. A miracle was indeed seen then for his whole body was as fresh, white and beautiful as if he had risen from the dead instead of having been dead for so many days.[2] There

---

[1] Ecclus. 44: 25
[2] cf. Sulpicius Severus, *Epistula III*, CSEL, I, p. 150 ; F. M. Powicke, *The Life of Ailred of Rievaulx* (N.M.T.) pp. 62, 77.

marcidum, nichil fuscum, nil non lacteum aut potius
liliosum renitebat. Manus eius et digiti, brachia quoque
et lacerti, non aliter quam pridem in uiuo, tunc *a* in
defuncto placabiles, molles et tractabiles erant. Balsamo
sola eius facies et manus eius dextera *b* fuerat delibuta.
De aliorum autem statu menbrorum nil inuestigauimus.
Digito enim anulum, chirotecas uirgamque *c* pastoralem
manibus eius et brachiis inserentes, de hiis solummodo ea
que diximus ita se habere deprehendimus. Omnibus
itaque pontificalibus rite insignitus, nudata facie, soporati
magis quam exanimati speciem pretendebat. Ita a
glorificantibus Deum refertur denuo in chorum.
Accurrunt undique turbe inspectantium, cereos manibus
ardentes preferentium, pedes eius et manus osculantium,
aurum et argentum lapidesque pretiosos offerentium.

Interea, dum paululum remotius cum uiro uenerabili
ipsius ecclesie decano consedissemus, inuicem de hiis
que circa christum Domini mirabiliter acciderant con-
ferentes, assunt quidam stupentes et attoniti, talia nobis
dicentes, ' Vidistisne et attendistis quanto decore uernare
iam cepit facies episcopi, ut rosis rubentibus genas
similes pretendat, ut dormientis, non defuncti, nuperque
de balneis egressi hylaritatem preferat ? ' Ad hec
decano admirante, hec nuntiantibus respondimus,
' Fallimini procul dubio, fratres karissimi. Reuera
enim candore mirabili nitet uultus eius, rubei uero
coloris nullum in eo uestigium elucet. Satis paulo ante
diligenter notauimus omnem eius speciem atque
decorem.' Tunc illi nos quomodo *d* reluctantes rapuerunt
et in cominus adductos ostendebant fide oculata uerissima
se fuisse de gratia ruboris quo micabat facies eius
prosecutos. Quod intuentes, nec ulterius ueritati
perfecte contraire ualentes, illud in Trenis de Nazareis

_____

a nunc QX   *b* om B   *c* baculumque Q   *d* quodammodo QX

were no traces of discoloration, pallor, shrinking or darkening, but rather milk-whiteness or lily-whiteness. His hands, fingers, arms and joints were as flexible, supple and as easy to manipulate as when he was alive though only his face and right hand had been besmeared with balsam. I did not examine the state of his other limbs, and it was when I was placing his ring on his finger, and his pastoral staff in his arms and putting on his gloves that I saw what I have described. When he had been robed in his episcopal vestments and his face was uncovered, he looked just as if he were asleep and not really dead. Then with hymns of praise to God he was borne back again to the choir, where a great crowd hastened from every part of the church with lighted candles in their hands, to view the body, and kiss his feet and hands, and to make offerings of gold, silver and precious stones.

As I was sitting a little apart with the reverend dean of the cathedral, and we were talking about the miraculous occurrences in connection with the Lord's anointed, certain people came up to us in a state of great excitement and wonder. 'Have you seen,' they asked, 'or noticed the lovely rosy hue of the bishop's face? His cheeks are as red as roses, and he has the fresh appearance of one who has fallen asleep after a bath and not that of a dead man.' The dean was utterly dumbfounded, and I answered, 'You must have made a mistake, my dear brethren. His face is certainly of a marvellous, gleaming whiteness, but without the least tinge of red; a little while ago I noted with particular attention its amazing loveliness.' They then, however, dragged us somewhat against our will up to the coffin, and made us see for ourselves that what they had reported about the fresh and ruddy hue of his face was completely

canticum a Ieremia, in eo non inmerito etiam corporaliter
notauimus adimpletum, ' Candidiores niue, nitidiores
lacte, rubicundiores ebore antiquo.' *a* Permansit autem
uerus idem sponsi celestis amicus ita candidus et rubicundus,[1] quamdiu mansit in sponse sibi commisse aspec-
tibus super terram manifestus.   Vtrum uero in sepulti *b*
corpore decor ille permanserit necne, non est modo nostrum scire ; scietur autem postea.   Qui si forte euanuit, et
cum Moyse euacuata est gloria uultus eius,[2] non erit
unde scandalizarentur quibus id forte scire donabitur,
cum sit iugiter conspicabilis et inexterminabilis *c*species
eius in nubibus celi ; unde non solum detur pacis formosi-
tas set et debilitatis sospitas fluere in euum non desistit.

    Hiis ea que sequentur iocundo satis auspicio astipulari
noscuntur.   Nam ingressis *d* nobis ad locum memorati
consessus, ueniunt celeriter ad decanum plures qui
dicerent mulierem quamdam, lumine annis multis
priuatam, primo corporis sancti attactu uisum recepisse.
Suggerunt ut *e* classicum pulsari atque ' Te Deum
laudamus ' uocibus altissonis dominus decanus iubeat
decantari.   Verum istud nos *f* uehementer dissuasimus,
quia ignota fuit eis ipsa mulier, ne forte, conficta cecitate,
lumen se mentiretur de nouo recepisse, quo iam annosa
nullo tempore caruisset, set ueritatem super hoc et super
aliis que procul dubio audiri contingeret signis, diligentissime semper inquirendam primitus et non nisi certissime probata quolibet modo propalanda et publice
predicanda nouimus.*g*   Dum igitur super hiis disceptatio
aliquantula inter nos et clericos haberetur, accurrunt et
alii de muliere altera indubitatum referentes miraculum.

---

a + saphiro pulchriores X (*as in* Lam. 4. 7)   *b* sepulto o ; sepulchro p
c exterminabilis B ; interminabilis X   *d* regressis X
e *om* B   *f* + fieri X   *g* monuimus QX

correct. When we had seen it we could no longer deny what was absolutely true, and saw that the passage in the lamentations of Jeremiah concerning the Nazarites, ' They were brighter than snow, whiter than milk, and ruddier than old ivory ' exactly described his physical appearance. This whiteness and redness persisted as long as the faithful friend [1] of the celestial bridegroom remained on earth visible to all beholders in the church committed as a bride to his care. Whether the beauty survived when his body had been buried is hidden from us at present but will be revealed hereafter. If perchance it should happen that like Moses the glory of his countenance vanished,[2] this should not scandalise those to whom perhaps knowledge of this shall be given, for in Heaven his beauty will always be manifest, where there will be a never-failing source of lovely peace and help for those in need.

This miraculous occurrence was soon followed and confirmed by what follows. After we had returned to the place where we had been sitting, several people came excitedly to the dean to relate that a woman who had been blind for many years had recovered her sight the moment she touched the saint's body. They asked the venerable dean to have the bells rung and the Te Deum chanted. I strongly opposed this because the woman was a stranger and had perhaps pretended to be blind and lied about recovering her sight which, in spite of being old, she had never lost. It was essential carefully to ascertain the truth about this and other miracles, which would assuredly be reported, and not have any proclaimed or published unless they were confirmed. A little later, whilst I and the clergy were still arguing

---

[1] cf. Lam. 4: 7
[2] cf. 2 Cor. 3: 7

Dum enim matrona quedam deuota, oblatione facta,
iuxta corpus insisteret piis precibus, crumenam sibi a
zona dependentem et solidos aliquot argenteos con-
tinentem, fur clandestinus repente inscidit. Qui mox,
nullo adhuc mortalium preter ipsum quod fecerat
agnoscente, percutitur subita cecitate. Hinc quo se
ferret, quo gressum tenderet prorsus nesciebat. Qui
nimio actus timore, cum aliquamdiu huc illucque tamquam ebrius et crapulatus a uino, nutandus *a* abire
temptaret nec posset ; cum iam oculos in se plurimorum
hiis gestibus in se conuerteret, et quidnam sibi esset ut
ita gesticularetur in loco tali inquirerent circumstantes,
manum cum bursa nil dicendo tetendit in altum, quid
egisset rebus ipsis manifestans et quid statim pertulisset
uoce lugubri subinferens. Inspicit et agnoscit mulier
loculum suum in manu sacrilegi inscisoris, cui ille
restituit quod abstulit, et lumen mox recepit quod
amisit. Recepit et illa pecuniam quam perdidit et
immensis attollit preconiis patroni clementiam quem
mente deuota adiuit.

De precedenti quoque muliere quod reuera diu *b*
ceca fuerit et amissum lumen ibidem receperit, in breui
post hec certius innotuit.*c* Tantus interea fiebat con-
cursus populorum ut infra modicum tempus quadraginta
marcarum summam oblatorum quantitas excederet.
Iacentem autem in medio filium lucis die et nocte
ambiebant uiri et femine, tenentes in manibus cereos
ardentes et in modum corone gloria et honore coronatum
a Domino continue cingentes.

Tunc magister Iohannes Leircestrensis, uir litteratus
et industrius, huiusmodi disticon ad pedes eius posuit, in

---

a nutando Q ; nutabundus X   *b* dum B
c X *insert* cure of knight from cancer (**Legenda**).

about this, others hurried in to relate an undoubted miracle which had happened to another woman. A certain pious matron who after making an offering was praying earnestly by the body, had had a purse hanging from her girdle, which contained a number of silver coins, cut off quickly and stealthily by a thief. No-one but himself would have known what he had done if he had not suddenly been struck blind, and could not escape because he did not know how to direct his steps. After a little while his unsuccessful attempts to get away, which caused him to stagger about aimlessly like a drunkard, attracted the notice of many of the bystanders who asked what had happened to make him behave so oddly in a church. Without saying anything, he raised up his hand holding the purse, thus showing what had occurred and then in a low voice broken with sobs confessed what had befallen him. The woman saw and recognised her pouch in the hand of the sacrilegious cut-purse, who recovered his lost sight after he had restored what he had stolen. She having recovered the money she had lost, loudly acclaimed the bounty of the patron whom she had visited with such devotion.

Soon afterwards we found out that it was true that the former woman had been blind for a long time and that her sight had been restored. Meanwhile the crowds had become immense, and within a very short time the offerings amounted to more than forty marks. Night and day men and women holding lighted candles in their hands walked continuously in a circle round the son of light lying in their midst, forming a garland to honour and glorify the saint crowned by God.

Then, an eminent and distinguished writer, Master John of Leicester, laid at his feet this short epitaph recording succinctly his many outstanding qualities :

quo multiplices uirtutum eius prerogatiuas breuiter expressit, dicens :

Pontificum baculus, monachorum norma, scholarum
Consultor, regum malleus Hugo fuit.

De hiis singulis, baculo scilicet et norma, consultore et malleo, etsi plurima que diceremus occurrant, tamen quia finiri longe prolixior quam sperabamus libellus expectat, hec latius aliis tractanda cedentes, lectorem interim presentium, ut ex minimis maiora coniciat, ad ea que iam superius dicta sunt animo retractanda destinamus.

Die postera dum portaretur ad tumulum, mutulatur hinc inde scissione crebra sacrarum quibus induebatur uestium. Sacrari *a* admodum se credebat quisquis tale sacrilegium committere ualuisset, ut in sacro sacrum de sacro aliquid rapuisset. Sepultus est, sicut ipse nobis preceperat, secus parietem non procul ab altari sancti Iohannis Baptiste, et sicut uisum est propter accessum confluentis populi magis congruere, a boreali ipsius edis regione.

Rex ipse ex hiis que diuinitus gloriose fiebant erga Dei hominem conpunctus, tunc primo sibi certius compertum esse perhibuit quanti penes Deum ordo monasticus loci fuerit, in quo ad tantam ipsius gratiam uir iste succreuit. Flexus etiam ad insperatam clementiam abbatibus Cisterciensis ordinis, quorum multitudo, que numerum excederet quinquagesimum, eo dicebatur conuenisse, exactionem pecuniariam quam ab eis diutius elaborauerat extorquere, funditus ad honorem sancti ipsis remisit. Monasterium preterea insigne se constructurum promisit ad gloriam Dei,[1] qui uiuit et gloriatur super omnia, Deus benedictus in secula. Amen.

a + uel sanctificari Q

Here lies Hugh, model of bishops,
Flower of monks, friend of scholars
And hammer of kings.

Although I could give many more examples showing the appropriateness of each of these descriptions of him, yet as this little work is much longer than I hoped and hastens to its close I will leave them for others to develop more fully, and in the meantime beg my reader to cast his mind back over what I have written, and conjecture the greater from the less.

The next day whilst he was being carried to his burial, frequent attempts were made to cut off pieces of the vestments in which he was arrayed.   Those who committed this act of sacrilege in a church believed that they would bring a blessing on themselves by stealing a holy relic connected with a saint.   He was laid, in accordance with his instructions to us, by the wall near the altar of St John the Baptist on the north side of the chapel, which seemed the best place because of the crowds flocking to his tomb.

Even the king was impressed by the miracles wrought by God to glorify his servant, and understood for the first time His predilection for the monastic order which had produced a man of such conspicuous holiness.   He was even moved by this to an unexpected act of clemency towards the Cistercian abbots, estimated at over fifty who were assembled there, for he remitted permanently out of veneration for the saint the tribute he had for a long time exacted from them.   He also vowed to erect a great monastery to the glory of God [1] who liveth and is glorified in all things, to whom be praise for ever and ever, Amen.

[1] King John fulfilled this promise by founding the Cistercian abbey of Beaulieu in Hampshire, in 1202 ; see S. F. Hockey, *Beaulieu : King John's Abbey* (1976).

The Diocese of Lincoln

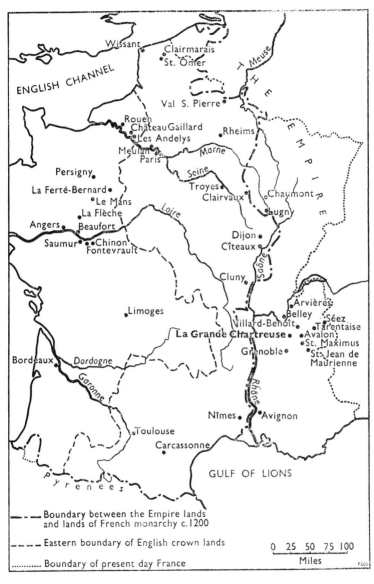

Map to illustrate St Hugh's overseas journeys

235

INDEX